READINGS
IN ART HISTORY

VOLUME I

Readings
in Art History

VOLUME I • ANCIENT EGYPT
THROUGH THE MIDDLE AGES

Edited by Harold Spencer

CHARLES SCRIBNER'S SONS • NEW YORK

Cover: 12th century Champlevé enamel plaque
attributed to Godefroid de Claire. 4 in. square.
The Metropolitan Museum of Art, gift of J. Pierpont Morgan, 1917.

Contents

CONTENTS

READINGS IN ART HISTORY

VOLUME I

INTRODUCTION

The aim of this anthology is to assemble a convenient and useful series of modern writings on several aspects of the history of art in the Western world. It is intended primarily, but not exclusively, as a supplement to the texts usually assigned in introductory courses in the history of Western art. To this extent it is a practical measure: the problem of providing multiple copies of supplementary readings on library reserve shelves has, at one time or another, haunted all who teach such courses. The paperbound anthology seems a reasonable answer, however partial the solution it offers. But this anthology's usefulness is not limited to introductory surveys of Western art. These selections provide a valuable set of readings for any student of Western civilization or of the creativeness of man; and although art history is not always presented in fine literary style, there are examples here of precision of expression and even of eloquence.

The selections in this anthology range from problems of style, technique, iconography, and theories of art, to the relevant stylistic and socioeconomic context within which a work of art acquires its form and performs its function. The sequence of the selections approximates customary chronology, so that the readings correlate with traditional periods. Some selections, however, reach beyond the limits of a single period or movement.

This first volume of the anthology covers the long period from ancient Egypt to the beginnings of the Renaissance, and attempts to achieve a reasonable balance between the ancient and medieval worlds while giving proportionate attention to sculpture, architecture, and painting. If the emphasis with respect to ancient art has been lavished on Greece and Rome it is not meant to imply for them a greater artistic accomplishment than the older civilizations of the Near East, but simply to recognize the preeminent role that classical antiquity has played in the subsequent history of Western art. If the art of the classical world can no longer exercise the claims

3

it once made on the heart and mind of Western man, its survival as an exemplar of beauty or grandeur for many periods of art can scarcely be denied. Variations on antique themes have sprung up again and again in generations grown aware of their inheritance or self-consciously seeking identity through the authority of their ancient roots. Other traditions, growing out of the institution of Christianity and the culture of the barbarian north, are the predominant ones in the selections from the latter half of this volume, and complete the major lines of influence that have lent their force to the shape and substance of Western art before the age of political and industrial revolutions.

The reader will find considerable variety among the selections in this anthology. Some, like the excerpt from Gisela Richter's *Sculpture and Sculptors of the Greeks,* are of a generalized nature, while others, like Walter Horn's article, "On the Origins of the Medieval Bay System," deal with specific problems. Some, like Paul Frankl's essay on Gothic mysticism, give focus to the philosophical ambience within which art performs its function, while others, like the selections from Millard Meiss, *Painting in Florence and Siena After the Black Death,* examine correlations between art and its socioeconomic context.

The excerpts from Émile Mâle's classic work on Gothic art deal with iconographical interpretations, as do those from Adolf Katzenellenbogen's fine study of the meaning of the tympanum at Vézelay, whereas the selections by Rhys Carpenter on Greek architecture and sculpture emphasize aesthetic and formal considerations.

There is yet another aspect to the variety encountered in this anthology. The editor has deliberately selected articles that range widely in the degree of difficulty they present to the reader, thereby increasing the flexibility of the anthology in meeting the diverse needs it must surely encounter in fulfilling its functions.

In many instances the footnotes that accompanied the original publication have been reduced or eliminated, sacrifices to the requirements of available space. In such cases, the function of this anthology as a series of supplementary readings in undergraduate courses of a generalized nature has been the guiding principle, but many footnotes leading to specialized study have been retained.

Although illustrations were limited by necessity, the editor has included as many as possible in an effort to enhance the usefulness of the anthology. They have been placed wherever possible adjacent to the relevant portions of the text, a welcome convenience. In some instances an illustration from one selection will be found to relate directly or peripherally to another reading. The choice of illustrations also permits comparisons and suggests problems of art history that lie outside the subject matter of the selections they illustrate.

The headnotes accompanying individual selections or groups of selections serve chiefly as bibliographical devices, and have been kept somewhat austere so as not to impinge on space better served by the selected readings than by pedagogical intrusions. Furthermore, each instructor who uses this anthology will have his own contextual devices for presenting problems in art history. The anthologist would, therefore, defer to the reader by allowing the selections to speak for themselves. The bibliographical references cited in the headnotes are limited to works in English since this anthology is intended primarily for the undergraduate audience.

Decisions as to what should be included were often difficult to make; and much important and attractive material was excluded when it appeared impossible to excerpt it without destroying the writer's purpose or the flow of his argument. In these selections every effort has been made to retain them as they originally appeared except in such cases where a lack of uniformity in spelling, capitalization, or punctuation might be confusing to the reader. Wherever a selection has been edited, the deletions are clearly indicated by ellipses. It was necessary to omit some of the illustrations and footnotes; the remaining ones have been renumbered.

No anthology can hope to serve fully the needs of every situation in which it might be used. There is a peculiar inevitability about this condition, and the following lines by A. A. Milne° epitomize both the dilemma of the anthologist and the refrain of his critics.

> It isn't really
> Anywhere!
> It's somewhere else
> Instead!

It would be ungracious to end this introduction without acknowledging the special contributions of a number of people: my teach-

---

° The lines from "Halfway Down" are from *When We Were Very Young* by A. A. Milne. Copyright, 1924, by. E. P. Dutton & Co., Inc. Renewal, 1952, A. A. Milne. Reprinted by permission of E. P. Dutton & Co., Inc. and Methuen & Company, Ltd.

ers, colleagues, and students over the years; Miss Sallie Pritchard, for her labors of typing and correspondence; and my wife, whose patience and criticism aided this project in so many ways.

HAROLD SPENCER

The University of Connecticut

1. EGYPTIAN ART

William Stevenson Smith

INTRODUCTION

From the edge of the eastern plateau that overlooks the modern city of Cairo the panorama that stretches far to the north and south and westward across the Nile to the desert can be read as a symbolic triad: the river which of old gave life to the valley, the great city affirming the continuity of that life, and far to the west on the edge of the desert, the eternal geometry of the Old Kingdom's pyramids. This heraldic confrontation of past and present to the axis of the Nile is a reminder that permanence was a basic dimension of ancient Egypt and the art it produced. So much of this art comes from the ancient tombs that the impulse is strong to view it as an art obsessed with death. But the statues of the dead do not close their eyes, servant statues administer to their needs, and the walls of the tombs celebrate the activities of life—the hunt, the harvest, and the feast. The life in the world of the tombs goes on like the unending cycle of the river's seasons.

The selection that follows, by an eminent Egyptologist, is an excellent introduction to both the forms and content of Egyptian art; but, more than that, the selection joins this art to the wider context of the eastern Mediterranean world, a direction the author has explored in detail in his more recent work, *Interconnections in the Ancient Near East* (1965).

For a general survey of the Egyptian civilization the best work is John A. Wilson, *The Burden of Egypt* (1951), available in a paperbound edition as *The Culture of Ancient Egypt*. An excellent brief survey of Egyptian art is Cyril Aldred, *Development of Ancient Egyptian Art 3200–1315* B.C., 3 Vols. (1949–1962). Other works are W. Stevenson Smith, *A History of Egyptian Sculpture and Painting in the Old Kingdom* (1946); Alexander Badawy, *A History of Egyptian Architecture*, Vol. I (1954), Vol. II (1966); E. Baldwin Smith, *Egyptian Architecture as Cultural Expression* (1938);

7

Arpag Mekhitarian, *Egyptian Painting*, translated by Stuart Gilbert (1956), a popular text especially useful for its color plates; Henri Frankfort, *Kingship and the Gods* (1948); and H. A. Groenewegen-Frankfort, *Arrest and Movement* (1951).

Ancient Egypt was protected by formidable desert barriers and confined to a narrow river valley. It was less subject to outside influences than the other great early civilization in Mesopotamia, and its culture presents, as one of its salient characteristics, a long, virtually unbroken continuity. In an almost rainless country the regular rise of the Nile every year provided the striking example of a renewal of life with each annual flood and gave the Egyptian a cheerful assurance of the permanence of established things, suggesting the acceptance that life would somehow continue after death in the same way. The peculiarly Egyptian concern with the continuity of life after death in a form similar to that which had been experienced upon earth provided an element in the development of the arts which was not present to such an extent in other countries. Thus, while architecture, painting, and sculpture ordinarily appeared in the service of the cult of a god or to glorify the wealth and power of a ruler, in Egypt we find emphasis laid upon providing a lasting dwelling-place for the dead, the re-creation of life magically in pictures to serve him, and lastly the provision of a substitute in stone for his perishable body.

This striving of the literal-minded and keenly observant Egyptian towards the re-creation of life for the dead man would seem to be intimately connected with the naturalistic elements in Egyptian art, and is primarily responsible for the impulse to produce portraiture which is a feature of the best of Egyptian sculpture. This worked against the formalizing tendencies which, particularly in Mesopotamia, led more towards the stylization of forms and the employment of geometric shapes. Its naturalistic elements lend a familiar quality to Egyptian art which never seems a wholly oriental creation, although it displays the same approach to representation which is common to all other ancient peoples before Greek times. All pre-Greek peoples give us a kind of diagram of a thing as man knew it to be, not as it appears to the eye under transitory circumstances. In spite of this attitude towards visual impressions, the Egyptian had an instinct to imitate closely what he saw about him. His natural disposition towards balance and proportion, combined with a long-

1. Limestone Statue of Zoser, Dynasty III, Old Kingdom
(Egyptian Museum, Cairo)

maintained tradition of orderly craftsmanship, strikes a sympathetic
note for the Westerner.

The availability of working materials is an influential factor which
must be taken into consideration. The abundance of good stone was
an advantage the Egyptian had over his contemporaries in southern
Mesopotamia, who had to import their stone. The shape and small
size of the slabs and boulders available to the Sumerian conditioned
the rounded forms and somewhat uneven quality of his sculpture.
The Egyptian early learned to cut blocks for building-stone, and
the sculptor had a plentiful supply of rectangular blocks from the
quarry for his work. This may well be a practical reason for his predisposition towards cubical form (Fig. 1) in contrast to the rounded,
conical shapes preferred by the Mesopotamian. It certainly allowed
for the largeness of scale which is another outstanding feature of
Egyptian work both in sculpture and architecture.

Egyptian Art

One is always conscious that the Egyptian has hewed his forms from the stone block and not modelled them from softer materials, as in Crete, where the only large-scale work that has survived is in plaster relief which assumes a plastic form in contrast to the stone-cutter's technique. This has a modelled projection from the surface which is opposed to the Egyptian tendency to maintain a flat plane in reliefs. In contrast to the timeless, static permanence of Egyptian statues, the instinct of the Cretan, who excelled in the fashioning of delicate small figures of ivory, metal, and faience, was to catch an impression of movement and lively action. The Cretan might be said to see things with a painter's eye. The modelling of his reliefs produces the same impressionistic results as does his painting.

The Mesopotamian, on the other hand, tends away from natural forms in his sculpture and towards formal patterns. There is nothing in Egypt like the way in which the surfaces of the human face of one of the great Assyrian bulls are enlivened by unrealistic but superbly decorative undercuttings and contrasts in planes. It is as though the craftsman's preoccupation with seal engraving impelled him to approach larger works with the formal equipment developed in that craft as well as in textile-making and metal-work. Metal seems to have been a particularly congenial medium, and it is probably no accident that one of the Mesopotamian's finest early creations in sculpture is the magnificent Akkadian copper head from Nineveh.[1]

The marvellous facility with which huge stones were handled became one of the outstanding characteristics of Egyptian architecture. Enduring stone forms were chiefly reserved for the building of temples and tombs, while secular architecture continued to employ sun-dried bricks and wood. This lighter construction has largely disappeared with the destruction of the cities in the Nile valley and the gradual accumulation of silt from the river's annual flood. More has survived of the domestic architecture of the New Kingdom than of other periods, particularly in the Palace of Amenhotep III and at Tell el Amarna. This material, much of which is not well known, helps to balance the impression gained from the overwhelming mass of evidence which is derived from tombs. The excellent preservation of so much which represents the peculiarly Egyptian emphasis upon tomb architecture might have produced a distorted picture if it were not for the beliefs which caused so many personal possessions to be buried in the tombs and so much of the daily life to be represented on the walls of the tomb chapel. A great deal is reflected of what must once have existed in the cities and on the country estates. In the stone buildings, as well as in the pictures, there is evident a particularly happy facility for the adaptation of plant-forms to conventionalized design, especially in the shapes of columnar support. The palaces of the New Kingdom have preserved also something of a purely decorative use of naturalistically represented plant and animal life in ceiling- and floor-paintings, as well as on minor wall-spaces. Something of this sort must have occurred earlier in house decoration.

The covering of wall-surfaces with scenes representing the ruler's relationship with the gods of the temple of the glorification of his acts on earth seems to have been common to all ancient peoples. However, the Egyptian's impulse to re-create life for the dead man, which caused him to make statues for the tomb, also suggested that he cover the walls of the chapel with representations of life on earth. A desire for permanence early led to the use of low relief carvings on the stone-lined walls of a tomb chapel or temple. Like the statues, these were painted to complete their life-like aspect. In praising the beauty of these carvings there has been a tendency to overlook the fine quality of the painted detail or the work in paint alone which sometimes takes the place of these reliefs. The usual Egyptian practice, which combined the skills of the sculptor and the painter in creating one unified whole in painted relief, has to a certain extent obscured the Egyptian's very real contribution purely as a painter. In early times he was rivalled in this respect only by the Cretan. Egypt has provided us with an amazingly preserved series of examples in the field of wall-painting which range over the whole long period of Egyptian history. The finest examples of Cretan work are limited to a fairly short range of time at the beginning of the Egyptian New Kingdom, while accidents of preservation have confined our knowledge of the painting of Western Asia to a few examples widely separated in time. Thus Egypt provides by far the largest body of evidence for the development of early painting. Moreover, the Egyptian, with his naturalistic approach and meticulous interest in recording the details of what he saw about him, developed an extraordinary dexterity of brushwork and a manipulation of a wide range of color which is hard to match in ancient times. This is most evident in the breaking up of flat surfaces of color by fine brush-strokes of different hues to suggest the fur of an animal or the feathering of a bird. The success achieved in indicating texture is immediately clear if one examines a rare example of such an attempt outside Egypt in the bull's head from the wall-paintings of the palace of Mari in northern Syria[2] or another head of a bull from the Cretan palace of Knossos.[3] In these the detail is indicated summarily by rather coarse dark lines. The emphasis on the thick outlines of the Mesopotamian example is even more apparent in the paintings of the early Assyrian palace[4] of Tukulti-Ninurta, where the strongly marked bordering of the different parts of the composition has been compared to the isolation of the various elements in the design of an oriental carpet. In contrast to this tendency to reduce forms to a decorative pattern, the Egyptian was interested in the outward look of living and inanimate things, and consequently endeavored to perfect his skill in indicating their surface details. He never loses, however, his sense of the clarity of their form or the use that can be made of line for this purpose. The Cretan, on the other hand, seems impatient with such detailed rendering of an animal or a plant form. He presents us with a creature instinct with life and movement, but his lively, instantaneous, impressionistic treatment will not bear too close analysis as to the accuracy of its details.

Thus, within certain limits of his conventions, the Egyptian approaches his subject with careful, painstaking attention to detail. He has a matter-of-fact rather than an imaginative attitude to the world about him, and when he deals with supernatural things manages with a kind of cheerful assurance to give them a familiar, everyday look. Even the most remarkable monsters are rather dryly conceived, and one of his most surprising achievements was the convincing naturalness with which were combined human and animal parts in composite form for the representation of his gods. The Egyptian mind did not run riot in imagining such strange and frightening spirits as appear on the seal designs of Mesopotamia or Crete. Instead there is an almost complacent acceptance of the orderliness and continuity of existence in a mild climate which was spared a good many of the more frightening caprices of nature. There is no expression of that anxiety with which the Mesopotamian regarded the harshness of nature, nor did the Egyptian's surroundings provide him with the broken mountain crags and seascapes that stirred the imagination of the inhabitants of the Aegean.

The rationalized approach to visual impressions developed by the Greeks was foreign to earlier peoples. The Greeks first contrived a consistent way of drawing figures so that their different parts were related to one another in the manner in which they appear to the eye. They then began to experiment with the placing of these figures against a background in which the lines correspond to a series of receding planes which appear natural to the observer. They ended by developing a system of aerial perspective. The absence of a desire on the part of the Egyptian to suggest depth and volume in his painting and reliefs is only one aspect of an attitude towards representation which prevailed throughout the ancient world. It tends to generalization according to the characteristics of the people who employ it, whether this takes the form of avoiding movement, as in Egypt, or crystallizes a typical aspect of lively action, as in Crete.

Specific historical events, if represented at all, are treated as the symbolical memorial of a victory or some other action of the ruler. Often when a battle is actually represented it is given a form which might be considered an enlarged hieroglyph signifying the idea. This is perfectly illustrated by the complementary use of early word-signs and figure representation on the Narmer palette at the beginning of Dynasty I, but the intimate connection between writing and drawing continues throughout all Egyptian monuments. The beautifully made hieroglyphs are small drawings in themselves and form an integral part of larger compositions, while the wall-scenes are really an extension of the written signs. Inscriptions are also a necessary part of the statues. They provided the essential identity of the owner by giving his titles and name, although the portrayal of his outward appearance is usually generalized without individual characteristics, except in certain outstanding works that we shall see appear throughout Egyptian history at periods of remarkable creative effort. Similarly, the subject-matter of the wall-scenes is restricted to typical aspects of Egyptian life which ordinarily lack the narrative element in the sense that they seldom refer to specific happenings. Backgrounds are summarized, with a few trees, a vineyard, the selected parts of a building, or the upright stems of a papyrus thicket to suggest the setting of a scene. At first there is little attempt to deal with the spatial relationship between these simple stage-props and the men and animals which they accompany. Emotion or individual feeling, and the dramatic relationship between the figures which this might engender, had little place, although we may find certain typified exceptions such as the mourners at a funeral or the dying forms of animals.

However, within this general framework we shall find a constant enlivening of the whole by freshly observed detail and an increasing interest in the treatment of landscape and architectural backgrounds with experiments in the more complicated grouping of figures and their relationships in space. This reached its most advanced stage in the huge compositions of the Ramesside temple reliefs, where topographical and even historical elements, which had first made their appearance in the Eighteenth Dynasty, are handled in a fashion paralleled only by the later Assyrian reliefs. The royal sculpture of the Twelfth Dynasty also shows a first attempt to portray something of man's inner feeling in the somber, careworn faces of Sesotris III (see Figs. 14, 15) and Amenemhat III. At the same time the painter brought an advanced technique and a more subtle color sense to the treatment of textures which had already interested the artists of the Old Kingdom. This was to be carried to a most sophisticated stage in the very extensive work of the Eighteenth-Dynasty painters.

Of course it is the significant changes which appear against the background of the long continuity of Egyptian civilization that quicken our interest. One of the fascinations of the study of Egyptian art is in learning to distinguish the variations in a style which is easily recognizable as belonging to that country over a vast length of time from the fourth millennium down to 332 B.C., when the conquest of Alexander the Great brought Dynastic Egypt to an end. Initially one may have the impression of an endless repetition of forms, but closer examination reveals definite characteristics of the Old, Middle, and New Kingdoms. Then we begin to realize the special qualities of the formative stages which led up to these great periods of achievement. First came that brilliant Archaic Period in Dynasties I–III, when civilization was developing out of the primitive conditions of Predynastic times towards a culmination in the Old Kingdom. This so-called Pyramid Age of Dynasties IV–VI began about 2680 B.C. and lasted for some four hundred years. The freshness of a new beginning appears again about 2100 B.C. in Dynasty XI, and shortly after 1600 B.C. in early Dynasty XVIII, when the Middle and New Kingdoms respectively emerged from the darkness of those times of political disintegration known as the First and Second Intermediate Periods. Once again, towards the end of the eighth century B.C. and after a long period of decline, we find new life poured into the old forms. This renewal was stimulated by the invasion of the Kushite kings of the Sudan (which the Greeks called Ethiopia and the Romans Nubia). It strikes us as a more conscious, archaizing effort, lacking in the spontaneity of earlier national revivals. . . .

In looking back over the tremendous span of Egyptian civilization, it should be remembered that from the beginning of historic times the king was always referred to as a god. He was sometimes simply termed the Good God. As Horus he was considered the earthly embodiment of an ancient deity of the sky whose worship was preeminent at the time of the establishment of united rule over the two lands of Upper and Lower Egypt in Dynasty I. As Son of Ra the king represented the direct descent of royalty from the creator sun god. Finally in his assimilation with Osiris he would continue to reign over the realm of the dead; for he was repeating the cycle of the god who was thought to be an ancient king who had passed through death to resurrection. Such a drastic simplification of the Egyptian conception of divine kingship presents ideas which were developed in succeeding periods, but which had been accepted by the end of Dynasty V when the earliest preserved body of religious literature, known as the Pyramid Texts, appears first on the walls of the burial-chambers of King Unas. These potent spells were compiled in order to assist in the king's translation from his earthly body into the world of the gods, and imply the recognition of his human qualities which must undergo transformation after death.

The manifold nature of Egyptian religious beliefs defies summary treatment.[5] We are accustomed to the attempt to resolve opposing views, but we must expect instead a many-sided approach to a phenomenon, with the result that unrelated explanations are accepted side by side. Formidable difficulties are presented by the accumulation of beliefs over the centuries through an additive process which was reluctant to replace one idea wholly with another or to discard the old. There is both continuity and extraordinary fluidity in this. Two gods may be assimilated with one another without losing their separate entities. Likewise there may be various manifestations of the same god, as in the case of Horus, who as avenger of his father Osiris, or the infant son of Isis, is quite a different being from the sky god whose wings span the heavens and whose eyes are the sun and the moon.

We find a mixture of popular beliefs and the attempts of learned men to explain the emergence out of chaos of that order which was personified by the Goddess Maat, who stood for justice, truth, and right. From the beginning the Egyptian felt that he was surrounded not only by friendly but also by hostile spirits which had to be propitiated. He also sensed the more remote and impersonal quality of the great forces of nature whose personifications were revered as well as the gods of each locality. The local deities had at first appeared in the shape of animals, or more rarely were represented by a plant or inanimate object. Later, when they assumed human form, the animal head was frequently retained, or else the original animal, plant, or object was borne as a symbol on the head. The Goddess Nekhbet wore a vulture headdress, and Hathor was shown with the horns of a cow, although she might still manifest herself in the form of that animal. There were a number of different Hathors, although these were generally associated with the idea of a mother goddess. Her worship was accompanied by dancing and sistra-playing, and she came to be thought of as the goddess of love and joy. As Mistress of the Sycamore she was identified with a tree-spirit in an old sanctuary near the Giza Pyramids and became the patroness of the royal family of Dynasty IV. In similar guise she is later found dispensing food and cool drink to the dead. Through an interchange of functions with the sky goddess Nut and the Goddess of the West she was associated with the western mountain at Thebes, where she received the sun at its setting.

In historic times the term "city god" describes what must have been an early conception of a local deity who presided over a community. Generally he formed the head of a family triad, such as we have in the case of Ptah of Memphis with his consort the lioness Sekhmet and their son Nefertem, whose symbol was a lotus flower. As one of the primitive villages assumed leadership over neighboring communities, its local god acquired supremacy in that district. Later political fluctuations might replace the god of such a district by another, or they might bring about his rise to national importance. In this process one god might take on the attributes of his predecessor or, if his worship spread throughout the country, he might assume the qualities of one of the great cosmic deities. In the latter case he was still associated with a particular place, of which he was considered the lord and in which lay his principal sanctuary. Something of this process can be learned from the sacred emblems on the standards of the Nomes or provinces which evidently reflect the independent districts of prehistoric times. Thus in Hermopolis the ibis-headed Thoth, the god of wisdom, had long supplanted Wenut, but her symbol, the hare, continued to be used on the standard of this Fifteenth Nome of Upper Egypt. Neith, on the other hand, always remained mistress of Sais, the capital of the Fifth Nome of Lower Egypt, whose standard bore her arms, a shield and crossed arrows.

The assimilation of one divine being with another is easier to understand if we can grasp something of the Egyptian's conception of a vital force which was present to a varying degree in all things animate and even inanimate. When, in the creation according to the doctrine of Heliopolis, the sun, Atum-Ra, brought into being Shu (air) and Tefnut (moisture), he spread his arms about them and his Ka entered into them. Here is suggested the transmission of a life-force which remained in continuous operation from the beginning of the world. It was thus that divine nature was imparted to the king, although its full potentialities could not be realized until after death. Lesser mortals were able to share some part of this force.

The Ka was one of three emanations of the spirit. It was related to, but separate from, the Akh and the Ba. These had all originally belonged only to the gods. They approximate to what we think of as the soul and were all associated with the personality of the individual. One could only become an Akh, a transfigured spirit, after death. Its place was in the heavens remote from the body. The Ba, on the other hand, was an animated aspect of the soul which could move back and forth from the dead body. From the Eighteenth Dynasty onward it is pictured as a human-headed bird, drinking cool water from a pool, perched in the branches of a tree, or fluttering down to join the body in the tomb chamber. The Ka is best viewed as a person's vital force which accompanied him both in life and in death. Certain of its qualities were intensified in the person of the king and they were fully possessed only by supreme beings. The Ka had a separate existence and in one sense can be thought of as a double or as a protective genius. It was closely associated with the tomb statue and with nourishment. Through it the dead man was able to avail himself of the food and drink that

18

he had contracted with his funerary priest to present on stipulated occasions at the false-door of his tomb chapel, and which could be supplemented by the offerings pictured on the walls of this chapel.

NOTES

[1] H. Frankfort, *The Art and Architecture of the Ancient Orient*, Pelican History of Art (Harmondsworth, 1954), plates 42 and 43.

[2] Frankfort, *op. cit.*, plate 69A.

[3] Sir Arthur Evans, *The Palace of Minos*, 1 (London, 1921), 529, Figure 385.

[4] Frankfort, *op. cit.*, plate 74.

[5] See H. Frankfort, *Kingship and the Gods* (Chicago, 1948); *Ancient Egyptian Religion* (New York, 1948); J. Vandier, *La Religion égyptienne*, 2nd ed. (Paris, 1949).

2. THE AESTHETICS OF GREEK ARCHITECTURE

Rhys Carpenter

INTRODUCTION

When it was first published in 1921, *The Esthetic Basis of Greek Art* was cited by one eminent reviewer as possibly the best study in English on the aesthetics of Greek art. Revised in 1959, it continues to occupy an attractive place in the literature. Its author's interest in the psychology of visual perception has often led him into controversial regions, but always he guides the reader to fresh—and delightful—insights into ancient art.

The standard books in English on Greek architecture are W. B. Dinsmoor, *The Architecture of Ancient Greece* (1950); Donald S. Robertson, *A Handbook of Greek and Roman Architecture* (1954); and A. W. Lawrence, *Greek Architecture* (1957). A recent and controversial study of the meaning of Aegean and Greek architecture is the eloquent work by Vincent J. Scully, *The Earth, the Temple, and the Gods* (1962). One should read, in conjunction with it, the review by Homer A. Thompson in *The Art Bulletin*, XLV, 3 (1963), to fix the outlines of the controversy.

The selection that follows is reprinted from Chapter IV in Rhys Carpenter, *The Esthetic Basis of Greek Art* (1959), with the permission of the publishers, Indiana University Press.

I must presuppose that the history and achievements of Greek architecture are sufficiently familiar to the reader. He will know, for example, that the dominant form or theme is the colonnaded temple; that this is built with wall, column, and horizontal beam; and that the structural elements are the square-hewn, close-fitting, mortarless ashlar block, and the various members of two distinct and characteristic "Orders," the Doric and the Ionic, to the latter of which is allied a sub-Order, the Corinthian, scarcely differing from the Ionic save in the form of its capital. He will know, further, that there are temple remains dating from the sixth century B.C. and remarkable for their vigor and simplicity; that in the fifth century were achieved the refined and powerful buildings on the Athenian acropolis, in which the Doric Order reached its formal perfection and the Ionic its first flowering on Attic soil; and that in the two succeeding centuries the Ionic style was perfected by Pythius and Hermogenes and their respective schools, on the west shores of Asia Minor in such notable exemplars as the Mausoleum, the Athena temple at Priene, the Artemis temples at Ephesus and at Magnesia on the Meander, and the long-travailled but never-complete giant temple of Didymean Apollo.

I must also assume that most of the technical vocabulary of the architect will convey its legitimate meaning to the reader, and that he has already noticed the obvious and salient virtues or limitations of the Greek style.

Thus he will know that it is a current precept that Greek buildings always express their purpose and the mechanics of their construction. A temple-plan is self-explanatory; its elevation never misleads us with any pretence—although it must be granted that it rather effectually disguises the building's interior conformation by spreading a flatly aligned colonnade in front of it. The entablature is not carved or molded to produce a merely decorative façade: the epistyle has horizontal stressings to show its function; we may guess that ceiling beams bed behind the frieze; the cornice is unashamedly a watershed; the pediment occurs of necessity because a sloping roof can end in no simpler or more obvious manner. The acroteria are the only structural nonessentials—and I am not altogether sure

23

that these may not have been survivals of weights to hold down the roof, like the stones on Swiss chalets, or the interlacing of rafters.

We can scarcely acquit the Greek architects of having followed a third popular modern precept by making their architecture express its material, since they not merely painted their marble, but in the members of the two Orders carved forms (such as triglyphs, dentils, guttae, regulae) which were clearly imitative presentations of timber construction. Yet they exploited the good qualities of their building material, by giving their marble walls that lustrous finish which still endures upon them, and by carving designs whose sharpness of line and shadow-free shallows emphasized those beauties which reside more in fine marble than in any other stone. On the other hand, they could not tolerate rustication or ruggedness (except for fortification walls and similar uses) but covered their coarser materials with a stucco of powdered marble which effectively gave the lie to its native qualities. That they sheathed exposed timber with terracotta or bronze cannot be instanced against them, since it was done not so much to disguise the material as to protect and preserve the wood.

There is a fourth precept to which good architecture is generally supposed to conform. It must express (it is said) the mentality and civilization of its builders—as though whatever man consciously makes could fail to be eloquent of himself! Even a Moorish tower upon a Renaissance palace built for the servants' hall of an American millionaire's countryplace is eloquent of its age and culture. Eclecticism is as much a style as any other—and as significant of its attendant civilization. The skyline of Fifth Avenue is very eloquent of the perturbed and composite culture that made it and enjoys it. But it is intended to assert by this particular precept, that the spiritual qualities of an age should somehow be deducible from the buildings which it produces; and it is clearly true of Greek architecture that it is ordered and logical, that it harmonizes part with part, and parts with whole, and that, to a most remarkable degree, it is unfantastic and, in all its elements and proportions, always implies a human use or service, and a mortal eye and a rational mind to observe and approve it.

There are no structural irrelevancies in Greek building, such as columns which are not the true supports of their superstructures, or façades which merely mask with decorative additions the disparate structure behind them. But though there are no structural irrelevancies, neither is there much structural inventiveness or ambition. The Greek temple is, in its intent, a one-story affair. The superposed colonnades in its interior were forced on the builder by the physical necessity of supporting the roofbeams and the aesthetic impossibility of doing so by means of a single story of columns (since these would have to be taller and so more massive than those of the exterior order). The two-story colonnade with ground floor and gallery, thus produced, was often employed to line marketplaces and open squares, but seems not to have incited builders to attempt a third or fourth stage of columns. The tower-like superposition of the Orders was reserved for Roman façades and the restless Renaissance to achieve. The stoa, thus limited by custom to two stages, was further restrained in its height by the characteristically Greek consideration that a column more than 12 feet high would seem out of proportion to the human beings for whose service and convenience it was intended. Here, as so often in things Greek, it seemed that "man is of all things the measure." The temples, being houses of gods or at least their images, were not cribbed and cabined by these demands of human proportion: their single story of columns (you would imagine) could swell to any height. But here another proportion stepped in to check their rise toward the colossal: the distance from column to column always bore some sort of established relation to the height of the shafts, and columns could not be too widely spaced lest they could no longer be safely bridged with horizontal beams of stone. The Greeks were timid engineers:[1] a 15-foot air-span gave them pause, and the lintel of Diana's temple at Ephesus was a gigantic achievement. And so when they strove toward the colossal in height, their columns were allowed but barely sixty feet.[2] Except for such exceptional forms as the lighthouse of Alexandria and the Mausoleum of Hali-carnassus, how many Greek buildings (like the Zeus temple at Girgenti) overpassed a height of one hundred feet? The theaters, to be sure, stretched up till their topmost rows might be more than this distance above the dancers' circle; but the seats were all bedded safely on the sloping hillside. For the Greeks before the Roman era, no hillside—no theater. Nothing is more surprising than to sketch the elevation of one of the great French Gothic cathedrals and to the same scale superpose upon it the façade of any of the greater Greek temples. Where the two buildings chance to agree in width,

25

as do the Parthenon and the cathedral of Chartres, it is all the more astonishing to see the Gothic pushing its nave to twice the Greek temple's height before ever it begins to stretch its tower and spires toward the sky.

Nor were plans varied or complex or ambitious.[3] The temple was the god's house and the depository for his possessions. What then should a god do with more than two rooms? When the cult-statue was housed and the dedications and sacred treasures were safely sheltered, nothing remained to do. A surrounding colonnade to accommodate the god's worshippers, perhaps; but nothing more. The altar, if only because of its smoke and fire, was in the open air and escaped housing. A peribolos wall, marking out the god's acreage, often shut in indiscriminately temple, altar, and *ex voto* dedications. The Greek architect had no idea of the mysterious in setting or approach; a few chthonian shrines in caverns is all that can be cited. Nor did it occur to him that his god might house, dark and inaccessible, beyond great walls and many rooms, approached through courtyard and hallway and stair, as the gods of the Pharaohs lived in the penetralia of Karnak or Luxor. Nor were there kings to dwell in magnificent palaces. Even a sixth century tyrant was a man among men. Pisistratus might take the Acropolis for his house, and Dionysius might have his dwelling on Ortygia; but these were fortresses, not palaces. Even the princes of Hellenistic Pergamon have only a paltry bit of the great hillslope for their private places. The "palace" of Pericles? There was none. And the great fifth century Athens, which was responsible for the masterpieces of the Acropolis, was only "a poorly laid-out town"[4] of small mud-brick houses and crooked narrow streets. The greatness of Greek architecture is certainly not domestic, but lies in temples and public buildings of the *polis*. Yet how monotonous are the plans of the Greek temples! and although their settings are often wonderful—on the windy sunrise cape of Sunium, among the waste grey folds of Arcadian Bassae, under the shining frown of the Delphic cliffs—how much reliance is placed on Nature and how little does Art contribute! Delphi is as idly and irrelevantly marshalled as the accretions of a cemetery; Delos is an architectural pepperpot; Olympia is unconsidered and fortuitous; the Athenian acropolis—a crown of splendor upon a head of tangled hair—owes much of its effectiveness to the lofty, clear-shining aloofness of its site. Neither in the planning of the individual building nor in its relation to other buildings does the Greek architect show invention or artistic imagination. I do not feel confident that he even considered this latter relation until the fourth century: the symmetry *à peu prés* in the arrangement of the buildings on the Acropolis may be very subtle—or very haphazard.

Mnesicles' unfulfilled design for the Propylaea, the town-plan of Halicarnassus and perhaps Rhodes, the carven giants against the gigantic masses of the Zeus temple of Acragas, the Erechtheum plan with its imperfect reaching-out toward a freer form[5]—a list of six or seven such items seems to exhaust the instances of original and powerful departures from the lucid but easy perfection of an established tradition. Two "Orders" and a variant—only that to show for the activity of centuries! Two entablatures and three kinds of capital—is that fecundity? is that inspiration? Is it then so hard for the human brain to invent, so impossible for it to create, that one of the most intelligent and aesthetically most sensitive of races should have only this to show? They are very fine of their kind, these Orders and these temple-, colonnade, tholos-, and theater-forms; but under what limitations and abnegation of originality was their perfection wrought! And how could so many generations of active architects remain content to copy and recopy from the same meager repertory, as though there were no other way to build, no other plans or forms, nor even any other moldings to be imagined, and as though to alter a proportion or to refine a subsidiary outline were achievement enough for any master?

How can we explain such absence of individual invention and artistic variety? Only by referring it to a deep-seated prejudice of the Greek mind. . . .

The impression that the Greek architects were merely seeking the right form, not striving to be original or emotionally expressive, occurs insistently. The proportions of the Doric Order change rapidly but consistently during the sixth and fifth centuries B.C. With the attainment of the right form in the Athenian Propylaea the process of development is almost entirely arrested. Later, the decidence of the Order from favor for temple-construction and the obvious need of a lightened entablature in the use of this Order for colonnades, entirely altered the ratios: the form was no longer right, an altered use had modified it. The profile of the Doric capital changes greatly during the sixth and fifth centuries; but after the time of the Propylaea the only important change is the slight straightening of the top of the echinus which makes the capital so much easier to cut—and entirely robs it of beauty. When the architects no longer appreciate rightness of form, the Practical and the Labor-saving are allowed to announce their wishes.

Until Hellenistic times there was only one important innovation among architectural forms—the Corinthian capital—and that was produced under logical pressure because of the inadequacy of the existing forms. The Ionic capital posed an insoluble problem at the point where a colonnade changed direction (as at the corner of a temple), while the Doric capital could not be extricated from its use with the Doric entablature whose triglyph was a tyrannous nuisance with its interference in the free spacing of columns. Moreover neither the Doric nor the Ionic capital strictly satisfied the logical requirements for the right form. The capital's function is to take the entablature weight and transmit it to the column-shaft. As an intermediary its shape should be consonant with those which it serves: it should be rectangular above and circular below in its cross section, and in the intervening part it must perform without effort the transition from rectangle to circle. The Ionic capital does not meet these requirements; the Doric lacks the transition; but the Corinthian will withstand the most rigorous criticism. It is a marvellous metamorphosis of a circle into a rectangle by a conventional device of leaves tied around a shaft.

The development of the Ionic column-base from the crude and unfelt forms of the Samian Heraion to the Attic or the fourth-century Asia Minor types is a coherent and gradual process. Contemplating it, we have the impression of beholding in operation that which the metaphysicians call a Final Cause, as though it were not each term in the series which occasioned the next, but the ultimate and perfect form like a magnet exerting its attraction through all the attempts of all the earlier builders. Compare, in particular, the Ionic bases of the Propylaea, of the east porch of the Erechtheum, and the north porch of the same building: the last form lies in the first, and progress is as unhesitant as though the path were known and the goal sighted in advance. Equally impressive is the abrupt cessation of experiments and changes as soon as the right form has been attained. The profile of the north porch bases recurs some eighty years later on the monument of Lysicrates, almost unmodified, and the form seems to have imposed itself upon the ancient builders almost as authoritatively as upon their modern imitators. The

Corinthian capital has much the same history; its form, once reached, undergoes little further change until late Hellenistic times.

This explanation for the extraordinary tyranny of the canonic form is manifestly inapplicable to all the elements of the Orders. The shape of a triglyph or mutule could not be deduced from the necessities of a roofed two-room shrine in trabeated stone or from any other intellectual formula or requirement. One could derive the column logically, but not its diminution; the capital, but not its profile; the architrave and perhaps the frieze, but not their scheme of decoration; the cornice, but not its profile. With the substitution of stone for timber in early times (for however much one may differ as to the detail of this timber prototype, it is impossible to refuse credence to it in some form or other) the structural justification for the appearance and pattern of regula, guttae, triglyph, mutule, fasciae, and dentils is their pretence of representing in conventionalized form the beam ends, planks, cleats, and even the nail-heads of timber-work transmuted into stone. Once established, these conventions survived through universal recognition of their artistic usefulness for articulating a structure which otherwise would possess little intelligible appearance. However inappropriate to limestone or marble for their material embodiment, and however irrelevant to the structural demands of squared and fitted blocks of stone, they supplied a recognizable norm for imparting to an assemblage of walls, ceilings, roofs, rooms, and corridors a unified, coherent, and shapely appearance—in short, they transformed mere masonry into a stoa or a temple. Precisely because strict architectural logic made no demand for the presence of most of the elements which composed the Orders and could not dictate to them either their shape or size or surface pattern, they escaped criticism, censure, or attack. They had come into existence in the early days of Greek architectural thinking and thereafter persisted in their own right as established species—much as there might be no discoverable inherent necessity for owls or weasels, but there they were, and each had its distinctive and established form. . . .

It is an impressive discovery when the human mind first catches glimpse of the eternal supersensuous laws ruling the seemingly casual appearances of the world of sense. This moment came to the Greeks early in their career in the course of Pythagorean and other geometric investigations. In musical theory its appearance was most striking. Sounds—those intangible and invisible occurrences, seemingly unruled by anything but a fortuitous concordance among themselves—suddenly admitted their allegiance to the tyranny of geometry and number. The consonance of two notes was shown to depend on the presence of a simple integral numerical ratio between the lengths of the strings which produced them. Beauty and ugliness of sound were but functions of Number and ratio, and therefore founded on something measurable, something intelligible. Everywhere, order showed its control within the universe—in the paths of the stars, in the structure of material things—and everywhere, order seemed to be traceable to the influence of Number. If the right and wrong in something seemingly so elusive and unmeasurable as musical tone was based on Number, was it not even more probable that a similar geometric or arithmetic basis should determine right and wrong in the appearance of seen objects, which were material things, measurable and directly amenable to geometric notions? Nature is orderly. The forms for which she strives are strikingly symmetrical and numerically rational. The accidents of matter obscure and confuse the simple geometry of her intentions; but if we compare enough specimens of any species, we can eliminate the individual accidents and construct the true form. Here then is a cardinal assumption of Greek aesthetic practice—that there is a true form for every class of objects and that such a true form is characterized by its geometric simplicity, by the commensurability of its component members. For if its parts be not simply commensurable, then complex and therefore less perfect numbers will enter and take the place of the more perfect ones which might have been employed. Commensurability of parts, $\sigma \upsilon \mu \mu \epsilon \tau \rho i \alpha$, is consequently a test of rightness of form, and it behooves the architect to work by the aid of its precepts.

The generative ratio of the Doric Order was fixed as 2 to 1 in the earliest times of which we have knowledge. In the round building whose architrave was discovered in the foundations of the Sikyonian treasury at Delphi this ratio was apparently not followed: in Hellenistic times the entablature (because so diminished in height) is frequently poly-triglyphal. But between these limits of time, the ratio of 2 to 1 served for what may be termed the generative formula of the Order in its horizontal extension. To every normal column span we find (enumerating the elements as they lie one above the other)

1 column,
2 regulae,
2 triglyphs + 2 metopes,
4 mutules,
4 lion's-heads,
(8 rows of cover-tiles?)

so that an ordinary Doric colonnade beats out a rhythm of full-notes in the columns, half and quarter notes in the entablature, and (frequently) eighth notes on the sloping roof, and even sixteenth notes in the floral ornamentation of the sima between the lion's-head water-spouts. In the Zeus temple at Olympia the measurements in ancient feet show how thoroughly and coherently the ratio was applied: the width of the roof-tile is taken as two feet, twice this measure gives us the width of a mutule with its *via* as well as the distance from lion's-head to lion's-head on the roof gutter, twice this latter measure gives the width of a triglyph with its metope, as well as the length of an abacus block, twice this measure gives the width from column center to column center, which is also the length of an epistyle block, and twice this last measure gives the height of a column. Finally, if the central acroterion of Nike was life-size, the total height stylobate to peak of gable-figure may very probably have equalled twice this last measurement. And so with $2 \times 2 \times 2 \times 2 \times 2$ ($\times$ 2?) the exterior of the temple is built up, and the tacit assumption seems to be that the eye, contemplating these forms, will be rhythmically affected by the simple numerical ratios inherent in them.

A more sophisticated employment of numerical ratio occurs in the colonnaded portico which the late fourth century architect Philon added to the Hall of Mysteries at Eleusis. There—as building inscriptions state and existing fragments of the architectural elements confirm—the columns' lower diameter was set at six feet while the open floor-space between the columns was set at nine feet; half of the former dimension was assigned to the triglyph width, half of the latter to the metope width; and half of this last measure was given to the overhang of the cornice over the frieze.

The giant columns of Persepolis clearly betray Greek influence, and not least in their careful observation of numerical symmetry. The two fore-parts of bulls which carry the rafters are supported by a four-sided theme, each side of which has four scrolls or volutes (each decorated with sixteen-petalled rosettes) into which a four-filleted band has been wound; this in turn is supported by a capital whose upper portion shows eight, while its lower portion shows sixteen, floral divisions; below, a shaft with forty-eight flutings is supported on a base whose petal forms number twenty-four.

There can of course be no doubt of the conscious use of this simplest of all numerical ratios as a generative formula in the Doric Order, but it should not be imagined that all the measurements therefore will be found to be mathematically exact—all equal or double or quadruple—in the ancient Doric temples. In the Sicilian temples[6] especially there occur the greatest irregularities in the spacing of the columns and the size of the various members. Much of this may be attributed to indifferent workmanship, since the eye really exacts only very general approximations to the mathematically correct in architectural ratios. But in the classic instance of the Parthenon it is a very difficult thesis to maintain that the irregularities are attributable to mason's errors or the architect's indifference to exactness. Rather it appears that the builders deliberately sought to temper the mathematically correct by slight departures from the "true" measurements, even carrying this ideal so far that they left no straight line straight nor any spacing equal.[7] We cannot fail to recall the practice of the sculptors contemporary to the Periclean architects, and particularly that reputedly Polyclitan saying concerning the "many numbers" which "*almost*" give perfection. The so-called "refinements" of Periclean architecture, the slight deviations from perfect regularity and symmetry, are not optical corrections for untrue illusions,[8] but are added in order to give life to the rigid mathematical correctness of the standard norm; they are departures from the "many numbers," out of which arises perfection. Certainly it is a very surprising thing that the Parthenon measurements cannot be reduced to feet and dactyls according to any common scale. A foot of .2957 meters will do fairly well; a foot of .3362 meters will apply with nearly equal success; but neither these nor any other unitary lengths will fit all the measurements, because they are integrally incommensurable. We can only conclude that the builders of the Parthenon (whether by intelligent imitation or by intuitive artistic taste) had applied to architecture the same secret of beauty which governs natural forms—the tempering of geometric accuracy by minute deviations in the interest of irregularity. I need only refer to the extraordinary mathematical precision which underlies natural forms in the vegetable and animal worlds[9] and to the patent observation that in any given individual of the species the precision of the underlying form is always tempered by the irregularities attendant upon the chance elements of environment and growth, and add that we are apt to find the actual slightly irregularized flower or shell more real, more "living," and more artistically moving than the cold geometrical perfection of the underlying form. The form only lives when it is irregularized in matter. In architecture the forms are man-devised; but if they are harmonized with mathematical precision and then irregularized in their material presentation, they will acquire a status analogous to that of a living thing in nature. . . .

I have dwelt a good deal on this numerical aspect of Greek architecture not only because it is philosophically interesting in its own right, but also because of certain remarkable implications which it involves. Out of Number come commensurability of lengths and surfaces and, by repetition, architectural beat and rhythm. But all these in Greek architecture are only effective upon the spectator if the matter in which they are embodied is seen as in one and the same plane.

The rhythm of a Doric colonnade with its measured recurrence of columns moving past, while the triglyphs double and the cornice and roof quadruple the same steady beat—all this is effective, indeed exists for the beholder, only if all these elements are felt to be on a single surface or area or plane. Theirs is an art of related lines and surfaces, not of solids. . . .

Instead of true depth, Greek architecture gives us successive and usually parallel planes. The stoa or colonnade presents the front plane of the exterior order, the middle plane of the columns which support the roof-beam, and the rear plane of the wall at the back. There is no sense of depth or enclosed space. Rather, the true depth has been converted into a succession of nearly flat and wholly disconnected surfaces—precisely as in Archaic Greek relief sculpture. Even the roof, thanks to the straight mounting lines of the cover-tiles, joins in the vertical planes. The human beings moving in this colonnade appear to the exterior spectator like bas-relief on the rear plane.

With the temple it is, of course, the same. On the long sides there are two parallel planes, that of the colonnade and that of the naos wall; on the short sides there are three planes, that of the exterior colonnade, that of the vestibule colonnade and that of the rear wall of the vestibule (with or without its doorway with door or hanging). More complicated vistas in agora or temenos only add other planes. In glimpses across angles of colonnaded squares, or through corners of dipteral temples, the masses are all presented at intervals so that the eye sees a series of superimposed surfaces sharply divided by an intervening break of perfectly indeterminate extent. It should be added that the Greek atmosphere encourages this impression by eating up the air's appearance of solidity, so that space loses its density and surfaces seem directly superimposed. . . .

And so there follows the most remarkable property of all in Greek architecture. Since its appearances all lie in parallel or perpendicular planes, it can only *define or bound solid space, and cannot enclose it.*

Just as there is no true depth to a Greek colonnade, but only the specious depth of Greek sculptured relief, so there is no sense of space shut in and contained in anything that the Greek builders made. Even the temple-interiors offered only more colonnades and walls in parallel planes, topped by a flat ceiling which was only another plane at right angles. Such a procedure bounds space, defines it; but though mechanically it contains space because it shuts it off, it is powerless to impart any such feeling to the human mind. Whereas a vault closes down upon space and makes space sensible, a panel ceiling merely ties the walls. In the terms of relief-carving, it acts like the straight edge or step between successive planes.

That these temple interiors were but half-lighted is perhaps an indication that artistically they were but half-felt or half-considered. They were but the space enclosed by the inner faces of the walls; they were the inside of the treasure-chest, serving to shut in the gold and the sacred heirlooms; and just as the outside of a chest has the craftsman's favor and gets the carving and gilding, so it was the exterior aspect of these enclosing walls which appealed to the ancient builder.

No doubt this is somewhat fanciful, and there exists a better reason for the opinion that interiors were the least successful aspect of Greek architecture. For it is of the utmost importance to note that Greek architecture had almost no need (of a direct practical kind) for trying to shut space in. Greek life was out-of-doors. The houses were mere sleeping-cells about a central patio, the theaters were unroofed gathering-places of the people upon the hillside; the marketplaces were open; even the shops were mere storehouses from which goods for the day's trade could be brought out to be spread in the open bazaar; the colonnades were but casual out-of-door shelters from wind and rain and sun; the schools were out-of-door palaestrae; the hospitals were colonnades in the sacred precinct of Aesclepius. Only the temples and the council-rooms so much as put the problem of enclosing airspace with encompassing masonry. Before the late Hellenistic age, domestic architecture hardly existed. It is not remarkable, therefore, that the architects devoted themselves wholly to external appearances or that, given the Greek conditions of atmosphere and light, they learned, as no other race has done, the secret of surface and line, but got no farther in the aesthetics of their art than the expression of support in vertical parallel planes.

We may assert, therefore, that the Greek architects had no comprehension of the artistic handling of space in interiors. That vast preoccupation of Gothic and modern designers was to them a book unopened. If a paradox is permissible, their only interior compositions were out-of-doors, where the roof was the blue sky. In town-square and temple-precinct they composed spatial complexities; but the picture is always made of overlapping surfaces moving across one another as the spectator moves. The intervening depths are lost, just as they were lost for the ridges and gulleys and forests of their own beloved mountains which still today show like flat bas-reliefs against the Grecian sky. . . .

Upon this two-dimensional character of its visual presentation Greek architecture based its artistic effects. Since support in the immediate vertical plane was all that such an art could present to the eye, all expression of weight sustained and held aloft must appear in the arrangement of lines and surfaces in the frontal plane of the Order. The entablature presses flat upon the columns and therefore can tolerate only horizontal or vertical lines in its decoration, since in this way the heavy uncomprising mass can be made directly intelligible. Our eyes follow the horizontal lines and our emotions instinctively interpret such lines in terms of mass in a state of rest. We have experienced just such a sweep of line in looking at the horizon of plains or of the ocean: it is the line of things outspread, heavy and immovable and enduring, held by gravity, but in no danger of falling. The columns express in their contour successful but not effortless resistance to this downward pressure, which weighs

35

squarely and heavily upon them until they bulge with the pressure. Here presumably is the psychology of entasis: it is the visible yielding to compression until a stable condition of resistance is reached. It establishes an analogy with human muscular effort and presents it directly to our emotional sensibility.

NOTES

[1] *The Greeks were timid engineers.* Consider the elaborate precautions taken with the central span of the Propylaea (W. B. Dinsmoor in *American Journal of Archaelogy*, [1910], pp. 145 ff). By applying the modern engineering formulae given in Kidder's *Architect's and Builder's Pocketbook*, I find that these precautions were superfluous.

[2] *These columns were . . . but barely sixty feet.* Cf. Athens, Olympieum; Miletos, Didymeum; Ephesos, "fifth" or Hellenistic temple of Artemis.

[3] Contrast the rich inventions of plan in late Roman times (Montano, *Scielti di varii tempietti antichi*, and *Raccolta di tempii*, etc.).

[4] πόλις κακῶς ερρυμοτομημένη Dicaearchos I. 1.12.

[5] I do not accept Dörpfeld's suggestion of an original symmetrical plan doubled on a north-south axis.

[6] Cf. Koldewey and Puchstein, *die griechischen Tempel in Unteritalien und Sicilien.*

[7] *. . . they left no straight line straight.* The material for the study of this question is to be found in Penrose, *Principles of Athenian Architecture* and Goodyear, *Greek Refinements.*

[8] *. . . not optical corrections.* Goodyear has abundantly proved this point in the book referred to in the previous note.

[9] Cf. T. A. Cook, *The Curves of Life;* d'Arcy Thompson, *Growth and Form;* A. H. Church, *Relation of Phyllotaxis to Mechanical Laws;* and the two (very popularly written) books by S. Colman and C. A. Coan, *Nature's Harmonic Unity* and *Proportional Form.*

3. THE GENERAL

CHARACTERISTICS OF

GREEK SCULPTURE

Gisela M. A. Richter

INTRODUCTION

Gisela Richter's *The Sculpture and Sculptors of the Greeks* has been one of the most useful studies of Greek sculpture since its initial publication in 1929. For years, students of Greek art have benefited from her research, published in such works as *Red-Figured Athenian Vases* (1936), *Kouroi* (1942, 1960), *Archaic Greek Art Against its Historical Background* (1949), *Three Critical Periods in Greek Sculpture* (1951), *Ancient Italy* (1955), and *A Handbook of Greek Art*, 4th rev. ed. (1965), which contains a fine selected bibliography on all phases of Greek art.

Miss Richter is one of those scholars who does not recoil from the risks of generalization. The selection in this anthology accepts such risks, and the result is surely one of the best introductory essays on the nature of Greek sculpture.

Other recommended readings on the sculpture would include Rhys Carpenter, *Greek Sculpture* (1960), which is not strictly speaking a history of Greek sculpture but a study of the techniques in their relationship to style; portions of his *The Esthetic Basis of Greek Art*, rev. ed. (1959), especially Chapter III; and Humfry Payne and G. M. Young, *Archaic Marble Sculpture from the Acropolis* (1936). For material on the techniques of Greek

37

sculpture one should mention, in addition to the above works, Stanley Casson, *The Technique of Early Greek Sculpture* (1933); C. Bluemel, *Greek Sculptors at Work* (1955); and, for a discussion of Graeco-Roman copies, Miss Richter's *Ancient Italy* (1955).

The selection that follows is reprinted from Chapter II in Gisela M. A. Richter, *The Sculpture and Sculptors of the Greeks*, rev. ed. (1950). Copyright © 1929, 1930, 1950 by Yale University Press.

We must remember that when the Greeks of classical times began their career civilization was still young. Everything that has happened in the last three thousand years was to them nonexistent. It is difficult to realize at once what this implies. It means that their artistic background was confined to the products of Egypt, Western Asia, and, in part, of Crete; and even of these their knowledge was limited, especially in literature, for what existed of Eastern writings was not easily accessible. Their own past was dimly remembered in the form of myths and legends. So practically the only literature they knew was Homer; the only history they were cognizant of was the Trojan war. In religion they had come in contact in the East with beliefs in heterogeneous gods and monsters, and from this they had developed the anthropomorphic religion found in Homer and Hesiod. In other words, most of the influences—artistic, intellectual, and religious—which act upon the modern man were as yet unformed. The background was simpler and the human mind had the freshness of youth.

In the centuries in which the classical Greek civilization was developed great changes happened. From its primitive beginning it passed through many stages to a more complicated outlook, and during this time it created a large part of what constitutes our Western culture. Nevertheless, it is possible to view the Greek mind as a whole. We will endeavor to do so and to see how its quality determined the character of Greek sculpture.

The three outstanding characteristics which strike us when we analyze the Greek mentality applied to art are directness, agility, and a feeling for beauty.

The directness was no doubt largely the result of a simpler outlook. It is a quality which we with our more complicated natures have lost; and when we come in contact with it, it affects us like a fresh breeze on a sultry day. It enabled the Greeks to keep their eyes on the essentials without the distraction of superfluous details. In literature this shows itself in their vivid similes, their keen observation, and also in a bald sincerity in stating facts.[1] Take such a description as Aeschylus': . . . ταχύπτεροι πνοαί, . . . ποντίων τε

κυμάτων ἀνήριθμον γέλασμα, παμμῆτόρ τε γῆ,[2] "Swift winged winds
. . . , and numberless laughter of waves, and earth the mother of
all." Could there be a truer and more beautiful description of the
much-besung wind and sea and earth? It reaches out to the chief
quality of each, transforms it into poetry, and creates thereby
something fundamental and permanent. Or take Clytaemnestra's
analysis of her emotions (in Sophocles' Electra[3]) when she hears of
the death of her son Orestes, whose vengeance she dreaded: "Are
these glad tidings? Rather would I say sad but of profit." It is a
simple statement of the case, without pretense or blinking of facts;
and perfectly concise. Greek literature is full of these pregnant,
clear-eyed sayings. The much-quoted epitaph, "His father Philip
laid here to rest his twelve-year-old son Nicoteles, his high hope,"[4]
is another example of this combination of sincerity and conciseness.
What could be added to the essential facts conveyed in "laid to
rest," "twelve-year-old," and "high hope" which would not be a
superfluity? And let us remember Aristotle's definition of superfluities, "That which makes no perceptible difference by its presence
or its absence is no real part of the whole."[5]

It is this feeling for the whole unencumbered by superfluities
which gives Greek art its peculiar greatness. At the very beginning
of his career the Greek sculptor went straight to the essentials. In
the early "Apollo" statues why is it that in spite of their stiffness
and faulty construction they are full of life? Because the important
functional parts of the body are properly accented, the details are
omitted, and each and every part passes into and connects with
the adjoining part. . . . The rendering is simplified; the important
parts are made to stand out and there are no incidents, no superfluities. The result is that we have the impression of an organic
whole which can function and live (Fig. 2). And this is true of all
Greek sculpture during its best periods.

The second outstanding characteristic of the Greeks we may take
to be their agility. It was stimulated doubtless by the geography
of the country. For the combination of mountains and sea tended
both to separate the Greek peoples from one another and to stimulate emigration. The mountains acted as barriers and the sea invited
adventures. Hence the formation of a number of separate communities distributed over a large area including Greece, western Asia
Minor, the Aegean Islands, southern Italy, and a few outlying places
in Spain and France. This double circumstance insured on the one

2. Kouros of Sounion, Archaic Greek, *c.* 600 B.C. (Marburg-Art Reference Bureau)

hand compact community life in small city states, on the other the variety of stimulus derived from heterogeneous peoples; all of which made for lively activity, because individual responsibility in a small state and rivalry with other states are apt to invite energy. This striving for adventure and for knowledge led the Greeks into many untried paths. It is responsible for the amazing number of their discoveries in almost every field of intellectual activity. "To be learning something is the greatest of pleasures, not only to the philosopher but also to the rest of mankind, however small their capacity for it," is Aristotle's definition of happiness[6] of which Plato's more imaginative rendering is, "He whose heart has been set on the love of learning and on true wisdom and has chiefly exercised this part of himself, this man must without fail have thoughts that are immortal and divine."[7]

In sculpture this agility of mind and this love of knowledge are likewise responsible for a great deal. They meant progress and development. Without them Greek sculpture might have remained stationary, never surpassing the attainments of Oriental artists. The Egyptian sculptor, for instance, with all his wonderful feeling for the value of essentials, practiced his art for thousands of years

41

without solving some of its difficulties. He followed throughout the old law of frontality,[8] his knowledge of anatomy remained primitive, and in his reliefs proper perspective was never attained. The agile mind of the Greek determined to wrestle with these problems. Not content with what had been accomplished before him, he was eager to solve new problems, and so he started out on his adventure of representing a human body in all manner of postures, constructed according to nature, with its parts in proper relation and perspective, both in the round and in relief. To a pioneer in the field it was a formidable task. But with remarkable perseverance the Greek artist accomplished it, and his solution of these problems was like the removal of shackles which had hampered the free development of art for generations. The human figure, by its movements and gestures, could henceforth express action and emotion. . . .

A love of truth and of knowledge could easily have made realists of the Greeks; but their realism was transformed into idealism by their third great characteristic—their feeling for beauty. Beauty to them was not something apart from daily life but interwoven into every phase of it. The beauty of their own landscape undoubtedly quickened their sensibilities in this direction. Its grandeur and suavity, its rich colors and fine contours, its elusive, subtle quality would inevitably influence a young, impressionable people. It would incline them to regard beauty as an integral part of their lives and to find their happiness in the loveliness of their immediate surroundings. And their sense for beauty grew so strong that it became the underlying principle in their lives. For they made a great discovery—one that we have lost since, perhaps through Puritan interpretations, but are beginning to realize again—that goodness and beauty are identical, not only figuratively but actually. "Virtue it appears will be a kind of health and beauty and good habit of the soul; and vice will be a disease and deformity and sickness of it," says Plato in his Republic;[9] and with the Greeks it was a generally accepted principle. "Then good language and good harmony and grace and good rhythm all depend upon a good nature, by which I mean a mind that is really well and nobly constituted in its moral character," Plato says again in his Republic;[10] and in his Symposion:[11] "From the love of the beautiful has sprung every good in heaven and earth." Most eloquent of all is the current Greek expression for a "gentleman"—καλός κἀγαθός, "beautiful and good." Greek and especially Athenian education was planned directly with this end in view; and athletics and music were given the most prominent places, one to foster the beauty of the body, the other of the mind. That exercise develops the body is easily accepted by us today; but that art and music make men good is not so generally believed. Yet the Athenians practised this creed with good results; at least they won a reputation, Plato tells us, "throughout Europe and Asia" "for the beauties of their bodies and the various virtues of their souls." [12] Let us learn from Plato how this can be accomplished. In dealing with the education of his guardians in his Republic, [13] he gives us a specific account. Socrates asks: "Ought we not to seek out artists who by the power of genius can trace out the nature of the fair and the graceful, that our young men, dwelling as it were in a healthful region, may drink in good from every quarter, whence any emanation from noble works may strike upon their eye or their ear, like a gale wafting health from salubrious lands, and win them imperceptibly from their earliest childhood into resemblance, love, and harmony with the true beauty of reason?" And when Glaucon assents Socrates continues: "Is it then on these accounts that we attach such supreme importance to a musical education, because rhythm and harmony sink most deeply into the recesses of the soul, and take most powerful hold of it, bringing gracefulness in their train, and making a man graceful if he be rightly nurtured?" And finally he sums up, "There can be no fairer spectacle than that of a man who combines the possession of moral beauty in his soul with outward beauty of form, corresponding and harmonizing with the former, because the same great pattern enters into both." Translated into conduct this aesthetic ideal became a reverence for sobriety and temperance. As an imaginative, southern people the Greeks no doubt had strong feelings difficult to control; but they recognized that temperance was a kind of harmony, and therefore desirable. So μηδέν ἄγαν, "nothing too much," became their motto, and ὕβρις "insolence," their abomination.

Naturally in the art of sculpture the Greek sense of beauty found a fruitful field. It is directly responsible for the most characteristic quality, idealism. The creation of beauty was the sculptor's chief interest and his types are selected with this end in view. "But when you want to represent beautiful figures," says Socrates to the artist Parrhasius, "since it is not easy to find everything without a flaw in a single human being, do you not then collect from a number

43

what is beautiful in each, so that the whole body may appear beautiful?" And Parrhasius admits that such is their practice. This sums up very simply the Greek point of view. It is not realism and truth to nature but perfection of form that the Greeks consciously strove for. And this beauty of form was further enhanced by their feeling for design, which gave to their work a highly decorative quality. It is particularly strong in the archaic period when stylization took the place of correctness of modeling, but it was not lost even in the more naturalistic periods, and always gives style to the whole—the style which distinguishes art from nature. Indeed it is this sense of composition which the Greek regarded as perhaps the most important element in a work of art. It is clearly brought out in the definition of beauty quoted by Plotinus (as the opinion of some):[14]

> What is it that impresses you when you look at something, attracts you, captivates you, and fills you with joy?
> The general opinion, I may say, is that it is the interrelation of parts toward one another and toward the whole, with the added element of good color, which constitutes beauty as perceived by the eye; in other words, that beauty in visible things as in everything else consists of symmetry and proportion. In their eyes, nothing simple and devoid of parts can be beautiful, only a composite.

This joy in "symmetry and proportion" can be clearly detected in all Greek art.

Another important factor in the "idealism" of Greek sculpture is its simplification. The Greek sculptor felt that to translate the human body into a work of art he must harmonize the multiformity and restlessness of nature and create a unity. We have spoken of his subordination of parts to the whole, his elimination of superfluous details, his restriction to the essentials. Equally important was his simplification of the design. His statue was contained in a unified space,[15] that is, a space with restricted depth. . . . It is important to understand and realize this characteristic of Greek sculpture; for it is very largely through this conception of space that a Greek statue acquires its dignity and grandeur. A figure thus carved can be taken in by the human eye without distraction, and thereby attains that sense of quiet and detachment which makes art a refreshment to the spirit.

This "relief conception," as it has been called by Hildebrand, was inherited by the Greeks from the Egyptians; it was stimulated by the universal practice of stone carving, in which both the figure and the space surrounding it were potentially enclosed in the block, by the demand for architectural sculpture with its uniform depths of pediments and metopes. That the Greeks recognized its importance from an artistic point of view is shown by their practice of it even when working in bronze or with figures in which no background had to be considered. It is not until the very latest period, in such creations as the Dirke monument, that this conception is given up, and the result is, we feel immediately, a certain restlessness.

Still another determining element in the idealistic impression of Greek sculpture is beauty of contour. So much of Greek sculpture was out in the open to be viewed from a distance that the outline counted for much; and it is the lovely undulating outline of a Greek statue which impresses us from the first. Indeed this feeling for contour was so strong in the Greek artist that it shows itself in all his work, not only in the design of the whole figure, but in every part of it—the oval of the face, the swing of the eyelids, the curve of the lips, the drawing of the muscles and of the folds of the drapery. It is an extraordinarily strong sensitivity for rhythmic line—which found expression also in the shapes of vases and in vase painting.

It is, then, sense of structure, simplification of form and design, harmonious proportion, and rhythmic contour that stand out as the salient features of Greek sculpture. By them it acquires the grandeur which we feel in its presence. They give it its spiritual quality. And since art is a spiritualization of nature it is this spiritualizing quality which is fundamental, and without which representation is not art. And so Greek sculpture, throughout its development, has the distinguishing trait of great art.

From our analysis of the Greek mind and its influence on Greek sculpture we must pass to the chief uses of sculpture in Greece; for the nature of the demand of course affects the character of the supply.

Sculpture in Greece was largely religious. Its chief use was for the decoration of temples either as pediment groups, friezes, or acroteria, for the cult statues of deities placed in the cella, and for votive statues and reliefs dedicated in sanctuaries. A large proportion of the sculpture that has survived is therefore architectural. This demand early developed the technique of relief as well as the composition of large groups. We should never have had the superb creations of the western pediment of the Olympia temple or the Parthenon frieze but for the long history which preceded them and which gave the sculptor ample opportunities of development. But these pediments and friezes could not vie in importance with the cult statues placed in the interiors of temples. It was round them that the popular worship centered and it was by them that the people obtained a concrete realization of their gods. And so to embody his vision of the deity in a great temple statue was the highest task of a Greek sculptor. Unfortunately hardly any of these statues have survived. We have only descriptions and small reproductions by which to visualize the colossal chryselephantine statues by Phidias, Polyclitus, and Alcamenes. In every estimate of Greek sculpture, therefore, we must remember that its finest creations have been irretrievably lost.

Another important demand for sculpture in Greek times was created by the custom of erecting statues of the victors in the athletic contests given in honor of Zeus, Poseidon, Hera, etc. The statues stood in the public places and in the sacred enclosures in which the games had taken place, and the young athletes were mostly represented nude, for that is how they had engaged in their contests. This practice and the athletic ideal which prompted it led to the development of the nude male type as a favorite form. Not only athletes but gods and heroes were so represented. In this series of nude male figures the ideal human form was gradually worked out and became one of the greatest achievements of Greek sculpture.

Commemorative sculptures which are so popular today also played an important part in Greece. A significant victory would be celebrated by the erection of a statue or group, like the Nike of Paionios at Olympia, or the bronze Athena of Phidias on the Acropolis which was an offering "from the spoils of the Persians who landed at Marathon." The group of the Tyrannicides set up on the marketplace would remind Athenians every day of their liberation from the tyrants and of the value of their democratic institutions. We hear also of large groups of several figures, e.g., statues of Athena, Apollo, Miltiades, Erechtheus, Cecrops, Pandion, Aegeus, and five other heroes, another offering "from the spoils of Marathon" by Phidias. Such groups in the round must have been remarkable achievements, and it is a grievous loss that they have disappeared. The erection of portraits of distinguished men became increasingly popular as time went on.

Besides these more or less public uses of sculpture there was a large private demand for grave monuments. The chief forms adopted in Athens were slabs with reliefs representing the departed, either alone or with sorrowing relatives, statues in the round, slabs crowned by finials, and vases decorated with reliefs. They supply us with some of the most touching and most "personal" representations we have in Greek art. These sculptured grave monuments remained in vogue until the end of the fourth century B.C. when the "anti-luxury" decree of Demetrius put a sudden stop to this artistic expression. Their constant use during three centuries greatly furthered the development of relief technique.

It is important to become familiar also with the subjects represented in Greek sculpture; for the Greek artist had an entirely different repertoire from our own. Early Christian, medieval, and Renaissance art are from this point of view much nearer to us, since they need little explanation; but when we enter the Greek field we are stepping into an unknown land; and we must be careful to leave behind us any preconceptions we may have.

We have seen how the athletic ideal helped to concentrate interest in the human figure. It accustomed people to seeing the human body in all manner of postures and to appreciating its beauty. Moreover, the Greek with his love of the normal had a tendency to humanize everything. His gods and goddesses are no longer monsters, as often in Eastern art, but assume human form; so do the Nymphs, Satyrs, Centaurs, Tritons, and the other personifications of nature. Even when these start with hybrid shapes they soon lose their animal characteristics and gradually become more and more human. And so Greek sculpture consists largely of figures of human beings representing divinities, heroes, and athletes. Animals and decorative motives find a place and an important one, but they are nevertheless secondary. The human figure is the theme par excellence.

Joined to this humanizing tendency the Greeks had a love for storytelling. Much of Greek religion consists of stories about gods and goddesses and heroes; and these manifold imaginative tales would naturally make a great appeal to the artist. They supplied him with the most varied material, which he used so constantly that definite standardized types soon emerged. Plato's words about litera-

47

ture apply also to sculpture and painting—that art must eschew novelty and be framed after the pattern of those foundation myths which the poets have made familiar. So we must become conversant with these foundation myths. And a delightful process it is; for these stories have the freshness and imaginative quality of a poetic people. In entering this world of Greek fiction with its contests of Lapiths and Centaurs and Amazons, its wonderful deeds of heroes, and its manifold adventures of gods and goddesses, we feel very near the beginning of civilization. We sense the vivaciousness and naïveté of youth. No doubt some of the myths have a historical background; some are certainly rooted in actual experience; but the poet when he took his material transformed fact into fancy and then the artist translated this fancy into a beautiful picture. And so in our interpretation of Greek mythology in Greek art let us endeavor to catch the lovely simplicity of these spirited stories directly and concretely told. It is easy for us with our modern, complicated minds to read our own thoughts into these representations and endow them with farfetched symbolic significance. But thereby we lose the early Greek flavor and become more like the late Latin commentators. . . . To the Greek artist the hero was always Heracles with his lion's skin and club or Theseus with his little chiton and his sword or Perseus with his distinctive paraphernalia, tackling in various ways these dangerous creatures. The whole interest lies in the contest, in the story, and in its artistic rendering. Its subjective significance was outside the artist's scope.

In this connection we may again quote Plato;[16] for in his analytical time a few learned people were beginning to lose the childlikeness of earlier days and search for farfetched interpretations. When Socrates is asked by young Phaedrus whether he believes in the story that Boreas carried off Orithyia he gives an illuminating answer, which it may be well to quote at length, for it states the case admirably: "If I disbelieved," Socrates says, "as the wise men do, I should not be extraordinary; then I might give a rational explanation, that a blast of Boreas, the north wind, pushed her off the neighboring rocks as she was playing with Pharmaceia, and that when she had died in this manner she was said to have been carried off by Boreas. I think, however, such explanations are very pretty in general, but are the inventions of a very clever and laborious and not altogether enviable man, for no other reason than because after this he must explain the forms of the Centaurs, and then that of the Chimaera, and there presses in upon him a whole crowd of such creatures, Gorgons, Pegasoi, and multitudes of strange, inconceivable, portentous natures. If anyone disbelieves in these, and with a rustic sort of wisdom, undertakes to explain each in accordance with probability, he will need a great deal of leisure. Now I have no leisure for them at all. . . . And so I dismiss these matters and accept the customary belief about them."

Surely our interest also lies in these customary beliefs of the people who produced and enjoyed the art which we are endeavoring to understand. So we cannot do better than follow Socrates' advice and not spoil a fairy tale with a laborious mind. We must remember, then, that the only symbolism we shall find in Greek art is the concrete one by which pebbles suggest the beach, a fish the sea, a growing plant the meadow, a pine tree the mountain, a reed the river bank, and a column the house. This practical symbolism was freely used, for such shorthand methods were useful and easily understood, and were thoroughly in line with the Greek tendency to simplification.

The large mass of architectural sculptures—the pediments of the temples, the continuous friezes, the metopes—have almost invariably mythological representations—either legends directly associated with the deity to whom the temple was dedicated (e.g., the birth of Athena and her strife with Poseidon in the pediments of the Parthenon), or the familiar contest scenes of Heracles, Theseus, Lapiths, etc. Only occasionally is there a scene from actual life, for instance, the Panathenaic procession in the Parthenon frieze; though here too the subject is lifted to a higher plane by the actual presence of the gods on the eastern side. The almost total absence of historical representations is striking. Even in single sculptures erected to celebrate a specific victory such subjects are rare; when Miltiades is introduced in Phidias' group commemorative of the battle of Marathon[17] he is associated with Athena, Apollo, and various heroes; the representation of Greeks and Persians on the frieze of the temple of Athena Nike is exceptional. We have not a single representation of the battles of Thermopylae or Salamis, of the Peloponnesian war, of the great plague, of the Sicilian expedition; in short, of the outstanding events which formed the chief preoccupation of the Greeks of the fifth century. How different the Romans or the Egyptians and Assyrians with their endless friezes recording their triumphs over their enemies; how different we ourselves with some of our war monuments and realistic pictures of contemporary battles! The Greeks, in order to convey the strife and stress of their time, had recourse to mythological contests, or to the semi-legendary events of the Trojan war.[18] These were far enough removed to admit of safe treatment, which with the constantly changing alignment of the Greek states was probably an important point. At all events, the Greeks knew that history with the strong partisan and bitter feeling it arouses is not an appropriate subject for sculpture. The same is true of contemporary political events. The Greek was distinctly a "political animal." Of all his contributions to mankind he prided himself most on his civic ideal. Every Athenian citizen was a representative in Congress and a legislator in the law courts. But that part of his life was passed over by the artist. And probably for the same reason for which contemporary wars were omitted—that controversial subjects do not belong to the realm of art.

There were some other aspects of daily life, however, which found a place in Greek sculpture. Not only single statues of athletes but chariot groups were popular dedications; and occasionally even in the fifth century we hear of such "genre" subjects as the statue by Styppax of "a slave roasting entrails and kindling a fire with a blast from his swollen cheeks."[19] In the Hellenistic period such themes greatly gained in vogue, especially in bronze and terracotta statuettes. But the most frequent representations of daily life occur on the grave monuments where the departed were shown in their favorite occupations, as their families liked to remember them. To us these pictures of Greek life are singularly precious; for they are contemporary illustrations of familiar happenings and as such eloquent and trustworthy. We see here men represented as warriors or athletes; women busy with their spinning or putting on their jewelry; children playing ball or caressing their pet animals; and in the family groups we gain a realization of a happy and affectionate family life. And, always, these renderings are simple and direct—with no trace of sentimentality or exaggeration, but with the Greek note of serenity which makes of them something typical and permanent. We are reminded of Nietzsche's famous saying: "Die Griechen sind, wie das Genie, einfach: deshalb sind sie die unsterblichen Lehrer."

NOTES

[1] For an excellent discussion of this subject, cf. Livingstone, *The Greek Genius and Its Meaning to Us.*

[2] *Prometheus Bound* 88 ff.

[3] 766.

[4] Callimachus, *Epigr.* 19.

[5] *Poetics* 8. 4.

[6] *Poetics* IV 4.

[7] *Timaius* 90 A.

[8] Frontality I take to mean a perfect symmetry in the two sides of the body, i.e., the equal distribution of weight on the two legs. This admits of the torsion of the body which we find adequately rendered in some Egyptian sculptures.

[9] IV. 444.

[10] III. 400.

[11] 197.

[12] *Timaius* 21 A–25 D.

[13] III. 401–402.

[14] *Ennead* I. VI. i. Though Plotinus lived in the third century A.D. his teachings are often borrowed from Plato and other philosophers of the fifth and fourth centuries B.C.

[15] Cf. on this subject Hildebrand's remarks in his illuminating book, *Das Problem der Form.*

[16] *Phaidrus* 229 D.

[17] Pausanias X. 10. 1. In Mikon's famous painting of the battle of Marathon, Athena and some popular heroes (Theseus, Heracles, and Echetlus) are likewise introduced (Pausanias I. 16).

[18] We have a few exceptions to this general rule in Greek paintings, for instance in the representation of the battle of Oinoe in the Poikile (Pausanias I. 15).

[19] Pliny, *N. H.* XXXIV. 81.

4. GREEK GEOMETRIC AND ARCHAIC ART

Sir John D. Beazley

INTRODUCTION

Greek Sculpture and Painting, initially the chapters on Greek art in the *Cambridge Ancient History,* has long enjoyed a reputation as an exemplary survey of Greek art from its Geometric beginnings to the Hellenistic period. The selections on the painting and sculpture of the Geometric and Archaic periods are the work of J. D. Beazley, whose prose style, like his analyses of the art, is as fine as it is precise. The early centuries of Greek art have seldom been better summarized than in this selection—and nowhere more memorably.

The Development of Attic Black-Figure (1951), by the same author, can be recommended for further reading on the subject of Archaic vase-painting. For vase-painting in general there is Ernst Pfuhl, *Masterpieces of Greek Drawing and Painting,* tr. by J. D. Beazley (1955); Ernst Buschor, *Greek Vase-Painting,* tr. G. C. Richards (1922); and Mary Hamilton Swindler, *Ancient Painting* (1929). R. S. Young, *Hesperia,* Supplement II (1939) is a valuable source for information on Geometric pottery, and for red-figure vase-painting one should consult Richter, *Red-Figured Athenian Vases* (1936), and her *Attic Red-Figured Vases, A Survey* (1946, 1958). The following contain useful discussions on the techniques of Greek pottery: Richter, *The Craft of Athenian Pottery* (1923); Beazley, *Potter and Painter in Ancient Athens* (1944); and Joseph V. Noble's article "The Technique of Attic Vase-Painting" in *American Journal of Archaeology*, LXIV, 4 (1960).

The selections that follow are reprinted from sections I–VII in J. D. Beazley and Bernard Ashmole, *Greek Sculpture and Painting to the End of the Hellenistic Period*, Rev. ed. (1966), with the permission of the publishers, Cambridge University Press.

I. EARLY GREEK ART

The early story of Greek art is concerned with three phenomena: the reign of a primitive Geometric art from the tenth century to the eighth; the assimilation of Oriental influences toward and after the close of that period; and the formation, assisted at first by these Oriental models, of a new national style, the Greek Archaic, in the seventh and sixth centuries. The culmination of this style, at the end of the sixth century and the beginning of the fifth, is attended by the collapse, for the first time in the world's history, of certain age-long conventions, and the way is thus prepared for an art of unprecedented freedom, the classical Greek art of the fifth and fourth centuries.

The literary sources for the history of sixth-century art are extremely scanty, and for the art of the preceding centuries there is hardly any direct literary testimony. Inscriptional evidence begins in the seventh century. But most of our knowledge is derived from the stylistic and other peculiarities of the objects themselves, and from the circumstances of their discovery. Sometimes an object can be connected closely or loosely with a datable person or event; and other objects can be dated relatively to the first.

Of the vast number of objects produced in antiquity, some had a better chance of surviving to our times than others. Some substances are perishable (wood, plaster, textiles), others comparatively durable but convertible (marble, bronze), others comparatively durable and comparatively inconvertible (well-baked clay, gemstones). Thus painted clay vessels must take the place, for us, of paintings on wood or wall; small bronzes, lost or discarded, for the most part, in antiquity, of the large bronze statues which remained in place to be melted down; and only a small proportion of marble statues has escaped utter defacement or the lime-kiln. For these reasons, and for others, such as the lack of exploration in many areas, there are great gaps in our monumental evidence. In the early period, however, our sources, though scanty, are untroubled: the

55

objects to be dealt with are almost exclusively originals, and not, as in subsequent periods, largely later copies or imitations: unearthed but lately, they have suffered little at the restorer's hands: lastly, we may feel confident that, on the whole, the best of them, whether sculptures or paintings, are equal in quality to the best of their time: for the Archaic sculptures of the Acropolis were buried in an age which paid little respect to the work of the past, and were not disinterred until our own days; and it was not till well after the Persian Wars that painting took such a leap as to leave the decoration of vases far behind: "the vases of the Classical period are but a reflection of classical beauty; the vases of the Archaic period are archaic beauty itself."

II. GEOMETRIC ART

Between the flourishing of the Creto-Mycenaean civilization, and the geometric period proper, there lies a long period which has been named, not very happily, the Proto-Geometric: a period of cultural decay, doubtless of invasions and incessant conflict. The remains are chiefly ceramic. The shapes and decoration of the vessels are commonplace. The material which the painter uses is still that lustrous black glaze which was invented by Middle Minoan potters, but his repertory is limited to groups of semi-circles and circles, triangles, straight and wavy lines.

Somewhere about the end of the tenth century, a new style arose, the Geometric style proper, which in the course of the ninth and eighth centuries conquered the Greek world. Its triumph was more complete in some districts than in others: in Crete and eastward, Proto-Geometric and even late Aegean elements lingered; old shapes, and old ornaments, such as the concentric circle, persisted; and old principles of decoration.

The analogies between Greek geometric work and the products of the Northern Balkans and Central Europe point to the rudiments of the style having been brought to Greece by Northern invaders. When life in Greece became a little more settled, the seed ripened: and the rudiments were formed into a distinctive Greek style. That this Greek style originated in a single center seems likely from the uniform character of early Geometric decoration in places so far apart as Crete and Thessaly, Athens and Rhodes. Where the center was is doubtful, but seeing that the development of the style is more consistent in Old Greece, especially in Attica, than elsewhere, its home probably lay in that quarter.

Geometric pottery reached its highest point in Attica, and the progress of the style can be traced better there than anywhere else. The earliest Attic Geometric vases are decorated with horizontal bands, row over row, of simple rectilinear patterns—meander, lozenge, chain, zigzag; a broader band being set between narrower, and the narrower symmetrically disposed. New shapes of vase came in with the new style of decoration, and others were added later. These shapes differ widely from the harmonious forms of sixth- or fifth-century vases; but they please by their strength, clarity, and sedateness. The early Geometric system of decoration was elaborated in two ways: first by a structural alteration in the ornamental scheme—the division of the main zone by means of verticals into rectangular fields; and secondly by the introduction of animal and human figures. A row of animals in single file is substituted for a pattern zone; the antithetic group, two animals facing, with or without a central object, is used to adorn a rectangular field; freer compositions appear, scenes of a general character from everyday life. The chief animals are birds, horses, deer: the scenes are mostly battles, often at sea or on the seashore, and funerals. The figures are schematized silhouettes. The men, for example, are very tall and thin, the trunk a triangle tapering to the waist, the head a knob with a mere excrescence for the face: toward the end of the style the head is lit up—the head-knob is drawn in outline, and a dot signifies the eye. The background of the picture is toned down by copious filling-ornaments.

The metalwork which has survived from the Geometric period consists mainly of bronze bands, incised with patterns, which formed part of vessels; gold diadems with embossed designs; incised fibulae; further, of small bronze statuettes, some of them votive offerings each standing on its own base, others portions of larger objects (staves, pins, vessels, stands). The engraved and embossed decoration resembles that of the vases. The statuettes are small figures of animals or of men, sometimes simple groups, mare and foal, rider, chariot. The best show artistic intention, decision, and some skill. The men are mainly arms and legs, but by the end of the period, the forms begin to round out a little and grow shapely: and in a small group of ivories found with geometric vases in an Attic grave,

3. Attic Dipylon Amphora, Late Geometric Style, 8th Century B.C. (National Museum, Athens)

the greater corporeity, and the studied symmetry of the attitude, give a presage of Greek Archaic sculpture.

This art of thin lines and sharp corners, this small, bleak, thrifty art, presents a strange contrast to the rich swell and swing of Mycenaean forms. But its achievement should not be underrated. Take one of those huge monumental vases (Fig. 3) which stood over Athenian graves: we cannot fail to admire the simple firm lines of the shape; the careful arrangement of the decorative elements to suit their places; and the clear, compact composition of the main picture—a dead man lying in state, with mourners to left and mourners to right of him, and mourners seated and kneeling beside the bier.

III. ORIENTAL INFLUENCES: AND THE EARLIEST ARCHAIC ART

Even in the Geometric period, the Greek world shows occasional signs of contact with the more ancient and far more highly developed art of the East: if more were known about early Ionia these signs would no doubt be more frequent. Toward the end of the eighth century foreign import and foreign influence increase greatly, and eventually contribute to the transformation of the aspect of Greek art. Products of Hittite and Syrian art, and of the mixed art created out of Syrian, Mesopotamian and Egyptian elements by the Phoenicians, reached the Greeks both overland and by sea. Few of these products were of fine quality; but they served to place the artistic experience of ages at the disposal of the untutored Greek craftsman. The Homeric poems bear witness to a general admiration for the works of art made or peddled by the Phoenician: and the old belief that the shield of Achilles is based upon Eastern metal-work, though often assailed, holds the field. Side by side with this Oriental influence, there are traces, but much fainter traces, of another: Creto-Mycenaean traditions may have lingered in some districts after fading out elsewhere: and it is always possible that in various parts of Greece, Cretan or Mycenaean objects, remaining in view, or discovered from time to time, contributed at least the decayed nobleman's mite towards the formation not only of the Greek system of ornament but of the Greek figure style as well.

Oriental motives find their way into Attica, as into Sparta, before the end of the Geometric period. Lion and griffin appear on diadems found with Geometric vases: a man fights with a rampant lion; two lions devour a hunter: and from time to time an Oriental creature strays into pottery, like a prospector before the rush. . . .

The pottery of the late eighth and the seventh century, from its plentifulness and variety, throws more light upon the history of Greek art during the period than any other class of object. The technique of vase-painting changes towards the end of the eighth century. The face, or parts of it, are now drawn in black outline, with black lines for inner details. The "reserved" spaces (those enclosed by the black outline) are often uncolored; but female flesh is sometimes filled in with white, male with white or brown. White and red are used for details as well as black. An alternative process was to retain the old silhouette of the Geometric period, but trans-formed by the use of incised lines for inner markings: the black is usually enlivened by touches of red. Both processes, "outline" and "black-figure," may occur on the same vase, even in the same picture; further, in the black-figured pictures, the female flesh is regularly "reserved," and the male sometimes brown.

Geometric painting was monochrome: the new art contrasts light with dark, and one color with another. The Geometric painter divided his field into many small areas, and decorated each with small oft-repeated units: the new art enlarges the areas by reducing their number; decorates them with bigger and bolder elements, connected by an ampler rhythm; lays more stress on the chief area; achieves unity of design by subordination not by diffusion.

In patterns and in figures the straight line gives place to the curved. Lotus-flower, lotus-bud, and other motives floral and spiral were borrowed from the East, and out of these borrowed elements new and complex patterns were constituted, the ancestors of classical Greek ornament. For a long time animals are no less, even more, popular than before; but the choice changes; the favorites are now the ferocious or fantastic creatures of the East, lion, griffin, sphinx, and new monsters invented to keep these company. Turning to the human figure, we find the meager schematic forms swelling out and acquiring volume. The arms are no longer match-like; thighs, buttocks and calves are big and strong: the joints are defined, breast, knee and ankle indicated, the facial features emphasized. In the Geometric period legs and head were always in profile, breast always frontal: now the breast may be either frontal or in profile: frontal if the arms are extended to left and right of the body, in profile if the arms are close to the body or both stretched forward. The head can now look back. The movement of the legs is freer and truer: Geometric figures are unsteady, especially when they would run: but seventh-century figures, standing, running or striding, have the steadiness of later Greek art. An interlocked group is hardly representable in the simple silhouette style: if two Geometric figures were in contact, they touched but gingerly: the seventh century, by its inner delineation and its color contrasts, can demarcate one figure from another in an intertwined group: animal can close with animal, man with monster or man. "Congruent" groups can also be formed, two figures side by side, one overlapping the other. The subjects alter: the battle pictures become more disciplined; hoplite faces hoplite in the prescribed attitude; in good order, a detachment advances at the double, or the victors follow up their success; the fallen are no longer ranged, one higher than the other, like specimens on a board, but lie grovelling or supine each on his own piece of groundline. The chariot-race supplants the slow funeral procession. Lastly, the Greek artist now sets himself to represent, on clay, metal or other material, the stories of the gods and the great men of old: and by the sixth century these "myths" will have become his favorite theme. Old types are enriched and defined by a mythical content, new figures created to embody a particular story. The scenes are still confined to the barest necessaries: and the passions represented are the simplest: the desire to kill or to escape death, the delight at the sight of a friend.

The vases of this period divide themselves into two groups, an eastern, comprising the vases of Greek Asia Minor, of the adjacent islands, especially Rhodes, and of Naukratis; and a less homogeneous western. The contrast between the two groups is instructive. The east uses the outline technique, and long avoids incision: the black-figure technique arises in the west. The east is conservative, the west experimental. The east is content with the ancient monsters of the Orient, the west devises new: the east likes uniform rows of animals, a whole row of goats, another of deer, the west mixes its animals: the western patterns are now wilder, now more complex than the eastern: the west is narrative, the east decorative: the east, having no tale to tell, retains the filling-ornaments, and needs no inscriptions: the west ends by clearing the ground for action and for word.

Geometric pottery, though exported was not exported widely, and beyond the Greek world hardly at all: the potter worked mainly for local demand: but by the seventh century pottery was one of the principal articles of Greek export trade. Eastern Greek pottery was sent north to the Black Sea colonies, south to Egypt, west to Sicily and Etruria. The circulation of Corinthian pottery was even wider. . . .

At the end of the seventh century, the black-figure takes the place of the outline technique in Attica: the exuberant ornament is

4. "Nessos" Amphora, Attic, c. 610–600 B.C. Heracles Killing the Centaur Nessos, Gorgons (National Museum, Athens)

reduced, the animals are powerfully stylized; the eccentricity disappears. The change is partly due to influence from Proto-Corinthian art. The chief example of this stage is the Nessos amphora in Athens (Fig. 4), where the group of Heracles and the Centaur yields to fine Proto-Corinthian work in deftness, surpasses it in force. Other works by the same painter have been preserved: he is perhaps the earliest Greek artist whose personality we can grasp.

IV. THE SIXTH CENTURY, TO 520 B.C.: EARLY AND MIDDLE ARCHAIC SCULPTURE

The figures and scenes with which we have hitherto been dealing were all small. In the later part of the seventh century large stone statues appear in Greece. The idea of making life-size or colossal statues came to Greece from Egypt, the home of grandeur, now open to the Greeks. There is no reason to suppose that the period of big stone figures was preceded by a period of big wooden figures: the material was probably stone from the beginning. Soft limestone could be shaped with the knife: marble needed hammer, punch, chisel, emery; but its clearness and brightness, and the high finish it would take, repaid the labor. Limestone is used by the sixth-century sculptor, but chiefly for the figures decorating buildings: free sculpture prefers marble. Large bronze statues could be constructed by attaching metal plaques to a wooden core: but in the second half of the sixth century improvements in the process of hollow casting enabled the Greek artist to *cast* large figures in bronze. Few such figures remain from antiquity: but from the late sixth century onwards, bronze was the favorite material for free statuary. Terracotta was used not only for metopes and other ornaments of buildings, but also for statuettes and even for larger figures.

There was plenty of work for sculptors. The custom of giving representations of living things to the gods was a very old one. The new figures, so large, so life-like, so handsome, yet so durable, would be bound to delight the divinity and make him love the donor: and so the Greek sanctuaries became peopled with men, women and animals in marble or bronze. The image of the god himself is installed in his stone house. The effigy of the dead man is set over his grave. Moreover, the development of the stone temple leads to a great extension in the range of decorative sculpture. Certain parts of the building call for decoration: the frieze is adorned with figures in low relief: a new kind of work, high relief, enlivens pediment and metope: the pedimental figures tend to become detached in part or wholly from the background, and thus to approximate to the nature of free statuary. Besides this applied relief-work, there are substantive reliefs, funerary and votive. For work on a smaller scale there was great demand: for metal statuettes—parts of vessels and other furniture, or dedications each complete in itself; and for engraved seals, and engraved dies to make coins with: the sixth century revived the old art of engraving in hard gemstones, and the practice of issuing coins had already reached the Greek world.

Free sculpture long confines itself to a few simple types, and its repertory is very small compared with that of painting or relief. The chief types are the upright male figure, usually naked, one leg, the left, set well forward; the draped female figure, with legs close together, or the left slightly advanced; the draped seated figure. The statue is intended to be viewed directly from the front: two side views are also contemplated, and usually a back view. Each side view is a complete profile, corresponding to the complete profile in painting. The transition from side view to front view is more or less abrupt, and the stone figure retains a measure of the quadrature of the block from which it was hewn. The attitude of the statue is rigid: one leg may be set forward, the arms have a certain limited freedom of movement, and in draped statues the lines of the clothing may cut across the figure: but trunk does not twist or bend, legs are alike in posture, head looks straight forward, inclining neither up nor down nor sideways. The main mass of the statue, now as before, is bilaterally symmetrical, the plane of symmetry being the median plane, that is the plane which passes through crown, nose, navel and fork.

The leading type is that of the naked upright man with left leg advanced, the "kouros." The kouros did not develop out of early Greek statuettes: it is something new in Greece, and the model was Egyptian. The hands may hold objects, but the arms usually hang down along the sides, with the fists clenched. The figure is fully corporeal. The main divisions of the body are clearly marked: broad shoulders, big buttocks, big thighs, and muscular calves are emphasized by wasp waist and neat hard knees: the trunk remains summary. The figure becomes lighter with time, the limbs more refined, the facial features smaller and more vivacious.

The earlier female figures ("korai") stand with legs pressed close together, the later take a little step forward with the left. In early western women, the drapery encloses the figure in a quasi-rectangular case, which may be diversified by patterns. The germs of a subtler system of drapery are observable in the Ephesian ivories, in which the lower part of the thin chiton is either covered with dense vertical lines, or divided by a plain central band or a group of central vertical folds in relief. In the sixth century, these devices were elaborated in eastern Greece and in the islands. In an Ionian bronze of the seventh century one of the hands grasps the central strip:[1] the motive found favor; but still more popular motive was that of the hand grasping the central strip and bearing it to the side of the body, thus drawing the chiton tight so that the legs show through, and setting up a system of long curving folds. For the upper part of chiton we must turn once more to Ephesus: here the upper part is sometimes drawn down over the belt at the sides, so that the lower line of the chiton is an arc, not a straight line. Later, the chiton is pulled farther down at one side of the belt than at the other, making the two sides of the garment uneven: later still, the unevenness is increased by the Ionic himation, the upper line of which cuts across the figure diagonally from shoulder to waist. Dense groups of rippled lines render the crinkling of the chiton, and both garments terminate below in series of step-like folds. The rendering of drapery thus developed is a complex one: it diversifies the surface by dividing it into a number of areas, each with its own system of curved or straight lines; and it vivifies the mass by revealing the bodily forms beneath.

Kouros and kore, to give them their conventional names, remain the principal types of free statue throughout the archaic period. It is not until about 480 B.C. that the two legs and the two sides of the body come to be differentiated, the weight resting on one leg, the axis of the trunk being thrown out of the straight, and the head beginning to bend to one side. Then we shall no longer be able to speak of kouros and kore: but that time is far hence. The scheme of the kouros is so simple, intelligible, and compact, that no kouros will ever be quite ugly: οὔποτε πάγκακον ἔσται. But we shall find great differences in quality as well as in execution, and the later will not necessarily be better than the earlier. Among the earlier kouroi, to which we are confining ourselves for the present, two stand out: the huge and very early kouros of Sunium [see Fig.

2], in his rude majesty, like Otus, the child giant who challenged the gods, or like Adam the first man; and the kouros of Tenea, spruce and fine.

The uniformity of substantive statuary does not extend to relief-work. Here subjects and attitudes are far more varied. In many of its uses, the relief is an alternative to the picture: the chief theme is narrative, and the figures have nearly the same rules as the figures of painting. In the decorations of metope and pediment the relief is often very high indeed, and pedimental figures are sometimes partly or wholly detached from the background: but however high the relief, it remains flattish: the artist long hesitates to avail himself of the opportunity which the depth of the block affords of rendering the third dimension: the modelling is confined, for the most part, to the neighborhood of the front plane, and the sculpture has something of a drawing on stone with the contours emphasized by being worked back from the surface. . . .

The effect of the stone figure was completed by the application of color, the predominant colors being a bright red and a merry blue. In limestone figures, male flesh was painted red or red-brown, and blue and red, occasionally other colors, used for the garments; backgrounds were now plain, now colored. In marble the colors, though bright, were used more discretely: the flesh was commonly left plain, with colored details—hair, lips, eyes; part of the drapery might be colored, but most of it was plain, with colored borders or a sprinkling of little patterns: in reliefs the background was dark, blue or red. Bronze was left in its natural tone; details sometimes inlaid in other material. . . .

V. THE SIXTH CENTURY, TO 520 B.C.: EARLY AND MIDDLE ARCHAIC PAINTING

What were the materials of sixth-century painting? The clay metopes from Thermon are virtually pictures, and votive pictures on clay tablets are common in the sixth century at Athens as well as at Corinth. A few paintings on marble slabs have survived from the later part of the century. Wooden panels we may take for granted, though no examples have reached us: but whether mural painting was already practiced in Greece is an open question. It was practiced in Etruria; moreover, the Etruscan tomb-paintings show overwhelming Greek influence: but of Archaic Greek wall-painting we have no fragment remaining, nor any mention in our scanty records. The black-figure method of vase-painting reached Attica, as we saw, at the end of the seventh century, and even penetrated into eastern Greece. During the greater part of the sixth century, the sway of the black-figure technique is almost undisputed: it is not till about 530 B.C. that a new method, the so-called red-figure, arises in Athens and gradually supplants the old. During the black-figure period, the outline method forms, as far as one can see, but an undercurrent: but our impression would no doubt be different, if our non-ceramic evidence were more abundant.

The drawing of the earliest red-figure vases does not differ, in essentials, from that of the black-figured work which preceded them: and the style of the black-figured work changed but slowly. New features appear between 600 and 525 B.C.: but what goes on is mainly the fulfillment of ideas initiated in the seventh century, and the refinement and systematization of older forms. Filling-ornaments, which declined in the seventh century, disappear by the middle of the sixth. The friezes of animals fall into comparative neglect. Narrative engrosses the painters: mythical or heroic pictures acquire greater volume and greater variety than before. . . . The emotions expressed by the figures are more varied than in the seventh century: the tragic dejection of the seer who knows that Amphiaraus will not return; the joy of Theseus' crew at the sight of land and home; the incorrigible impudence of the satyrs who form the bodyguard of Dionysus and his bride. If there are more moods than there used to be, there are also more kinds of people. The world no longer consists of bearded men, beardless youths, women, animals and monsters. The old man and the child become more frequent; the workman appears, and with him the capitalist; the foreigner also, the eastern or northern barbarian in trousers and quaint hat, the flimsy Egyptian, the . . . negro; the lover; the man of pleasure; and most important of all, the wild man, the satyr, with horse's ears and horse's tail, the incarnation of our less serious moods, and one of the chief vehicles of Greek humor for many a day.

In the drawing of the figure, and even in the shapes of the vases, there is a tendency to make the forms more precise, and usually, to refine them: to proceed from the ideal expressed by Kleobis and Biton to that of the kouros of Tenea. The types of figure are the same as before, full profile, or profile legs joined to frontal breast;

but a step is sometimes taken towards the three-quarter view of the succeeding period. . . .

Not long after 600 B.C., Attic vases appear in Naukratis, in south Russia and in Etruria: by the middle of the sixth century they have penetrated everywhere, and above all, the great Etrurian market is in the hands of the Athenians. Their monopoly of fine pottery

5. Attic Amphora by Exekias, *c.* 550–540 B.C. (Vatican Museum)

a) Dioskouroi welcomed home

b) Achilles and Ajax playing draughts

67

remained almost unchallenged for over a hundred years. Signatures of artists and of potters and owners of fabrics, hitherto rare in Greece, now become common in Athens. The earliest Attic artist whose name we know is the vase-painter Sophilos. Sophilos was by no means a dolt: but it was not such men as he who beat the Corinthians forever from the field. It was men like Ergotimos and Klitias, the maker and the painter of the François vase, a nobly-shaped crater decorated with row upon row of pictures, chiefly scenes from myth, comprising hundreds of thin, angular, extra-ordinarily varied, elegant and expressive figures: a marvel of minute yet masculine work. The François vase was found in the far west, at Chiusi in Etruria: a cup signed by Klitias has been found far in the east at Phrygian Gordion. It is on cups that the style and the spirit of Klitias continue: in the "little-master cups" with their tiny exquisite figures. Larger pictures were painted side by side with these, and the black-figure technique may be said to culminate in the Vatican amphora signed by Exekias (Fig. 5). The technique: for the style is already past its prime: the spirit which is able to express itself through silhouette and incision is departing, and the time has come for a new and freer means of expression, the red-figure style.

VI. LATE ARCHAIC SCULPTURE

In considering the sculpture of the Late Archaic period, we may begin, for the sake of simplicity, with the naked male figure and the clothed female figure of the types which we have learned to know as kouros and kore; for it is not until the time of the Persian Wars that these two simple but happy creations cease to be the dominant types of substantive statue. . . .

For all the beauty and variety of the Late Archaic kouroi and korai, it is not in these that Late Archaic sculpture finds its most perfect expression, but in the action-figures—men not being but doing—common as before in groups, especially in decoration of buildings, and becoming common now as substantive statues. . . .

The west pediment [of the Temple of Aphaia at Aegina] is dis-tinctly less advanced in style than the east, and it is plausibly conjectured that the west belongs to the years just before 490, the east to the years just after. The excellence of the several figures has long been recognized, and wonder expressed, that the Aeginetan sculptors, best known in antiquity as bronze-casters, should have been masters of marble as well: but not until the new excavations of 1901 was it possible to form an accurate idea of the composition. Many-figured battle-scenes, dense yet clear; each man eager, light of foot, and trained to the last ounce; and all the freedom of a picture in the attitudes—darting, dying, and even falling. The theme of the pediments is one upon which Pindar loved to dwell in his Aeginetan odes: how the sons of Aiakos had twice taken Troy: once with Heracles, and again with the Atreidai. . . . If a single figure had to be chosen to represent ripe Archaic sculpture, would it not be the archer Heracles, himself tense as a drawn bow, from the east pediment at Aegina?

VII. LATE ARCHAIC PAINTING

. . . In the course of the sixth century the Attic potters drove their competitors from the field. About 525, a new technique came in. The old black-figure method long survived, never quite died out, and produced masterpieces down to the end of the sixth century, but it waned gradually before the new red-figure method, in which the figures are not painted in black on the clay of the vase, but left in the color of the clay, and the background painted black: the minor details are in brown lines; a purplish-red is used very sparingly; and the color-effect is thus very sober. That manly precision, which is one of the chief characteristics of Greek vase-painting, is now imparted not by incised lines as previously, but by the wiry unerring "relief-line." In its relation to nature, the drawing of the earliest red-figure vases does not differ in essentials from that of the black-figured vases signed by Exekias or Amasis. The great change sets in fully about ten years after the introduction of the red-figure technique. The characteristics of the new style are first, a profound interest in the individual forms of the human body, and second, a new conception of the body in space, a conception of which the most obvious manifestation is the love of certain violent yet definite foreshortenings. The first of these characteristics we know from the sculpture of the time: in painting it may be illustrated by the Antaios of Euphronius (Fig. 6), which stands at the beginning of the movement, and is full of the enthusiasm of the pioneer: the artist delights in collecting and recording the very smallest facts. Such extreme profusion of detail is hardly found in later works: by the end of the Archaic period the knowledge now being amassed is common property, and though used is not displayed. The second characteristic has no exact equivalent in sculpture in the round, but it naturally occurs in low relief, and to some extent in high relief. Hitherto the figures making up a picture had moved past the beholder on a plane parallel to the plane of his eyes: either the legs had been in profile and the breast frontal, or the whole figure had been in profile. In the new style of the later sixth century the figures are apt to turn towards the spectator and front him, partly or mainly: there are figures in which one leg is in profile and the other leg and the trunk frontal;

6. Attic Krater Painted by Euphronius, *c.* 510–500 B.C. Heracles Wrestling with Antaios (Louvre, Paris)

70

and figures in which both legs are in profile and the trunk three-quartered. Such figures do not merely make more variety in the representation: the foreshortenings lead the eye onward beyond the surface of the picture, and by suggesting the third dimension give the bodies more solidity and substance. The frontal figure is not a mere vehicle of action: it invites the beholder to contemplate its mass. The Thorykion of Euthymides is a good example; in which we notice further that the two halves of the body are differentiated by the frontal leg, that the head, though still in profile, no longer perches rigid on a rigid neck, but bends on to the shoulder, that one hip is higher than the other, and the trunk on the eve of turning with the bend of the head. Thus, and by the turn toward us, the figure falls into line, in some degree, with the new kind of statue which we shall find taking the place of the kouros at the beginning of the next period: an earlier manifestation of the same revolutionary idea.

Besides figures seen from the front, we have figures seen from behind: with profile legs and the back three-quartered; or with one leg in profile, and trunk and the other leg in full back-view. The head is still nearly always in profile: the full face remains rare, and three-quarter faces are not attempted till after the beginning of the fifth century, and then only occasionally and for a long time unsuccessfully. Three-quartered hands add life to the gesture; the foot may make a three-quarter turn. Finally, the artist no longer shrinks from obscuring important parts of the body: the thigh of Antaios occludes the lower half of his leg.

Thus, by purely linear devices, the painter contrives to give his picture a certain depth in space. Toward the end of the Archaic period, a device of different kind but with a kindred tendency makes its first appearance: shading. It is used very seldom and very sparingly: a flat wash of brown to give the hollow of a hat or of folds, hatched brown brush-strokes to model the rotundity of a vessel or a shield. But it is the first step towards the abolition of the linear contour and towards the replacement of outline drawing by what the modern world calls painting.

The chief interest of the vase-painter remains action. Narrative subjects—mythical and heroic—are as popular as ever, but pictures from everyday life become commoner than before, and there is a special love of athletic scenes with their straining muscles, intense movements, and countless postures; for scenes of revelry, the "komos," where men rush, dance, quarrel, lust, vomit, shout, and sing; and for the counterpart of the komos in the ideal sphere—the thiasos, Dionysus with his satyrs and maenads. For all its variety, humor and unconcern, this art is not naturalistic: apart from some very old persons, crookbacked and borne-over, from a fat belly or so, a wrinkled brow, a bald head, a bad beard, or a blobby nose; god and man, Greek and barbarian, athlete, drinker and amorist, have the same well-formed bodies and the same untainted vigor.

NOTES

[1] A. Furtwängler, *Olympia* 4, pl. VII, 74.

5. GREEK TEMPLE PEDIMENTS

Rhys Carpenter

INTRODUCTION

The selection from Carpenter's *Greek Sculpture* was chosen for the emphasis it places on two key monuments of pedimental sculpture, the warriors from the Temple of Aphaia at Aegina (too enthusiastically restored by Thorwaldsen) and the fine marbles from the Temple of Zeus at Olympia, together representing the crucial era of Late Archaic and Early Classical sculpture. Carpenter's observations in this selection on the development of pedimental sculpture weave together three significant phenomena: the relationship pedimental sculpture bears to both painted and relief decoration, the connections between bronze and marble statuary suggested by the Aegina groups, and the mimetic aspects of Greek sculpture. It is instructive to read, in conjunction with this selection, Gisela Richter's *Three Critical Periods in Greek Sculpture* (1951), which highlights other significant turning points in the evolution of Greek sculpture, and Carpenter's article "Tradition and Invention in Attic Reliefs," *American Journal of Archaeology*, LIV, 4 (1950).

The selection that follows is reprinted from Chapter V, *Greek Sculpture* by Rhys Carpenter, by permission of The University of Chicago Press. © 1960 by The University of Chicago.

In ancient Greece as in later Europe during the Romanesque and Gothic period and, for that matter, in any age when the major contribution to building was the stonemason's concern, sculpture and architecture were intimately allied. In Greece, both arts employed the same material medium of white finely crystaled marble, trimmed and carved with the same tools, finished in equally exact precision, and with brightly colored detail added in the same wax-base pigments. The Greek architect conceived his task in the same visual terms and aimed at the same artistic effects as did his sculptural fellow. Indeed, sculptors and architects were often one— Scopas and the younger Polyclitus being conspicuous examples of this dual role. In consequence, it is not far wide of the truth to say that a Greek temple such as the Parthenon, with its perfection of jointing and coherence of contour and organic unity of structural form, would have seemed not so much assembled out of separate blocks as carved in a single huge mass of marble. It is not surprising that Greek architecture (again like Romanesque and Gothic) relied greatly on sculpture for decorative aid.

Apart from the carved and colored moldings which were introduced to crown and separate the various structural elements, the sculptural adjuncts to the Greek orders had their origin in two unrelated types of ornamentation. One of these was painted design applied to blank surfaces; the other was modeled clay for finial plaques and figurines along gutters and gabled ridges. Since roofs were covered in terracotta tile, their decoration with terracotta figurines or modeled plaques along their eaves and against the sky line was a wholly appropriate invention. In another category, the smooth surfaces of the marble walls and the various other blank elements incident to a temple structure presented panels to attract the painter's art. But glyptic monumental sculpture in-the-round had originally no congenial place on a Greek building. Here it was carving in relief which acted as the intermediary in converting the painter's contribution into sculptural enterprise.

In timber construction, a framework of parallel beams laid horizontally carries the ceilings, and sloping (or "raking") beams are set as rafters to support the roof. In the horizontal rack, the open intervals at the outer end of the ceiling beams could be closed with thin slabs to keep out the weather. These slabs might be made either of thin wooden plank or of terracotta when that material was in use for sheathing exposed woodwork. On either of these the application of a whitewash slip would provide a suitable ground for painted design. It was from such painted panels that the carved metopes of the Doric order were evolved.

Along the flanks, where the horizontal ceiling beams and the sloping rafters converge, there were only the overhanging eaves above the metopes; but at the narrow ends of the building the sloping rafters, rising from either side to a central ridgepole, formed a large gaping triangle above the ceiling level. Since this opening, too, needed to be closed against the weather, a screen wall was inserted—the *tympanon* of Greek architectural parlance—and this presented an attractive field for painted design. It was not the open space under the sloping roof but the closing wall behind it, not the pedimental gable but the tympanon screen, which at first received decoration. From the reinforcement of such tympanon designs by carving them in relief, pedimental sculpture was initiated on the Doric temple. But it was not until relief gave place to fully detached statuary that the shallow shelf in front of the closing wall was utilized. In this manner the Greek tradition for pedimental sculpture was evolved.

This is not a theoretical reconstruction of an assumed series of events; for the earliest pedimental sculpture which has survived is all relief-work; and the earlier its date, the shallower is its carving and the more dependent is it on drawn outline and flat, colored surfaces. The tiny pediment showing Heracles' combat with the Hydra, from the Athenian acropolis, is very faithfully a carved-out Attic black-figure vase design. And the transition from tympanon relief to detached sculpture in-the-round is convincingly demonstrated on the Siphnian Treasury at Delphi, where the upper half of the various pedimental figures is fully cut away from the ground while their lower portion remains imbedded in it, carved only in relief.

By all odds, the most spectacular relief-pediment to survive is the well-preserved series of tympanon blocks from an early sixth-century temple to the local Artemis of Corcyra, the island today generally known as Corfu. In utter disregard of consistent scale, the carved figures swell from tiny prostrate or seated figures in the corners of the gable to huge spotted leopards flanking an enormous, hideous-faced Gorgon at the center. The available height of wall under the sloping roof has alone determined the varying sizes of the occupants of a common spatial frame. The artist's mind was seemingly undisturbed by any suspicion that such a loftily set and sharply isolated situation demarcated a spatial world of its own, which imposed a self-contained orderliness of coherent size, pertinent action, and relevant meaning. All this the Greek sense of artistic fitness might be expected to reason out fully and find for all its problems of scale and composition and subject matter their appropriate solutions—not abruptly and at a single cast, but only after repeated trial and effort.

What explanation can be offered for the substitution of sculptural for pictorial decoration on the Greek temple?

On the blank rear walls of public colonnades such as lined the open plaza (or *agora*) of a typical Greek city or enclosed a sheltered porch (or *lesché*), paintings were often executed in wax pigment upon the polished or stuccoed marble surface. This tradition was not altered in favor of adornment in carved relief for such a location, nor were statues set to embellish such a background wall. Similarly, within the temples and public buildings, painted designs were applied to the stone screens and perhaps to the interior faces of the walls (as seems to have been the original intent for the Hephaisteion in Athens). Was it merely the danger of impairment by sunlight, wind, and rain which deterred a similar pictorial treatment of the exposed exterior surfaces of a building? Such an explanation would hardly apply to a tympanon, where heavy eaves offered adequate protection for painted decoration. In order to explain the shift from pictorial to sculptural decoration in Greek architecture, which produced the carved metopes and the pedimental statuary of the classic temple norm, we must postulate a powerful, though perhaps not wholly conscious, preference for sculpture as against pictorial representation, the very reverse of the condition in Renaissance Italy when painting was the favored art, with sculpture by and large a poor second. In Greek appraisal, painting was more appropriate to interiors with low illumination, sculpture in-the-round to the full light of out-of-doors, while relief (the intermediary between the two arts) was cut in greater salience when intended to be seen in strong daylight and more weakly

7. Detail, Cella Freize, *c.* 442–438 B.C., Parthenon, Athens (Alison Frantz)

limned where the light was less. So, on the Parthenon, the figures on the exterior metopes were as completely detached from their ground as the medium permitted, whereas the sheltered frieze within the colonnade, dimmed by the ceiling above it, was carved in much slighter projection (Figs. 7, 8). The technical reasoning here is sound. The higher the protrusion of relief carving, the deeper will be the shadow cast by and upon the figures and the greater will be the illumination required to dispel it. *Per contra,* where diffused shade prevails and daylight is dimmed, relief must avoid adding to the obscurity and must therefore use only low-projecting masses devoid of heavy shadow. For the harsh, sun-struck reality of a Greek temple standing in the open against a Grecian sky, although flat color could profitably be added to clarify the individual structural members, any painted composition spread flat upon an exposed surface would have possessed insufficient spatial actuality, in contrast with the vividly real structure of the building. Here only solid sculpture had adequate material existence. Likewise, a carved and colored relief upon a tympanon, viewed from far below and at a considerable distance, would appear scarcely

78

more than a painting on a shadowed screen, too weak for the heavy frame of roof and cornice.

Yet the introduction of solidly substantial figures in the niche of built-in space between entablature and roof, while it better suited the architectural environment of sharply defined structural shapes, entailed an esthetic objection of a different order. Whereas painted representations were only visual evocations as unreal as the incidents in a storyteller's tale, statues in their full and firmly solid actuality must seem as real as the temple on which they were stationed. The Aeginetan warriors, fighting and stumbling and lying wounded on their corniced shelf high up above unclimbable columns within a starkly uncomfortable triangle beneath an irrelevant roof, could hardly fail to suggest something illogical and even ludicrous in their embattled presence, encamped on a temple front.

We have no way of knowing whether the irrationality of thus representing convincingly human beings in a setting manifestly impossible to them ever disturbed the Greek artist or his public. But it raises the interesting query whether the Greeks' insistence on visual realism had not here led them astray. And it is perhaps pertinent that the architects addicted to the Ionic order, though

8. Detail, Cella Frieze (Alison Frantz)

they ultimately accepted the Attic practice of setting between epistyle and cornice a frieze of sculptured figures in relief, resolutely resisted the introduction *more Dorico* of statues in their pediments.

Because the roofs of temples were carried on central ridgepoles running the length of the building to form symmetrical gables at either end, sculptors were confronted with the task of filling two triangular fields of identical shape and size. For this reason, Greek pedimental sculpture was produced in twin sets of closely contemporary execution and hence, it is to be expected, of comparable style and similar composition.

This being the norm, it was extremely surprising and no less bewildering to discover on closer study of the remains of the early fifth-century sanctuary of the deity Aphaia on the island of Aegina opposite the Attic shore that not two but *three* series of pedimental figures were represented, with no other possible source than the one isolated Doric temple. The most plausible explanation for this anomaly assumes that, during the Persian invasion and at the time of the enemy's naval blockade of the Saronic Gulf before Salamis, a hostile landing party severely damaged the statuary on the eastern front of the newly erected temple but did no harm to the western gable, whose figures may not yet have been set in place. After the Persian defeat, the Aeginetans would have replaced the damaged statues with a new set of figures and buried the discarded series within the sanctuary, just as the Athenians at that time interred the shattered dedications on their acropolis. Such an explanation, if correct, lends new importance to the Aegina statues. Despite the havoc which Persian rage, the indifference of time, and the oversanguine restorations of Thorwaldsen have inflicted on them, their contribution to the chronology of stylistic development during a crucial phase goes far to compensate for the disappointments attendant on a visit to the famous *Aeginetensaal* in Munich.

Although the correct restoration of many of the figures is debatable and their arrangement within their respective pediments is still by no means entirely certain, there is much to be learned from them. Compared with any known marble work from the period (even if that period is a decade later than the handbooks on sculpture assume), the variety of poses is surprisingly great. This richness of compositional resource must have been derived from the Aeginetan bronze-casters' experimentation with piece-cast figures. There is abundant evidence for an important school of sculpture in bronze on Aegina by the close of the sixth century, but little or nothing to suggest a flourishing industry in marble. Yet for the sculptural adornment of a marble temple there was no other choice than marble, since it was seemingly unthinkable to the Greek mind that bronze should be employed. The compulsion to essay a branch of the sculptor's art with which the Aeginetans were not conversant explains their adherence to technical procedures from working in metal. This is revealed not only by the highly active poses such as could with difficulty be cut from single blocks or kept in balance or insured from breakage when made of solid stone, but also by the abundant recourse to metal accessories for the statues. Spears and shields, bows and arrows, helmets and plumed crests, all occur as separately cast additions to the marble hands and heads of the warriors. A further borrowing from bronze technique, which greatly affected the stylistic quality of the work, is the sharp, shallow engraving for the hair of head and beard and for the detailed elaboration of such costume and armor as had not been supplied in metal.

It should be remarked that this intrusion of actual armor and weapons into a make-believe company of stone was entirely consonant with the realistic ambition of the Greek sculptors, whether Archaic or not, who saw no logical objection to putting genuine swords and spears in the hands and helmets on the heads of figures intended to be seen so accoutered. The resultant "mixed metaphor," which confused physical reality with artistic imagery, was greatly mitigated where the addition of bronze, whether left blank, artificially patinated, or gilded over, produced no further visual effect than that of an extra color in the palette of bright hues habitual to Greek marble sculpture.

A significant advantage in borrowing from the bronze-caster's more extensive repertory of poses was the unity of scale and subject matter which could be achieved—probably for the first time in sculptural history—within the awkward spatial limitations of a full-size temple gable. By judicious choice of attitudes—reclining, kneeling, stooping, falling, lunging, striding, or standing erect—the designer could meet all the exigencies of pedimental headroom without introducing any discrepant size in the figures. It was of course incumbent to choose some applicable theme to justify the simultaneous occurrence of so many different postures. But such a theme was ready at hand in the combat scenes of contemporary pictorial tradition. The melee of battle included every moment for such a scene. That the arrangement which resulted was wholly impossible in actual combat hardly weighed against the sculptural coherence and visual harmony attained. Whatever else might be said against such a carefully ordered display of arbitrary action in conflict, at least it solved the formal problem of pedimental composition with exemplary consistency and without any surrender of artistic sense or fitness.

It is hardly sound aesthetic criticism to object that in such a situation it is the pre-established external frame which has supplied the unifying bond to the composition; for the frame belongs to the architecture, and if this dominates the sculpture, it correctly emphasizes the subordination of decoration to structural design. Even so, it must be the sculptor's task to compose so adroitly that the figures seem to determine the shape of the frame rather than to allow it to be apparent that, in fact, the reverse is the case. Herein the Aeginetan masters signally succeeded.

Greek temples faced the sunrise, toward which the cult statue of the enshrined divinity looked out through a great doorway and the eastern row of exterior columns. In consequence, the eastern pediment crowned the open entrance front while the western pediment adorned the rear of the god's dwelling. At Aphaia's temple on Aegina the absorbed interest of the sculptors in their new formula of composition seems to have precluded any thought of distinguishing sculpturally between the two façades. But at Olympia, with the next great commission for temple pediment statues only a decade later than the last of the Aegina triad, east and west were emphatically and brilliantly contrasted. This finely conceived distinction might well have become an accepted tradition for the Doric temple; yet it seems to have been an isolated trait of Greek artistic inventiveness. No comparable difference of mode between front and rear pediment is discernible in the later temples, whether in the Parthenon at Athens or the rebuilt shrines for Apollo at Delphi and Athena Alea at Tegea in Arcadia. However, since the last two are known to us by little more than a description of their statues, no dogmatic statement may be made.

In Elis beside the river Alpheus, where the foremost of the Greek athletic festival contests were ceremoniously celebrated every fourth summer, Zeus, lord of the games, had long held his sanctuary yet possessed no proper temple of his own. He shared with his wife Hera an old-fashioned, squat-columned, but in no sense mean or unworthy building. The god's share in the booty from the richly caparisoned Persian host in the great defeat at Platea provided the funds, as the tremendous victory provided the moral incentive, for building an ambitious new temple. (At Athens, where a sadly ruined town had first to be rebuilt and adequately fortified with encompassing walls, the city goddess' new temple had to wait forty years for its dedication; the Parthenon, following at an appreciable interval the temple of Zeus, is the next great sculptural undertaking.) At Olympia the funds seem to have been exhausted before crowning statues had been set against the sky line for acroteria above the pediments or a worthily rich and duly impressive cult statue of the god could be placed in the interior chamber. In consequence, the completion of the sculpture for the temple lagged for more than thirty years. The twelve metope reliefs for the front and rear vestibules—the exterior order was left blank—were the first to be finished; next, the two pediments were filled with statuary by masters unidentified; thereafter, but not immediately, the enormous gold and ivory cult statue of the seated Zeus was fashioned by Phidias and installed within the temple; and, last of all, the acroterial figures of Victory were carved by Paeonius, an Ionian-born sculptor resident in Athens. Of this splendor of sculptural adornment, several of the metopes and most of the pediment statues have survived in intelligible condition; but of the acroteria and the great chryselephantine statue no fragments remain. Thanks to the clean river sand in which the marble has lain embedded, whatever has been recovered preserves a surface texture such as few ancient statues can rival. Most of the classical marbles now on display in museums were found encrusted with a lime deposit or otherwise discolored and damaged from century-long repose under rain-soaked soil. Because they were thoroughly cleaned, often with acid to loosen the crust, scoured, and burnished without pity during the Renaissance and in even quite recent times without due regard, the original texture is usually lost. But from this misfortune the marbles from the Zeus temple at Olympia are exempt. Broken as they are, whatever remains has lost nothing save its coloring in wax and still shows the original touch of the stonecutter's hands. And since these pediments mark the highest surviving achievement of a particularly inventive phase in stylistic progress and self-conscious artistry, a pilgrimage to Olympia today is as obligatory on the lover of Greek art as ever it was in the past on the enthusiast for athletic contests.

As immediate successors to the artists of Aphaia's temple on Aegina, the sculptors at Olympia might be expected to have followed the excellent Aeginetan formula for pedimental composition, but in fact it would be difficult to imagine nearly contemporaneous productions more profoundly different in mood and manner than those which adorned the two sanctuaries.

It is completely uncertain who were the masters charged with the metopes and pediments at Olympia or even from what part of Greece they and their helpers were called to Elis. To be sure, Pausanias in describing the famous temple, still standing undamaged in his day six centuries after it was erected, records two familiar names of the Attic school, Alcamenes and Paeonius, as masters of the two pediments. But the proven date and apparent style of these sculptors render his testimony unacceptable. Yet he may have correctly indicated the home land of the sculptural school responsible for the work. It is mistaken to suppose that there were a great many important centers of sculptural activity in Greece at this time or many workshops equipped and experienced to execute so great a commission in marble (just as, in this same period, statues in bronze were probably being produced at only a comparatively small number of foundries—at Samos, Aegina, Argos, Athens, and perhaps Chalcis, as well as at Rhegion on the Sicilian strait, to name those for which we have most certain evidence). Of this much at least we may feel convinced, that the artists who carved the statues for the Olympia pediments had been apprenticed and schooled to work in marble, not bronze, and that they were intimately familiar with the Attic sculpture of their day. The head of the huge Apollo who stood protectingly in the center of the western pediment has often been likened to that of the *Blond Boy* of Athens; the heroic nudes on either side of the god, striding with weapons raised, are reminiscent of the Attic *Tyrannicides,* the famous bronze pair made to replace Antenor's figures carried off by the Persians; beyond these, the centaurs assaulting Lapith women and boys resemble those of the earlier metopes which were (perhaps) even then being carved at Athens to await emplacement on the great new temple projected for Athena Parthenos; and finally some of the attendant figures in the east pediment show contracted poses of much the same silhouetted character as Myron's *Discobolus.*

At Olympia the two pediments are deliberately and dramatically contrasted one with the other. On the entrance façade the ordering of the figures is calm and tranquil with each statue set openly apart from its neighbors, whereas the rear gable is filled with a remarkably agitated arrangement of symmetrically balanced groups tightly interlocked. It is presumably an accidental result of such a disposition of the figures rather than the deliberate intent of a geometrically minded artist that, when projected, the axes of all the major figures in the east gable run vertically parallel without intersecting or converging, while in the west the projected axes converge toward two rather vaguely defined areas situated about forty feet above and below the pedimental floor level (the latter convergence agreeing, by coincidence, perhaps, with the location of a spectator standing before the temple front). When examining Greek art, and most especially that of the fifth century, it is difficult to decide how many of its geometrical and other mathematical qualities were deliberately introduced by the artist; for, as already noted, there can be no question that the sculptors and architects of the period were highly sensitive to numerical and geometrical relationships of form and much concerned to employ them in their work.

Certainly, there is a deliberately contrived contrast in mood and manner between the two pediments at Olympia. In the ceremonially aloof poses of the east gable the central statues continue the *kouros* tradition of the motionless pier-hewn figure, while the attendants crouch or otherwise contract themselves into immobile blocks, humanly articulated rectangles surmounted by slumbering heads; and in the corners, recumbent youths, interpreted by Pausanias as divinities of the two nearby rivers, emerge from tightly wrapped sheaths of clothing, as slow-moving as mollusks in their shells. A local legend fraught with violence and threat of murderous disaster—the tale of the chariot pursuit of Pelops by his grim, unwilling father-in-law—has been drained of all incident and action in order to transmute it into changeless statuary. It is as though, before acting out a drama of deceit and flight and lovers' triumph, a company of players had aligned themselves at the footlights to bow to their audience. Those who incline to esthetic dogma in the spirit of Lessing may detect herein a fundamental aversion to pictorial narrative which properly distinguishes the sculptor's from the painter's art. But to conclude that Greek sculpture avoided the immediate representation of dramatic action is to overlook the rear pediment of the same temple where all is turmoil and impassioned strife.

Perhaps it will be objected that here, in this astonishing array of interlaced bodies, sculpture has become pictorial narrative; but if so, it constitutes a peculiarly Greek sort of pictured presentation, since there is no indication of scenery or setting, of spatial or material environment, but only living actors upon an empty stage, set side by side against a common ground. It is true that Greek painters might have portrayed a centauromachy in similar terms of vivid silhouettes against a blank background; but this would suggest either that Greek painting had a strong sculptural bias or that Greek sculpture drew on graphic precedent, but not that Greek sculpture had here transcended its proper domain and trespassed on painting's legitimate preserve. If in the east pediment all action has dropped from the myth and no story is being told, and in the west the incidents of a drama of violent struggle are displayed in vivid detail, in neither case is there transgression beyond the representation of sculptural themes in sculptural terms. Architectural space—the solid triangle on the shallow shelf between horizontal and raking cornice—has been accepted and utilized as sculptural space without conversion into pictorial illusion of inactual depth and distance. It is the supreme logic of Greek sculpture and the best proof of its sound artistic sense that it confines itself to sculptural space.

If it be inquired what may be meant by "sculptural space" and what warrant there is for its existence, a straightforward answer can be given:

Whenever we concentrate our attention on a piece of sculpture, we deliberately segregate it mentally (and hence visually) from its objective environment. Amid the depth and distance in which our visual world extends, a sufficient amount of these commodities will accrue to the sculptured solid; and, in addition, it will attract to itself enough of the surrounding aerial vacancy to insulate itself from the rest of the visual scene. It demands adequate living-room for its activities. According as it is seen to be thin or thick, flat or cylindrical, cubical or otherwise constituted, it will occupy varying amounts of visual space; and according as it presents motion or implies any similar reaching-out beyond itself, it will assimilate sufficient enveloping space for action. There is thus a subjective factor in sculptural space which differentiates it from the measurable volume which a physicist would assign to the configured material mass of a statue. The material mass is never identical with the apparent volume as seen—and still less so if we add the sculpture's attracted environment, its spatial "aura." Sculptural space is accordingly definable in terms of apparent volume and assimilated surrounding "aura," and hence is not fully identical with physical or (as we are apt to call it) "real" space.

On inquiry it will be found that architectural space has a similar subjective character; but it is sufficient for our present understanding to note that sculptural space may coincide with architectural space accurately enough to prevent any sensible discrepancy; whereas pictorial space, because it is created through the substitution of an artificial visual field with its own presentation of depth and distance, cannot be made coextensive with either architectural or sculptural space, both of which partake of the spatial world of our normal waking sense-experience. There is nothing recondite in such a formulation, which corresponds to everyone's awareness that buildings and statues are spatially real while that which we see in a painting is spatially illusionary. But it is less generally appreciated that the spatial structure of sculptural representation depends primarily on vision and not on physical measurements. It is what it is *seen* to be; and since it is also seen as something other than its material self—being, for instance, the god Apollo as well as a nine-foot mass of marble—how it seems to be shaped is greatly affected by visual presentation and suggestion. It is this distinction between the carved block and the seen statue which the fifth-century sculptors were beginning to appreciate. At Olympia we may see them working their way to an optically effective solution to an extremely subtle visual problem.

On this problem—if we are not to misapprehend or miss completely one of the most extraordinary properties of Greek sculptural art—we must concentrate our attention.

The Greeks understood sculpture as an art of direct visual presentation; what one saw, when one looked attentively and intelligently, was the entire intent. Statues were not meant to be symbolic suggestions of something other than themselves, illusive and allusive in their impact on the imagination of the spectator. They were fully objectified existants in the same world of sense as the rest of the spectator's sensuous experience (even if some mental concession had to be made to explain their immobile presence out-of-doors in a temple precinct or a public market place). This should not be construed to imply that the Greeks had no recognition of a statue's independent status as a work of art or were unaware of its essential unreality as a block of carved marble or a piece of cast bronze; they cannot be accused of thus confusing subject matter with esthetic experience. But it serves to justify the struggle for mimetic truth which through six centuries of seldom-diverted effort determined the course of their sculpture's stylistic development.

6. HELLENISTIC ART

George M. A. Hanfmann

INTRODUCTION

George M. A. Hanfmann's article "Hellenistic Art" was written in conjunction with Ernst Kitzinger's "Hellenistic Heritage of Byzantine Art," selections from which are also included in this anthology. Both articles derive from papers presented at an exploratory symposium on the Hellenistic origins of Byzantine civilization held at Dumbarton Oaks in May 1962. Quite apart from its original purpose of providing background for Professor Kitzinger's discussion of Hellenistic elements in Byzantine art, the selection that follows can stand alone as an excellent introduction to Hellenistic art, its thematic range, and stylistic variety; and, as the reader will soon discover, it is not without considerable relevance to developments in Roman art.

The standard work in English on Hellenistic sculpture is Margarete Bieber, *The Sculpture of the Hellenistic Age*, rev. ed. (1961). Chapter II of Gisela M. A. Richter's *Three Critical Periods in Greek Sculpture* (1951) surveys the various trends of the last third of the fourth century B.C. which saw the formation of Hellenistic (as distinct from Hellenic) art. E. Schmidt, *The Great Altar of Pergamon* (1962) and D. Thimme, "The Masters of the Pergamon Gigantomachy," *The American Journal of Archaeology*, L (1946) examine a key monument of Hellenistic art. Other aspects of Hellenistic art, further emphasizing its international character, are discussed in W. A. Lawrence, "Rhodes and Hellenistic Sculpture," *Annual of the British School at Athens*, XXVI (1923–25), and, by the same author, "Greek Sculpture in Ptolemaic Egypt," *Journal of Egyptian Archaeology*, XI (1925).

The selection that follows is reprinted from George M. A. Hanfmann, "Hellenistic Art," *Dumbarton Oaks Papers*, XVII (1963), pp. 83–94, by permission of the author. Several passages, footnotes, and illustrations have been omitted in this reprint. Footnotes and illustrations have been renumbered.

FACTORS LIMITING A COMPARISON OF
HELLENISTIC AND BYZANTINE ART.
ESSENTIAL TRAITS OF HELLENISTIC ART

In an attempt to make the vast subject manageable, Professor Kitzinger and I have agreed to limit our discussion to certain major themes. I shall try to combine this attempt to seek out what was and what was not of interest to Byzantine artists with some intimation of what I conceive to be some of the essential traits of Hellenistic art. Thus we may hope to avoid an undue displacement of emphasis. Nevertheless, some of the major limitations of this procedure must be indicated. To make any useful comparisons with Byzantine art, we must emphasize pictorial media; yet the basic intuition of Hellenistic art was still plastic, and the plastic, three-dimensional human figure held the center of the stage. Then again, the focal themes of Byzantine art are the Sacred Image and the Sacred Cycles of the Old and New Testament. Neither the cult image nor the mythological, biographical cycle are the most expressive vehicles of Hellenistic creativity. Its full grandeur and splendor revealed itself in divinely hallowed, sacral but not sacred, atmosphere of heroic myth, and, on a more comprehensive scale, in complexes in which nature, architecture, sculpture, and probably painting were united for the sake of the total effect in a new sense of an immediate (as against the Classic distanced) nature-given reality. The Victory of Samothrace sweeping down from a mountain to alight on a "real" ship over the real water of a fountain pool, the Gauls of the great Attalid dedication fighting their defiant battle against the backdrop of the grand vistas of the eagle eyrie of Pergamon, and the Eros, asleep on his "real" rock, these seem to me to represent the essence of Hellenistic achievement.[1] If we look for their common denominator, it is vitality, *vis vitalis*, heroic or idyllic, manifesting itself within the framework of the vast diversity of nature, which is the true hero of Hellenistic art.

EROTICISM

Eroticism pervades Hellenistic art. If any divine powers other than Tyche enjoyed universal and popular interest, it was Eros, Aphrodite, and Dionysus. Hellenistic poetry played countless variations on the theme of the mischievous god of love, sometimes baby, sometimes a small boy, who hits indiscriminately with his arrows, burns lovers with his torch, and is in turn punished, his bow broken, his wings clipped.[2]

A world of infantile fantasies transforms myth and daily life, as when erotes play at adult work.[3] Starting from the theme *omnia vincit Amor*, the erotic invasion of myth brings before us erotes who take away the armor of the god of war and the club of the strongest of mortals, Heracles.[4] In myth after myth, heroic couples are turned into sentimental lovers.[5] . . .

There is frank and joyous love-play, especially among satyrs and maenads, now interpreted as nature's children;[6] but in much of Hellenistic art we sense an overtone of sophisticated perversion. It is the only art which has openly glorified the hermaphrodite.[7] . . .

HUMOR AND LAUGHTER

From Archaic times on, the burlesque, the fantastic exaggeration, the parody was the great vehicle of Greek humor. It is the essence of the gusty, lusty, riproaring laughter of the Old Comedy. In the Late Classical age, this tradition lived on in the Phlyax.[8] Hellenistic humor is first and foremost an extension of this theatrical humor into the reality of daily life. In an amazing outburst of caricature, Hellenistic artists portrayed slaves, dwarfs, misshapen people, and barbarians as real-life cousins of the fantastically ugly and ridiculous people of theatrical comedy. These grotesques combine the traditional satyric approach of the comedy with keen observation, replace the stylized exaggeration of the masks with nature's quirks, and bring the new naturalistic and scientific approach to bear upon the traditional types and situations. This humor is not always good-natured. The Hellenistic world thought funny what we may consider cruel and brutal.

Laughter and smile, on the other hand, were glorified as expressions of an uninhibited, desirable natural state best embodied in Dionysiac beings and children. Laughter as an expression of ebullient vitality achieved a positive value which was not, however, permitted to invade the traditional solemnity of heroic myth—except in little byplays involving satyrs or erotes.[9]

GENRE

With the grotesques, we have already touched upon one kind of Hellenistic genre. Let us consider briefly some examples of other types. Despite their intensive observation of "low life" the "Street Musicians" by Dioscurides of Samos are conceived in the spirit of the satyric grotesque.[10] The brilliantly painted "Woman and Shepherd" on the other hand, have been conjectured to represent a mythological scene from the Wanderings of Demeter.[11] Daily life or humanized myth?—that this question can arise is characteristic of the Hellenistic age. Certainly humanization of myth was progressing in the arts. This desire to make the divine tangible, detailed, and concrete need not lead to lack of belief. Thus it has been said of Dionysus that while the divine child becomes ever more sacred, its representations become ever more human.[12]

The theme of mother and child, on which Professor Kitzinger will touch in his paper, discloses something of the Hellenistic approach to humanization of myth and, at the same time, reveals some interesting traits of the attitude of the artists toward the theme of motherhood. There is genuine human appeal in such pictures as that of Danae nursing little Perseus[13] after she and her baby have been rescued from their floating box by the two fishermen, who look on with astonishment and sympathy; but the picture is not primarily a symbol of tender relation between Mother and Child. Rather it is a humanized visualization of a certain incident important for the mythological story. That nursing mothers are often figures of the Dionysiac thiasos, that tender scenes of women fondling babies show not mothers but benevolent nymphs, that Eros and Aphrodite are the son and mother most frequently shown, that scenes of tenderness sometimes turn out to be erotic—as in the baby cupid sitting in Psyche's lap[14]—all of this suggests that motherhood as such was not being glorified. Indeed, in a recent study on Birth and Childhood of Divine Children[15] J. Laager has concluded that in the Olympian mythology the mother-child relationship tends to fade into the background in favor of a male protector of the child—a Hermes, a Silenus. Hellenistic art impartially humanizes and sentimentalizes both—the mother as well as the male protector.

ENLARGEMENT OF THE PHYSICAL WORLD: LANDSCAPES AND ARCHITECTURAL SETTINGS

One of the most striking creations of Hellenistic art are the so-called "sacral-idyllic landscapes" which lie in a border land between genre and myth. Here the mythical and sacral overtones are an integral part of the vision of an idyllic land of shepherds and wanderers, not the real shepherds and wanderers but the shepherds of the Theocritean idylls. Sometimes this idyllic land is shown for its own sake.[16] Sometimes it forms the setting for a mythological narration such as Odysseus' wanderings through the countryside, the portrayal of which became fashionable in Late Hellenistic Rome. The very sketchiness of the pictorial technique enhances the dream-like quality which is still ideal in a thoroughly Greek—but not in a Classical—way. What is missing here from the point of view of genre is not naturalistic observation but the direct, factual statement such as we encounter in untutored Roman folk art and in the Vienna Genesis where camels behave like real camels, sturdy and mean, in contrast to the evanescent vision of a camel as seen in the Yellow Frieze of the House of Livia.

The "sacral-idyllic" landscapes bring us to the problem of Hellenistic landscape in general. No subject is more controversial. This discussion must center on the famous Odyssey landscapes, certainly the most highly developed renderings of landscape which have come down to us from antiquity. P. H. von Blanckenhagen has argued that these pictures are derived from an earlier frieze-like Hellenistic painting which was not interrupted by columns or pilasters; the Yellow Frieze in the House of Livia and some other "sacral-idyllic" landscapes have been cited in support of this view.[17]

These putative Early Hellenistic landscapes remain phantoms. We must, I believe, accept this astonishing performance for what it is—a monument of the Hellenistic landscape painting in its latest, Roman phase. The most significant aspect of the Odyssey pictures is the sense of pantheistic vastness of nature, a nature which achieves importance equal, if not superior to the myth. This nature still receives its final animation from men; but the heroic mood is now nature's, not man's. The perennial life of the universe will go on, even when the Odyssey has ended.

In their comprehensive scope and sweep, the Odyssey landscapes are unique; but something of the same marriage of myth and nature in a poetic mode occurs in the various "sacral-idyllic" or "idyllic-mythological" paintings. In literature a similar chord, struck first in the descriptions of the Isles of the Blest, echoes in the "Blessed Landscapes" of Hellenistic romances.[18] In the celebrated picture of Paris on Mount Ida the theme is "an ideal shepherd in hallowed solitude of the mountains," not the hero or the villain of the tragedy of Troy. It is this overtone of ideality of a dreamland as remote as Paradise which seems to have inspired Byzantine artists in Ravenna to adopt such a "Landscape with Shepherd" for the portrayal of the Good Shepherd;[19] but as may be readily seen by the Roman rendering of the subject in Hadrian's Villa, the Christian mosaicists drew their inspiration not from the pantheistic interpretations of Hellenism, with their small figures and large, panoramic landscape, but from the simplified "middle-scale" interpretations of the Roman period.[20]

In other Late Hellenistic representations, the ideality of the framework is less obvious and the specific character of the setting is elaborated, with some borrowings from the cartographic tradition. Civilized urban life is made part of this picture of the *oikoumene* when the so-called "city formula"[21] is added to panoramic vistas of sea and rock. Here again, in varying degree, the setting is more prominent than the action. The fall of Icarus is only an incident in the continuous life cycle of man and nature (Fig. 9).[22]

Potentially, this kind of animated landscape was adaptable to historic narration. In the Jonah scene of the Paris Psalter (Fig. 10), the artist seems to have been strongly impressed by the vision of an ancient "city by the sea" (Fig. 9). Indeed, the miraculous delivery from the belly of the whale becomes almost incidental. There are other striking resemblances; the little boat with the spectators here turned into boatmen who throw a sacklike Jonah overboard, the upward thrusts of gesturing hands transformed from astonished comment into pious urgency of prayer, the lofty place of the luminous divinity in the upper regions of the picture—in one Helios,

9. Pompeii, House of Amandus, Wall Painting, *Fall of Icarus*, First Century A.D.

in the other the hand of God in sunlike orb. Here, for once, one feels that a Hellenistic model may have been the immediate source.[23]

We can recall here only briefly the great variety of other Hellenistic experiments in suggesting spatial, physical setting. What we know of Greek geometry and optics confirms the ancient tradition

10. Paris Psalter, *Jonah*, c. 900 A.D. (Bibliothèque Nationale, Paris, after H. Omont, Fac-similés des miniatures des manuscrits grecs de la Bibliothèque Nationale, 1902, pl. 12)

11. Pompeii, House of the Little Fountain, Wall Painting, *View of Imaginary Town and Landscape*

that architectural drawing applied to theater backgrounds was the primary vehicle for the only consistent optic constructions which ancient painting had achieved. We are fortunate in having a Tarentine vase of the Late Classical period a reflection of an early stage in this process.[24] Its final phase is seen in such pictures as that of Iphigeneia on Tauris set against a magnificently Baroque stage background in the house of Pinarius Cerialis.[25] Other solutions show cities climbing up mountains, and bird's-eye views of cities (Fig. 11), intimate close-ups of civilized nature in Roman villas, and rising rocks peopled with heroic, monumental figures as in the Orpheus painting from Pompeii—which is rather strikingly related in its composition to the rendering of Moses on Sinai in the Paris and Vatican Psalters. This experimentation also comprises architectural backgrounds for narrative friezes such as are shown in scenes from the Iliad on the jug from Bernay and in the stucco frieze from Casa del Criptoportico in Pompeii.

Enlargement of the physical world was thus, in the main, a Hellenistic achievement.[26] It remains to point out its obvious limitations. Despite their knowledge of axial perspective, Hellenistic

97

painters never managed to detach this geometric construction from the representations of architecture and to apply it consistently to nature-made elements of landscape. The relation of landscape and figures remains in a kind of labile flux which enhances the sense of unreality. It is the unity of coloristic treatment, the dynamic play of highlights, and the sustained harmony of moods that holds this world together.

ILLUSIONISM

"Illusionism" is a term often used to describe the great advance made by the Hellenistic painters in conveying the impression of a world rich with color, spread out in space, and enlivened with light and shade. The term is not unambiguous—ever since Plato antiquity had felt that there is involved in pictorial representation on a two-dimensional surface an element of illusion in the sense of delusion and deceit, of showing what is not. On the whole, Hellenistic art took a positive attitude toward this deceit. To ancient critics, the pictorial achievements of what we would term Late Classical and Early Hellenistic painting were nothing short of miraculous. To understand their enthusiasm, we must not forget that these were discoveries made for the first time in the history of mankind. A Late Hellenistic theorist, whose views are preserved by Pliny (XXXV:29), states that painting at long last differentiated itself from other arts, discovered light and shade, explored hue, value, and gradations as well as contrasts of colors, and then added something described as *splendor* and specifically said to be different from light (*splendor, alius hic quam lumen*). This is usually translated as "glow"; what it appears to mean is the general heightening of optical effect attained by the use of highlights as well as by coloristic devices.

From our vantage point of Post-Impressionism and highly developed color photography, the achievements of Hellenistic painters seem curiously incomplete. Yet, even in the provincial reflection by Pompeian wall painters, such is the somnambulistic certainty in the evocative handling of the brush that a critic of the rank of a J. Burckhardt felt himself "seduced into impieties toward the Renaissance" by the brilliance and brio of the ancient Campanians. In their best work, the new pictorial means are utilized to endow

12. Pompeian Wall Painting, Detail: Head of Omphale, First Century A.D. (Museo Nazionale, Naples)

the human body, by color and highlight, with a pulsating life and a juicy opulence which sculpture cannot attain.

"If there are any first-rate paintings in Pompeii, they are these," says a sensitive critic of this famous picture of Heracles and Omphale (Fig. 12), part of a triptych or trilogy celebrating the power of Dionysus. The picture is quite certainly by one of the best Pompeian painters of the Fourth Style. It is equally certainly a close rendering of a Hellenistic composition of the third century B.C. At the very least it is a testimonial for the ability of painters in the Late Hellenistic-Early Roman phase of illusionism to create an effect of rich coloristic contrasts modelled in broad strokes and enhanced by generalized light. . . .

Ancient painters never accomplished what Correggio and Rembrandt were to achieve—the visualization of vaporous atmosphere and the completely unified rendering of chiaroscuro. That they attempted night scenes at all was a revolutionary venture. What they did manage to convey with their strange and inconsistent flashing white lights is the drama of the night. The picture of the Trojan horse[27] with its ghostly little silhouettes and vague masses of people is perhaps the most far-reaching attempt of antiquity to dissolve its usually plastic figures; and in the moving rendering of Priam guarding the body of Hector, the dark quiet of the night is used to enhance the mood of the sad vigil.[28]

99

That landscape and still life emerge as independent if subsidiary themes is characteristic of the interpenetration of the scientific interest in nature and the vitalistic attitude of Hellenistic painters. The sunlit solitude of heroic mountains was perhaps never more charmingly evoked than in the picture of the shepherd and ram; the very sketchiness of the landscape, the insubstantiality of the figures in the background emphasize its poetic unreality.[29]

To find that close-up segments of nature were considered subjects valid in their own right is even more remarkable in an art which was still anthropomorphic in essence. Hellenistic painting interprets still life not as *nature-morte* but as nature alive with a pantheistic life of which the carriers are light and color. Thus in a typical Pompeian "still life"[30] the glass, with its miraculous property of responding to light, is even more alive than the animate bird. This truly is "glow and shimmer."

Such Hellenistic splendor, however, is always a heightening of the natural, not a quest for the radiance of the supernatural. Hellenistic monarchs were noted for luxury and the kings of Pergamon had a monopoly on gold-woven textiles, *Attalicae vestes*. Gold was used to depict gold objects and to increase effects of ornamental details; but to my knowledge neither gold nor silver was ever used to produce the effect of unearthly light, not even in representations of the halo which in Pompeian paintings was already used as a symbol of divine effulgence.[31]

EMOTION

The Classical art of Greece had inaugurated a new approach to the portrayal of emotion which was made possible by the discovery of organic art and the resultant ability to establish a convincing relation between the soul and the body. Following up this breakthrough in many directions, Hellenistic artists enormously enlarged the scope and diversity of emotional situations which art might portray. Their precise observation of physical appearances and their careful studies of the relation between somatic and psychological factors enabled them to diversify the portrayal of emotions to an extent which, at first glance, appears infinite. Relaxed sleep[32] and blazing breathlessness[33] are as much within the power of Hellenistic artists as are the skillfully graduated responses in the crowd of spectators commenting on the expiring Minotaur.[34] Nevertheless, within and underneath this seemingly realistic precision, there is always present a typical element, a belief that the general transcends the specific. Apart from the province of the grotesque, Hellenism continues to uphold the Classical belief in the beauty of man—only the human body is now fleshly and sensuously rather than neutrally and ideally beautiful. The heroic gesture still dominates, even when the emotional situation calls for brutality, suffering, and anguish (Laocoön, Sacrifice of Iphigeneia),[35] subjects the ancient critics would describe as scenes of pathos, *pathe, animi perturbationes.*

For Byzantine art, the treatment of the scenes of death, grief, and lament is of particular significance; and for this reason, it may be relevant to end this discussion with some Hellenistic interpretations of the same theme. Following the precedent set by Classical art, the great majority of sepulchral monuments was concerned not with scenes of grief and lament but with perpetuation of the memory of life.[36] The exception—and this is of interest for Byzantine art—are memorials of women who died in childbirth, as did Hediste, commemorated on the Hellenistic stele from Pagasai.[37] It is not impossible that such funerary scenes influenced the portrayals of death and burial in mythological illustrations; in an Ilias cycle, the corpse of Patroclus swathed in a shroud seems to echo the prostrate forms of dying women—and to anticipate curiously scenes of both death and nativity in Early Christian art.[38] From literary sources we learn that the pathetic contrast of an infant and a dead or dying mother was emphatically presented in famous Hellenistic paintings and sculptures.[39] This, however, is only an extension of that theatrical spirit of pathetic tragedy which Hellenism introduced into such legends as the myth of Pyramus and Thisbe. In general, the heroic and mythical sphere interprets death in the spirit of life defiantly ebbing away or as transition to eternal sleep.[40] This grandiose, pathetic tradition is in Roman art transformed into scenes made urgent and drastic to the point of grief-torn ugliness; and it is from this less formalized, "drastic" tradition that some of the Early Christian artists may have drawn their inspiration.[41]

One type of mythological situation, however, did evoke a more "internalized," subdued, and moving interpretation. On an Etruscan urn from Volterra,[42] there is preserved the reflection of a great Hellenistic composition showing the dead and broken but still beautiful Patroclus being lifted from the chariot. Compassion and pity speak eloquently in the group of Patroclus and the two warriors who gently lower the body of the fallen hero. A comparison with Byzantine representations of the Descent from the Cross, as for instance with the fresco of Nerezi,[43] underlines both the common denominator in the motif and the difference in the treatment—the quietly beautiful, subdued, in a sense objective, approach in the Hellenistic work, which excludes the spectator from immediate participation, and the poignantly expressive but also symbolically demonstrative power of the Byzantine masterpiece.

EPILOGUE

In these perfunctory remarks I have sought to indicate something of the range of Hellenistic art which made it such a treasure house for the Romans and the Byzantines. Elaborating and enlarging the anthropomorphic art created by the artists of Classical Greece, Hellenistic art extended the potential of the Classical tradition by searching observation of the variety and diversity of human types and experience. Going beyond the Classic, Hellenistic artists discovered for the ancient world the largeness of nature and the possibility of envisaging a universe in which humanity is but a small part of a larger order. To this expanded cosmos, Hellenism added the new dimensions of textured local color, of light and shade, of splendor designed to heighten the feeling of life. Hellenistic art is a world of realistic unrealities—its major concerns are the defiant heroism of mythical and semi-mythical supermen, the sensuous and sentimental delights of love, the dream of a children's world where children play with gods and heroes; of grotesques uglier but also more exuberant than life; and—perhaps most comprehensively—the image of a sacral-idyllic world of pantheistic landscapes peopled with simple folk, whose worship of their rustic gods is uncorrupted by philosophic doubt, and whose peaceful, natural existence knows neither ambition nor strife. Religion in Hellenistic art is diffused and dispersed through all phases of existence, its myth is an afterglow which, like poetry, serves to elevate man's view of his past and his present. With all this yearning for the Golden Age of innocence and for escape to bucolic nature, the general tenor of Hellenistic art is life-affirming; even death is sleep, not decay. The hedonistic view of *KTO KHRO* parades its skeletons to encourage the spectator to live, not to die.[44] In contrast to Byzantine art, Hellenistic art is entirely and enthusiastically of this world, *huius mundi*, with all the good and evil this might imply for devout Christians.

This Hellenistic art, authentically Greek in essence,[45] was doomed even without the Roman conquest—artistically, by the limits set to any naturalistic cycle; psychologically, by the lack of any powerful religious impetus; biologically, by its enormous geographical expansion from India to Spain, with the resultant thinning out of its carriers and the increasing erosive impact of the native attitudes and traditions. Its Roman heirs understood much of it, but not that *élan vital* which was the unifying idea of Hellenistic creativity. In the three centuries when the Roman Empire prospered (A.D. 100–400) and held sway over men's thoughts, the entire vision of life and the world changed from the heroic superman to the *civis Romanus;* and he in turn was transformed into a citizen of the City of God, as the *interpretatio Romana* of Hellenistic heritage was succeeded by *interpretatio Christiana.* Yet Hellenistic art "dying died not." To assess the share of Hellenistic elements in the medieval image of the Classical world and to trace the persistence of Hellenistic art as a latent force which, especially in the Eastern part of the former Roman Empire, could stimulate creative revivals, is a task which presents fascinating challenges to students of Byzantine art and culture.

NOTES

[1] Gauls: as proposed by A. Schober, *RM*, 51 (1936), pp. 104 ff., and *Die Kunst von Pergamon* (1951), pp. 46, 54, pls. 20 f., 80. Bieber, pp. 108 ff., Figs. 281–283, 424–427. Sleeping Eros: Bieber, p. 145, Figs. 616–618. G. M. A. Richter, *AJA*, 47 (1943), pp. 365 ff., Figs. 1 ff. R. Martin rightly notes that the "monumental urbanism" of Pergamon, which is of one piece with the Pergamene style in sculpture, works toward the heightening of nature rather than against nature, *L'urbanisme dans la Grece antique* (1956), chap. 3.

[2] On poetry, F. Lasserre, *La figure d'Eros dans la poésie grecque* (1946), pp. 150 ff. A. Furtwängler, in Roscher, *Myth. Lex.* (1884), Vol. 1 : 1, pp. 1365 ff., and *Antike Gemmen* (1900), III, pp. 167 f., 280 f.

[3] Best known from the amorini paintings of the Casa dei Vettii, Herrmann-Bruckmann, *Denkmäler der Malerei*, pls. 22 ff., 35. Their Hellenistic character is discussed in detail by F. Matz, *Ein römisches Meisterwerk* (1958), pp. 169 ff., pl. 36. Cf. those shown in Delos, Curtius, p. 78, Fig. 45.

[4] Although the purpose is different, much material has been collected by F. Matz, *op. cit.*, pp. 62 ff., which also includes amorini with thunderbolt of Zeus, trident of Poseidon, and quiver of Apollo. Amorini and Ares, Curtius, pl. 1., Matz, pl. 7b.

[5] As in groups of Ares and Aphrodite, Perseus and Andromeda, Dionysus and Ariadne, Curtius, Figs. 149 f., pl. 1. E. Simon, *Jahrbuch d. k. d. arch. Inst.*, 76 (1961), pp. 130 f., Fig. 15. L. Richardson, *Mem. of the Amer. Acad. in Rome*, 23 (1955), pl. 20.

[6] Alinari 28 080. Museo Comunale, Antiquarium. Bieber, p. 147, Fig. 627.

[7] Sleeping hermaphrodite, Louvre. Cf. Vigneau, *TEL: Encyclopédie photographique*, III, p. 231; B and C. J. Charbonneaux, *La sculpture du Louvre*, (1936), pl. 45 f.; Bieber, pp. 146 f., Figs. 623, 625 ff., and p. 124, Fig. 492.

[8] Ample illustrations in M. Bieber, *The History of the Greek and Roman Theater*, 2nd ed. (1961), chaps. 3, 7, 8, 10.

[9] Cf. H. Kenner, *Weinen und Lachen in der griechischen Kunst* (Oesterreich: Akademie der Wissenschaften, Philosophisch-Historische Klasse, *Sitzungsberichte* 234 : 2 [1960]), p. 89, Fig. 21. Kenner, pp. 93 f., emphasizes the rarity of laughing figures and concludes that only satyrs, centaurs, comedy masks, and children— non-human, or not-yet-human beings—were permitted to display laughing faces because an ideal of emotional restraint dominated Greek art. This does not quite do justice to the situation in the Hellenistic age.

[10] Curtius, pp. 337 ff., pl. 9, considers it a theatrical scene. Fig. 14 is after E. Pfuhl, *Malerei und Zeichnung der Griechen*, 3, Fig. 684.

[11] Richardson, *MAAR*, 23 (1955), p. 126, pl. 23 : 2, "Io Painter." Cf. Curtius, p. 316, Fig. 181.

[12] By M. Seiger in her report on Birth and Childhood of a God in Hellenistic Art.

[13] Richardson, pl. 49 : 1, "Iphigeneia Painter."

[14] A. S. Arvanitopoulos, *Athenische Mitteilungen*, 37 (1912), pp. 76 ff., pls. 2–3. H. Fuhrmann, *JdI*, 65–66 (1951), pp. 103 ff. L. Leschi, *MonPiot*, 35 (1936), pp. 139 ff. A. Maiuri, *La Casa del Menandro* (1932), pp. 335 ff. Morgoulieff, *Monuments antiques representant les scènes d'accouchement* (1893), and the literature quoted by J. Laager, cf. note 39. For the bathing scene, much discussed since the discovery of the Baalbek mosaic, there are not only Hellenistic but even Archaic forerunners. Cf. M. Lawrence, *De Artibus Opuscula XL: Essays in Honor of Erwin Panofsky* (1961), I, pp. 323–334, II, Fig. 13. K. Weitzmann, *Ancient Book Illumination* (1959), pp. 55 ff., Figs. 62 ff., Achilles. E. Simon, *JdI*, 76 (1961), pp. 160 f., Figs. 32, 34 f. For a typical Dionysiac "mother" who is actually a nymph, cf. the Farnesina painting, Curtius, Figs. 64 f.

[15] J. Laager, *Geburt und Kindheit des Gottes in der griechischen Mythologie* (1957).

[16] Yellow frieze, House of Livia, after P. Marconi, *La pittura dei Romani* (1929), Fig. 78. Cf. *Monumenti della pittura antica scoperti in Italia*, Sez. III : III, pl. 7 (color plate). The most recent, sensitive appreciation of "idyllic" landscapes is at hand in P. H. von Blanckenhagen and Chr. Alexander's *The Paintings from Boscotrecase*, *RM*, Suppl. 6 (1962). Von Blanckenhagen's evaluation, pp. 60 f., agrees so closely with mine that it is perhaps relevant to observe that neither of us had an opportunity to consult the work of the other.

[17] Rizzo, *Le pittura ellenistico-romana* (1929), pl. 163. P. H. von Blanckenhagen,

AJA, 61 (1957), pp. 79 f. K. Schefold, *AM*, 71 (1956), pp. 211 ff.

[18] M. Hadas, *Hellenistic Culture* (1959), chap. 16, "Blessed Landscapes and Havens," pp. 212 ff.

[19] Curtius, Fig. 208. Ravenna: C. R. Morey, *Early Christian Art* (1942), pp. 158 f., Fig. 168 (Galla Placidia).

[20] E. Pfuhl, *Malerei und Zeichnung*, 3, Fig. 695. Color plate in S. Aurigemma, *Villa Adriana* (1961), p. 169, pl. 18.

[21] F. M. Biebel, *Gerasa* (ed. by C. H. Kraeling) (1938), pp. 341–351, pls. 67b, c; 68 a, b; 75a, 86 ff.

[22] Fig. 9 after Alinari 39 387. P. H. von Blanckenhagen, *AJA*, 61 (1957), p. 82, pl. 32, Fig. 11.

[23] Fig. 10 after H. Omont, *Fac-similés des miniatures et des manuscrits grecs de la Bibliothèque Nationale* (1902), p. 9, pl. 12, MS graec. 139, fol. 431. For the motif of figures emerging from the door, cf. Curtius, p. 250, Fig. 145. and K. Weitzmann, *Ancient Book Illumination* (1959), p. 61, pl. 31, Fig. 69.

[24] H. Bulle, "Eine Skenographie" *94. Winckelmannsprogramm Berlin* (1934), pl. 2. M. Bieber, *History of the Greek and Roman Theater*, 2nd ed. (1961), p. 68, Fig. 266.

[25] Pinarius Cerialis: Bieber, *op. cit.*, p. 231, Fig. 774.

[26] For the situation in Classical Greek art, cf. G. M. A. Hanfmann, *AJA*, 61 (1957), pp. 75 ff.

[27] Made famous as an example of illusionism by F. Wickhoff, *Roman Art* (1900), pp. 149 f., pl. 12.

[28] House of C. Decimus Octavius Quartio. Spinazzola, *Pompeii*, 2 (1953), Fig. 1049.

[29] Alinari 39 135, Curtius, Fig. 213. Color: B. Maiuri, *Museo Nazionale di Napoli* (1957), p. 108.

[30] From Herculaneum. B. Maiuri, *op. cit.*, p. 134.

[31] On the use of gold, cf. E. Pfuhl, *Malerei und Zeichnung*, 2 (1923), pp. 582, 586, 591, 710, 712. For early empire, cf. A. Boëthius, *The Golden House of Nero* (1960), pp. 102 f., 112. Halo: cf. G. M. A. Hanfmann, *AJA*, 43 (1939), pp. 234 f.

[32] Sleeping Eros, n. 1 . . . Metropolitan Museum, New York, neg. 131094, cf. Bieber, p. 145, Figs. 616–618.

[33] Jockey from the sea near Cape Artemision, E. Buschor, *Vom Sinn der griechischen Standbilder* (1942), pl. 25. Cf. Bieber, p. 151, Fig. 645.

[34] B. Maiuri, *Museo Nazionale di Napoli* (1957), pl. 95, cf. L. Richardson, *MAAR*, 23 (1955), p. 121, pls. 21 f., "Dioscuri Painter." Curtius, pp. 213 f., Fig. 126, thought, probably rightly, that the spectator group goes back to a Late Hellenistic version derived from the same Late Classical original as the superior painting from the Basilica of Herculaneum . . . ; Curtius, Figs. 7 f.

[35] Laocoön in new reconstruction, after F. Magi, *Il ripristino del Laocoonte*, Pontif. Accademia Romana di Archeologia, *Memorie*, 9 (1960), pl. 41. Sacrifice of Iphigeneia, . . . Curtius, pp. 290 ff., pl. 5. Richardson, *MAAR*, 23 (1955), p. 148, pl. 47 : 1, "Iphigeneia Painter." The "beautiful" concept may have been modified to some extent by psychological associations of the kind indicated by references to color of skin and hair as reflections of character in Pseudo-Aristotelian *Physiognomica* and Pollux's catalogue of masks.

[36] For the Classical tradition, cf. K. Friis Johansen, *The Attic Grave-Reliefs of the Classical Period* (1951).

[37] Hediste: Pfuhl, *Malerei und Zeichnung* (1923), pp. 902 f., 907, Fig. 748.

[38] The corpse of Patroclus: House of C. Decimus Octavius Quartio, Spinazzola, *Pompeii*, 2, Figs. 1030, 1032 f. Cf. K. Weitzmann, *The Fresco Cycle of S. Maria di Castelseprio* (1951), pls. 5, 27, Nativity; pls. 3, 29, Joseph's dream; P. Buberl, *Illuminierte Handschriften in Wien* (1937), pl. 34:27, death of Isaac; pl. 44:48, death of Jacob.

[39] Aristeides of Thebes, painter, Pliny, XXXV:98, "a mother lying wounded to death in the sack of a city; she appears conscious that her babe is creeping towards her breast." The picture was taken by Alexander the Great to Pella. Epigonus, Pergamene sculptor, Pliny, XXXIV:88, "infant piteously caressing its dead mother."

[40] . . . Head of giant from copies of "Small Attalid Dedications," German Archaeological Institute, Rome, 36. 1150. Bieber, Figs. 434 f. Sleep—Bieber, Figs. 425, 432.

[41] Meleager sarcophagus Louvre-Borghese. Cf. A. Paoletti, *Materiali archeologici nelle chiese dell' Umbria, Sarcofago con il mito di Meleagro* (1961), pp. 44 ff., where other examples of drastic, "ugly" scenes of grief on Meleager sarcophagi are reproduced. I owe the reference to C. C. Vermeule. On the increase of drastic, desperate grief in rendering of mourners in Roman art, cf. H. Kenner, *Weinen und Lachen* (1960), pp. 57 f. For Early Christian art, cf. Vienna Genesis, Buberl, *Illuminierte Handschriften* . . . (Wien, 1937), pl. 33:26, death of Deborah.

[42] Photograph, Soprintendenza Antichità, Firenze, no. 5463, Cf. D. Levi, *Rivista del R. Istituto di Archeologia e Storia dell'Arte*, 4 (1932–3), pp. 7 ff., pl. 2b.

[43] P. Muratoff, *La peinture Byzantine* (1928), pl. 153. UNESCO, *Yugoslavia: Mediaeval Frescoes* (1955), pl. 9.

[44] K. Schefold, *Die Bildnisse der antiken Dichter, Redner, und Denker,* (1943), pp. 166 f., 216 (goblets from Boscoreale) with references. Photograph, M. Chuzeville. This side shows Zenon (left) pointing at Epicure, who is taking a cake from the table. The scene is inscribed: *to telos hedone,* "pleasure is the [highest] end."

[45] I do not wish for a moment to deny the historic significance and aesthetic potential of forms developed in Egypt, Syria, Mesopotamia, and India through fusion of Hellenistic with native elements, but the center of gravity, the artistic leadership remained in a small area—essentially the Greek islands and the Greek cities in the coastal areas of Asia Minor, with a wider "secondary" zone taking in Athens, Sikyon, Tarentum, Syracuse, Antioch, and Alexandria.

7. THE PROBLEM
OF ROMAN ART

Otto J. Brendel

INTRODUCTION

When the spirit of Anchises speaks to Aeneas in the sixth book of Virgil's *Aeneid*, he projects a Roman destiny in which the fine arts are left to the talents of others: it would not be the Roman's destiny to fashion bronze into softer forms and to draw life from the marble. The Roman's charge would be to maintain dominion over the lands of the earth, to keep the peace, to be merciful to the vanquished, and to humble the proud. If there was an art in this, it was the art of government.

Nevertheless, authentically Roman though this Augustan view might be, it is qualified by the presence of an impressive body of architecture, sculpture, relief, and painting produced within the Roman sphere for their patrons over many hundreds of years. How to both define and evaluate this Roman art bears directly on the aesthetic, historical, and terminological problem presented by Professor Brendel in his important article "Prolegomena to a Book on Roman Art," first published in the *Memoirs of the American Academy in Rome* in 1953.

The selection in this anthology is taken from the opening sections of this article. Here the basic questions that must be asked in this process of definition and evaluation are formulated, and here also they are given a historical locus. For a sound introduction to the history of the problem of Roman art from the Renaissance to the 1940's the reader should consult the full essay by Professor Brendel.

Among works in English which deal with various aspects of Roman art, Franz Wickhof, *Roman Art* (1900), still holds a special place in the literature. This work is a translation, by Eugénie Strong, of the introductory essay in Wickhof's *Wiener Genesis* (1895). His work, together with that of Alois Riegl, *Die spätrömische Kunstindustrie* (1901), was influential in modifying the unfavorable view of Roman art established by the eighteenth-century historian, J. J. Winckelmann, in his *Geschichte der Kunst des Alterthums* (1764). For a general view of changes in the criticism of art, there is F. P. Chambers, *The History of Taste* (1932). A discussion of the aesthetics of Roman art can be found in R. L. Scranton, *Aesthetic Aspects of Ancient Art* (1964), pp. 265–315. Mention should also be made of Eugénie Strong, *Art in Ancient Rome*, 2 Vols. (1928), and G. M. A. Hanfmann, *Roman Art* (1964), which is handsomely illustrated.

The selection that follows is reprinted from Otto J. Brendel, "Prolegomena to a Book of Roman Art," *Memoirs of the American Academy in Rome*, XXI (1953), by permission of the author and Indiana University Press.

History has imparted a curious double meaning to the words "Rome" and "Roman." If we say "Rome," we refer at the same time to a city and a state. The city lies within geographically well defined boundaries, between the Alban hills and the mouth of the Tiber in central Italy. The state grew far beyond these limits and eventually became the Roman empire. The city of Rome still exists. The Roman state on the other hand belongs to the past, so that we have become accustomed to speak of the Roman empire as a historical period. Yet all these complex facts, the city and the state, the empire and its time in history, we call by the same name, "Roman." Our very language becomes a potential source of confusion with regard to everything Roman, and from this condition art is not exempt.

The salient point is that all accomplishments to which Rome lent its name are not "Roman" in the same sense nor to the same degree. For instance, "Roman history" traditionally comprises the total evolution of the Roman state from its origin to the end of the empire and consequently much more than a mere city history of Rome, while the medieval and later affairs of the city are not usually included in this term. Roman law was eventually collected and codified at the behest of a Byzantine emporer, Justinian; yet it is "Roman." The ancient bridges and aqueducts of Spain or southern France were built under the Empire, though probably not by natives of Rome only, nor can it be asserted that the technical knowledge employed in these structures was all owed to Romans. Yet to us these buildings constitute monuments of Roman enterprise and engineering. On the other hand, rather paradoxically, the most intimate and direct expression of the Roman spirit, its language, was never called "Roman." It is "Latin." Thus the credit for this accomplishment is given not to Rome but to a regional civilization, now extinct, of which Rome once formed a part.

We must understand from the outset that the same uncertainty is bound to reappear in the study of Roman art. It has indeed determined the course of these studies, especially in their latest stage during the past fifty years. The name itself, "Roman art," requires explanation. What do we really mean by this expression? Conceivably we may so designate the art of the city of Rome in the same sense as one speaks of "Roman" Baroque. But we may also with the same expression refer to the art of the Empire and call "Roman" all works of art produced during the imperial epoch anywhere. Again, the attribute "Roman" may be limited to such works of art as were produced by Romans only, not by Greeks working in Rome or under the Empire, or a certain type of art may be defined as stylistically "Roman," as another type is "Gothic," regardless of its place and time of origin. The problem is inherent in all investigations stipulating or negating the existence of a "Roman" art as the case may be. Yet few writers have stated this expressly. Alois Riegl, for one, perceived the necessity of explaining the term "Roman" in the title of his *Spätrömische Kunstindustrie.* He declares in the introduction: "In selecting the word 'Roman' instead of 'antique,' I had in mind the entire Roman empire but not—as I wish to emphasize strongly from the outset—the city of Rome or the Italic people or the nations of the western half of the empire only."[1] This, of course, represents only the deliberate choice of a single writer; other definitions are just as possible.

Three characteristic problems arise from the peculiar conditions of Roman art. One regards its *aesthetic evaluation,* which has proved remarkably uncertain almost from the beginning; the second its *historical development,* about which very little authentic documentary evidence has come down to us. Obviously, moreover, by modern standards, in order to deal with either one of these questions, we must first decide what to call "Roman." Both involve the initial, *terminological* difficulty. Past experience has amply shown that these three questions are closely connected with each other. Together they form the "Roman problem" in the modern literature on art.

All three loom large in the recent discussions of ancient art. They have stimulated factual research and theoretical thought alike. Some of the most brilliant recent contributions to art historical method and the critical analysis of art have been dedicated to the Roman problem. Indeed, this controversy represents a characteristically modern interest, as one can sense from its growing intensity. Roman art, now more than ever, constitutes a controversial matter. We still have no real mastery of all the seemingly disparate and often uncoordinated materials which claim our attention as "Roman art."

We lack ascertained facts, and we also lack adequate critical tools to deal with the variety of these materials. It has proven especially difficult to evolve those generally valid, comprehensive principles, which seem required in order to separate effectively all works of Roman art from the other arts with which they are so closely allied, the Etruscan and the Greek.

Numerous factual discoveries mark the progress of knowledge through the past hundred years of archaeological research. Roman art has had its share of these discoveries; nevertheless, the recent discussions in this field have probably made their greatest contribution by bringing into focus the general problem of Roman art. As to the answers suggested, no agreement is yet in sight. At least it is evident today that one cannot write a history of Roman art, as one can set out to write a history of Egyptian or Greek art, by starting from a recognized, coherent body of works of art, which present an obvious unity of style, of intentions and of means of expression. The terms "Egyptian," "Greek" have an established meaning in the field of art; the meaning of the word "Roman" cannot so be taken for granted. The unity of Roman art is not obvious as a style or approach to artistic representation, like the Egyptian style. If a similar inner coherence existed at all in Roman art connecting its various manifestations, it must still be uncovered in the diversity before us. The decision is mostly up to the modern student, as to what to call "Roman" and why, and the burden of proof rests on the critic. A history of Roman art cannot merely present and explain; it must first define its subject matter.

In this respect the case of Rome is not unique in the history of art. Critics of "Renaissance" art likewise must define the term "Renaissance" and demonstrate its usefulness as a historical category, before they can deal with the various productions of this period as a closed group. Their task may be less difficult than the problems presented by Roman art, insofar as the nucleus of Renaissance art, in Italy at least, defines itself well by way of its style and intellectual climate. Questions arise, however, as to the limits of the category. Shall we say that Renaissance art begins with Giotto or Masaccio? Is it a purely Italian movement or are we justified in speaking of a "Northern Renaissance"? What modifications are needed to impart to the latter term a meaning consistent with reality? The answer to these questions is not self-evident; they require clarification. Similar questions are in place, and even more pressing, with regard to Baroque art. Where does it begin? Where are its limits? What, in fact, is "Baroque," a historical period or merely a trend within a historical period, the seventeenth century? Such questions are not unlike those which Roman art puts before us. The term "modern art" is similarly ill defined and in need of discussion, in spite of the fact that its object forms a part of our contemporary existence. Not all contemporary art is "modern." In each of these instances the validity of a critical or historiographic category must first be proven, and its precise limitations defined before actual materials can be ascribed to it. We must draw the line between that which is or is not "modern" or "baroque" in art. So we must decide what we wish to call "Roman." The distinction expresses our own critical evaluation of a work of art. Additional examples are not hard to find in the history of art.

Still, however, the puzzle of Roman art would remain. For one thing, most of the arguable, critical classifications of the kind just mentioned result from conditions typical of the post-Classical periods, Medieval or later. In these periods it surprises us less that artists choose freely between various modes of expression. In ancient art we are accustomed to find the distinctions much more sharply drawn—more objectively, it would seem. The style of Egyptian paintings or statues, for instance, is highly characteristic. It is easily recognized, because its approach to artistic representation is permanent as to fundamental principles and exclusive of all other ancient styles. As a rule there can be little doubt whether or not a work of art is Egyptian. Greek art, similarly, in review exhibits a distinctive and self-contained character, in spite of the evolutionary energy which led it through so many different phases from the archaic to the Hellenistic. Yet even in antiquity instances occur which may cast a doubt on the certainty with which we use these historical categories. Greek artists worked for Persians. Shall we call the results Greek or Persian art? Intermediary arts existed between the great styles of Egypt, the Near East and early Greece, like the art of the Phoenicians. Such "mixed" styles are now commonly treated with disrespect, as lacking in originality. But they, too, had their share in the growth and expansion of our civilization. An objective evaluation of the archaic Phoenician style has yet to be given.

However, all these were but minor incidents in the early history of Mediterranean culture. What makes the case of Roman art so baffling is the fact that in this one instance we are confronted with a main branch of ancient art, of long tradition and extraordinary productivity, yet surprisingly deficient in those exclusive, constant and definite stylistic traits, which differentiate most other ancient arts from each other like so many different languages. Moreover the Roman accomplishments in other fields are both distinctive and outstanding. One expects to find a Roman art comparable in importance to the Roman military achievements or government administration, which built the famous Empire, or to the classical Latin literature which infused the political structure with a spiritual meaning of its own. Instead, one finds an art of quite uneven tendencies, uncertain in origin, oscillating between a "neo-classic" acceptance of Greek standards and an often crude "popular" realism, and eventually issuing in the seemingly "anti-classic," formal rigidity of the late Roman style.

The dilemma is critical as well as historical. When modern criticism wishes to do justice to a display of art so contrary to modern expectations, it is first of all confronted with the problem of *aesthetic evaluation*. But this cannot long be separated from the *historical problem* of evolution. Therefore, to reconstruct the evolution of Roman art as a process in history has long been, and still is, a pressing task. And this task, in turn, leads to the problem of definition, as explained above. We must define what we mean by "Roman art." This is the *terminological problem*. Recent criticism has tended to concentrate especially on the question what, precisely, is Roman in Roman art.

THE HISTORY OF THE PROBLEM

One must know these three aspects of the problem—the *aesthetic,* the *historical,* and the *terminological*—in order to understand the modern literature on Roman art. All three undoubtedly derive from the real conditions of Roman art. Yet only gradually have modern students and critics become aware of these conditions. Each one of these questions, thought inherent in the material, moved at one time within sight of modern criticism, and upon its discovery gave rise to a fresh approach to Roman art. Thus the *historical* problem of Roman art was first formulated during the Renaissance; the *aesthetic* evaluation became problematic during the seventeenth and eighteenth centuries; and the *terminological* definition of a Roman style concerns the most recent research. These changes of viewpoint each time accompanied an increase of factual knowledge and a more direct contact with the original materials. They are also symptomatic of other more general changes in European thought. In this, as in other fields, it appears that discoveries are not made at random but when the time has come for them. Through the past centuries the varying reactions to Roman art have faithfully followed not only the dominating preferences of taste but the development of ideas in general. In this way, from time to time, by the intuition of one writer or the efforts of a whole group of scholars, the entire problem has been reformulated and recast in a radical manner. Whenever this has happened, the result has been a new theory of Roman art. The fundamental ideas incorporated in the earlier approaches are not as yet extinct, nor is their usefulness exhausted by the observation that some theories owe their origin and impact to intellectual constellations different from the present.

NOTES

[1] A. Riegl, *Die spätrömische Kunstindustrie* (Vienna, 1901), 10. (Author's translation).

8. VERISM IN ROMAN PORTRAITS

Gisela M. A. Richter

INTRODUCTION

In this selection Miss Richter surveys the various theories explaining the origin of verism in Roman Republican portrait sculpture, giving particular attention to the theory that the dry realism of Roman portraiture derives from the influence of Egyptian portraits. This theory she finds inadequate. The answer for Miss Richter lies in Greek portraiture: that it was the combination of Greek artists long skilled in naturalistic representation and the Romans themselves, with their interesting faces and their taste for uncompromising realism, that produced the phenomenon of Roman verism.

For further reading consult G. M. A. Hanfmann, "Observations on Roman Portraiture," *Collection Latomus*, XI (1953); Margarete Bieber, *The Sculpture of the Hellenistic Age*, rev. ed. (1961), the chapter on the "Transition from Hellenistic to Roman Sculpture," and, by the same author, *Alexander the Great in Greek and Roman Art* (1964), a revision of her earlier article, "The Portraits of Alexander the Great," *Proceedings of the American Philosophical Society*, XCIII (1949); and Gisela M. A. Richter, *The Portraits of the Greeks*, 3 vols. (1965). Jale Inan and Elisabeth Rosenbaum, *Roman and Early Byzantine Portrait Sculpture in Asia Minor* (1966), in so far as Roman portraiture is concerned, deals primarily with works of the Imperial periods and does not include works of purely Hellenistic manner. R. P. Hinks, *Greek and Roman Portrait-Sculpture* (1935), dealing only with works in the British Museum, is a good introduction; and Ludwig Goldscheider, *Roman Portraits* (1940) is a well-illustrated picture book.

The selection that follows is reprinted from Gisela M. A. Richter, "The Origin of Verism in Roman Portraits," *The Journal of Roman Studies*, XLV (1955), by permission of the author and the Society for the Promotion of Roman Studies.

W as the verism of Roman Republican portraits due to Italic, Etruscan, Roman, Egyptian, or Greek influence?[1] This question has been much discussed, especially of late.[2] Of particular interest is the recent theory that late Egyptian portraits played a decisive part. In this article I want first to discuss the evidence for the various influences that have been considered potent in the creation of Roman verism, and then try from this evidence to deduce which factor, or which factors, were the most potent. I shall examine in particular the Egyptian and the Greek theories, for in these fields I may perhaps have something new to say,[3] whereas the Italian side has been thoroughly explored.

The question at issue is an important one; . . . the birth of Republican Roman portraiture was as momentous a happening in the history of art as was the birth of individualistic representation in Greek art. The many different views that have been held regarding the origin testify to the complexity of the question. If a convincing solution could be obtained, it would clarify, I think, our whole understanding of that great phenomenon—the origin of Roman art.

First I must define the word "verism," which has only comparatively recently entered our archaeological vocabulary. Verism I take to mean a somewhat dry realism, a realism which shows the person portrayed as he really is, without idealizing tendencies, with wrinkles and warts and other physical defects, and also, what is more important, with an expression not of a philosopher or poet or visionary, but of what might be called a man of affairs.

As I have said, the influence of Italy on Roman art is so well-known that it need not detain us long. A few words will suffice. Some have thought that the ancient Italic peoples already had an inclination to veristic representation and that this had some influence on Roman art. They refer us, for instance, to the early Canopic jars of the seventh and sixth centuries B.C. with lids in the form of heads. These heads, however, even if intended to represent the deceased whose ashes were placed in the jars, are so primitive that they do not, in my opinion, enter into our discussion. Moreover,

117

this ancient Italic art is separated from Republican portraits by several centuries. All that one can say is that these Italic "expressionist" products already show a style that is not idealizing, and that a realistic outlook remained a dominant characteristic of Italian art.

There is also a theory that a number of bronze heads, perhaps datable in the second century B.C.—for instance those from Fiesole in the Louvre, from Bovianum Vetus in the Bibliothèque Nationale, and from Etruria in Florence—are Italic forerunners of the Republican portraits. Others, however, would assign these heads not to Italic but to Etruscan artists; and this seems to me more likely, for the ability of Etruscan sculptors to create realistic portraits is attested by the figures on Etruscan third-to-second-century urns and sarcophagi.[4] Occasionally, indeed, the heads of these figures show so powerful and so dry a realism that it could really be called verism. I refer to the well-known group from Volterra[5] and other examples like it. But the importance of this possible Etruscan influence on Roman Republican art must not be exaggerated, for various reasons. First, it must be remembered that the art of Etruria in the third and second centuries B.C. reflects the international Hellenistic Greek style that pervaded the whole of Italy; it was not an independent phenomenon. Moreover, by the first century B.C., according to the present evidence at least, Etruscan art was in its last phase. Furthermore, the Etruscans rarely worked in marble, the material of most of the extant Roman portraits. It is, therefore, doubtful if this tired art, without experience in the working of hard stone, could have initiated the great Roman portraiture of the first century B.C. Some influence there certainly must have been. Italic and Etruscan traditions doubtless played a part. But in addition there must have been some other potent factor.

The ancient Roman custom of making wax portraits of their ancestors, placed in houses and carried in processions, was long thought to have had a decisive influence on Roman Republican portraiture. Recent research, however, has thrown doubt on this theory.[6] Here again the chronology does not seem to fit. Moreover, it is one thing to make wax portraits, perhaps molded from actual faces, and another thing to create portrait busts and statues in marble. Nevertheless, one may deduce from the testimony of Polybius, Pliny, and others, that the Romans early took an interest in portraiture. Furthermore, it is known from history that the Roman character was essentially practical. This practical sense, and Italic and Etruscan heritage, undoubtedly paved the way, one might say, for the creation of verism in Roman portraits. But, again, they cannot have been the only factors. We now know better than before (from the researches of Rizzo,[7] Vessberg,[8] Miss Toynbee,[9] and others[10]) that in the first century B.C. Roman sculptors could not have been the great innovators of Roman art. Our evidence indicates that the sculptors of that time who worked for Roman patrons were chiefly foreigners, especially Greeks. As is well known, the Romans, after their conquests of Greece, Asia Minor, and Southern Italy, became enamored of Greek art. Many Greek sculptures were brought to Italy as loot, and when this importation of originals more or less ceased, there began an era of copying. It is also known that for this work Greek artists came to Italy. But then we may ask was it really these Greeks who created the verism of Roman art? It has seemed difficult to many to accept this; for the theory has always been, and we encounter it also in recent books, that the realism of the Greeks was always idealizing. How then could they have created this new verism in Italy? It was really this very argument, I think, that started the theory of Egyptian influence. For in Egypt realistic portraiture existed from the time of the Old Kingdom, and in the late period it became what may be called veristic. The theory has, therefore, been advanced, not only by Egyptian archaeologists but by authorities in our own field,[11] and it is increasingly gaining credence, that it was not Italic, Etruscan, Roman, or Greek, but Egyptian influence that started the verism of Roman portraiture.

In order to be able to gauge the truth of this new theory we must examine Egyptian portraiture, and see what was the conception that the Egyptians had of individualistic representation during their long, distinguished history. For each period I shall select a few outstanding examples and try to deduce from them the characteristics of their time. I should add that if I, a classicist, venture to discuss Egyptian portraits, my excuse is that I am able to look at them with Greek eyes.

There is no doubt that in Egypt portraiture, that is, the individualization of a specific person, was practiced much earlier and for a much longer period than elsewhere. Stupendous portraits exist from the third millennium B.C. until Ptolemaic times. We all know the magnificent wooden statue of Ka-aper (Fig. 13), of the fifth dynasty (c. 2480–2350 B.C.). It is generally called Sheikh El Beled; for when it was unearthed the workmen recognized a striking resemblance between it and their own sheik, that is, the chief of their village. This story is very instructive. If we compare the head of this statue with the more generalized sculptures of the same epoch, we find that the "Sheikh" shows exactly the same type. The features are similar, the shapes of mouth, nose, eyes are the same, likewise the structure of the head; and the same applies to the body. But to the "Sheikh" the artist has given more plumpness, and more modeling round the eyes and mouth. In this way, and with the inlaid, gleaming eyes, that are still marvelously preserved, the artist has obtained an extraordinary sense of individualization. Nevertheless, this individualism is founded on a generic type; and this is true also of other portraits

13. Ka-aper, Called "Sheikh-el-Beled," Wood, 3'7" High, 5th Dynasty (2565–2420 B.C.) (Egyptian Museum, Cairo)

14. Sesostris III, 12th Dynasty, Middle Kingdom, 3⁹⁄₁₆" High (Berlin Museum)

15. Fragment of head of King Sesostris III (Se'n Wosret III), Quartzite, 6½″ High (The Metropolitan Museum of Art, New York, Carnarvon Collection, Gift of Edward S. Harkness, 1926)

of the Old Kingdom. The head always represents the racial type with a few individual features *applied*. It is not a psychological study of an individual. . . .

When one examines the portraits of the Middle Kingdom, those of Sesostris III (1887–1850 B.C.), for instance (Fig. 14), one sees that also here the type rather than the individual is the fundamental thing. To the generic type has been applied what one may call a formula of old age, of melancholy so to speak, with upper eyelids lowered, prominent cheekbones, and some modeling round eyes and mouth. This formula is used not only for Sesostris III, but for his successor Amenemhêt III (1850–1800 B.C.). The same type is used for both, as well as for others, so that it is often difficult to know who is represented. Only an inscription can teach us. And this is true also of two masterpieces of this period—the obsidian head in the Gulbenkian Collection, generally called Amenemhêt III, and the fragmentary head in the Metropolitan Museum in New York, called Sesostris III (Fig. 15). With all their remarkable realism and

121

sensitiveness, they are based on the same type and the same formula.

How little was thought of individualization in portraiture at the time is also shown by the numerous instances in which a portrait of a preceding period was "usurped" by a person of a later time. In these cases almost always only the inscription was changed. The face was left as it was.

In the New Kingdom there is the special case of Akhenaten (1370–1352 B.C.), whose portraits are what may really be called individualized. The head with its strange shape and with features different from the generic, is represented with a real feeling for a specific personality. It is a unique phenomenon in the history of Egyptian art, as were the philosophy and religion of Akhenaten. Only at that one time were the rigid laws of Egyptian thought broken and new ideas introduced. But this revolution lasted less than twenty years. With Tuthankhamen (1352–c. 1341 B.C.) there was a return to the ancient religion of Amun and of multiple gods. This is shown also in the portraits. They become again generic, typical, with now and then individual features applied. . . .

It is well known that during the New Kingdom there was a great expansion of Egypt. Nubia, Lybia, Asia Minor, Assyria were conquered. The prisoners of these various conquered nations are sometimes represented. Each is shown in a realistic manner, but this realism is generalized. The race, not the individual, is differentiated. It is the same conception that one finds in the portraits of the time.

To the twenty-fifth dynasty (c. 715–656 B.C.) belongs the famous portrait of Mentuemhat, prince of Thebes and governor of Southern Egypt. It is a masterpiece. The formula of old age that we encountered in the Middle Kingdom, with modeling round the eyes, is here used so successfully that the portrait really seems to be that of an individual. But it is almost unique in that epoch. The majority of the heads show the usual generalization with perhaps a few individual features indicated. And this applies also, and especially so, to the succeeding Saitic period (663–525 B.C.).

To the epoch of the Persian conquest and domination of Egypt (525–404 B.C.) several interesting portraits can be assigned. They have serious faces, with narrow, elongated eyes, protruding chin, and modeled lips, drawn inward at the corners. The formula used is no longer that of old age and melancholy that was current in the Middle Kingdom, but rather of perturbation, of worry one might almost say. It is well-known that the period of Persian domination was a difficult one for the Egyptian people.

Looking at these Egyptian portraits created during a period of over 2,000 years two things above all strike us. One is that there was no gradual, systematic development. There is no continuity. From time to time individualized portraits appear, but they are isolated products among many others of a generic type. The second thing that impresses us is that in all these centuries in which the Egyptians worked with so much ability, with that extraordinary sense for volume and delicacy of contour, they always adhered to conventionalized renderings of the human figure and observed frontality. This was the accepted system, not only with the Egyptians but with all ancient peoples. It was the Greeks who changed this age-old conception. In a single century, from about 600–500 B.C., they effected step by step a momentous change, and opened the way for a new art—a new art also in portraiture. These Greeks knew very well that before they had changed the ancient conventionalized renderings of the human anatomy, and before they had conquered the ancient frontality, which inevitably imparted a certain rigidity to their figures, neither movement nor portraiture could be properly represented. Thus, naturalistic representation in Greek art began after 500 B.C., that is, at the end of the Archaic period. From that time one can observe a continuous development also in portraiture. In the period of the Ptolemies, in the third and second centuries B.C., this realistic representation had been fully realized.

What happened to Egyptian art during the Hellenistic Greek period, when the Ptolemies were the masters of Egypt? It is most interesting to observe how the old tradition, founded on the Egyptian religion, was still strong enough to resist, to a certain extent, the new ideas introduced by the Greeks. Egyptian sculpture even then remained frontal, with individual parts generalized. There is no movement to the right or to the left. The bodies and heads remain quasi-cubic, with only four principal sides observed. The stance, with left foot advanced and arms held close to the body, is the same as it had been for two or three thousand years. The old conventionalized renderings of hands, knees, feet, shoulders (without indication of the trapezium), etc., are retained. Furthermore, the large majority of the portraits continue to be generic as before. Relatively few are individualized. These, however, sometimes show so surpris-

16. Ptolemaic Statue, 19¼″ High
(Staatliche Museum, Berlin [Lost
in World War II])

17. Head from Dimeh, 8⅝″ High
(Staatliche Sammlung, Munich)

ing a realism that one could call it verism. But—and this seems
to me important—this verism is limited to the face; the form of
the head and of the figure retain the old frontality and conventionalized renderings. That is why Egyptian portraits of this period
appear so strange to us. They show a mixture of two irreconcilable
styles . . . (Fig. 16).

Occasionally, however, among these Egyptian portraits in hard
stone appear some that are more or less rounded and have realis-
tically modeled features, like the contemporary Greek heads (Fig.
17). They present a great contrast to the Egyptian products. They
were evidently influenced, or perhaps even worked, by Greek
sculptors; for there is no reason to think, as some do, that the Greeks

124

were not capable of working hard Egyptian stones, and that, therefore, all sculptures in granite and basalt—found not only in Egypt, but in Greece and Italy—were worked by Egyptian sculptors.

If after this necessarily summary examination of Egyptian portraits, one returns to Roman art, one is immediately conscious of a fundamental difference. The Roman portraits are not cubic, rounded only at the corners, as are the Egyptian statues. Instead of being quadrilateral, they are observed from many sides. Stances and modeling are naturalistic.

This fundamental difference throws doubt on the theory that the dry realism of the late Egyptian portraits initiated Roman Republican portraiture. It does not seem possible that these Egyptian artists who in their own country still worked in the old system of frontality and conventionalized renderings should have created heads and statues of an entirely different system elsewhere. Perhaps the Romans, with their taste for reality, liked these Egyptian portraits and demanded similar veristic portraits of themselves. But to initiate an art as great as that of Republican portraiture more than pleasing models and a taste for verism are necessary.

To find an answer, therefore, in our quest we must search elsewhere. As I have said, for a long time it was thought that the Greeks created only an idealizing, not a veristic, realism. But does this old theory really still hold? I think that there is evidence that puts it in doubt.

First I want to recall the gems published by Furtwängler in his *Antike Gemmen* that he dated in the third and second centuries B.C. The most important is a gold ring, found in Capua and now in the National Museum in Naples. On it is the portrait, evidently of a Roman, signed by Heracleidas: Ἡρ]ακλείδας ἐπόει. Another is an aquamarine (beryl) in the Archaeological Museum of Florence,[12] also with a Roman portrait, signed by Agathopous: Ἀ]γαθόπους ἐποίει. The two other gems, which are not signed, are in Boston and London[13] (Fig. 18), and resemble the signed ones stylistically. All four portraits show considerable verism. The date given by Furtwängler to these gems has been accepted by other archaeologists, including Beazley and Lippold.[14] Not only is the style different from that of the portraits on the Graeco-Roman gems of the first century B.C. and A.D., but the forms of the letters in the two signatures are those current in the third to second, and in the second to early first century B.C. respectively.[15]

18. Gem (British Museum)

19. Coin of Antimachus of Bactria,
c. 185 B.C. (British Museum)

If this evidence is accepted, one must conclude that Greek artists made Roman portraits before the late Republican period and that they, too, were capable of creating verism.

Moreover, the gems do not stand alone. There is also the indisputable evidence of the portraits on the Hellenistic coins that can be dated by the names inscribed on them to the late third and the second century B.C.[16] A number of them show what may certainly be called dry realism. I may mention in particular the superb heads of Ariarathes III of Cappadocia, 235–220 B.C.; Antimachus of Bactria, *c.* 210 B.C. (Fig. 19); Mithridates III of Pontos, *c.* 220–185 B.C.; Pharnakos I of Pontos, *c.* 185–169 B.C.; Eukratides of Bactria, 180–150 B.C.; and his son Heliocles of Bactria, after 150 B.C.[17]

The portraits on these gems and coins bring before us personages who had not the familiar Greek physiognomies. They show the beginnings of a veristic style, introduced by Greek artists when faced with the novel task of portraying new types—those of Roman officials living in Greek lands, and those of the princes in the Asian principalities. . . .

The most important consideration, however, in our quest is the following: In Greece, in the Islands, and in Asia Minor there have

20. *Head from Athens* (Ny
Carlsberg Glyptotek, Co-
penhagen)

been found Roman portraits of the Republican epoch (Fig. 20) which
show the same style as those found in Italy. As more and more are
being published they are becoming better known.[18] All these heads
show the dry realism or verism in resolute Roman faces familiar
from their Italian counterparts. But one can hardly imagine that
in that epoch Egyptian or Roman sculptors worked in Greek lands
where there were many Greek artists with long experience in
working marble, a material which was practically unknown in Egypt
or Italy before the first century B.C. It seems more probable that
the sculptors of those heads were indigenous, as indeed the many
signatures on the statue bases from Delos indicate.[19] This would
again show that Greek artists were able to introduce verism into
their portraits.

There is still another observation that may shed light on our
problem. When one examines the portrait heads that appear for
the first time on Roman coins a little before the middle of the first
century B.C.,[20] one sees that in those representing the great Romans
of the past—whose likenesses had, of course, to be imaginary—the
style is idealizing, whereas in those of more or less contemporary
personages the style is veristic. . . .

According to Vessberg (and his arguments seem convincing), the artists who made these portraits on Roman coins were immigrant Greeks. It was natural, therefore, that when these men were called upon to portray Roman heroes of bygone days they used their familiar idealizing Greek style; but when they were confronted with the task of portraying actual personages, with characteristic, practical Roman faces, they made real portraits. The result was verism.

It would seem, then, that in addition to the ability of the artist to create an exact likeness, there is another important factor that produced veristic realism in Roman Republican portraits. We archaeologists often do not sufficiently take into account that in a portrait the physiognomy of the person represented has importance. In our attempts to date portraits or to assign them to local centers, we have sometimes grouped together heads with similar features or expressions. It seems likely, however, that such characteristics actually belonged to the persons represented, for in a realistic portrait the physiognomy of the individual is, of course, a determining factor.

If one takes all these arguments into account, the most probable explanation of the verism of Roman Republican portraits seems to be the following: When the Greek artists, after the conquests of their countries during the third and second centuries B.C., began to work for Roman clients, who had a taste for realism, and in addition were practical, realistic people, with faces very different from those of the Greek philosophers and poets who had oftenest been represented in past times, it was then that veristic Roman portraiture was born. It was the Greeks with their long experience in naturalistic representation and in the carving of marble, and the Romans with their faces of a lively verism and with their taste for realism, who together created the great epoch of Republican portraiture. Italic and Etruscan traditions doubtless played a part, and it is possible that the late Egyptian veristic portraits exercised some influence.[21] But the most important factors responsible for the masterpieces of Republican portraiture were the veristic faces of the Romans themselves, and the interest of the Greek artists in representing these novel types—which they doubtless found inspiring.

It has long ago been ascertained that late Hellenistic art was the foundation of Roman Republican portraiture. If one goes a step further and recognizes the uninterrupted continuity from late Greek to Roman art, much, I think, becomes clear. The naturalistic style evolved by the Greeks was continued by the same types of artists that had created the late Hellenistic portraits; only the conception changed with the new requirements. The Romans introduced a new concept which became dominant throughout their vast empire.

NOTES

[1] This article is based on a talk I gave at the "Sodalizio tra Studiosi dell' Arte," in Rome on 24th April, 1955.

[2] Of the extensive literature it is sufficient to cite the two recent fundamental contributions by Vessberg, *Studien zur Kunstgeschichte der römischen Republik* (1941), (henceforth quoted as *Studien*), and Schweitzer, *Die Bildniskunst der römischen Republik* (1947), (henceforth quoted as *Bildniskunst*). The subject of the origin of Republican Roman portraiture, however, has still not been solved to everybody's satisfaction. . . .

[3] I had the opportunity in the early months of 1955 of studying the Egyptian portraits in the Museum of Cairo, where a wealth of material is presented. I also had the privilege of discussing many problems with Bernard V. Bothmer, of the Museum of Fine Arts, Boston, and Director of the American Research Center in Cairo. He is engaged in the important task of preparing a Corpus of late Egyptian sculptures, some of which can be dated by inscriptions.

[4] Cf., e.g. D. Levi, "L'arte etrusca e il ritratto," *Dedalo* XIII, 1933, pp. 222 ff.

[5] Cf. now the fine illustration of the heads of the group in the Catalogue of the *Mostra dell' arte e della civiltà etrusca* (Milan, 1955) pl. CI.

[6] Cf. especially Vessberg, *Studien*, pp. 40 ff., 97 ff.; Schweitzer, *Bildniskunst*, pp. 19 ff.

[7] "I Romani e l'arte greca," *L'Urbe* x, 1947, pp. 3 ff.

[8] *Studien* pp. 46 ff., and *passim*.

[9] "Some Notes on Artists in the Roman World," *Collection Latomus* VI, 1951, pp. 5 ff.

[10] Cf., e.g. F. Poulsen, "Die Römer der republikanischen Zeit und ihre Stellung zu Kunst," in *Die Antike* XIII, 1937, pp. 125 ff.; Chamoux, *L'antiquité classique* 1955 (to appear presently); my *Three Critical Periods in Greek Sculpture* (1951), pp. 37 ff.; my article entitled "Who made the Roman Portrait Statues, Greeks or Romans?" in *American Philos. Soc. Proc.* Vol. 95, 1951, pp. 184 ff.; and my forthcoming *Ancient Italy*. To the signatures by Greek sculptors on Roman works cited in *Three Critical Periods*, may now be added that of Publius Licinius Demetrius, freedman of Publius, who made a relief with two portraits in the early Empire. On it are represented his own portrait and that of a fellow freedman, with the tools of his trade. The relief was found at Tusculum and is now in the British Museum. Cf. *Fifty-first Annual Report of the National Art-Collection Fund:* 1954, no. 1749; Vermeule, *Numismatic Circular* LXI, no. 11 (Nov., 1953), and LXII, no. 3 (March, 1954).

[11] On this subject cf. especially L'Orange, *Röm. Mitt.* LIV, 1929, p. 167; Brendel, *Die Antike* LX, 1933, pp. 130 ff.; F. Poulsen, "Probleme der römischen Ikonog-

raphie," *Det kgl. Danske Videnskabernes Selskab., Archaeologisk-kunsthistoriske Meddelelser* ii, 1, 1937, pp. 6 ff., and *From the Collections of the Ny-Carlsberg Glyptothek* ii, 1938, pp. 30 ff.; Snijder, *Mnemosyne* ser. iii, vol. vii, 1939, pp. 241 ff.; Boëthius, *Acta Archaeologica* xiii, 1942, p. 228; Drerup, *Aegyptische Bildnisköpfe griechischer und römischer Zeit* 1950; Vessberg, *Studien* p. 255; Schweitzer, *Bildniskunst* pp. 76 f.; Kukahn, "Sobre les origines del retrato romano," *Archivo español de Arqueologia* xxvi, 1953, pp. 249 ff.; B. V. Bothmer, *Bulletin of the Museum of Fine Arts, Boston* xlix, 1951, pp. 69 ff.; Andrén "Greek and Roman heads in the Malmström Collection," *Skrifter Utgivna av Svenska Institutet i Rom,* 4°, xx, *Opuscula romana,* ii, 1955.

[12] Furtwängler, *Antike Gemmen,* pl. xxxiii, 9.

[13] *Ibid.* pl. xxxiii, 16, 14; Beazley, *Lewes House Gems* no. 101, pl. vi; Walters, *Catalogue of Engraved Gems in the British Museum* no. 1190 (15 by 14 mm.).

[14] Beazley, l.c.; Lippold, *Gemmen und Kameen* 178, pl. lxix, 2.

[15] Furtwängler, *Jb.d.I.* iii, 1888, pp. 208, 211 f. Professoressa Guarducci, whom I consulted on this point, agrees with Furtwängler's findings.

[16] Cf., e.g. Imhoof-Blumer, *Porträköpfe auf antiken Münzen hellenischer und hellenisierter Völker* pls. vi, vii; Waddington, *Receuil des monnaies grecques d'Asie Mineure* 1, i, pl. 1, nos. 2–13; *Catalogue of Greek coins in the British Museum, Pontus, Paphlagonia, Bithynia, Bosporus,* pl. viii, 2, 3; Bieber, *The Sculpture of the Hellenistic Age,* Figs. 310, 314–16, 321–26.

[17] [See Richter, *The Journal of Roman Studies,* xlv (1955), Plate vii, 26–29, for illustrations of this series.]

[18] [*Ibid.,* Plates viii, 33, 40; ix, 35; x, 37–39.]

[19] Roussel, Délos, *Colonie athénienne* (1916), 288, n. 4; Roussel and Launey, *Inscriptions de Délos* iv, 2 pp. 330 ff., nos. 2489 ff. The large number of Roman portraits erected in the East in pre-Imperial times can also be gauged by the list given by Raubitschek, *JRS* xliv, 1954, pp. 65 ff., of inscribed pedestals made for statues of Julius Caesar. They come from the mainland (Athens, Megara, Thespiae, and Demetrias), the Islands (Delos, Keos, Chios, Samos), and Asia Minor (Ephesus and Pergamon).

[20] Cf. on this subject the illuminating discussion by Vessberg, *Studien,* pp. 115 ff.

[21] This problem will doubtless be clarified by the results of the researches by B. V. Bothmer (see above, n. 3).

9. ROMAN ARCHITECTURE

William L. MacDonald

INTRODUCTION

During the course of the first and second centuries A.D. a new vaulted architecture, predominantly secular in function, developed in the Mediterranean world. In all parts of the Empire it became a testimony of the Roman presence. Unlike the architecture of the Greeks, this Roman style emphasized enclosure, the interior hollow, thus providing a principle from which later centuries would continue to draw precedent.

William L. MacDonald's first volume on Roman architecture, concentrating on four monuments, the Pantheon, the markets of Trajan, and the palaces of Nero and Domitian, is a detailed study of the major forms that define the Imperial architecture. The portions selected for this anthology discuss the materials and methods of construction as well as general characteristics of this new architecture of Imperial Rome.

Other works on Roman architecture are W.J. Anderson and R.P. Spiers, *The Architecture of Greece and Rome,* 2 Vols., rev. by Thomas Ashby (1927), and G.T. Rivoira, *Roman Architecture,* tr. by G. McN. Rushforth (1930). *Brickwork in Italy,* ed. G.C. Mars (1925), and N. Davy, *A History of Building Materials* (1961) are good sources for technical information. F.E. Brown, *Roman Architecture* (1961) is a brief, popular survey. Ward Perkins, *Roman Architecture* is forthcoming in the Pelican History of Art series.

Footnotes in the selections that follow cite, in abbreviated form, the following works:

AJA	*American Journal of Archaeology*
Atti	*Atti del . . . congresso* (sometimes *convegno*) *nazionale di storia dell' architettura.*
BC	*Bulletino della commissione archeologica communale di Roma.*

Blake *1*	M.E. Blake, *Ancient Roman Construction in Italy from the Prehistoric Period to Augustus* (1947).
Blake *2*	M.E. Blake, *Roman Construction in Italy from Tiberius through the Flavians* (1959).
BollCentro	*Bolletino del centro di studi per la storia dell' architettura.*
CIL	*Corpus Inscriptionum Latinarium.*
Durm	J. Durm, *Die Baukunst der Etrusker. Die Baukunst der Römer,* 2nd ed. (1905).
EncIt	*Enciclopedia Italiana.*
ESAR	*Economic Survey of Ancient Rome,* ed. T. Frank, 6 vols. (1933–40), reprinted in 1959.
Meiggs	R. Meiggs, *Roman Ostia* (1960).
Middleton	J.H. Middleton, *The Remains of Ancient Rome* (1892).
NS	*Notizie degli scavi di antichità*
Rostovtzeff	M.I. Rostovtzeff, *Social and Economic History of the Roman Empire,* 2nd ed., 2 Vols. (1957).

ECONOMY OF CONSTRUCTION

Architecture properly includes the art of building, and to omit it would be to suggest a division of knowledge and responsibility that Roman imperial architects would not have recognized. Labor, materials, and methods of building were efficiently organized in an economy of construction second only to principles of design in the formation of the new architecture. Roman attitudes toward making, assembling, and using materials produced the orderly rhythms of preparation and construction essential to success in large buildings of brick and concrete. The great architects had at their disposal ready trains of supply and assembly that reached from the distant clay pits and quarries to the tops of their towering scaffolds, where brick and aggregate, by reversing the processes of nature, were bound by mortar into rock-like structure. . . .

The labor force formed the base of this economy. Unskilled workmen were enrolled or impressed in gangs, and craftsmen and semiskilled workers were organized according to their specialties into corporations or guilds (neither term is very satisfactory; what had begun as mutual assistance associations and funeral colleges were increasingly regulated by the government as the *étatisation* of society deepened).[1] Statius, enthusiastically describing Domitian's new road across the Volturno marshes into Naples, gives a glimpse of Roman divisions of labor and orderly method.

> The first work was to prepare furrows and mark out the borders of the road, and to hollow out the ground with deep excavation; then to fill up the excavated trench with other material, and to make foundations ready for the road's arched bridge, lest the soil give way and a treacherous bed provide an unstable base for the heavily loaded stones; then to bind it with blocks, set close on either side, and with frequent wedges. How many gangs are at work together! Some cut down the forest and strip the mountain sides, some shape beams and boulders with iron tools; others [cement] the stones together . . . others work to dry up the pools and [dig canals] to lead the minor streams far away. These men could cut the Athos peninsula.[2]

. . . There was even a *collegium subrutorum* or guild of demolition experts.[3] During the period under discussion, labor of all kinds seems to have been plentiful in Rome.[4] The proportion of freemen to slaves is not known; we have no document such as the building contract for the north porch of the Erechtheum in Athens, which records that out of a hundred and seven men at work at least forty-two were metics (registered aliens) and twenty were slaves (all of the latter were masons or carpenters).[5] Whatever their status Roman laborers and craftsmen were bonded firmly in groups to which their individualities were largely submerged, just as the small units of materials they put into position were essential but standardized parts of a coherent structural whole. This shaping of manpower and knowledge into a system both orderly and flexible explains certain characteristics of the new architecture. The imperial architect could command a large and well-organized labor force, and with its help he gave monumentality to his ideas and permanence to his buildings.

MATERIALS

In all vaulted buildings of imperial date, with the exception of some provincial work in cut stone, materials were used in a consistent way. Small individual structural elements were combined with mortar to obtain, after the fabric had dried out and cured, structurally continuous and enduring solids. Piers, walls, and vaults were made of concrete, and brick facing was used on piers and non-foundation walls. Wood and stone were as important in erecting buildings as lime, sand, and brick, and a fair amount of metal was used, though not in structural members. These materials will be considered in an approximately ascending order of their significance.

The extensive use of metal in ancient architecture is sometimes overlooked. In addition to decorative elements such as bronze capitals, rosettes, and cornices metalworkers and foundrymen made doors, conduits, pipes, and a wide variety of fittings and hardware.[6] Metal roof tiles, of the kind used on the Basilica Ulpia and the Pantheon, were not uncommon. Within the structural fabric of ancient stone buildings massive iron clamps, often secured in lead, were frequently used.[7] The timbers of the roof of the Pantheon porch may have been encased in metal, and there were probably other instances of protecting wooden members with metal sheathing. For hanging ceilings of cement and tile, Vitruvius prescribes the use of large iron bars, hung from iron hooks in the beams above, to carry the suspended weight.[8] In the piers and walls of Roman vaulted buildings a great deal of iron and bronze was used, in the form of cramps and plugs, to insure a permanent bond between marble facing, setting beds of cement, and the brick-faced structure proper. . . .

The various colors of Roman bricks and decorative terra-cottas are important. By using different kinds of clay and by varying the length of firing, colors were deliberately produced for visual purposes. Contrasts of color were common. At Ostia, for example, external pilasters of dark red and capitals and moldings of yellow, all of terra-cotta, appear in Trajanic and Hadrianic tombs and buildings. At Isola Sacra, near Ostia, there are many examples of multicolored decorative terra-cotta inserts in external walls. If these details were meant to be stuccoed over, it is difficult to understand why pieces of various colors were produced and then carefully assembled in architectural and decorative patterns. It is apparent that at least some terra-cotta exterior surfaces were meant to be seen.

In and near Rome, and in those parts of the provinces where suitable materials were available, terra-cotta manufacture became an industry. Huge quantities were made by coordinating the several production processes, a high degree of standardization was achieved, and stocks were laid up in excess and in ignorance of requirements. The standard tile and brick sizes and the fixed shapes and sizes of terra-cotta fittings and parts facilitated planning and helped architects and builders to increase the efficiency of construction. Layout and dimensioning were simplified. The extensive interchangeability of terra-cotta parts, so obvious today, was a radical innovation. They were fully utilized in the economy of building, to the extent that each brick was put to more than one use during construction.

Metal, wood, stone, and terra-cotta were all used, temporarily or permanently, in connection with mortar. The word is used here to indicate all materials of mixed composition that were in a semi-fluid state at the time of actual use in construction: the mortar for brickwork, the mix in which aggregates were placed to make concrete, and the various types of aggregate-free cements such as *opus signinum,* a mortar containing both crushed brick and pozzolana that was used to line structures carrying or containing water and to protect the exteriors of vaults.[9] Plasters and stuccoes, being non-structural, belong in another category. They were used chiefly for facings, interior moldings, and decorative reliefs.

In Roman times mortar was already of great antiquity. Greek mortars were famous for their strength and quality. Before developing concrete the Romans had used mortars for many purposes, for example to level courses of stones not cut and finished precisely.[10] By the second century B.C. the properties of mortar were quite fully understood and the development of true concrete construction was well underway. When in the next century kiln-fired brick began to replace unfired brick, and pozzolana came into regular use, mortar became an essential material. The lengthy modern discussions of the various types of Roman wall facings are somewhat misleading, for mortar is the most important structural material in Roman non-trabeated architecture. Facings changed, and the changes give some indication of date, but the facings are not the walls themselves.

Vitruvius says that in making mortar, sea sand should be avoided. Good sands, he adds, crackle when rubbed and do not stain white cloth.[11] Lime, after burning, should be set aside to age.[12] By his day the Romans had mastered the use of pozzolana, which they added to the dry mix in lieu of part of the sand. Pozzolana is a friable volcanic material, found in thick beds of chunks and gravel-sized pieces in Latium and Campania and easily reduced to usable form.[13] It often has a distinct reddish or yellowish hue and has the property of forming hydraulic silicates in combination with lime, quartz sand, and water. The importance of pozzolana can be exaggerated, for some large Roman concrete buildings were built without it, but mortar made with it will set readily underwater, an advantage Roman engineers made good use of. The architects and builders of the high empire must have been convinced that pozzolana improved their concrete, for it was used in all the buildings described above and is rarely absent from high imperial construction in Rome and its environs.

Making mortars and using them in the building processes was in effect a process of dehydration—the burning of lime—and subsequent hydration. Because water could be added to the granular substances at the convenience of the builders, the construction of walls and vaults was much facilitated. The amorphous, dry ingredients could be easily measured and divided into manageable quantities. No highly skilled labor was required. The amounts of mortar needed for use during a given period of time could be readily calculated, and the consecutive steps of preparation and use suited Roman habits of orderly procedure. Mortar gave the architect the basis for structural materials that could be cast in a variety of architectural shapes, and its importance lies in its inherent potential of form. Doubtless there was a long period of trial and experiment. By the early first century the basic problems had been mastered and sound knowledge accumulated empirically. The ruin of part of old Rome in the summer of 64 provided the first city-wide opportunity for the use of mortar, which for nearly three centuries thereafter was the essential substance of vaulted architecture in the capital.

The ultimate synthetic product of Roman experiments with mortars, aggregates, and structural problems was the durable concrete of imperial times. . . . Basically it was a material for casting on a monumental scale. When correctly made and poured it could provide structurally continuous solids from foundations up to the crowns of vaults. The necessity of repeating bearing surfaces was much reduced. Ideally speaking, seamless and jointless structures were made possible. Architects and builders were largely freed from the necessity of thinking and planning in terms of beams and isolated bearing points, and could concentrate upon less fragmented structural and visual forms. Inevitably this led to an architecture more modeled than assembled, and it helps to explain the proliferation of curves in both plans and sections from the middle of the first century onward.

In the economy of vaulted design, shapeless raw materials were transposed into building solids by inverting natural processes.[14] Sand, lime, and pozzolana were made into rock, and clay was baked almost as hard as stone. But the small scale of the individual bricks, and the timing of bringing together the ingredients of mortar, meant that the new materials were pliant and flexible. They were the chief structural resources the great architects of the period had in mind when designing, the equivalent of stone for the Greek masters and steel and reinforced concrete for architects today.

In the use of materials two essential features stand out. One is organization, the result of applying administrative talent to problems of reliable procurement and methodical sequences of construction. Order and system were brought into complex situations involving the mutual adjustment of many variables and the fairly efficient deployment of thousands of men. The Romans learned much about such things from their predecessors, but the mastery of the economy of vaulted construction was peculiarly their own. From this point of view the method of erecting the Palace of Domitian or the Pantheon was as characteristic of Roman civilization as the law or the army. The second and more significant point concerns the inherent connection between the nature of the materials and the space-geometry of the buildings. Roman builders did not subtract from materials to obtain form, as a stonecutter does when he fashions a squared block or a cornice, but added materials together, binding them freely with mortar and building up steadily around and over a space to give it definition. It was in this sense that bricks and concrete were flexible, occupying and forming with ready adaptability the volumetric boundaries conceived by the architect.

METHODS

The building process was largely derived from the nature of the materials, which, because the fabric had to dry out and cure, were unfinished at the moment of use. In order to obtain secure and stable buildings, construction had to proceed according to rhythms of work determined by the setting time of the mortar. The speed with which a portion of newly made structure reached sufficient bearing strength was the key factor both in planning construction and in actual building. Brick-faced walls and piers were built, without shuttering, a horizontal layer at a time, and as soon as a layer could bear enough weight the process was repeated and the building rose another few feet. For both stability and efficiency, timing was all.

In order to obtain better siting or footings the Romans were willing to alter natural contours extensively. Valleys were filled and hills were cut back. By Flavian times it was normal practice to place important buildings on level vaulted terraces or deep concrete mats.[15] Long experience with roads, aqueducts, bridges, ports, and other massive utilitarian works provided a sound knowledge of sinking foundations for stable arcuate and vaulted construction. Foundations tended to be deep and extremely substantial. The Esquiline Wing of the Domus Aurea stands upon a vast, thick sheet of concrete, poured in part at least over preexisting houses. This increased the elevation of the building on the hillside and gave it a substantial base. Rabirius, to obtain his two desired floor levels, filled depressions, cut the Palatine rock back where necessary, and extended his upper platform to the desired limits on lofty vaulted substructures. Again, earlier buildings were filled in or their structure utilized.[16] The vertical staging of Trajan's Markets is composed of vaulted terraces that rise as much as four stories above the slope of the Quirinal. The Pantheon rotunda and drum stand upon a massive ring of concrete. Because of these precautions, evidence of settlement in these buildings is rare. They were quite well prepared to meet the threat of outside forces such as earthquake, subsidence, or extraordinary wind pressure.

The care taken in monumental building to obtain firm footings and to distribute loads fairly evenly is also evident in the supports for bearing walls. The normal practice was to excavate to a depth of two or more meters—foundation walls five and six meters deep are not unknown—and then pour the concrete wall between wooden shutterings. Many of these walls can be examined today. Some have been exposed to the weather for many years, but the negative forms of the shuttering posts (usually placed on the wall side) and of the boards as well are sometimes so clear that the grain of the rough-sawn wood can still be read.

Foundation walls were rarely faced. Once the concrete had cured sufficiently the shuttering was removed and the brick-faced wall was begun above ground level. It is not likely that shuttering, properly shored, was much used to help support faced walls, although a contrary opinion has been held.[17] The use of shuttering against brick-facing would have been difficult. First, the brick wall would have to be built up to a sufficient height to take advantage of vertical timbers long enough to give support to a considerable number of horizontal shutters. Short vertical timbers, supporting only a few boards, would not have kept the wall true. If high shuttering were put up first, the bricks would have had to be laid from the inside, a very unlikely procedure even for thick walls. Since the brick-facing is always very shallow, a mere skin a brick or half-brick deep on the surface of the concrete, it would have become increasingly unstable as it rose without its intended concrete core, and extremely difficult to keep true even if erected from inside up against the shuttering boards. Finally, the risk would be run of having the lower courses of mason's mortar stiffen too much before the concrete was

139

poured in, preventing the two mortars, which were applied separately, from setting together properly.

The only woodwork that seems to have been required for building brick-faced walls was the scaffolding for the masons and the ladder and ramp systems needed for bringing up bricks, mortar, and aggregate. Since the brick-facings did not function structurally once the mortar had hardened, and since shuttering was impractical, speed of erection and accuracy of construction were functions of the stiffening and drying rate of mortar. The unrestored portions of the walls of such buildings as the Markets and the Pantheon, being absolutely uniform, give no indication of the levels at which construction may have been temporarily halted for drying, for the assembly of new scaffolding, or for the end of the working day. If the mixing of mortar and its delivery to the masons, and to the mouth of the wall, were timed so that it would start to stiffen shortly after it was put in place, then perhaps both of the brick skins and the concrete core could all go up more or less together. The operation could then continue for some distance before it was necessary to halt and allow the wall to gain enough strength to carry an additional load safely and without risking distortion.

The vertical distance between halts that might be accomplished under these circumstances cannot be calculated because the most important variables are unknown. It is likely that the mortars stiffened rapidly. The rows of putlog holes for the horizontal members of the scaffolding indicate that about twenty to twenty-five rows of bricks were laid from a given level. The so-called bonding courses, discussed below, may possibly mark the end of a day's work. What is more important is that true and stable walls and piers could be built accurately by this leap-frog method. Concrete was poured between low, thin retaining walls of brick, and as soon as it set sufficiently to bear the load of the next layer, the process was repeated. Nice adjustments in timing and the supply of materials were required if the labor force was to be used with efficiency. The best masons and practical builders alone could not make the system work, for the details as well as the broad outlines of the planning had to be completed in advance. In practice this probably meant that everyone knew their job from long experience. Even so the Roman genius for order and system lay behind all the day-to-day work.

The facing bricks, from Nero's time onward, were usually sawn or broken into triangles before they were used.[18] Laying and jointing, especially in the principal Trajanic and Hadrianic monuments, can only be characterized as nearly perfect. Yet much of this meticulous work was not intended to be seen. Presumably it cannot have been done to protect the concrete, for foundation walls were usually left unfaced and many of them, little damaged by nature, still support their original loads. Also, inside walls as well as peripheral walls were faced. The facing did not provide a sufficiently rough surface for stucco or cement to adhere to satisfactorily, and the hardness of the bricks and the pozzolana mortar made it difficult to attach anything to the wall at all. Yet the bricks were necessary. They formed temporary, low formwork while the wall was going up in stages. At the lower levels this could have been done more easily and economically with shuttering properly shored. But the higher the wall went the more difficult this would have become and, above a certain height, it would have been all but impossible. Walls fifteen and twenty meters high were built, and for these heights no shoring or other form of counterpressure could have been readily provided. Also, the triangular bricks exposed rough and somewhat porous surfaces for marriage with the mortar of the interior concrete core, for by laying the bricks in simple bond a pocketed interior wall of irregular points was produced. In this sense bricks were used simply as another form of aggregate. Since they were evenly dressed on the outside, the task of keeping the wall in alignment was facilitated.

Early Roman experiments with concrete evolved from the use of relatively uncompacted rubble fills placed between ashlar or other types of stone walls. Facing materials grew thinner and progressively less structural, and cores became increasingly able to bear heavier loads. This evolution intersected the discovery of pozzolana mortars and, later, the quantity production of high-quality kiln-fired brick; the builders of the imperial age made the most out of combining tradition and invention. The multiplicity of functions assigned to brick-facing, which in some cases included a purely aesthetic and visual role, is typical of the economy of vaulted design. The reciprocities established among materials and their functions both during and after actual construction were ingenious. Orderly procedures are necessary to all successful monumental construction, but the Romans mass-produced building materials and investigated their efficient and appropriate uses to a greater degree than any pre-industrial people. The ancient Latin principle of order, the instinctive habit of trying to put men and things in their proper places of service, lay behind this. . . .

Once the formwork of a vault was in position the actual construction was relatively simple. Mortar and aggregate were raised to the pouring level and put into position.[19] Usually the extrados was given a coat of waterproof pozzolana cement, though terra-cotta tiles were sometimes laid directly upon the concrete, and the huge Pantheon vault was finished with a thin covering of brick. If an oculus was required a stout wheel-form was built. This was positioned horizontally at the open crown of the vault, and rings of bricks, set vertically, were laid around its circumference. The last pours of concrete then brought the fabric of the vault up to this brickwork, and construction was complete. After a period of drying and curing the formwork could be dismantled and the structure given over to the decorators and marbleworkers.

STRUCTURAL FEATURES

Roman engineering was empirical, based upon deductions made from observation and experience. Not all of these deductions can be reached today by studying the buildings, and important data for the analysis of vaulted-style structure and statics are missing. The drying times and curing rates of the mortars, crucial factors in obtaining stability and in the economy of construction as well, are unknown. The true physical composition and precise structural nature of the concrete itself is uncertain.[20] Yet the basic structural principle is clear: stability depended not upon pressure or friction, as in unmortared arches or vaults of cut stone, but upon something very different, the cohesion and homogeneity of the cured concrete mass.[21]

This principle and its application explain many features of vaulted-style construction.[22] The concrete cores, invisible once the buildings were finished, were in theory continuous bearing solids. Vaults were cast by pouring down upon wooden forms in order to fill up the volumes and obtain the surfaces the forms described, and this was done without any thought of voussoirs or other discrete internal divisions of structure. These vaults were physically continuous with their piers and walls, for there were no intervening bearing surfaces. But in practice the problems raised by giving shape and support to the initially formless concrete led to methods of construction that made the finished fabric structurally less simple than theory indicated. In addition, the procedures followed by the builders often caused the ideal continuity of the fabric, inherent in the basic principle, to be interrupted. By using brick to give shape to the concrete walls and piers until they hardened to bearing strength, certain secondary structural problems were introduced. At the beginning these bricks functioned as shuttering, but as the mortar cured they became an inseparable part of the structure, preserving the concrete core within a thin, weatherproof crust to which new outer finishes could be applied when needed. . . .

Although concrete did most of the work, bricks were essential both to construction and structure proper, and in thin walls the facings are probably as important structurally as the concrete. In monumental buildings the facings were falsework, weatherproofing, and structure all in one, and their various infixed devices were developed to solve the problems inherent in constructing permanent formwork, inseparably bonded to the main structure, at great scale. . . .

In a sense a structure grew out of itself because of the relationships among facings, cores, and compression devices (paradoxically, the bulkiness of vaulted designs was the result of a rather clever and economical way of building). The system helped in answering quite readily and efficiently the need for great quantities of construction. The way buildings were put up assisted in making the act of architecture a social one, no inconsiderable achievement and until then unknown in the ancient world. The Romans were able to build functional, permanent structures of many types by means of one architectural technology. Partly because of this, great buildings for public use became commonplace, and architecture of some consequence was brought into daily life and to ordinary towns far more than in the past. In this the economy of construction was an essential force. Its simplicity and method, synchronized to the needs and purposes of an age of cities, facilitated planning and realizing public building programs. Because of these things, and because of what the buildings inspired in later generations, the economy of imperial construction is a significant part of the history of architecture.

Behind it lay the attitudes and talents of the new architects. The predetermined order and timing of events meant that they had to direct large groups of men and insure that they did their work without appreciable error. Each of these workmen, like each brick in the walls they made, performed as a soldier under orders. The economy of the new architecture derived maximum efficiency and utility from each element in relation to its neighbors, an expression of an inherent Latin trait. The unknown military tribune, who at the battle of Cynoscephalae in 197 B.C. "judged on the spur of the moment what ought to be done" and detached twenty maniples with which he broke the phalanx of Philip V, expressed the same trait.[23] He had the training to give him judgment, and the materials of his contribution to Flaminius' victory were prepared to respond in an orderly way to his decision. Under difficult conditions he was able to move two thousand infantry quickly, efficiently, and successfully. So it was also with imperial architects, their materials and men.

THE NEW ARCHITECTURE

What the palaces, the Markets, and the Pantheon show above all else is the maturity of the concept of monumental interior space. The strength and dynamism of imperial civilization were so great that the need for a suitable architecture could not be denied. The Romans, always building, quite naturally sought for forms that would express this ecumenical experience. Vaults were not in any way new when Severus, Rabirius, and their contemporaries gave architecture a fresh beginning with their great buildings. Yet they fashioned the new style with vaulted spaces, and in the last analysis it is the meaning and effects of these spaces that more than anything else give the style its identification and individuality. In Timgad as in Tralles, at Baia as at Bosra, the Roman stewardship of all antiquity and the imperial hope for one inclusive society—coerced or free—were proclaimed by an architecture of splendid interior spaces.

Rome itself was the nexus where many strains of design and technology were gathered together. There, seen in the light of imperial social and political aims, these strains were adapted and reworked as the new style evolved. The forms and effects of this architecture served the capital and the provinces alike until during the fourth and fifth centuries they were gradually translated into the artistic languages of the early middle ages. In this way Roman concepts of interior space lived on in both East and West. The palaces, Markets, and Pantheon alone cannot carry the whole burden of this complicated story, but they record accurately its first and in many ways most creative chapter and vividly mark the stylistic and emotional distance between the new architecture and that of the past. The inherent value of these buildings as examples is magnified by the long life, after the dissolution of imperial authority in the West, of their architectural principles and the associations evoked by their forms.

CHARACTERISTICS OF DESIGN

The transcendent characteristic of the new architecture was its space-shaping, space-bordering quality. Whatever the decor, however integrated the trabeation, this quality predominated. Its omnipresent, generative force was the circular curve, occasionally modulated to polygonal shape, upon which progressive architects based their volumetric and spatial creations and with which they resolved and fixed their axes and vistas. The curve gave them the radial focus that more than anything else established the viewer's relationship to their designs. Not only the major vaulted spaces, but their entrances, openings, niches, and decor were evolved from a preoccupation—almost an obsession—with the embracing and focusing qualities of circular lines and surfaces. The indispensable curve gave Roman vaulted architecture its overwhelming sense of place, and its use in three dimensions as the boundary of architectural space is the quintessential feature of the style. Although the formal structure of the style was geometric, a number of shapes were used together in every building. Even the Pantheon, the most unitary of Roman monumental designs, is composed of triangles, a prismatic block, a cylinder, a hemisphere, and apsidal recesses. The imperial architect, unlike a designer such as Ledoux, was not attracted by basic, unadorned geometric shapes standing alone as buildings. Shapes in combination interested him, shapes arranged significantly and harmonically as to scale and meaning, and articulated by an elaborate but consistent system of decoration and well thought-out lighting.

145

Although in this way Roman design "became absolutely emanci-pated from precedent, and was pursued as research into the possi-bilities of form and combination,"[24] the ancient principle of sym-metry was not abandoned. Few vaulted-style buildings erected before Hadrian's death in 138 depart to any considerable extent from a basic, underlying frame of mirror or bilateral symmetry. The geometric interior volumes were themselves symmetrical, and were combined symmetrically in plan. Eccentricity of plan and therefore of elevation was extremely rare. Dominant axes and balanced silhouettes, and the almost complete lack of any noncircular curves, explain as much as the solidity of their construction the impression of strength and permanence these buildings give. The stability implied by simple geometric forms was exploited to the full, both through the persistent revelation of their inherent symmetry and by combining them, as for example when a semidomed apse was placed at the end of a barrel-vaulted room. This hyper-symmetry, this unwillingness ever to admit any ambiguity of axis, was so positive a force that even the external axes leading to the entrances of monumental buildings were defined by courtyards or other axially parallel features. By such means even open spaces could be given a certain feeling of interiorness. Unlike the projected axes of Greek monumental architecture, which frequently passed unhindered out across the natural landscape, the center lines of Roman buildings tended to be stopped and fixed by architectural solids nearby—an apse, a nymphaeum, even a gate would do (in a space of centralized plan, another major axis was self-contained within the building itself). Embracing, curved shapes were used to catch and cup the central lines of architectural force as the basin of a fountain catches its jet of water. Against a vertical half-cylinder capped by a shell-form or semidome the movement of an axis was both marked and resolved. The parallel side walls or other bordering features of a central axis, whether of a single space or a large composition of many elements, were almost always exactly alike. As in the atrium house the path along a controlling axis might be interrupted, but this rarely diluted its visual and directive power. The devia-tions introduced were only temporary, for no real choice of routes was offered and the compelling symmetry of the design was unaffected. . . .

An environment of controlling forms preempted attention and rigorously limited freedom of movement, characteristics inherited from the past. For centuries the open sacred precinct, with its altar and its looming cult building beyond, had given form and direction to the most fundamental rituals of Roman life. The early imperial fora, with their elevated marble temples dominating elongated enclosures, expressed the same. principles in more sophisticated fashion. In the vaulted style the evolution of this traditional directionalism and focus was brought to its logical conclusion. One was now either guided toward a focal concavity or brought into an axially terminal space, a large and well-lighted architectural volume from which the natural world was excluded, where enveloping and radially focused surfaces suggested permanence, stability, and security.

IMPERIAL CIVILIZATION AND ARCHITECTURE

. . . The vaulted style was infused with the same hortatory quality found in official statuary and reliefs, upon coins, and in the panegyrical literature. This insistent rhetoric of Roman state art reflects the sharp paternalism upon which the coherence and preservation of society was thought to depend. In the buildings this quality is evident in the way the senses were instructed by axis, symmetry, and the properties of concavity. These characteristics of design and sensory instruction also reflected the balance and order, the almost choreographic clarity, of Roman ritual and liturgy. In these ways the vaulted style was a mimesis of the state, a metaphor in tangible form upon its traditions and its claims to all-embracing sovereignty. Naturally it arose in Rome, the center of these traditions and claims, where after Nero's time it was used to create an *urbs pro maiestate imperii ornata*.[25]

All of the great vaulted buildings were charged with the property of expressing unity. Encouragement to individualism was missing because choice was missing. Vaulted architecture was no more permissive than the state itself. Axis, symmetry, and the terminal feature or volume kept everyone *en face* in fact or in mind with the focal, symbolic shape; there were no true alternatives. Roman architecture might be defined as a body of law in masonry, governing human responses by didactic forms whose expressive force was intended to be recognized or apprehended immediately by the sensory faculties. Grace and elegance were sacrificed to this drive to persuade one and all to conform, and this could explain the preoccupation with the primary geometric shapes so readily yielded by the economy of imperial construction. The age of truly personal expression in architecture lay in the future, for the architecture of Rome, like that of Egypt and Greece, spoke of a particular way of life and the institutions it fostered rather than of the independent opportunity and taste of any single individual.

The nature of imperial society was also expressed in the very orderly way in which diverse human and natural resources were directed toward the end in view. The success of the solution to these essentially logistical problems is evident in the ability of the Romans, during the first and second centuries, to erect large numbers of buildings simultaneously without straining either their knowledge or their economy of construction. Their capacity to move almost as one man toward a desired goal was exploited in an atmosphere of bureaucratic expansion and increasing state regulation, but this made possible that supple manipulation and control of each unit of action and substance that insured the continuity of the necessary rhythms of construction. Bricks and aggregate were deployed through the buildings like maniples and centuries of infantry in the sense that each anonymous unit obeyed the commands of the architect and was dependent upon the proper functioning of exactly similar units assembled in a strictly disciplined order. The hundred foremen, each directing a gang of a hundred men, who are said to have supervised the construction of Hagia Sophia, were the inheritors in Justinian's age of Roman working methods.[26]

The government influenced the new architecture in other practical ways. It largely controlled finances, could focus talent and labor upon architectural objectives if and when it chose, and concerned itself with building codes and schedules of maintenance. Apparently a fair proportion of architects and builders were trained during military service, and many were kept on the government rolls either in the army or in the civil service to be posted to various locations around the Empire as the need arose. The guilds, at first only supervised by the government, were gradually absorbed into its ever expanding, infinitely graded hierarchy. The government was in a position to orchestrate the architectural resources of the whole realm. Sparse as the written evidence is, it suggests that this was done for architecture as for law, the administration, and the army.

That the emperors and their governments used the vaulted style as an instrument of propaganda can hardly be doubted. All official architecture was used in this way. The proliferation in the provinces of large baths based upon first- and early second-century designs in Rome is the most obvious case, but many other vaulted building types were used in the provinces, such as markets, warehouses, amphitheaters, and municipal nymphaea. Districts and towns in Italy were embellished with an apparent generosity that the emperors surely regarded as a sound investment in the future of the state. Though the financial resources of the Empire were primitively managed there was always money for building after the armies and the supply of Rome had been provided for. The doors of the treasuries were open to provincial governments as well. Astute provincial officials and citizens knew how to take advantage of the government's predisposition to build.[27] The pax romana kept communications open, allowing the style to spread and change as it was conditioned, in both Rome and the provinces, by non-Latin concepts.

What happened in Rome and many imperial cities during the years 54 to 138 is very much like what is happening in industrial countries today. Even making necessary allowances for the profound technological changes of the last two centuries, the Roman experience of architecture and building in the High Empire was more like our own than that of any other age. Both periods are marked by a drive to surpass the old led by men who want the new. Both are concerned with the visual as well as the social condition of the municipality. Today, when imitation Georgian and nondescript buildings are razed by the block and replaced by innumerable variations on the rectilinear silhouette, something of what happened in Rome, Ostia, Leptis Magna, Pergamon, or a hundred other cities of the Empire is taking place. Even the smallest town was given some architectural token to represent the imperial peace. In general the Romans built more slowly and more permanently than we, but they had the same compulsion to make their cities conform, in their public buildings at least, to the modern age. And the modern age was the new imperial order, which uprooted hundreds, sometimes thousands, of families to make way for new housing and municipal buildings.

Unlike the Egyptians and the Greeks, the Romans of the Empire built most of their major buildings for the social commonwealth. The importance of the temple, from the architectural point of view, was challenged by the attention given to secular buildings. Since imperial society and the state were shaped in the same image, the new vaulted architecture was essentially social in nature. The concept that Roman architecture is basically utilitarian, so popular for so long, is correct with respect to its emphasis upon social utility. What the Romans wanted were places where they might either act upon or debate and consider the very real and never entirely solved problems that arise among men. Roman architecture is the tangible shape of an innermost Roman trait—the desire for the adjustment of one thing with another. For the Romans this adjustment had to take place in a prescribed place ordered in such a way as to facilitate the means adopted. Because the Romans persisted in interpreting this need, the skyline and visual register of central Rome changed ceaselessly for more than two hundred years and the ancient cities of earlier societies, in many cases already extremely rich architecturally, were rebuilt or enlarged with Roman designs. In less ancient lands miniature Romes sprang up. London and Dougga, Ostia and Dura, whatever their rank in the multinational fabric of Roman imperial civilization, all make this clear: neither earlier styles nor traditional forms could alone express and house what Rome hoped to accomplish.

Western Europe and the lands around the Mediterranean still brim with architectural documents of these intentions. The principles of this architecture, for centuries an effective instrument of Roman culture, were not lost when the political framework of ancient society collapsed. They survived the transition to the early middle ages, and together with Roman literature and law have continued ever since to give inspiration and instruction. And Roman architecture has never ceased to be relevant to the study of the nature and meaning of architectural form, for it was an expressive and powerful art, defining a critically important experience of Mediterranean and Western man.

Roman Architecture

NOTES

[1] Rostovtzeff, *1*, 379–92, 462; Meiggs, p. 319; cf. *ESAR*, *5*, 246–52. The fundamental work on the guilds is J. P. Waltzing, *Étude historique sur les corporations professionnelles chez les Romains*, 4 Vols. (Louvain, 1895–1900).

[2] *Silvae* 4.3.40–58.

[3] The *collegium subrutorum* appears in *CIL* 6.940. Cf. Meiggs, pp. 311–36, esp. p. 319.

[4] *ESAR*, *5*, 234–36.

[5] R. H. Randall, Jr., "The Erectheum Workmen," *AJA*, *57* (1953), 199–210.

[6] See for example Durm, pp. 344–352; *Oxford History of Technology*, *2* (1956), 236, 419; F. Kretzschmer, *Bilddokumente römischer Technik* (Düsseldorf, 1958), pp. 53–58; R. Calza and E. Nash, *Ostia* (Florence, 1959), Fig. 80.

[7] Vitruvius 2.8.4; cf. 1.5.3. See also Middleton, *1*, 40; W. B. Dinsmoor, *The Architecture of Ancient Greece* (London, 1950), pp. 104–05, 174; Blake, 2, 90, 92, 93.

[8] 5.10.3; cf. Middleton 2, 119–20.

[9] Roman mortars are discussed in detail by Blake, *1*, Chap. 9.

[10] Blake, *1*, 145.

[11] 2.4.1. For Roman screening of sand, see N. Davey, *A History of Building Materials* (London, 1961), p. 127.

[12] 7.2.2. The flare kiln used for burning limestone today is almost exactly like the kiln described by Cato, *On Agriculture* 38.

[13] Vitruvius, 2.6; Strabo, 5.4; A. Maffei, *Enclt* s.v. "Pozzolana"; L. Crema, "La volta nell' architettura romana," *L'Ingegnere*, *16* (1942), 941; Blake, *1*, 42–43.

[14] Vitruvius is at some pains to explain the properties of lime and pozzolana in 2.5.2 and 2.6; for the place of such subjects in his scheme of architecture, see F. E. Brown, "Vitruvius and the Liberal Art of Architecture," *Bucknell Review*, *11.4* (1963), 105.

[15] G. Lugli, "Nuove forme dall' architettura romana nell' età dei Flavi," *Atti*, *3*, 95–102, discusses this among other innovations of Flavian times.

[16] Lugli, *Roma*, pp. 493–508; A. Bartoli, "Scavi del Palatino (Domus Augustana)," *NS* (1929), 26. Very recently an immense concrete foundation of imperial date, 11 m. high, has been found; it is saw-toothed in plan (cf. Vitruvius, 6.8.7).

[17] Middleton, *1*, 57–58; cf. Blake, *1*, 294.

[18] Blake, 2, 162–63, gives a good summary of this development; cf. Lugli, *Tecnica*, *1*, 584.

[19] These materials were carried up in baskets. The wheelbarrow, which was in use in China in the third century, did not appear in the West until many centuries later; J. Needham, *Science and Civilization in China* (Cambridge, 1954), *1*, 118; *Oxford History of Technology*, *2* (1956), 642. For cranes, etc., see Vitruvius, 10.2; Kretzschmer (above, n. 6), pp. 23–26; J. Rougé, "Ad ciconias nixas," *Revue des études anciennes*, *59* (1957), 320–328 (a study of *CIL* 6.1785, concluding that the inscription refers to a guild of crane operators; I owe this reference to the courtesy of Professor Lionel Casson); A. G. Drachmann, *The Mechanical Technology of Greek and Roman Antiquity* (Copenhagen, 1963), pp. 142–48, 199. For

the huge construction crane, operated by a treadmill, that appears on a relief from the tomb of the Haterii, see A. F. Burstall, *A History of Mechanical Engineering* (London, 1963), p. 88; cf. F. Castagnoli, "Gli edifici rappresentati in un relievo del sepolcro degli Haterii," *BC*, 69 (1941), 59–69.

[20] For the technical literature, see above, n. 13. On the drying rate of mortars see Vitruvius, 2.4.2; Frontinus, *Aqueducts* 123; Ward Perkins, *The Great Palace of the Byzantine Emperors, Second Report*, ed. D. T. Rice (Edinburgh, 1958), p. 79; cf. *AJA*, 65 (1961), 328; Blake, *1*, 316, 352; Fitchen, *Construction of Gothic Cathedrals* (Oxford, 1961), pp. 262–265. I have never seen anything resembling an expansion joint, even in the largest structures. There is no evidence as to whether the concrete was ever compacted after being tipped into the brick or wood forms, but cf. Vitruvius, 7.1.3. The question of the monolithic character of Roman imperial concrete is much debated. In general it appears that small thick vaults can properly be spoken of as monoliths, but large and relatively thin vaults probably cannot; see Ward Perkins, p. 80; cf. Fitchen, pp. 64–65 and citations.

[21] In the strictest terms these buildings are not entirely in compression, for there is a certain amount of beam and tie action within them.

[22] Among them the "hanging" quality of certain vaults which have partly fallen, for example in the Large Baths of Hadrian's Villa (S. Aurigemma, *Villa Adriana* [Rome, 1961], pp. 90–95), and the large flat slabs of concrete flooring that just may have been used to span small distances but which are more probably the layered pieces of floors of upper stories which have separated from the vault concrete. These slabs can be seen for example at Hadrian's Villa in the three-apsed hall by the Poikele, and in the lower level of the Domus Augustana; cf. Vitruvius, 7.1.3. See also Middleton, *1*, 64, 70–72, *2*, 121, 245.

[23] Polybius, 18.26.1–5.

[24] W. R. Lethaby, *Architecture, an Introduction to the History and Theory of the Art of Building*, 3rd ed. (Oxford, 1955), p. 94, Cf. G. Lugli, "Nuove forme dall' architettura romana nell' età dei Flavi." *Atti*, *3*, 101–02 . . . L. Crema, *Significato della architettura romana* . . . (Rome, 1959; = *BollCentro*, 15), pp. 14–22.

[25] The phrase is from Suetonius, *Augustus* 28.3.

[26] A. Banduri, *Imperium orientale, sive antiquitates Constantinopolitanae*, in the *Corpus Byzantinae Historiae*, 25.1 (Paris, 1711), 69.

[27] See R. MacMullen, "Roman Imperial Building in the Provinces," *Harvard Studies in Classical Philology*, 54 (1959), 209–210.

10. THE GENESIS OF
CHRISTIAN ART

Charles Rufus Morey

INTRODUCTION

For many years the little book, *Christian Art*, by Charles Rufus Morey has been a model *sui generis* as an introduction to the history of art in the service of Christianity. Developed from a series of essays that appeared in *Liturgical Arts*, it distills into some sixty-two evocative pages the course of Christian art from its earliest forms to the seventeenth century. To be sure, there are many tensions impacted by such drastic compression, but every page is a delight to read.

The content of the selection chosen for this anthology is examined in detail in Morey's later work, *Early Christian Art*, 2nd ed. (1953). Another excellent survey is Ernst Kitzinger, *Early Medieval Art* (1940), originally published as a guide to objects in the British Museum, and now available (with some revisions) in a paperbound edition (1964, 1966). Only slightly longer than Morey's little book, Kitzinger's survey ends with the Romanesque art of the twelfth century. Two reviews of the first edition of Morey's *Early Christian Art* are useful supplements: those in *The Art Bulletin*, XXV, 1 (1943) and in the *American Journal of Archaeology*, XLVII, 1 (1943). Other readings are Richard Krautheimer, *Early Christian and Byzantine Architecture* (1965), especially Parts I–III; Earl Baldwin Smith, *Architectural Symbolism of Imperial Rome and the Middle Ages* (1956); and Wolfgang Volbach and Max Hirmer (photographer), *Early Christian Art* (1962). Walter Lowrie, *Art in the Early Church* (1947) is useful for iconography, and Josef Strzygowski, *Origins of Christian Church Art* (1923) emphasizes the contributions of the East.

The selection that follows is reprinted from C. R. Morey, *Christian Art* (London, 1935), pp. 5–19, used by permission of David McKay Company, Inc.

Christianity has been so long a permanent factor of experience that it is difficult to imagine the time when it was not. Yet such a time there was; and once craftsmen essayed to paint, or carve, or build for the first time something that was to be Christian, with nothing to show them how it should look.

But around them lay the panorama of Hellenistic art, the cumulative result of the expansion, dilution, and adaptation of Greek architecture, sculpture, and painting. The earliest Christian craftsmen possessed, or were possessed by, habits of design and visualization rooted six centuries deep. Small wonder that the first works designed for Christian purposes have nothing Christian in their form or decoration.

The early Christian congregations met, like any new society, wherever meeting was possible: in the larger dwellings of the members of the community, or in a "hall" secured for the purpose. Later on, as church-building acquired self-consciousness and integration, we find survivals of these early expedients; the *atrium* of the house became the *paradisus*, the *parvis*, of the medieval cathedral; from the "hall," which in the Graeco-Roman language of the beginning of our era bore the name "basilica," came the name for the earliest and most important churches, and the inner disposition of nave and aisles.

The earliest of the Christian tombs that have survived to us—the subterranean chambers of the catacombs of Rome—are decorated with the same kind of impressionistic vignette that one finds frescoed on the humbler walls of Pompeii, with subjects sometimes of naïvely pagan content. About 100 A.D. the Christian subjects commence: a Good Shepherd, adapted from Graeco-Roman renderings of Hermes or Aristaeus; an orant woman, belonging to the class of Hellenistic personifications and doubtless standing for the departed soul; and finally the first unmistakably Christian type—Daniel standing between his lions. The preponderance in catacomb frescoes of the second and third centuries of Old Testament figures and scenes over those of the New is very marked, but not at all surprising.

155

The Old Testament had been translated into Alexandrian Greek long before the Christian era; its themes were known and its stories told in the Jewish colonies of every city of the Roman world. The New Testament was scarcely written when Christian art began; the figure of the Founder, clear in moral significance, was still obscure as a physical image; His deeds were still too variously recounted, and His sufferings too sacred, to become as yet themes for graphic representation. The idea that dominates the art of the catacombs, viz., deliverance from sin and death, could be and was at first embodied in the familiar stories of the Old Testament: Jonah made a satisfactory symbol of the Resurrection; Noah standing in his Ark (a mere box!) recalled the hope of salvation from the deluge of sin.

The miracles of the Savior, guaranty of salvation, begin to appear in the catacomb frescoes of the second century, but only such miracles as the Multiplication of the Loaves and Fishes, or the Healing of the Paralytic, which could *omit* the Wonder-Worker; it sufficed the early believer that there be painted on his tomb the feasting multitude alone, in which he saw himself, symbolically, partaking of the sacrament which the scene connoted, or the paralytic walking away with his bed upon his back, as token of the Savior's power that would be exerted for him as well as for the sick man of Bethesda. It is after 200 A.D. that, in those frescoes which can be identified with certainty as depicting the miracles, the figure of Christ appears—a youth of beardless face and short hair. It is in the third century that we find the first certain examples of the miracle of the Water Turned into Wine, of the Healing of the Blind Man, of the Leper, of the Woman with the Issue of Blood, in which may be seen this earliest artistic representation of Christ. He was also depicted as a beardless, short-haired youth at Alexandria, just as we see Him on a famous ivory box from that city, now in the Berlin Museum, seated among His disciples and teaching. Later the Alexandrian Church visualized Jesus, especially when performing His miracles, as carrying a short cross in the manner of a scepter, and sometimes standing on the beasts of Psalm xc, like Horus on his crocodiles. In Asia Minor there was a variant of this youthful type which gave Him long hair flowing down upon His shoulders (Fig. 22). From the second half of the fourth century the Asiatic East and Italy began to add the beard that made from this type the head which has become traditional in Christian art.

21. Joshua Rotulus (Biblioteca Vaticana). 9th–10th C. Copy of 5th–6th C. ms.

There is still another reason why the Old Testament preceded the New in furnishing the themes of the nascent Christian art. It is becoming more and more evident that the early centuries of our era were familiar with *illustrated* copies of the books of the Old Testament, and that these picturebooks were first produced in Alexandria where the first Greek version of the Old Testament was made. The earliest books of this sort were of course in roll form, and a copy of one of them, the famous *Rotulus of Joshua* (Fig. 21), still exists in the Vatican Library. Before its parchment membranes were detached from one another, the Rotulus was thirty feet long, and bore an uninterrupted frieze of drawings that told most of the story of the Hebrew conquest of the Promised Land. The Hebrews in these drawings are pictured as an army of Roman soldiers, and Joshua as their *imperator,* all wearing costumes which are the same as those of the soldiery depicted on the spiral reliefs of the Columns of Trajan and of Marcus Aurelius in the second century. The original from which the Rotulus was copied, directly or through one or more other copies, cannot be dated later than the Columns. The landscape background against which the military scenes are enacted is indeed more akin to the landscapes that one sees on the walls of Pompeii

157

than the landscapes of the reliefs on the Columns; it is composed of mountain ranges on the summits of which mountain-genii recline, with here and there impressionistic, distant views of cities, or groups of buildings, or gardens enclosing shrines. To this early Alexandrian illustration of the Old Testament can be traced all the early Christian illustrated books thereof at present in existence, such as the Genesis of Vienna and the remains of the Cotton Bible in the British Museum. These Old Testament pictures performed a strange role in medieval art: the Pompeian settings in which their scenes were cast were preserved from century to century by the persistent and faithful copying of the Alexandrian originals. That is why we meet in Byzantine painting, far down in the eleventh and twelfth centuries, those fresh landscape-vistas, Hellenistic-looking architecture, and the typical slopes of rocky hills that later made their way into Italian painting *via* Duccio and the Sienese, and still form the habitual background of the sacred episodes on Russian icons. A singular case of the survival of early Old Testament illustration is furnished by the Genesis mosaics of the thirteenth century that decorate the vaults of the narthex of Saint Mark's at Venice; they were copied quite accurately, though with a certain Byzantine stiffness of style, from the illustrations of an Alexandrian Book of Genesis written and illustrated seven hundred years before.

The themes of the Old Testament, owing to this early standardization in Alexandria, became fairly well fixed in Christian art at an early date, and were apt to follow the same formulae all over the Mediterranean world, wherever the prized Greek texts of the Septuagint, the Alexandrian version of the Old Testament, were used. Not so with the subjects of the New Testament. The different churches, Alexandrian, Syrian, Ephesian, African, Italian, Gallic, all had their own versions of the Gospels and their own images of the episodes narrated therein. A singular instance of this has recently emerged from A. M. Friend's investigation of the portraits of the Evangelists in the Greek and Latin Gospel-books. He has found that in Egypt the Evangelists were originally represented as standing figures, in Ephesus as philosophers seated in profile, in Italy as author-types sitting frontally, like the portrait of Virgil in a famous manuscript of that author in the Vatican Library.

The same local variation is found in the representation of incidents in the life of Christ. The Jesus who enters Jerusalem in the early Christian art of Egypt rides over a rug which is spread in

His path, while elsewhere in the Roman world a mantle takes its place. In Egypt representations of the Nativity were unique in including the curious figure of Salome, the midwife, who doubted the virginity of Mary and was punished by the withering of her hand, restored only after it had touched the swaddling clothes of the Infant. An angel accompanies the Magi as they approach the Christ Child in Egyptian Epiphanies; in Palestine the same is true, but the scene is symmetrical, with one Magus and the angel balancing two Magi on the other side of a frontally seated Virgin and Child. The very number of the Magi was still uncertain in the Christian art of the fourth century; a fresco in the Catacomb of Domitilla in Rome shows us four of them, and another of the third century in the Catacomb of SS. Peter and Marcellinus represents only two. The Annunciation was variously conceived; in Egypt the Virgin received the angelic salutation seated, while the Asiatic church conceived her as standing on that occasion. Christ seated on the globe of the world is a type found only in Latin works throughout the range of early Christian art; out of the Vision of Ezekiel the Eastern Church gradually evolved, instead, its own notion of Christ in Majesty, surrounded by a circular glory and seated either on a throne or on the arc of heaven.

Most interesting and puzzling of all the early modes of rendering sacred subjects are those that were in vogue, during the fifth and sixth centuries, in that belt of Latin culture which in late antiquity included northern Italy, distinguished from central and southern Italy, and spread across the southern part of Gaul into Spain. Here we find distinctive usages, ecclesiastic and liturgical, which once prevailed throughout the "belt," but which later were crowded out of Italy and Gaul into Spain and formed the basis of the constitution of the early medieval church in Spain and of its Mozarabic liturgy. In the period of which we speak, the south of Gaul and Spain were united in the Visigothic kingdom, and culturally at least allied with the north of Italy, newly important by reason of the transfer of the political capital of the peninsula from Rome to Ravenna. The individuality of this cultural belt is reflected in its ecclesiastic art. Here one finds, for example, our earliest existing representation of the Crucifixion (fifth century), depicting the Savior nude save for the loincloth and differing widely from the extant Asiatic renderings, which come about a century later, wherein Christ is clothed in a long tunic. In our Latin school above mentioned we also discover that the lance-wound in the body of the Savior was thought to be in His left side instead of His right, where it is put by the otherwise invariable rule of medieval art, and consequently in pictures or reliefs that represent the doubting Thomas approaching his Master, the disciple comes from the spectator's right, advancing to touch the wound in the Savior's left side. In Italo-Gallic Baptisms of this school the Baptist is conceived as a shepherd and given a crook. Most curious of all is the manner of showing the Massacre of the Innocents, the slaughter of the children of Bethlehem, for in southern Gaul the soldiers do not stab the infants, but dash them to the ground—a distinction which is preserved in the Mozarabic liturgy when it marks the lesson for the day with the rubric: "in *allisione infantium*."

These Italo-Gallic peculiarities perpetuated themselves in Western Europe in some cases far into the Middle Ages; Irish artists, for example, even as late as the ninth and tenth centuries, still sometimes place Longinus, the centurion who pierced the side of the Savior, on His left. Carolingian miniaturists and ivory-carvers continue also another peculiarity of early Christian Latin iconography in picturing the Holy Sepulcher as a two-storied affair, a cubical lower portion supporting a rotunda. The origin of this notion is obscure, but it was undoubtedly helped by the existence of so many structures of this type in Provence, such as the tomb of the Julii at Saint-Rémy. The actual appearance of the Tomb of Christ as it looked *c.* 600 is preserved to us in the painted cover of a wooden box that was found among the relics of the Sancta Sanctorum at the Lateran in Rome, when its altar was opened in 1905. This box was filled with an amalgam of resin and sand in which were imbedded pieces of wood and stone picked up by some pilgrim to the holy places in or near Jerusalem at the end of the sixth century. The objects are all labeled with the names in Greek of the places from which they came, e.g., "from Bethlehem," "from the Mount of Olives," etc. The scenes painted on the cover have reference to some of these places; they show the Crucifixion, the Resurrection, the Ascension, the Nativity, and the Baptism. In the Resurrection we see the Sepulcher as a circular shrine with a conical roof and an altar in front of it, above all of which is poised the dome of the Anastasis, the church which Constantine built above the Tomb. The same picture of it appears on the little leaden phials in which pilgrims put the oil they took from the lamps that burned in front of the Tomb and the other *loca sancta;* some of these phials, dating also from the end of the sixth century, are still preserved in the treasury of the cathedral of Monza near Milan. In 614 the Persian Chosroes raided Jerusalem and destroyed the Sepulcher. Save for the obscure descriptions of early pilgrims, these phials and the painting on the lid of the reliquary box are our only record of the Holy Sepulcher as it appeared to visitors to the Holy City in the first Christian centuries.

The standardizing of the themes of the New Testament proceeded hand in hand with the standardizing of its text. Both processes were the result of the steady pressure of the Graeco-Asiatic church upon the rest of the Christian world. But the fact that the source of authority for Old Testament iconography was Alexandria, while that for the New Testament was Nearer Asia, produced a difference in the two sections of biblical illustration that was never completely obliterated, the one preserving its spatial background and pictur-esque landscape accessories, the other inclining more and more to a neutral setting for the Gospel episodes, which finally issued in the plain gold background of Byzantine mosaics.

Alexandria, in late antiquity, was the stronghold of what there was of realism, and of the realization of space, in Hellenistic art. The conceptions of the Alexandrian school are well reflected in the paintings of Pompeii; there we can see the freedom with which the movement and posture of the human figure were rendered, the expansiveness with which its surroundings were conceived, in short, the three-dimensionality of the world as viewed by these sophisti-cated artists, seeking, as metropolitan genius has ever sought, an escape to the "open spaces" from the complications and irritations of city life. In Greece and Asia, on the other hand, we find that the last phase of Hellenism takes a negative turn; evoking the past, it seeks by imitation to revive the glories of the Athenian art of the fourth and fifth centuries before our era. This classic style was two-dimensional, eschewing depth of background, and shutting in its space by an architectural treatment or by a sheer neutral wall (Fig. 22).

There could be no question as to which of these two styles was to become the principal artistic vehicle of the new religion. Chris-tian hope was fixed on the next world, not on this; its conceptions of ultimate reality transcended material experience. As the spiritual significance of the mysteries depicted was better understood, there was not felt the same need for minutely concrete representations, nor the same desire for that illusion of material existence which could be imparted by the Alexandrian indications of specific locality and time. The trend of Christian style was therefore in the main toward the two-dimensional, Neo-Attic wing of Graeco-Roman art.

The effect of this was at first to make it ugly. The antique ideal, the Greek quest, was one of material beauty, the presentation of life in typical completeness and perfection, but bounded by the bourne of the sensible world. The Christian painter and sculptor, child of centuries of Hellenic and Hellenistic naturalism, groped blindly through his inherited materialistic style toward an expression of his own immaterial concepts; it is no wonder that the early phases of Christian art destroyed the beauty of the past without achieving that of the future. Only in the sixth century do we find the new ideal successfully rendered in fitting form; in the mosaics and carved

22. Early Christian Sarcophagus, 5th Century A.D., Sant'Apollinare in Classe, Ravenna

ornament of that period in Ravenna a new principle of composition is visible which achieves unity not through the traditional Greek insistence on a central motif, but by rhythmic repetition of accents. If one compares the processions of saints on the walls of S. Apollinare Nuovo, or other mosaics at Ravenna, with any Greek pedimental group, the new concept of unity emerges clearly. The Greek effect is static; in the mosaics of the sixth century the integrating principle is movement, conveyed by a succession of color accents that perform the function of a musical beat.

This change from the principle of balance and symmetry to one of rhythm as the source of unity and beauty involved the introduction of series and sequence and thereby of unlimited extent, albeit in the two dimensions of classic style. The same revolt against the limitations of Greek unity was accomplished in the architecture of late antiquity by the introduction of the factor of space. Space is the element whereby the interior of a building may be made to suggest the romance of the unlimited, which the solids of the structure deny; its development in Christian architecture, like the shift toward rhythmic composition in the representative arts, measures the progress the new cult was making toward the adequate expression of its spiritual content. Antiquity had avoided the inclusion of space in architectural effect; the classic example is the Egyptian pyramid with no interior space at all. The Greek temple had used space, not indeed for internal composition, which was the least of the classic builder's preoccupations, but for the proper relief and isolation of the colonnade of the porch. It is only in the Roman phase of Hellenistic architecture, as in the Pantheon, that we find a building actually composed as an interior.

Even here the antique prejudice against the unlimited, the incommensurable, in short the infinite, toward which the Christian cult was oriented, produced a curious inhibition. The interior of the Pantheon is geometrically conceived, a half-sphere with no windows save the *oculus* in the top, promptly measured by the eye and therefore finite and controllable. In Hagia Sophia at Constantinople, built four centuries later, we see the same result, save that the geometry is more subtle, and the builders have done away with the carefully colonnaded walls and coffered ceiling which still in the Pantheon betokened the antique preoccupation with solids rather than voids. The supports are evasive, leaving somewhat the impression that the half-spheres and quarter-spheres of emptiness which

163

the domes and semidomes inclose, are themselves the realities of the building, and the ceilings but their weightless definitions. But they are half-spheres and quarter-spheres none the less, commensurable and therefore not transcending the limits of experience. The Greek element in Byzantine art thus shows itself still strong enough to confine Christian concepts within the limits of a rationalized art.

The complete exploitation of interior space toward the Christian ideal of union of the finite with the infinite, of the interior with all of out-of-doors, was accomplished much later, in the Gothic cathedral, and lay at the end of a long evolution of Christian architecture in the Latin West. Nevertheless the germ of the cathedral and the statement of the space problem which it solved with so much beauty can be found in the early Latin basilica (Fig. 23), at the beginning of the evolution. The very orientation of this structure shows the stirring of a new purpose. Antique buildings of this kind were usually symmetrical, with their interior colonnades running across the ends as well as along the sides. While the semicircular apse was already a feature of such pagan plans, it was usually paired with another in the interest of balance. The Christian interior was focused by its single apse and by the altar in the sanctuary, toward which the eye ran rapidly along the closely spaced columns of the nave; above the nave wall was the clerestory letting in a flood of light from without. The Christian basilica had thus produced an axis of movement within the equilibrium of the antique interior; it had also, in its opening of the clerestory, posed the problem of space without as related to space within. But the roof of the basilica was of wood, impermanent, and symbolic of the inchoate character of this unsatisfactory architectural form. The substitution of the Romanesque masonry vault for the Early Christian wooden roof responded hardly more to considerations of safety from fire than to aesthetic need. This vaulting of the nave started the Christian interior of the West toward its goal. The heavy piers and the wide bays of vaulted construction produced a slower rhythm than the early colonnade, conducting the eye with a greater awe toward the sanctuary; and the gradual emphasizing of the internal supports led to a vertical axis which competed with the antique horizontal axis. Finally nothing was left but to invent the ribbed vaulting of Gothic construction, that made the walls unnecessary and opened up the clerestory again, this time to admit a light transfigured by color,

23. Sant'Apollinare in Classe, Ravenna, 533–549 A.D.
View of Interior Looking Toward Apse

and transforming the interior from mere emptiness into mystically
significant volume.

The early Latin churches arrest our attention therefore more for
their implications of beauty desired than for their evidence of beauty
accomplished. Hagia Sophia is witness to the crystallizing and
rationalizing of the representations of Christian concepts in the
Greek East at an early date; in the West these concepts integrated
much more slowly, since the motive power in this evolution was
far more emotional than intellectual. Latin art was therefore in the
early Middle Ages less articulate than Greek, and for this very reason
subservient to the more civilized formulae purveyed by early Byzantine style. But these formulae could not in the end satisfy the
ecstatic piety of the West; the Byzantine is static in its ultimate

165

effect like the classic, and the West was committed to an expansive style from the moment it conceived the apsidal orientation of its first churches. It is the intent and striving of early Christian art in the West that fascinates the student who studies its ugliness enough to understand it; in its impulses lies the genesis of the most expressive religious art that history knows, which came to full flower in the Gothic cathedrals a thousand years after the first Christians painted their obscure hopes on the walls of the catacombs in Rome.

11. THE HELLENISTIC HERITAGE IN BYZANTINE ART

Ernst Kitzinger

INTRODUCTION

As Ernst Kitzinger points out in the opening section of his discussion of Hellenistic elements in Byzantine art (not included in the excerpt that follows), nineteenth-century scholarship had generally emphasized the Roman contribution to the origins and early developments of Christian art. With the publication of D. V. Ainalov's *The Hellenistic Origins of Byzantine Art* (1900), the original in Russian, now available in English translation (1961), and Joseph Strzygowski's *Orient oder Rom* (1901), attention was drawn to the role of the eastern Mediterranean regions in the history of Early Christian and Byzantine art. Professor Kitzinger notes, however, in the opening section referred to above, that there was a direct continuity between the art of Rome and that of Byzantium, and that the Byzantine contact with Hellenistic art may have come through intermediary channels. Nevertheless, whether through contact with authentic Hellenistic works or Roman intermediaries, there is present in Byzantine art a considerable heritage from the Hellenistic world, and this is examined with fine discrimination by Professor Kitzinger in the selection that follows.

For further reading on Byzantine art, there are Otto Demus, *Byzantine Mosaic Decoration* (1948); Kurt Weitzmann, *Greek Mythology in Byzantine Art* (1951); two popular, well-illustrated works, André Grabar, *Byzantine Painting* (1953), and David Talbot Rice, *The Art of Byzantium* (1959);

Richard Krautheimer, *Early Christian and Byzantine Architecture* (1965); and O. M. Dalton, *Byzantine Art and Archaeology* (1911), still a valuable survey of a wide range of Byzantine art forms, and now available in a reprint (1965). Charles Rufus Morey's *Early Christian Art*, 2nd ed. (1953) has valuable sections on the art of Ravenna, and Cyril Mango's *Materials for the Study of the Mosaics of St. Sophia at Istanbul*, Dumbarton Oaks Studies, VIII (1962) is of particular interest, not only for its treatment of the existing mosaics, but for its publication of various documents relating to them. S. K. Kostof's *The Orthodox Baptistry of Ravenna* is a fine monograph on an important monument of Ravennate art, and stresses the relationship it bears to the art of Byzantium. Earl Baldwin Smith, in *The Dome: A Study in the History of Ideas* (1950) traces the origins and meaning of this important feature of both Byzantine and Islamic architecture.

The selection that follows is reprinted from Ernst Kitzinger, "The Hellenistic Heritage in Byzantine Art," *Dumbarton Oaks Papers*, XVII (1963), pp. 98–115, by permission of the author. A number of passages, footnotes, and illustrations have been omitted in this reprint and the remaining footnotes and illustrations renumbered.

In many ways Hellenistic art seems a most unlikely source of inspiration or norms for Byzantine religious painting and sculpture. With its predilection for the grandiose and the pathetic, the romantic and the idyllic, the humorous and the grotesque, for genre and eroticism, Hellenistic pictorial art embodies the pagan world at its most pagan. Yet there are unquestionably many, and very prominent, works of Byzantine religious art in which the Hellenistic element is very strong. We need think only of the paintings of Castelseprio, the miniatures of the Paris Psalter, or the mosaics of the Kariye Djami. In what precise sense, however, do such works deserve the epithet "Hellenistic"? What are the sources and carriers of the Hellenistic elements which appear in them? And—most elusive problem of all—what do these elements mean in the contexts in which they come to be used? We do not always face up to the paradox which is implied in the formula "Hellenistic foundations of Byzantine art." We tend to forget how odd it really is to see episodes in the life of the biblical David or prophetic visions of the Old Testament enacted in the midst of a romantic landscape, originally created to delight the leisure classes of Pergamon, Ephesus, or Alexandria; or to find the writers of the Gospels seated against backdrops of fantastic architectures closely akin to those which in the first century B.C. were painted on the walls of a villa at Boscoreale. Is all this Hellenism in Byzantine religious art so much ballast, dried up formulae, meaningless trappings? Or, if it is not meaningless, what was its function? Such problems tend to get lost from sight in the debate over models and prototypes in which those of us who study the history of Byzantine art are perpetually engaged. They seem to me worthy of an hour's reflection. For it is certainly true to say that, to our generation at least, the Hellenistic features in Byzantine art often are a source of greater puzzlement (albeit, in many instances, unrecognized and unarticulated puzzlement) than the "abstract" and "medieval" ones which caused difficulties to earlier generations. We may not be able to reach any firm answers, but at least we shall have asked some questions which perhaps should be raised more frequently.

My procedure will be to take up one by one a number of elements that are specifically characteristic of Hellenistic art and to consider their subsequent fortunes in Byzantium. The selection of these elements was made in consultation with Professor Hanfmann, whose own paper, printed in this volume, provides a discussion of these same elements within the context of Hellenistic art. In effect, the two papers represent a joint effort on the part of two specialized scholars to isolate some significant strands in the complex web of connections between their respective fields and to do so without unduly distorting the overall image of either Hellenistic or Byzantine art.[1]

Some of the topics discussed by Professor Hanfmann may be given short shrift. There is no eroticism in Byzantine art—religious or secular. Nor is there anything that could be properly called humor. The absence of the latter element is noteworthy, considering the strength of the Hellenistic precedent and the amount of humor that emerged in the art—even the religious art—of the West in the course of the Middle Ages, at least by way of byplay. But, at any rate, here already a measure of selectivity becomes apparent in the Byzantine approach to the Hellenistic heritage.

I turn to *picturesque and idyllic genre,* for which there was considerable scope in Byzantine art. Pastoral idyls, for instance, found a natural place not only in the illustration of the lives of Old Testament heroes, such as Jacob, Joseph, and David, but also in connection with such texts as Psalm 32[2] and Gregory of Nazianzus' homily on New Sunday,[3] and most commonly, of course, in the portrayal of the shepherds of Bethlehem receiving the glad tidings of the birth of Christ. Again, in depicting the sick healed by Christ and His saints, artists were able to draw on the repertory of pathetic types which Hellenistic art had delighted in creating. As an example, I quote the young man with matchstick limbs on the Carrand Diptych in Florence[4]—one of the sick Maltese being brought before St. Paul (Acts 28:8–9)—whose artistic ancestry is beautifully exemplified by the bronze statuette of an emaciated man in the Dumbarton Oaks Collection.[5] The accounts—canonical or apocryphal—of the infancy of Christ and the Virgin Mary gave the illustrating artists occasion to preserve or revive something of the imagery of babyhood which Hellenistic art had so lovingly explored.

These are all themes in connection with which Hellenistic survivals and revivals occurred naturally.

I want to single out, however, for a somewhat more detailed discussion one motif from the last-named sphere, whose presence in Christian art was not entirely a matter of course, namely, the Child's first bath. The representation of this intimate detail from the life of the nursery is not called for either by the Gospels or by any of the apocryphal accounts habitually followed by the artists. Yet it came to be practically *de rigueur* even in the most solemn, "iconic," and monumental of Byzantine "feast cycles." I single out this motif because, not being warranted by the texts, it can serve particularly well to illustrate the power and impetus of the Hellenistic heritage in the *artistic* sphere, and can, moreover, lead us to an understanding of some of the factors and motivating forces that helped to ensure the survival or revival of such elements.

The Child's bath was not originally part of the iconography of the Nativity of Christ. The earliest dated representation is in the early eighth-century mosaics of the Oratory of Pope John VII in Old St. Peter's in Rome.[6] Certain other examples may be somewhat earlier, but we have a sufficient number of sixth-century representations of the Nativity to be able to say that at that time the bath was not yet a normal element in the iconography of the scene.[7] It had been, however, a stock motif in the representation of childbirth which often formed part of "biographical" picture cycles in antiquity. It figured in the birth of divine or divinely begotten infants—specifically Dionysus, Achilles, and Alexander the Great— but also in that of ordinary, anonymous mortals. In one instance, the episode was included in the representation of the birth of an imperial prince, or at least in a poetic description of such a representation.[8] While extant ancient works depicting the baby's bath all date from Roman times, the invention is undoubtedly Hellenistic and in its ultimate origins perhaps even older.[9] Its inclusion in life cycles of divine and heroic persons in all probability preceded its appearance in the pictorial biographies of ordinary mortals.

Several scholars have sought to prove that Christian artists took over the motif specifically from representations of the birth of Dionysus.[10] One at least of these Dionysiac examples—a textile from Antinoë in the Louvre—is as late as the fourth or fifth century.[11] The assumption would be that in this case an artist of the sixth,

or more probably the seventh, century sought inspiration in surviving illustrations of a pagan mythological subject to introduce a
new—and henceforth almost obligatory—element into the Nativity
scene. It would be an interesting example of the spell exercised by
the Hellenistic heritage even in a period of Byzantine art history
which does not rank among the principal "renaissance" phases, and
of the abiding importance of representations from ancient mythology (which, of course, were reproduced in Byzantium even much
later) in transmitting the ancient heritage to Byzantine religious
art.

I do not rule out the possibility that this is indeed the correct
interpretation of the data at hand. But it seems to me much more
likely that a link is missing in this genealogy. For one thing, the
fact that the child's first bath figured (poetically, at least) in *imperial*
iconography should give one pause, in view of the manifold instances
of an "imperialization" of Christian religious art. It was the newborn
child of Honorius and Maria whom Claudianus, the contemporary
poet, pictured as having been thus portrayed.[12] Supposing that such
pictorial renderings of imperial births actually existed at the time
and continued to be in vogue also in the fifth, sixth, and seventh
centuries, would not these be a likely source of inspiration for those
who added the baby's bath to the Nativity scene? But what is
probably more important, and, at any rate, somewhat more tangible,
is the presence of the motif in birth scenes relating to figures from
the Old Testament. The extant examples are of relatively late date,
and in many instances the representation of the bath is probably
due to a reverse influence from scenes of Christ's Nativity or other
New Testament birth scenes.[13] This, however, is not likely in the
case of the cycle of scenes from Genesis in the atrium of S. Marco
in Venice, where the bath motif occurs in the birth of Ishmael and
in the birth of Isaac. Because the iconography of the S. Marco
mosaics follows so closely that of the Cotton Genesis Manuscript,
there is an *a priori* probability that the midwives with baby and
washbasin (grouped, incidentally, in S. Marco in a manner which
strongly calls to mind the bath of the infant Dionysus in the textile
in the Louvre) were present also in that fifth-century manuscript,
in which the relevant details have not survived.[14] Thus Old Testament
illustrations of early date emerge as a possible carrier of a
Hellenistic motif subsequently incorporated in New Testament
iconography.[15] There will be occasion in this paper to make other

parallel observations. We need not here go into the question as to whether Old Testament illustrations came into being during the Hellenistic period itself, or only in Roman times. For Byzantine artists these illustrations provided a readily available and, so to speak, self-perpetuating reservoir of Hellenistic traditions. Awareness of this factor may serve as a corrective to an excessive reliance on "Hellenistic revivals."

But there was a revival, too. It has been observed that in all early representations of the bath in Nativity scenes, i.e. in all examples earlier than the tenth century, the Christ Child is shown upright in the basin.[16] Usually He is being held up by one of the midwives seated on the side. This is the arrangement even in Castelseprio, which in rendering and mood is by far the most "Hellenistic" of all the early examples.[17] Beginning with the tenth century, however, we find the Child reclining in relaxed fashion either in the basin or on the nurse's lap.[18] Quite often the Child, when reclining in the basin, is held by a midwife seated not beside but behind Him and, as it were, enveloping Him in a protective pose. This does appear to be a case of reversion to a Hellenistic type, as exemplified by the "Birth of Dionysus" on one of the silver cups from the Casa del Menandro in Pompeii. In the tenth century there also appears, or rather reappears, the charming touch of the nurse trying out with her hand the temperature of the bath water,[19] a detail which will then be repeated in many other Nativity scenes down to the end of the Middle Ages.[20] I say "reappears," because the designer of a Roman floor mosaic found some years ago at Baalbek imagined the nymph who bathed the infant Alexander to have taken the same precaution.

Thus the bath scene is a good test case with which to demonstrate both the *survival* of Hellenistic elements in Byzantium (with biblical and possibly mythological iconography acting as important means of transmission) and the *revival* phenomenon characteristic of certain phases, and most especially of the period of the "Macedonian Renaissance."

To what extent, however, are we justified in dealing with the baby's bath under the general heading of "genre"? Charming and touching as the details may be, does there not lie concealed within them a deep and solemn meaning, both in the Hellenistic and the Christian versions? I have said that at the outset the representation of the first bath probably belonged exclusively to the life cycle of gods and heroes. Although this was no longer the case in Roman times, the theme may have retained certain esoteric connotations —and acquired others—without which it could not have found a place in the portrayal of the epiphany of the Incarnate Word. In discussing the literary treatment of divine infants in Virgil's Fourth Eclogue, in the Egyptian cult of Horus, and in the apocryphal Infancy Gospels, Eduard Norden aptly speaks of a "Bewegung des stilistischen Pendels zwischen tändelndem Spiel mit dem Knäblein und ehrfurchtsvoller Prädikation seiner Göttlichkeit."[21] Do not both factors also enter into the adoption of the bath scene in Byzantine art?

Actually, from a dogmatic point of view the motif was questionable.[22] The Child was pure, as was His Mother. *Purus pure puram aperiens vulvam quam ipse puram fecit,* says Irenaeus,[23] and the same concept is present, at least implicitly, in the great majority of texts in which the birth of Christ is described or discussed. Yet I do not believe that in adopting the bath motif Byzantine artists and their clerical patrons and advisers were unmindful of dogma. They adopted the motif the more emphatically to demonstrate the humanity of Christ and the reality of the Incarnation. I cannot furnish documentary proof for this interpretation, since I do not know of any Early Christian or Byzantine text referring explicitly to the bath scene.[24] But I can quote at least one Byzantine author who provides this interpretation for a closely related—and, from a dogmatic point of view, equally questionable—motif, namely, for the Virgin Mary in the Nativity being represented as fatigued by the labors of childbirth. "She lies on a mattress," says Nicholas Mesarites in his description of the Nativity scene in the mosaics of the Church of the Holy Apostles, ". . . showing the face of a woman who has just been in pain—even though she escaped the pangs of labor—in order that the dispensation of the incarnation might not be looked upon with suspicion, as trickery."[25] The same reasoning undoubtedly accounts for the depiction of the Child as in need of ablution. Though born miraculously and spotless, He submits to the cares that human infants require and thus shows that the Word has indeed become flesh. Excessive heat of the bath water might hurt Him like any human baby. The more genre-like the elaboration of the theme the better, from this point of view.

Here, then, is an instance of a reinterpretation and revaluation of a Hellenistic theme in terms of specifically Christian needs and concerns.[26] Even the mundane, the playful, and the anecdotic proved valuable in this sense and thus gained a new lease on life. The very breadth of its human range made Hellenistic art a rich source of inspiration for artists striving to proclaim in visual language the fact that God has become Man. Undoubtedly here lies one of the keys to the power of the Hellenistic tradition in Byzantine art in general. If at times Hellenistic motifs that are retained or revived may seem paradoxical—or even faintly ludicrous—it is not for lack of meaning, but rather because of the solemnity, the weight of the new message with which they are invested.

Certain basic concepts and categories which have emerged from this analysis will be useful in considering other aspects of the Hellenistic heritage. Survival and revival, and particularly also the grafting of a revival on a surviving tradition—these are phenomena familiar in many areas of Byzantine art, though they are not always demonstrable as clearly as in this instance. Mythological and Old Testament subjects stand out as carriers of the Hellenistic survival again and again. And the distinction between a natural continuation or resumption of Hellenistic elements in the context of Christian religious art, on the one hand, and a revaluation and re-elaboration of such elements in the light of new meanings and new purposes, on the other—this distinction, too, will be found to be of larger significance. Not that I intend to construct from these categories a rigid framework into which to press all available material. Rather, may they serve as guide posts in our further investigations.

Consider *landscape painting*, for instance, which is one of the most important and most characteristic fields of endeavor of Hellenistic artists. The extent to which Byzantine artists made use of the ancient repertory of idyllic groves and running brooks, sunlit cliffs and soaring mountains, solitary porches and columns and picturesquely complex villa structures as settings for religious subjects is familiar to all. Yet, even in its most elaborate confections of this sort, Byzantine art does not achieve the sense of nature heroically animated, romantically unified, and pantheistically hallowed, which was the original *raison d'être* of these motifs. The imitation remains labored and self-conscious. It could hardly be otherwise given the fact that the emotional, religious, and philosophic trends to which these artistic forms responded had long since spent themselves. The

175

wonder is that so much of the artistic tradition survived in spite of this.

Perhaps I should qualify the negative statement I have just made by a reference to the frescoes of Castelseprio. This is one instance where a Byzantine artist not only uses motifs from Hellenistic landscape painting, but succeeds in evoking a sense of nature gently enveloping the human action. Here, as nowhere else in Byzantine art, the Gospel story is endowed with a poetic, dreamlike quality. But Castelseprio is an exception and I strongly suspect was an exception in its own time. For, in general, it was much more in the illustration of the Old Testament, rather than of the Gospel story, that the repertory of Hellenistic landscape painting survived at all. The fact is striking and has been observed repeatedly. Whether we think of the fifth-century mosaics of S. Maria Maggiore, the illuminated purple codices of the sixth century, the wall paintings of about 700 in the chancel of S. Maria Antiqua, or the splendidly illuminated manuscripts of the Macedonian era—it is usually the Old Testament subjects that provide an opportunity to develop outdoor settings with a greater or lesser amount of Hellenistic motifs, while the events from the Gospels tend to be displayed against a more neutral and abstract foil.

This, of course, is simply another aspect of a phenomenon already referred to. Old Testament illustration again is seen to be a carrier of the Hellenistic tradition. But we may use this aspect to probe a little more deeply the reasons for the phenomenon. In part, surely, these reasons are simply historical. Old Testament iconography was developed, and to some extent codified, before Gospel iconography was, and probably at a time when Hellenistic standards of narrative depiction were still universally practiced. It is safe to say this without going into controversial questions of the chronology and morphology of early Bible illustration, and more particularly of the extent and nature of its roots in the art of Hellenistic Judaism. A certain amount of landscape setting came to be traditionally and conventionally accepted as a normal garb for Old Testament subjects. . . .

I turn to an aspect of Hellenistic painting highly relevant to these idyllic and romantic landscapes but of much wider scope and application, namely, the quality often referred to as *illusionism*. The term denotes a technique which by purely pictorial means—by color, shades, and highlights—produces an illusion of three-dimensional shapes and, at the same time, suffuses these shapes with light and suggests their envelopment in "real" space. That Byzantine painting owes much to this aspect of Hellenism is generally recognized. But, again, there is the question of the exact role and meaning of this heritage.

At the very least, Byzantine painting owed to this tradition some of its flexibility as a visual language. In all centuries from the fourth to the fifteenth one finds innumerable instances in which highlights and shades help to convey an impression of physical presence, of movement, and sometimes of inner life as well. However routinely this pictorial language may be handled, however trite and worn-out its formulae may have become, it was an essential prerequisite for making of art—and painting in particular—the highly articulate instrument for complex and increasingly differentiated messages which it was in the hands of the Byzantine church and the Byzantine state. Much of the abiding appeal which Byzantine painting had for the Latin West also is due to this quality.

But illusionism in Hellenistic art meant more than the creation of optically convincing images. It meant the creation of a dream world. Glowing colors and shimmering lights not only give shape and heightened life to figures and objects, but often also dissolve them and make them transparent. The real hallmark of Hellenistic illusionism (as of nineteenth-century impressionism) is its ambivalence: it enhances and, at the same time, transfigures reality.[27]

That this is an important element in Byzantine painting also will be generally agreed. In the best of the seventh-century frescoes in S. Maria Antiqua, in which the techniques of Hellenistic illusionism are handled with surprising mastery, figures are lifelike yet insubstantial. The same is true of the frescoes of Castelseprio. Indeed, the blending of plausibility and elusiveness is the very essence of these remarkable paintings. Figures are alive and humanly convincing, but move in an airy and luminous world utterly beyond our grasp. On an earlier occasion I have drawn attention to instances where *angels* are singled out for a particularly bold and striking display of illusionistic technique. The frescoes of S. Maria Antiqua and the encaustic icon of the Virgin on Mount Sinai afford examples of this. I have suggested that illusionism in these instances may have been a means of characterizing angels as spiritual beings, as ἀσώματοι.[28] However this may be, illusionism in

Byzantine painting certainly was much more than a convenient idiom—let alone just a mechanically repeated technique. It was a positive aesthetic element deeply tied to new spiritual values and content. Here, in fact, is a prime example of Byzantium appropriating a segment of the Hellenistic heritage for its own particular purposes, investing it with a new meaning and a new mission; revaluating it, in other words, and, we must add, developing it in the process. For the web of highlights that ultimately emerges and spins a subtle pattern over surfaces of paintings and mosaics is far removed from anything the classical age had known. It becomes a kind of grid or armature for figures or even for entire panels.[29] Most literally is this true in the case of enamels where the metal cloisons containing the colored glass mass are an armature in the technical sense, but may indicate highlights at the same time.[30] However, the clearest proof that in the Byzantine aesthetic scheme these highlights have become a new aesthetic value is the fact that they are so frequently rendered in gold; and not only in enamels, where gold is the metal normally employed, but in paintings and mosaics as well.[31] Gold, of course, had many different uses in Byzantine art, and a discussion of all these uses and their relationships to classical or other antecedents would lead us far afield. Suffice it to say that so far as gold highlights are concerned, I find no clear-cut examples earlier than the fourth century A.D.[32] It was then—at the beginning of the Byzantine era—that figures and objects first appeared suffused with gold as though bathed in a light that is not of this world. The full aesthetic potential of the device, however, was realized subsequently in mature Byzantine art, when webs of gold utterly transfigure those whom they invest.[33]

The last aspect of Hellenistic art discussed by Professor Hanfmann is the *expression of emotions and mental states*, a sphere in which that art had particularly excelled. Exploring to a degree never previously attained in the visual arts the potentialities of pose, gesture, and, most particularly, facial expression, Hellenistic sculptors and painters had vastly increased the range, variety and, above all, intensity of the emotions displayed by human figures. How much of this achievement was retained and perpetuated in Byzantine art and what was its role?

This may not appear to be a very promising line of enquiry. Many Byzantine pictorial representations are totally unresponsive when approached from the point of view of the artist's concern with the emotional experiences of the figures portrayed. Even representations of moments of high drama—moments in the relating of which the biblical text itself describes the psychological reactions of those involved—may be found sadly wanting in this respect. In other instances, one is painfully aware of an originally meaningful pose or gesture having been drained of all genuine feeling through endless repetition. Thus, the butler and the baker, who in the prison scene of the Vienna Genesis (Fig. 24) display their reactions most violently as Joseph foretells them their respective fates, reappear in the corresponding scenes in the Byzantine Octateuchs as lame replicas of their former selves (Fig. 25). No doubt, lack of empathy is one of the reasons for the low esteem in which Byzantine art was held during periods which sought in the pictorial arts an adequate portrayal above all of a full range of human sentiments. Today we tend to lean too much toward the other extreme and to exclude this as a valid criterion altogether. . . .

In an attempt to assess more specifically the Hellenistic heritage in this sphere, one soon becomes aware of certain limitations. For one thing, the range of emotions that find expression—even fossilized expression—in Byzantine art is, on the whole, much reduced compared with Hellenistic art. I feel fairly safe, for instance, in asserting that in all Byzantine painting and sculpture there is not a single laughing figure. When one considers the popularity of such figures in Hellenistic art one realizes again that the survival of the ancient heritage was far from automatic. Probably the widest range of emotions that can be found anywhere in Byzantine art is in the miniatures of the Vienna Genesis. By any standards—not only Byzantine, but even classical, or, for that matter, modern—the illuminators of this famous manuscript were quite exceptionally successful in portraying with great poignancy a wide variety of psychological situations.[34] In the matter of psychological insight they outstripped by far most of the works that commonly figure in the discussion of their supposed sources, works such as the illuminated papyri and the bulk of Late Classical mythological representations. However important the role of such models may have been, here is a case—quite early in the history of Byzantine art—where one must reckon with real empathy intervening in the copying process on a considerable scale. The same is true, if to a lesser extent, of certain other narrative cycles, not only of this period but of some other periods as well.[35] But, by and large, the emotional and psychological range in Byzantine art is rather restricted. Its most important sector is the expression of grief and pain, and this is the area where the role of the Hellenistic influence can be most readily seen. But additional limitations also become apparent here.

The essence of the Hellenistic portrayal of emotion was that it was not only emphatic, but at the same time grandiose, noble, and beautiful even when expressing adversity. This combination is rare in Byzantine art. When Christian art, after its laconic and sternly inexpressive late-antique beginnings, first introduced a measure of empathy, it used for the expression of grief facial distortions that are, to be sure, ultimately of Hellenistic origin, but the figures as a whole totally lack the Hellenistic pathos. Here, if anywhere, it is important to bear in mind that Byzantine artists had far less contact with true Hellenistic art than with a Graeco-Roman koinē;

24. Vienna Genesis (Cod. Theol. gr. 31, p. 33): Joseph in Prison, Early 6th Century (National Library, Vienna)

25. MS # gr. 746, fol. 122v: Joseph in Prison (La Biblioteca Apostolica Vaticana)

a distinction, which in this instance means the difference between the heroic, noble, or poetic, and something that can best be described as drastic.[36] This epithet also applies to the far more emphatic display of grief in the Vienna Genesis (Fig. 26). The emphasis is soon reduced, particularly in scenes depicting the mourning over Christ and the Virgin; but what emerges then—especially in the so-called Second Golden Age of Byzantine art—is a restrained and lyrical mood that has more affinity with the art of the fourth century B.C. than with characteristically Hellenistic art. Thus, in a sense, the Hellenistic phase is by-passed, or, perhaps one should say, transcended.

This is an extremely important point. Not only does it serve to illustrate the limitations of the influence of the Hellenistic heritage, but it also illuminates in a broader sense the relationship of Byzantine art to the whole of the classical past. The Hellenic ultimately is more important than the Hellenistic. In calling to mind the art of the fourth century B.C. I have, however, advisedly spoken of an affinity and have avoided the term influence. For the restrained lyricism which emerges is an autonomous growth within Byzantine art and is not, or at least not primarily, a result of copying from ancient Greek works. It is distilled from the heritage of Graeco-Roman art, and here again, so it would seem, the tradition of Old

181

26. Death of the Virgin, Mosaic, 12th Century, Church of Martorana, Palermo (Alinari-Art Reference Bureau)

Testament illustrations plays an important part as an intermediary or carrier. The Koimesis, for instance, as it becomes tangible in the art of the Macedonian and Comnenian periods (Fig. 26), is surely an adaptation—a toned down adaptation—of a death scene such as those we find in the Vienna Genesis (Fig. 27). How methodical and purposeful the adaptation was can be seen from the fact that in subjects outside the most sacred sphere of Christ and the Virgin *more* of the drastic gesticulation of the kind found in the Vienna Genesis survives. . . . As late as the thirteenth century, in the frescoes of Sopočani, grief is much more emphatically expressed at the deathbed of Jacob (Fig. 28) and of Queen Anne Dandolo than at that of the Virgin.[37] The distinction is reflected also in the ekphraseis which stress the point that too excessive a display of grief is not appropriate to sacred figures.[38] The tender, lyrical mood which Byzantine art reserves for the most exalted expressions of grief and pain is of its own making and is rooted deeply in Byzantine religious mentality. Parenthetically, I may refer here to the emergence of the same kind of specifically Byzantine lyricism in another

27. Vienna Genesis (Cod. Theo. graec 31, p. 48) Death and Burial of Jacob, Early 6th Century (National Library, Vienna)

28. SOPOČANI Monestary Church: Death of Jacob (École des Hautes Études, Collection Chrétienne et Byzantine, Paris)

emotional sphere, the sphere of motherly affection. The image of
the Tender Virgin in which this theme finds its most perfect expression has certain antecedents in genre-like Hellenistic representations.[39] But here again the ethos is wholly new and the pensive,
introspective mood which informs the image is more akin to that
of works of the fourth century B.C. than to anything characteristically Hellenistic. . . .

The expression of pain and grief and of certain other emotions
was one of those aspects of ancient art for which Christian religious
subject matter offered a natural field of survival and revival. As I
have pointed out, however, Byzantine artists were far from taking
advantage of all the opportunities thus offered. The case is perhaps
somewhat parallel to what we found earlier in regard to certain
genre motifs. Like the latter, the expression of emotions became
a concern of artists at particular stages in the Byzantine development and may have served not simply to humanize the Gospel story,
as is often said, but in a very precise sense to bring home the reality
of Christ's life on earth, the reality of the Incarnation. I refer once
more to the passage in Mesarites in which the fatigue displayed
by the Virgin of the Nativity—and there are many Byzantine
representations of the subject in which fatigue is expressed, if not
in the young Mother's face, certainly in her pose—is interpreted
in this sense.[40] Yet this cannot be the whole explanation. Byzantine artists' interest in the ancient repertory of poses, gestures,
and facial expressions ultimately goes beyond both mere illustration
and the service of a religious doctrine however central and sacred.
The repertory in and by itself must have had meaning for them,
a meaning perhaps best defined by the term "life force," the *vis
vitalis* of which Professor Hanfmann has spoken.[41] How else, for
instance, is one to explain the disjointed use and seemingly arbitrary
combination of single figures or groups from that repertory on the
ivory caskets of the middle Byzantine period?[42] . . . Byzantium
never entirely ceased to respond to the life force that animates all
Greek art and that had found its most varied and emphatic expressions during the Hellenistic period.

We conclude that the Hellenistic heritage in Byzantine art is
neither a dead ballast mechanically carried along by unthinking,
robot-like craftsmen, generation after generation, through eleven
hundred years, nor a collection of curios unearthed and refurbished
from time to time to satisfy an antiquarian bent. There is a definite

rationale in what does and what does not survive, in what is and what is not revived during the various "renaissance" phases. In particular, many of the paradoxical aspects seemingly inherent in the use of the Hellenistic heritage for the purposes of religious art disappear upon closer study. Christian art offered a natural scope for a number of characteristic forms and themes developed in Hellenistic times. Many such forms and themes proved adaptable to serve new causes and to express specifically Christian concerns. Ultimately, however, the strength and nature of the heritage cannot be explained or understood unless one also recognizes that there were still operative in Byzantium impulses from that same life force that had shaped Hellenistic art many centuries earlier.

This life force also helps to account for the peculiar relationship between survivals and revivals which we have encountered. The seemingly fossilized forms that were carried along through the centuries were not quite so dried up as they often appear to be. Nor, on the other hand, were the revivals, the returns to the ancient sources, as sudden or as comprehensive as is sometimes claimed. Old Testament and, to some extent, mythological imagery were particularly important as agents of continuity. The whole problem perhaps can best be summed up by invoking the simile of the "sleeping embers which will rise in flames"—from time to time.

Lest I be accused of overemphasizing the Hellenistic element in Byzantine art, let me close with two reminders. First, I want to stress once more the importance of Roman art, which formed both a link and a barrier between Hellenistic and Byzantine art. Rome had preceded Byzantium in applying processes of selection and reinterpretation to the Hellenistic heritage, though it was instrumental also in preserving and transmitting a measure of the Hellenistic *vis vitalis*. Second, it is essential to maintain a sense of proportion and to realize that even in the aggregate the Hellenistic survivals and revivals in Byzantine art involve only a fraction of the Hellenistic achievement. Let us remind ourselves once more of an obvious fact which my selective approach may have tended to obscure, namely, that Byzantine art, viewed as a whole, has a focus, an orientation totally different from Hellenistic art. Only fragments are inherited, and these fragments are transformed, transfigured, and transcended in the service of Byzantium's own aesthetic ideal; or, perhaps one should say, polarized by two powerful magnets which shaped that ideal: the medieval and the essentially classical.

NOTES

[1] I wish to record here my gratitude to Professor Hanfmann for agreeing to this collaborative effort and for his unfailing helpfulness and stimulating criticism throughout its progress.

[2] J. J. Tikkanen, *Die Psalterillustration im Mittelalter* (Helsingfors, 1895), p. 21 and Fig. 16 (British Museum, MS Add. 19352, fol. 36ʳ).

[3] H. Omont, *Miniatures des plus anciens manuscrits grecs de la Bibliothèque Nationale* (Paris, 1929), pl. 104, Figs. 2–5 (MS gr. 533); pl. 117, Figs. 17–19 (MS Coislin 239).

[4] W. F. Volbach, *Elfenbeinarbeiten der Spätantike und des frühen Mittelalters* (Mainz, 1952), no. 108 and pl. 32.

[5] G. M. A. Richter, *Catalogue of Greek and Roman Antiquities in the Dumbarton Oaks Collection* (Cambridge, Mass., 1956), no. 17 and pl. 14.

[6] M. van Berchem and E. Clouzot, *Mosaiques chrétiennes du IVᵐᵉ au Xᵐᵉ siècle* (Geneva, 1924), pp. 209 ff., especially p. 212. See P. J. Nordhagen, "The Mosaics of John VII (705–707 A.D.)," *Institutum Romanum Norvegiae. Acta ad Archaeologiam et Artium Historiam Pertinentia*, II, 1965, pp. 121 ff., especially pp. 131 ff. and pl. 7b.

[7] P. J. Nordhagen, "The Origin of the Washing of the Child in the Nativity Scene," *Byzantinische Zeitschrift*, 54 (1961), pp. 333 ff. M. Lawrence, "Three Pagan Themes in Christian Art," *De artibus opuscula XL: Essays in Honor of Erwin Panofsky*, I (New York, 1961), pp. 323 ff., especially pp. 329 f.

[8] See *infra*, note 12.

[9] Hanfmann selection, note 14 (p. 86, note 38, in original article).

[10] Nordhagen, *op. cit.*, p. 334 (with further references); Lawrence, *op. cit.*, pp. 327 ff.

[11] Nordhagen, *op. cit.*, p. 336; Lawrence, *op. cit.*, p. 328 with note 30.

[12] Cl. Claudianus, *Carmina*, XXII (= *De consulatu Stilichonis*, II), 345–7 (ed. by Th. Birt, *MGH, Auctores Antiquissimi*, 10 [Berlin, 1892], p. 215). Cf. A. Frolow, in *Études byzantines*, 3 (1945), p. 80.

[13] Cf., e.g., miniatures in the Byzantine Octateuchs depicting the birth of Isaac and Moses (D. C. Hesseling, *Miniatures de l'octateuque grec de Smyrne* [Leyden, 1909], Figs. 72, 152; *Izvestiia of the Russian Archaeological Institute in Constantinople*, 12 (1907), Album, pl. 19, Fig. 92); or the scenes of the birth of David discussed and illustrated by K. Weitzmann, *Illustrations in Roll and Codex* (Princeton, 1947), pp. 151 f. and Fig. 140 f.

[14] For the birth of Isaac in S. Marco and the fragment of the corresponding miniature in the Cotton MS (a fragment which is defective in the area crucial for our purpose), see J. J. Tikkanen, *Die Genesismosaiken von S. Marco in Venedig und ihr Verhältnis zu den Miniaturen der Cottonbibel* (reprinted from *Acta Societatis Scientiarum Fennicae*, 17 [Helsingfors, 1889]), p. 106 and pl. 13, Figs. 98 f. The miniature depicting the birth of Ishmael is lost altogether, as Professor Weitzmann has kindly informed me.

[15] Such a chain of transmission was suggested long ago by M. Schmid, *Die Darstellung der Geburt Christi in der bildenden Kunst* (Stuttgart, 1890), pp. 94 f.

[16] K. Weitzmann, "Das Evangeliar im Skevophylakion zu Lavra," *Seminarium Kondakovianum*, 8 (1936), pp. 83 ff., especially p. 90.

[17] G. P. Bognetti, G. Chierici, A. Capitani d'Arzago, *Santa Maria di Castelseprio* (Milan, 1948), pp. 586 f. and pls. 48–51. M. Lawrence (*op. cit.*, p. 330) mistakenly states that "the Child sits in the lap of the midwife."

[18] Weitzmann, *op. cit.*, p. 91.

[19] The earliest dated example of this motif in Byzantine art seems to be in the scene of the birth of the Virgin in the Menologium of Basil II (MS Vat. gr. 1613): *Codices e vaticanis selecti*, 8: *Il Menologio di Basillio II*, 2 (Turin, 1907), p. 22. Cf. also our Fig. 8, [Kitzinger].

[20] E. Panofsky, *Early Netherlandish Painting* (Cambridge, Mass., 1953), p. 38.

[21] E. Norden, *Die Geburt des Kindes* (Leipzig-Berlin, 1924), p. 74.

[22] Cf. Didron's interesting account of a conversation on this subject with a learned monk on Mount Athos (*Manuel d'iconographie chrétienne* [Paris, 1845], p. 158, note 2).

[23] *Adv. haer.* IV, lv, 2 (ed. by W. W. Harvey [Cambridge, 1857], II, p. 266).

[24] Didron, *op. et loc. cit.*, states that the scene figures in a legend reported by Symeon Metaphrastes, but fails to give a reference. Other scholars have repeated Didron's statement.

[25] Nikolaos Mesarites, *Description of the Church of the Holy Apostles in Constantinople* (G. Downey, ed.), Transactions of the American Philosophical Society, N.S., 47, pt. 6 (Philadelphia, 1957), pp. 877 f. Mesarites' description is incompletely preserved. It may well have included a reference to the bath scene, which in all probability was represented in the mosaic.

[26] I mention only in passing the interpretation of the bath scene as an antitype of Baptism, for which I know only Western evidence; cf. a relief on the façade of St. Trophime in Arles, on which a dove is seen descending on the Child in the wash basin (Fig. 9), [Kitzinger].

[27] Hanfmann, pp. 98 ff.

[28] See E. Kitzinger, *Byzantine Art in the Period Between Justinian and Iconoclasm*, Berichte zum XI. Internationalen Byzantinisten-Kongress, IV, I (Munich, 1958), p. 47; also C. Bertelli, *La Madonna di Santa Maria in Trastevere* (Rome, 1961), pp. 31 f.

[29] This quality cannot be conveyed adequately in black and white illustrations; see color reproductions such as those on pp. 157 and 191 of A. Grabar, *Byzantine Painting* (Geneva, 1953), or pp. 69, 71, 73, 75, 77 of D. Talbot Rice, *The Art of Byzantium* (London, 1959).

[30] Grabar, *op. cit.*, pp. 188 f.; Rice, *op. cit.*, pp. 25, 33, 49.

[31] Grabar, *op. cit.*, pp. 53 highlights on rocks and plants), 113, 117 (highlights on rocks and plants), 158, 174, 177; Rice, *op. cit.*, p. 39.

[32] W. F. Volbach, *Frühchristliche Kunst* (Munich, 1958), pl. 130 (mosaic of Sta. Pudenziana; note the clouds, the rock of Golgotha and the roof tiles, though the latter may be meant to be materially golden).

[33] The concept of "Eigenlicht," in which W. Schöne (*Über das Licht in der Malerei* [Berlin, 1954]) sees the key to an understanding of the role played by light in Christian and medieval painting from the fifth century on (see especially pp. 20 ff., 49 f.), does not entirely fit the phenomenon of these gold highlights which

are so striking a feature of Byzantine painting. Though strongly ornamentalized, they retain something of the character of what Schöne calls "Fremdlicht" (cf. p. 27 f.); that is to say, they are reflections, but reflections of an unearthly light. On the relevant metaphysical concepts and their development in Hellenistic and Christian thought, see the summary statement, *ibid.*, pp. 55 f., and especially R. Bultmann, "Zur Geschichte der Lichtsymbolik im Altertum," *Philologus*, 97 (1948), pp. 1 ff.

[34] H. Gerstinger, *Die Wiener Genesis* (Vienna, 1931), pp. 172 f.

[35] Cf., e.g., the Chludoff Psalter and other Byzantine psalters with marginal illustrations.

[36] Cf. Hanfmann, p. 101.

[37] G. Millet, *La peinture du moyen âge en Yougoslavie*, A. Frolow, ed., II (Paris, 1957), pls. 19–21; 27, 2; 47.

[38] Cf. Mesarites on the figure of Christ in the Raising of Lazarus in the Church of the Holy Apostles (Downey, *op. cit.*, pp. 880, 907).

[39] . . . Hanfmann selection, pp. 93–4 (p. 86 in original article).

[40] See *supra*, p. 174. For the pose and its Hellenistic antecedents, see Hanfmann selection, p. 101.

[41] *Ibid.*, p. 91.

[42] A. Goldschmidt and K. Weitzmann, *Die byzantinischen Elfenbeinskulpturen*, I: *Die Kästen* (Berlin, 1930), pp. 13 ff.

12. THE ELEVENTH CENTURY AND THE ROMANESQUE CHURCH

Henri Focillon

INTRODUCTION

Henri Focillon's life with art began in childhood: his father, Victor Focillon, was an engraver and a friend of such artists as Monet and Rodin. In the method of Henri Focillon there is always the recurring motif of the relation between style and technique which could find no better evocation than his reference to the tools in his father's studio as being "warm with humanity and bright with use." The best introduction to his method is probably his *Vie des Formes*, published in 1934, and available in English translation as *The Life of Forms in Art*, issued shortly before his death in 1943. In this work he defines his concept of the evolution of styles, expressed in a format analogous to organic growth and implying some reproductive potentiality within the forms themselves. The application of this method—and the realization of its flexibility—is apparent in *The Art of the West in the Middle Ages*, in which the development of the forms of art takes place in a medium compounded of the inheritance of past traditions, the influences of the contemporary moment, and the experimental thrust into the future. For another schema treating the evolution of style, one should read George Kubler, *The Shape of Time* (1962).

Other readings are Arthur Kingsley Porter, *Medieval Architecture*, 2 Vols. (1912), now available in a reprint (1966); by the same author, *Romanesque Sculpture of the Pilgrimage Roads*, 10 Vols. (1923), also available in a 1966 reprint; K. J. Conant, *Carolingian and Romanesque Architecture 800–1200* (1959); George H. Crichton, *Romanesque Sculpture* in Italy (1954); Corrado Ricci, *Romanesque Architecture in Italy* (1925); E. W. Anthony, *Romanesque Frescoes* (1951); Carl Nordenfalk, *Romanesque Painting* (1958), with numerous color plates; and Denis Grivot and George Zarnecki, *Gislebertus, Sculptor of Autun* (1961).

The selections that follow are reprinted from Henri Focillon, *The Art of the West in the Middle Ages,* I, edited and revised by Jean Bony, translated by Donald King (1963). Published by Phaidon Press, Ltd., London, New York. Footnotes marked with an asterisk indicate additions by Jean Bony.

THE GREAT EXPERIMENTS: THE ELEVENTH CENTURY

The Middle Ages were from the first involved in a clash of traditions. In one aspect, the history of the period may be envisaged as a long-drawn effort by the West to resolve the conflict of forces resulting from the barbarian invasions. Two kinds of humanity were at grips, of which one had advanced through a long and glorious era of civilization, while the other had remained attached to the most primitive systems of social and cultural life. One built cities of stone, the other temporary shelters. One regarded architecture as an element of prime importance in man's activity, and, in artistic representation, respected the appearances of life, while for the other art was ornament and consisted in abstract composition. Nor was this the only conflict. The axis of the Mediterranean world had long been shifting, and this movement was now accelerated and stabilized by a combination of new factors—the peace of the Church (the official recognition of an Oriental religion), the importance of Constantinian Jerusalem, the foundation of the Eastern Empire, the decline of Rome as against metropolitan Byzantium and the still prosperous Hellenistic cities, the prestige of the great Sassanian empire, and the submergence of the West beneath the barbarian hordes. Asiatics were the missionaries of Christianity, especially to the Gauls. Egypt gave birth to monasticism, which built its first monasteries and churches there and was then diffused abroad. In Syria, Anatolia and Transcaucasia, where Christianity was recognized from the third century, an intense religious life, strongly colored by local genius, led to the erection of great numbers of buildings, very various in plan and structure, in which the ancient forms of Mesopotamia and Iran were adapted to Hellenistic techniques. The barbarians, too, played their part in the Orientalization of Europe, for their art was not only a repository of those less evolved Oriental motifs such as had long been incorporated in the La Tène style, but it was also in contact with, and transmitted,

191

elements of remoter origin, from beyond the steppes. The advance of Islam to the Pyrenees, the exodus of Syrian monks during the iconoclastic disputes, the travels of merchants and pilgrims, introduced a succession of new factors. Thus the Middle Ages were from the first confronted with the problem, Orient or Rome?—and with this was indissolubly linked the further problem, Mediterranean or barbarian culture? The history of medieval art recounts the manner in which the West, after a period of dependence on Mediterranean, Oriental and barbarian forms, established a judicious equilibrium, created its own forms, its architecture, its humanism, and defined its own specific culture.

The period following the invasions, during which the new political groupings were consolidated, shows not so much a sudden radical breach with the antique tradition, as a kind of shifting of values.[1] The towns continued to shelter within their walls, under the tutelage of the Bishops, institutions inherited from the Empire, and in some districts these survived for long periods. But the tone of civilization ceased to be urban; it absorbed rustic habits and primitive social formulae. Henceforward objects meant more than buildings, and symbols were more interesting than human figures. The newcomers, even those who had been clients of Rome and associates of her fortunes, retained their seminomadic ways, their mistrust of towns, and their taste for ornament and luxuriant, symmetrical, linear composition. On the rural estates, their life differed little from that of their forebears; they imposed new laws of property, a novel juridical system, and their own conception of the relationship of man with man. In the towns themselves, the decay of the crafts, and the shrinking of wealth and of trade, all contributed to a kind of narrowing of the patterns of life and of the scope of mental activity. By the time a conditional security had been restored, the tone of historical life was changed for centuries to come. The Roman buildings still stood; but often they had served as quarries when stone was needed for the ramparts, and it was long before they ceased to be despoiled for their columns for the adornment of Christian basilicas.[2] A few workshops of funerary sculptors remained faithful to the traditions of the Italian marble-workers, for all the arts this is the slowest to renew itself and lives longest on its conventions and formulae. Princes were not antagonistic to the conservation of antique culture, some indeed prided themselves upon it, but they were concerned only with its external trappings, and their best-meant efforts to direct the life of the spirit remained unfruitful, the caprices of amateurs.

It is by no means certain that the invasions merely accelerated an already inevitable decline. It is true that antique art, in most of its official manifestations under the late empire, seems watered-down by the academism of copyists, but it still retained its capacity for self-renewal under the influence of regional traditions. This is apparent in Gaul, in the vitality of the popular genius as shown in the best of the small-scale sculpture—rightly considered to be a contributory factor in the genesis of medieval art.[3] Moreover, the architecture, sculpture and metalwork of imperial times was not unsympathetic to those influences, which, from the sixth century, came to dominate the West; indeed Rome had had a taste for them, and ever since the time of her first expansion into the Hellenistic cultural area had remained in close touch with the Orient; perhaps, even before she went to school with Greece, some older, remoter impressions had come to her by way of Etruria. In later times Asiatic traders had brought to her coasts and provinces a special kind of Christianity, a mixed bag of merchandise, masterpieces of cunning metalwork, and a number of decorative motifs which are found alike on the lintels of Syrian basilicas and the tombs of Merovingian hypogea. But Roman art powerfully consolidated all these exotic contributions into its own substance, its own development, even as it were into the very mortar of its masonry, and from these disparate factors constituted the luxuriant and massive unity of its mighty buildings.

When one considers the art of the Goths in Italy, that of the Visigoths in Spain, or that of the Franks in Gaul, they seem all to be put together from the same elements and display more or less identical characteristics. Fragmentary survivals or hard desiccated copies of antique art rub shoulders with Eastern motifs and with the ornamental vocabulary of the nomads, which was now sometimes transcribed into stone for purposes of monumental decoration. Upon these uneasy juxtapositions, a mosaic rather than a style, Byzantine stereotypes became encrusted. Architecture, known to us largely from texts, is hard to visualize. If the chroniclers may be believed, it was audacious and brilliant; but the crypts of Jouarre and Grenoble display mean technique and an unambitious program. Clearly the keynote of the period is not to be found here. The decadence of the arts of stone is however counterbalanced by a

wonderful development of the arts of ornament. The abolition or
schematic reduction of the human figure coincides with a new skill
and fertility in abstract design. This is the vital factor. It is this
which characterizes the true interregnum between the two kinds
of humanism. An encyphered conception of the universe, rejecting
the human figure as inessential or even repugnant, replaces a plastic
vision which had been entirely dominated by man and which had
based itself on the realism and actuality of its images. When we
come to examine the origins of Romanesque sculpture, we shall see
the parts played by the East, by the North, and by prehistoric
cultures in the creation of this geometrical absolutism, its significance for Islam, and the manner in which the West reintegrated
it into the monumental scheme by allying it with living forms. It
must be realized that it was from the first an essentially innovating
element.

Carolingian art was less concerned to change the elements of this
complex than to modify their proportions. The restoration of the
Western Empire, the work of learned clerks, who, to recompense
the signal services rendered to Christianity by a great family, seized
the opportunity of reviving a title and a formula associated in their
minds with so much recollected splendor, naturally inclined the
minds of men to consult the examples of ancient Rome and to
emulate Byzantium. On the basis of traditions already several
centuries old and within the framework of a composite Oriental-
barbarous style, the art of the period is characterized by two dominant factors—a return to monumentality and a renaissance of the
human figure. The former affected not only architecture, but also
the development of the great cycles of history-painting in the
palaces of the Rhine and the Moselle, and even, as was demonstrated
recently, the mode of setting cabochon gemstones, which in other
respects departed little from the traditional system.[4] As for the
human figure, it did not—for reasons which will appear—assert itself
in stone-sculpture. We have only insecure evidence of the way it
was handled by the bronze-founders of the Aix workshops, but it
abounds in the manuscripts, where, in certain presentation-minia-
tures, it is treated with the amplitude of monumental painting.
Meantime, an ancient Celtic culture was maintaining and developing figure-art in quite another direction. From the seventh to the
tenth century, the Irish manuscripts bring before us in their strange
cypher a mysterious dream and a disconcerting logic which envelop

man, beast and plant in the convolutions of their interlace—a kind of chaos preceding genesis.[5] Palmette-man, interlace-man and spiral-man confront the togaed evangelist and the count in ceremonial chlamys. They are opposing worlds, but they tend to interpenetrate. For a time Carolingian art resuscitated humanistic programs, setting the human figure once again in the field of the painted page, and transporting an equestrian emperor from the Eternal City to stand before the palatine chapel. But it did not prepare or secure the future of medieval art by such means; rather would it have condemned it to the monotonous repetition of exhausted themes. A greater promise lay in contact with that spirit of ornamental fantasy wherein the human figure seems bound and paralyzed but where in fact it is extending the range of its experiences and, as it were, testing its capacity for the astonishing diversity of life.

. . . Carolingian architecture can show us buildings which are vaulted throughout—Aix and Germigny—as well as the vaulted ground storeys of the monumental porches. These latter are massive blocks, their upper storeys often of complex elevation, which comprise both western entrance and a chapel dedicated to the cult of the Savior or some saint. Highly individual creations, they foreshadow the vast Romanesque porches and, in their tower development, the future of the harmonic façade.

It might appear that the components of Romanesque art were already present in this period, and that the beginnings of that art must therefore be put back beyond the eleventh century to the advent of the Carolingian architects. Yet, however important the groundwork which they laid, however interesting their experiments and however promising their results, they left untouched the problem of vaulting in stone the great basilican naves, together with the associated problems of abutment and direct lighting. These questions, on the other hand, were the major preoccupation of Romanesque research from the eleventh century onwards. There is moreover a fundamental distinction to be made between Romanesque and Carolingian art, for the latter did not incorporate its monumental decoration in the substance of the stone, but continued to apply a veneer of ornament—mosaic or painting—or employed substitute materials, especially plaster. The various techniques still led separate existences and were not yet dominated and molded by a unified architectural thought. It cannot be said that the sculptors of the period lacked the capacity for figure work—the skill displayed in great numbers of lovely ivories proves the contrary—but the taste for monumental stone sculpture was still dormant in the West, though certain Asiatic Christian communities were already creating, especially in the Transcaucasian churches, important figures and grand compositions.[6] A pictorially biassed Middle Age, which hid the stone beneath a glittering surface decoration, hung plaster reliefs like precious ex-votos on the line of the imposts, or ran their soft and delicate lacework along the string-courses and into the window-embrasures, was the immediate predecessor of a Middle Age which expressed itself completely in stone, and whose sculpture and painting also were architecturally conceived.

It must, however, be acknowledged that the Carolingian ivory carvers, whose works are so various in composition, sentiment and handling, occasionally foreshadowed and perhaps pointed the way to certain decisive experiences of Romanesque monumental sculpture. They do at any rate display two principles which, when applied to monumental sculpture, endowed it with precision and originality—the principle of close adaptation of the design to its frame, and that of ornamental figure composition. On a comb from Cologne, pierced with rosettes and decorated on the reverse with foliage scrolls, figures are arranged and twisted so as to respect and even emphasize the very irregular outline and peculiar form of the field in which they are inscribed. Again, the ivory at St. Gall attributed to the famous artist-monk Tuotilo[7] has, in the upper part of a Crucifixion composition, figures of angels arranged precisely in the manner of ornamental foliage stems, a decorative conformation which recurs in its original guise in the band of foliage which runs along the top edge of the plaque. What we see here is no coincidence, but a conscious stylistic procedure. . . .

THE ROMANESQUE CHURCH

I

Even the most homogeneous style is defined only by the sequence of its development. As early as the eleventh century, Romanesque architecture had taken on a characteristic form marked by the systematic use of wall-arcades and flat pilasters, but it was simultaneously elaborating, in the course of a long series of experiments, the classic Romanesque forms whose apogee fell in the first third of the twelfth century. Historically significant monuments, ambitious programs, a single conception individually expressed by various regional groups and a beautiful and abundant sculpture dominated by the laws of the architecture—these were the main features of this superb moment of equilibrium, when images of God and of man, wrought from the building stone of the churches, mingled with the strangest fantasies of the human mind. The dreams of the most ancient East were reanimated, and embodied once more in figure-compositions; but the primacy of architecture imposed on them a logic, a profound harmony, which were the authentic expression of the West. This equilibrium, once achieved, was not overthrown by a sudden onset or insidious infiltration of new forms. Its stable principles and balanced clarity had emerged out of the flexible and many-sided researches of the experimental period, and they eventually lapsed again into a period of decline, marked by disorganization, ossification, and forgetfulness of the inherent laws of the style. We shall see that Romanesque art had its Baroque phase—using the word not in the limited sense of the historical period which followed the Renaissance, but as a designation for a state of mind whose recurrent manifestations appear in the lifetime of every style. It may be characterized on the one hand by academic dryness and the mechanical repetition of prototypes or, on the other, by forgetfulness of proper functions, profusion of ornament, and extravagant experiments, which call in question the value of acquired experience and the authority of the fundamental stylistic laws. But these destructive variations, these signs of weariness, incomprehension and forgetfulness, are in some sense a confirmation *a posteriori* (one might say, by *reductio ad absurdum*) of the value of the principles which they distort and deny. They are part of and they demonstrate the vitality of a style. If we were to content ourselves with a mere enumeration of the characteristics of Romanesque architecture and sculpture as if they were invariable data, neglecting the fact that they were in constant development from the late tenth to the early thirteenth century and beyond, we should be unable to appreciate all their aspects, which would often seem contradictory, and we should fail to perceive how those contradictions were harmonized by the hidden links which were forged between them by the evolution of the thought and life of the time.

In the monuments of the last third of the eleventh century and the first third of the twelfth, the Romanesque style is seen at the height of its powers. It was no mere passive expression of its place and time. Romanesque man comprehended himself through Romanesque art. The spirit of a great system of architectural thought was the keynote to which poetry, science, philosophy and language were attuned. Then, as never before, the spirit of form determined the form of the spirit. This stylistic maturity coincided with a historical maturity, which furthered it by the consistency of its aims, the boldness of its policies, the abundance of its resources and the moral force of its institutions, particularly those of urbanism and monasticism. Both the latter are forceful illustrations of the twofold character of the Middle Ages, at once sedentary and nomadic, local and European. Each town acted as a focus and magnet of its surrounding countryside, distilled its qualities, and concentrated in itself the peculiar local traditions and experiences. But at the same time the towns were all linked together by trade, and by the identity of their statutes, brought about by copying each other's charters—a fact of which we shall find remarkable confirmation in the Gothic period and which was not without influence, for example, on Burgundian art. Monasticism favored the interpenetration of localities to an even greater extent. By filiation, it propagated itself over enormous distances, and the monasteries were not only the refuge of exemplary Christians, detached from the life of their time, nor mere centers of meditation and culture, nor yet—in accordance with the spirit of their first foundation, renewed by the Cistercians—agricultural stations set up near a source of water for the purpose of tilling the virgin soil of desert places. For besides being planned, as they had already been in the Carolingian era, on the scale of towns, complete with schools, industrial and artistic workshops, scribes, blacksmiths and masons, they also intervened powerfully in the temporal destinies of the world, they cast a fine-meshed net over all Christendom, they were an organizing force and a focus of action. We should have a very inadequate understanding of the history of the early Middle Ages if we failed to take account of the expansion of Irish monarchism. Similarly, in the Romanesque period, the political and moral stature of Cluny was outstanding.[8] It was a monarchy of monks, a monarchy of the spirit, ruled over by the abbot of Cluny, the abbot of abbots, whose moral authority was effective even beyond the organization of which he was head. The greatest of these abbots were both saints and leaders of men. Their community gave the Church several popes, numerous theologians, and a number of those great figures who, like St. Odo and St. Hugh, epitomize, and at the same time transfigure by their virtues, the age in which they live. Cluny, said Émile Mâle, was the greatest phenomenon of the Middle Ages. The modern development of orders vowed to contemplation or charity, and lying rather aside from the main currents of spiritual action (even when one takes into account the revival of institutions more exacting in their demands on the life of the spirit), provide no basis for our understanding of this immense priestly organization and its relations with the kings, emperors and popes, whom it often welcomed and entertained within the walls of its principal house. These great abbots were artists, not after the manner of princes enamored of pomp and architectural splendor, but in a more profound and fundamental way. They loved music so greatly that when they came to decorate their church they caused the capitals of the sanctuary to be carved with figures symbolizing the various modes of plainsong. They loved nobility and dignity of form even as embodied in corruptible flesh, and one of them extolled a predecessor for the perfection of his beauty. These men stand in the foreground of the history of Romanesque art, not indeed as initiators of its morphology and style, for the roots of those lay deeper, but in the capacity of organizers. They it was who chose the sites of its activity, or at least it was they who animated the roads along which stand its most important monuments.

Cluny organized the pilgrimages, and thereby became the moving spirit of that nomadic middle age which rolled in wave after unceasing wave down the roads which led towards Santiago de Compostela and the oratory of San Michele on Monte Gargano.[9] This does not mean—far from it—that Romanesque art is exclusively Cluniac and that its leading features are to be traced back to Cluny itself, nor even that it was strictly dependent on the geography of these far-flung routes. The significance of the pilgrimage roads lay in the fact that they traversed various regions, beckoning always towards foreign horizons and intermingling the sedentary and the travelling populace; while acting as channels for the propagation of artistic types, they also attracted to themselves the forces and traditions of the localities through which they passed and these tended both to swell and to modify the character of the waves of influence. At the stages of the journey they fostered the dissemination of the *chansons de geste*,[10] and in doing so they mingled one aspect of the Middle Ages with another. They magnified local saints into saints venerated throughout the Western world, and by permitting the transmission of images over great distances, they enriched the universal language of iconography. The old Roman roads had been instruments of Roman penetration. The pilgrimage roads had a twofold action. They may have contributed to the unity of Romanesque art, but they also ensured its variety.

II

In embarking on the study of the architecture which took its place in this system it is more than ever necessary that we should bear in mind the basic factors of the art of building.[11] A building is composed of plan, structure, composition of masses, and distribution of effects. The architect is simultaneously and to a greater or less degree geometer, engineer, sculptor and painter—geometer in the interpretation of spatial area through the plan, engineer in the solution of the problem of stability, sculptor in the treatment of volumes, and painter in the handling of materials and light. Each type of talent and each phase of a style lays stress on one particular aspect of the art; the perfect harmony is attained only in the great periods. The importance of the plan is primarily sociological, for it is the diagram, the graphic representation, of the program. The proportional relationships are indicative not only of the spirit of the style but also of the practical needs which the building is called upon to serve; the circlet of chapels radiating from the apse is not simply harmonious form but is necessitated by religious practice, while the curving ambulatory is designed to ensure a free flow of movement. For an eye accustomed to the study of architecture and the realization of the plan in space, the plan will suggest much more, and will even indicate the structural solutions. But one must remember that a building is not simply a matter of fitting a suitable elevation on to a pre-arranged plan, and the similarity of two plans does not necessarily and in every case entail the similarity of the composition of masses. Even though the plan is in some sense the abstract basis of these latter, yet they possess their own essential values, especially in a style which lays stress on the beauty of the masses, as does the Romanesque architecture of the twelfth century. They contribute to the stability of the building (here we are considering not a visual harmony, but actual resistance to thrust) and, arranged in order of size and of greater or less projection, they superimpose on the relationships of plane geometry a system of monumental relationships without which there would be no architecture, but only a diagram drawn out, like a flower-bed, on the ground. It is essential, particularly in Romanesque studies, to make the effort of considering a building as a collection of solids and of gauging the relationships between them. This manner of approach is doubly sound, since in Western architecture, at least in the period under discussion, the exterior masses invariably correspond with the internal distribution of parts and their three-dimensional relationships, so that the plan may be deduced from them, though the converse is not true. The truth of this observation may be demonstrated by a single example: a transept which does not project beyond the aisle-walls is hardly apparent on the plan. Finally the silhouette of a building, that most significant of values, results from the composition of masses.

The problems of structure and equilibrium, which are so important in large, complex, lofty, vaulted buildings such as those of the Romanesque period, arise mainly from the use of a stone covering, but this is not necessarily true in every case, since lofty walls surmounted by a wooden roof also require buttressing, though to a lesser extent, and northern and northeastern France, not to mention other areas, can show examples of this type of structure which are completely faithful to the spirit and style of their time in plan, mass and effects. A building is not carved or hollowed out of a monolith, but *constructed*, that is, composed of separate elements, assembled according to rules in which the architect figures as an interpreter of the force of gravity. The Greeks opposed the action of gravity in the vertical direction only. The medieval masters in most cases had to solve a problem involving oblique components and the counteraction of thrust, and, by an admirable process of reasoning, they progressively specialized each member of the structure according to its function, and devised for it a form which was at once the most suitable and the most expressive of its purpose. It is in this respect that their architecture is most truly an art of logical thought, whereas the Greeks, having adopted once for all the straightforward solution of verticals and horizontals, were thereafter interested only in melodic variations of the proportions.

Besides being an interpreter of gravity the architect is also an interpreter of light, by virtue of the calculation and composition of his effects. This question must not be limited to the problems of lighting, though they in themselves are of capital importance, and we shall see how intimately they were linked with the problems of structure and equilibrium, and how their solutions evolved throughout the Middle Ages in step with the structural solutions. But the study of effects is of wider scope. It concerns the relationships of void and solid, of light and dark, and—perhaps most important—of plain and decorated. Again, a building is not an architect's drawing or a photographic print, it is composed of solid matter. It is obvious that this fact has specific and far-reaching effects on every detail of the treatment. It is of fundamental importance for the structure, since the various kinds of material have their own peculiar qualities and requirements, and these determine the functions which they can perform, the types of masonry for which they can be used, and the extent of the program to which they can be applied. Materials, moreover, have texture and color, and with these they make a pleasing and powerful contribution to the life of architecture, which is not intended merely for technical analysis and dissection but for the delight of the eye. They play their part within the system of relationships which we have just outlined, here stressing the solid, the broad luminous surface, the monumental economy of ornament, and there emphasizing the void, the equivocal effect of light and shade, and the profusion of carving; thus, though the vocabulary of forms may be constant, syntax, language and poetry are constantly recreated.

The elements can be isolated intellectually, but it must not be forgotten that they exist together, and that it is their organic interconnection, not their juxtaposition, which makes the building. We already have some idea of the interdependence of plan and structure, plan and masses, masses and equilibrium, and masses and effects. The architect conceives his building synthetically. Even in the first flash of an idea, his thought includes the diversity of the parts. Admittedly, of course, the genius of a school, a locality or a master may concentrate on one particular aspect. There are builders and there are decorators. But a medieval building is a harmony of living forces which mutually penetrate, amplify, restrain, modify and define each other. The interrelationship of the masses, and the various relationships by which the effects are qualified, are transformed from top to bottom, from pavement to rooftree, and in every dimension of the architecture. Each individual member shares in the life of the organism as a whole. And what is true of the Gothic skeleton of arches and ribs is no less so for the massive Romanesque structure of compact vaults and thick walls, as a more detailed examination will show. We are compelled to deal with the elements one by one, but we must never lose sight of the fact that these elements are all functions of each other. And when we analyze the regional varieties of Romanesque architecture, which testify so strikingly to its historical vigor, we shall find that they owe their individuality not so much to what may perhaps be called their superficial features, or to the treatment of details, as to modifications of the interrelationship of parts. In this respect they constitute dialectal varieties comparable with the various romance idioms.

The program of the Romanesque basilicas was that of an enormous reliquary open to all comers. The monastic church of the time served both monks and pilgrims. It sheltered the bodies of the saints and attracted the devotion of the faithful. Renowned relics, the miracles wrought by them, the pious legends which surrounded them, the cult which exalted their virtues, the enhanced value of prayer uttered beside them—all this intense spiritual fervor created the prosperity of the great abbeys, and at once necessitated and made possible the grandeur of their scale. As in the progress of cities, demand created supply. The plan of the pilgrimage churches is as if drawn by the immense throngs which passed through them, by the order of their going and of their standing still, the places where they stopped and the places where they moved onward. Sometimes a great narthex, a survival of the old church of the catechumens, precedes the church, and serves as its vestibule, though large enough, with its central nave, aisles and upper storey, to form a separate church. The church proper has three, and sometimes five, naves. It was thus enabled to impose order on the multitudes within, by cutting parallel furrows in the moving mass. One or two transepts, with oriented chapels opening off them, form two or four projections on the plan, each one so large that it seems an additional church set at right angles to the first. But they did not interrupt the progress of the pilgrim. They provided the throng with auxiliary entrances and exits, and they formed part of that architectural topography of pilgrimage which permitted of uninterrupted circulation within the building, from the west front to the chapels of the apse and from the chapels of the apse back to the west front. Sometimes, as in Saint-Sernin at Toulouse, a continuous aisle surrounds the transept arm, extends along the choir, makes the circuit of the apse, and so returns. The long choir favored the development of ceremony. But it was the east end which, in both plan and elevation, in both the establishment of the program and the treatment of the masses, was the vital part of the church. Here are disposed the chapels which sheltered the relics of the saints, in addition to those which in some cases were preserved in the crypt, as in the martyrium of the primitive basilica. The most frequent arrangement is that in which small apses radiate from the ambulatory, a scheme whose earliest examples we have already noted in the second half of the tenth century; this was the best arrangement from the point of view of circulation. But a whole family of churches preserved the orientation of the apses by disposing chapels of diminishing scale in echelon; and this plan was best from the point of view of presentation, the chapels being parallel to one another and opening directly on to choir and transepts. This scheme is known as the Benedictine or Berry plan, though it is not confined to that province. The finest and most characteristic example is perhaps that of Châteaumeillant. But it was the radiating plan which prevailed, and Romanesque art, which had received it from the Carolingian tradition, bequeathed it in due time to its Gothic successor. . . .

ROMANESQUE DECORATION

I

. . . At first sight how remote from us [Romanesque sculpture] seems! Is it possible that this is ours—this strange vision, entwined so mysteriously with the stone and inscribing the walls of the buildings with fancies which are often indecipherable, like the characters of a lost language? Can it be that our conception of man, life and the world is divided by such an abyss from that of our forebears? In Gothic sculpture we recognize ourselves, we find our own kind of humanity; it remains our contemporary, almost our neighbor—much more so than Renaissance sculpture, which was based upon the resuscitation of an earlier age for which we can no longer feel more than an intellectual sympathy and admiration. The endless ranks of images which fill the Gothic cathedrals evoke in us a kind of spiritual kinship, which we freely acknowledge; in many ways even, they are like a vivid recollection of our past life, our own past, and that of our towns, our suburbs and our country-side. We can name the animals and the plants, and the saints with their workingmen's faces who stand in the doorways are of the same race as our own fathers. But wherever we turn, the images of Romanesque art disconcert us by their composition and their senti-ment. It is an art abundant in monsters, visions, and enigmatic symbols. It seems at first sight much older than the age which it so faithfully expresses and the architecture to which it so exactly conforms.

Let us study it first as a system of signs before we attempt to interpret it as a system of forms. Every art is language, in two ways—once by its choice of subjects, once by its treatment of them. Iconography floodlights the life of the spirit. It is not a collection of symbols, a vocabulary, or a key; the novelty of M. Mâle's studies[12] consists in the widening of its horizons and the deepening of its perspectives, both historical and moral, to form a broad and detailed panorama of the spiritual life of the past. Romanesque iconography was epic. It bestowed super-human proportions on God-made-man and man-in-the-image-of-God; sometimes even it gave them an appearance divorced from humanity. It surrounded them with a cortège of monsters which entwine them in their coils. To expound and present them to the people it chose, as a terrible warning, the most extraordinary page of the whole Bible. The story of the Last Days, foretold in words of fire by an enthusiast filled with the afflatus of the Jewish Bible, inspired it with majestic terror. The seer roused the visionaries. The faithful entering the church were not welcomed by the evangelic Christ of the thirteenth-century *trumeau*, but compelled to file beneath the tympanum of the Last Judgment as if they themselves were about to hear their sentence from the mouth of the inflexible Judge. At La Lande de Cubzac, the sword of the Word flashes from the lips of the Apocalyptic Christ, who stands beside the symbolic candelabrum, holding in his hand the book sealed with seven seals. In a less strange guise, alone or flanked by two angels who seem to fan the flames of the glory which surrounds Him, it is this same God of the Apocalypse who figures on the old Aragonese tympana, at Perrecy-les-Forges in Burgundy and Mauriac in Auvergne, and who finally, in the second half of the twelfth century, appears again and again in monotonous profusion, accompanied by the tetramorph of Evangelists, above the portals of northern France. But it was particularly in the tympana of Languedoc, in the first half of the century, that the theme was developed with the full amplitude of the epic. Christ the Judge, whose kingdom is founded on the destruction of the universe and the punishment of sinners, emerges from the mystery of the end of time like an apparition suddenly risen before the eyes of His terror-stricken followers. Surrounded by convulsive shapes, He is accompanied by the twenty-four Elders carrying lamps and viols. At Beaulieu there appears behind Him the cross of His sacrifice, and of the redemption of mankind. Even when, as at Vézelay, He is the Christ of Pentecost, charging the Apostles with their mission,[13] He is still a terrible God. The Oriental Potentate of Moissac is Lord of a world from which the Good Shepherd of the catacombs, the Christ of Psamathia, and all those figures of Hellenistic Christianity who still combined divinity with youth and harmonious beauty have passed away. One might believe that the Romanesque Apocalypse trembled still with millenarian terrors, passed on by Beatus' illustrated commentary, which served as its guide through this Divine Comedy in stone. There is a breath of the East in these strange figures, this fearful conception of the Master of Days. Yet the same epic spirit, the same legendary disproportions, the same superhuman quality, are characteristic of the tales of knightly prowess created, at the same time and often at the same places, out of the recollection and imagination of the peoples of the West. The God of the sculptors and the heroes of the poets are ornaments of the same horizon of thought: the visionary theology of Scotus Eriugena, if it did not directly inspire the iconography, helps us at least to understand its intellectual climate. The unity of the period is not founded on a congeries of completely heterogeneous borrowings; unfamiliar elements were welcomed because they responded to a need, and we shall see how they were subsequently elaborated.

The stories of the Gospels and the lives of the saints, and still more the representation of the world, are touched with the same strangeness, and many details betray the remoteness of their origin. Sir Arthur Evans has recently shown that the theme of the Adoration of the Kings goes back to the remotest antiquity,[14] and it should be observed that already on Sumerian monuments it is accompanied by the motif of the guiding star. In Syria, Mesopotamia, Transcaucasia and Egypt the East Christian communities were the heirs of an iconographical tradition built up over thousands of years; they in turn devised new elements and established stereotypes which fixed the images for the future. The three cycles of Nativity, Passion, and Parables, the essential chapters of the iconography of the Gospels, are full of Oriental features, whose history and diffusion can be followed from the throne of Maximian and the ampullae of Monza down to Romanesque times. The Byzantine drama *Christos Paskon*,[15] whose influence is vouched for by numerous manuscripts, spread the knowledge of the *mise en scéne* of the Resurrection and the other episodes centered on the Tomb. The prophets of the Coming of Christ were born of the Biblical East and insinuated themselves into still older Oriental forms. Daniel standing between the lions who lick his feet is Gilgamesh, the master of animals in Assyrian art. An Oriental silk at Saint-Maurice d'Agaune in Valais, the national sanctuary of the Burgundians, shows the manner in which these themes were able in the early Middle Ages to penetrate the West and to become invested with a Christian significance, before they made their appearance on Romanesque capitals. Thus we find the Biblical and Gospel figures intimately linked with the oldest images of Asia,[16] and even when they are of more recent origin, they have very often been composed and fixed in the East. Hence the indisputably exotic tonality in the choice and treatment of subjects.

This quality of Romanesque iconography strikes us still more forcibly when we consider the number and the strangeness of the monsters which inhabit it. Man himself loses his identity and, obedient to the law of metamorphosis by which this universe is constantly created, broken down and recomposed, he also assumes a monstrous guise. Even when probability is respected, the animal life is of bewildering variety. The bestiary of the steppes, which had been diffused by the invasions, and the Asiatic fauna which had filled Visigothic manuscripts such as the Sacramentary of Gellone and now reappeared, often in copies after Arabic ivories, introduced into the churches the menagerie, the "paradise" of the Oriental monarch. But, seized by that hidden power which remolded living creatures to its own needs, and conferred on them a multiple existence more mobile and passionate than life itself, the animals are subdivided, reunited, acquire two heads on one body or two bodies for one head, gripe one another, devour one another, and are again reborn, all in an indecipherable tumultuous *mêlée*. What name can we give, what meaning assign to these fancies, which seem to emanate from the caprice or delirium of a solitary visionary and which yet recur throughout Romanesque art, like the images of some vast collective nightmare? Of what virtues, what sins are they the incarnation? At times we seem on the point of penetrating these symbols, but immediately they flicker away into the monstrous inanity of the compositions.

Such are the general characteristics of this iconography. It is rich in Oriental elements. It is epical and teratological. It gives us the epic of God, the epic of the end of the world, and the epic of chaos. Is there not a singular contradiction between the order of the churches and the tumult of these images, between the rules of an architecture whose strength, stability and logic we have been at pains to demonstrate, and the rules of an iconography between whose transfiguration of God and deformation of His creatures one may scarcely find a middle term, between structures dominated by a conception of plan and masses which is purely Western, and an iconography which derives most of its resources from the East? Only the study of the forms permits us to resolve this apparent contradiction; it will likewise assist us to make a true assessment of influences, and it will also demonstrate the profound harmony of thought between the technique of the Romanesque decorative artist and the intellectual technique of his period.

II

This technique had a twofold character: it was architectural, in that the figures were made to conform to their architectural setting and it was ornamental, in that the figures were drawn and composed in accordance with ornamental schemes. In our brief study of the experiments carried out in the course of the eleventh century we have already caught a glimpse of some of the earliest applications of these principles and of the manner in which they tended—in opposition to the academic forms of antique art and in alliance with the abstract repertory which had become diffused through Europe—to substitute for the verisimilitude of the images their just adaptation to a surrounding frame, and to replace the harmony and proportions of life by the harmony and proportions of an abstract system. The forms of architecture and the forms of life being fixed, what compromise could be established between them? Romanesque architecture did not offer indifferent fields to the decorator, but fields whose shape and function were clearly defined. The genius of the style lay in its association of sculpture with these functions. By adopting once for all the frieze-system, which had flourished in the eleventh century alongside more adventurous lines of research, it would have renounced its fundamental originality. It might also have allowed sculpture to flow indifferently over the wall-surfaces, and assimilated it to those severe and powerful masses in truly monumental beauty: but sculpture in architecture and for architecture demanded a much stricter economy. Where is it found, in a twelfth-century church? On capitals, tympana and archivolts. True, it did not altogether abandon the friezes and the arcades, but its development depended on the more tyrannical constraint exercised by frames which were ill-adapted to receive the image of life. Yet these frames seized upon sculpture, bestowed on it a new passion, imposed on it movement, mimicry and drama. To enter the system of the stone, man was forced to bend forward or lean backward, to stretch or contract his limbs, to become a giant or a dwarf. He preserved his identity at the cost of unbalance and deformation; he remained man, but a man of plastic material, obedient—not to the caprice of an ironical idea—but to the exigencies of a system which comprehended the entire structure.

Romanesque art was to make the church "speak"; space had to be found for an abundant iconography, without disturbing the architectural masses and their functions. It was necessary to set on top of the columns, at the same time avoiding the appearance of meagerness and insignificance, not one or two figures—Christ in Majesty, St. Anne and St. Elizabeth, Adam and Eve—which could easily be disposed axially or confronted, but the more numerous actors of the Nativity, the Flight into Egypt or the Last Supper. We must remember that it was in the Corinthian capital that human figures first began to be inserted; they were abducted from the charms of continuous narrative, the storyteller's dispersal of effects, and wedded to architecture, grouped in a colleret of figures or assigned the role of atlantes. In the course of this treatment the living organism was twisted out of shape and out of proportion, but it gained thereby an unexpected eloquence. Bound by every limb to the block of stone, and bound by the continuity of the movement to its companions, which are a prolongation and multiplication of itself, it gave rise to compact systems from which the removal of a single element would entail the ruin of the massive unity of the whole. The loose narrative of the frieze-style was succeeded by the complex strength of drama, with its concentrated impact, and its mimicry accentuated by the deformation of the actors. This architectural conformity did not operate only within the framework of the Corinthian capital. The cushion capital also, when it accepted figure decoration, submitted it to the same discipline. So too, did the capital formed like a truncated and inverted pyramid; and when the capitals of conjoined or adjacent columns were adorned with a single composition, the bridging of the gap between the two masses produced some unexpected but logical applications of the same principle.

A similar problem, but with rather different data, was set by the decorations of the archivolts. How could the image of man, and, in a more general sense, the image of life, be accommodated within the arch-moldings which curve around the semi-circular tympanum? . . . The decoration of the moldings is sometimes disposed radially, while at other times it follows the curve of the arch. In the former case, each voussoir is treated as a unit and closely contains the figure or ornament which it receives—bearers of offerings following one another in procession up to the keystone and down again on the other side, horses' heads, and ornamental frets worked in the stone as in ivory or ironwork. In the latter case, the figure occupies several voussoirs, bending with the arch; a body may cross the keystone, or the heads of two symmetrical bodies may be confronted there; the living creature becomes an architectural curve and is identified with the molding itself. The whole of southwestern France is rich in these surprising configurations. . . . Human figures sometimes try to escape to some extent from this narrow bondage. Instead of the radial or circumferential position, they take up a tangential one, forming with the curve of the arch an angle which hardly ever varies. The elongated bodies stand erect or bend over within the arch, their bellies slightly prominent, and punctuated by a spot of shadow between the thighs. . . .

The composition of a tympanum is not determined by a vague symmetry. Its elements must be both deployed and concentrated. Its lower and wider part extends to very nearly the same length as the lintel on which its rests. The upper segment narrows rapidly. The two parts are held together by the radii of the arch. A fan-shaped composition would seem to be the most favorable and harmonious solution, but the Romanesque sculptors by no means restricted themselves to that alone. Sometimes they made it more complex by the insertion of a triangular pediment, which is not outlined by projecting moldings, but is visible in the lines of heads which rise toward the central axis (and emphasized, as at Vézelay, by the fiery rays emanating from the hands of Christ), or may be suggested, in less elaborate compositions, by the movement of the mandorla-carrying angels as they bow down before the glory of God. Sometimes they subdivided it so as to obtain, with the help of some curvilinear triangles, a collection of rectangular frames, as at Cahors, and Carennac. Sometimes the composition blossoms like a flower or a palmette, with living figures forming the lobes. It was the special function of the monsters to contort themselves to suit these various schemes, but man also conformed. In accordance with a kind of morphological perspective, which, though equivalent with hierarchic perspective, yet precedes it in the structural and logical order, and is more insistent in its demands, the witnesses and actors of these impressive scenes, the attendants of the throne of heaven, increase in scale in proportion to their nearness to the Deity, who alone occupies the center and towers up to the full height of the tympanum.

. . . Finally, we may mention a class of rectangular panels, decorating *trumeaux* and doorjambs, which reveal to us one of the most curious aspects of this technique. The principle of exact conformity to the frame, strictly applied, results (there are many examples) in creatures of absolutely geometrical shape—the circle-men, like the delightful acrobat on the keystone of the archivolt at Vézelay, above the Zodiac, the lozenge-men, and the rectangle-men. But this last shape, once defined, could never satisfy the manifold demands of the iconography, which required other heroes than these massive witnesses, and especially they were unfitted to share in that restless movement with which Romanesque art is filled. Hence the figure conterminous with its frame was displaced by the figure which touched its frame at the greatest possible number of points. With elbow, shoulder, knee, and heel the body, whose parts are disposed on multiple axes, makes contact with the limits of the enclosing field, and thus describes a whole series of triangles. In this way there was produced a family of figures which, even in their immobility, enliven the firm and ponderous masses of Romanesque architecture with ceaseless movement; this sculpture, though dominated by the laws of a massive equilibrium, presents itself in the guise of a series of experimental studies in motion. . . . To a superficial observer this interpretation might seem a product of vain ingenuity, and this geometric grid a device to support a preconceived system. But the album of Villard de Honnecourt[17] provides, *a posteriori*, a brilliant confirmation. This Picard master-mason, whose notebook testifies to an insatiable curiosity, fed by wide experience, and foreign travel, resurrected some aspects of the "lost art," whose rules had been forgotten by his contemporaries and of which, after him, there seems to be no trace. By insisting on the interest of what he calls the "art de jométrie" and by divulging the secret of the triangulation of figures, he confirms the historical importance, the authenticity, and the systematic character of the processes which we have analyzed.

Architectural conformity and the use of geometric schemes, even if they are the fundamental characteristics of Romanesque technique, do not in themselves account for all its aspects. This essentially architectural sculpture was devised for particular positions and for frames which determined its arrangement and movement; but it is also ornamental—it established or rather modeled its image of life in accordance with the forms of ornament. The man, the beast and the monster are not only volute, medallion, molding, wall-mass, or function, they are not assembled only in accordance with the broad lines of a geometric scheme; they are also palmette and foliage-scroll. Recent research,[18] the point of departure for which was provided by the juxtaposition of a design composed of ornament in the pure state, and a figure composition in which its main lines are exactly reproduced, as if the sculptor wished to leave beside his work the key to its understanding, has brought to light the prodigious decorative "underpainting" of Romanesque sculpture. Moreover, if we envisage the ornament not as a static vocabulary or a collection of invariable formulae but as a dialectic or multiple development in which each term may be deduced from its predecessor, we find that the dialectic of the figure sculpture reproduces, in its movement and variety, that of the ornament. Three primary motifs—the foliage-scroll, the heart (with or without a palmette), and the motif formed by setting two foliage-scrolls back to back about a central axis—give rise to a large number of ornamental variations whose forms and interrelationships reappear in many of the figure compositions of Romanesque sculpture. If it were merely a question of explaining in this way the symmetries of confronted and addorsed objects, or the genesis of the monsters with two heads or two bodies, this fact would amount to no more than evidence of a very common and widespread habit, though it would still be noteworthy, since it was abandoned by European art after the twelfth century. But in fact there is a complete system, an immense variety of forms which can only be explained by the dialectic of ornament. An inexhaustible vitality, differing from organic life, and of even greater richness and multiplicity, but as highly organized, arises out of, and owes its diversity to, these abstract devices, and modulates its variations according to their variations. Very ancient motifs, such as the sea-siren with the double tail, were also admitted to this realm of forms, not as alien elements arbitrarily inserted or passive recipients of influence, but because they, too, had originated in an ornamental idea, whose shape and aptitude for life they still preserved, and were ready participants in the play of metamorphoses. In the setting within which this process of transformation operates, it links together all the movements, leaving no single gesture unconnected, and ensures that all the parts interlock and interpenetrate, so that each block of ornament in pictorial guise is like a small separate world, close-knit and compact, a law unto itself. The great complex compositions of the tympana are very often the expanded and diversified, yet quite regular, version of an ornamental motif which runs through the whole, controlling and influencing every detail. The epic of the Last

Day, the Adoration of the Kings, and all the other stories and visions, adorned the stones of the churches with a mysterious flora, with the characters of a hidden language, by which their own poetic content was enhanced. Thus the study of the technique of Romanesque sculpture has revealed to us a poetry and a psychology. The feeling and subtlety of the dialectical process as applied to these forms runs parallel with the dialectic of pure thought. It is not without significance that both church-decoration and the scholasticism of the period were equally dominated by the philosophy of abstraction, and that both groups of purist logicians were given to the spinning of elegant formal patterns. But whereas the dialectician lost himself in a labyrinth of unprofitable composition, the sculptor, in conjunction with the architect, was creating a new world, extending the limits of man's experience, and giving shape and form to his wildest fantasies.

NOTES

[*1] These ideas have been expanded by H. Focillon, *Du moyen-âge germanique au moyen-âge occidental, in Moyen-Age. Survivances et réveils* (Montreal, 1945), pp. 31–53.

[2] At Lyon, for instance, the columns of the Temple of Augustus were utilized for Saint-Martin d'Ainay. Similarly in the crypts (Jouarre, Grenoble) and baptisteries (Poitiers, Riez, Le Puy, etc.). See C. Enlart, *Manuel*, 2nd edition, I, p. 414, note 1, and p. 145.

[3] L. Bréhier, *L'art en France, des invasions barbares à l'époque romane*, p. 9. Examples of indigenous survivals are the pediment-shaped lintels which are common in Auvergnat and Belgian Romanesque, the geometrical motifs of Gallo-Roman mosaics, and, in figure-sculpture, the god with the purse from Lezoux (Musée de Saint-Germain), the mother-goddesses, the god with the hammer, etc.

[4] J. Seligmann, *L'orfèvrerie carolingienne, son évolution*, Institut d'art et d'archéologie de l'Université de Paris, Travaux du groupe d'histoire de l'art, 1928, p. 137.

[5] See L. Westwood, *Miniatures and Ornaments of Anglo-Saxon and Irish Manuscripts* (London, 1868); P. Gilbert, *Facsimiles of the National Manuscripts of Ireland*, 5 vols. (London, 1874–84); H. Focillon, *L'art des sculpteurs romans*, p. 97, 102, 103. [*]See also G. L. Micheli, *L'enluminure du haut Moyen-âge et les influences irlandaises* (Brussels, 1939); F. Henry, *Irish Art in the Early Christian Period* (London, 1940); F. Masai, *Essai sur les origines de la miniature dite irlandaise* (Brussels, 1947), (whose conclusions have not been universally accepted).

[6] See J. Baltrusaitis, *Études sur l'art médiéval en Géorgie et en Arménie* (Paris, 1929). In Georgia, the tympana of Djvari and of Ateni (seventh century), of Ochque (ninth century), and of Koumourdo (946); in Armenia, the stelae of Haritch (fifth to sixth century), the reliefs of Zwarthnotz (seventh century), etc.

⁷ A. Goldschmidt, *Die Elfenbeinskulpturen aus der Zeit der karolingischen und sächsischen Kaiser* (Berlin, 1914 etc.), 1, 163. °See E. de Wald, *Notes on the Tuotilo Ivories in Saint-Gall*, Art Bulletin, 1933, pp. 202 ff.

⁸ E. Mâle, *L'art français et l'art allemand du moyen âge*, pp. 93–4. Gregory VII, Urban II and Paschal II had been Cluniac monks. On the constitution of Cluny see V. Mortet, *Note sur la date de rédaction des Coutumes de Farfa* (Mâcon, 1911). °More recently: G. de Valous, *Le monachisme clunisien des origines au XVe siècle* (Liguge and Paris, 1936); J. Evans, *The Romanesque Architecture of the Order of Cluny* (Cambridge, 1938), and *Cluniac Art of the Romanesque Period* (Cambridge, 1950); to which must be added: Société des amis de Cluny, C. Oursel, ed., *A Cluny, Congrès scientifique . . . , 9–11 juillet* 1949 (Dijon, 1950).

⁹ The *Book of St. James*, a fine copy of which is preserved in the chapter-library at Compostela, was written to assist pilgrims, probably by the monks of Cluny, at some date after 1139. See J. Bédier, *Légendes épiques*, III, p. 75; E. Mâle, *L'art religieux du XIIe siècle en France*, p. 291 and notes 3 and 4. The fourth book of the Compostela Codex was published by Père Fita, Paris, 1882. In addition, see Lavergne, *Les chemins de Saint-Jacques en Gascogne* (Bordeaux 1887) Dufourcet, *Les voies romaines et les chemins de Saint-Jacques*, Congrès archéologique de Dax et Bayonne, 1888; Abbé Daux, *Le pèlerinage de Saint-Jacques de Compostelle* (*Paris* 1898), cited by Mâle, *op. cit.*, p. 289, note, and Ginot, *Les chemins de Saint-Jacques en Poitou* (Poitiers, 1912). The part played by the pilgrimage roads in the history of architecture was first studied by the Abbé Bouillet, the historian of Conques and Sainte-Foy, in Mémoires de la Société des Antiquaires de France, 1892, p. 117. The Via Tolosana linked Provence with Languedoc, and leaving Arles, continued by way of Saint-Gilles du Gard, Toulouse, and the Somport pass. The stages of the Auvergne route were Le Puy, Congues, Moissac. A third route connected Burgundy and Aquitaine, from Vézelay to Saint-Léonard and Perigueux. The fourth and last, leaving Tours, traversed Poitou and Saintonge, and passed by way of Bordeaux to join the two preceding routes at Roncevaux, where they crossed the Pyrenees. Each route was an unbroken chain of sanctuaries. The pilgrimage road from France into Italy, crossing the alps by the Great St. Bernard or Mont Cenis passes, joined the Emilian Way via Modena, then the Cassian Way at Arezzo, reaching Rome by way of Viterbo. Influences travelled back and forth along the roads of St. Michael just as they did along those of St. James. On the relationship between Sant' Antimo in Tuscany and Conques, see J. Vallery-Radot. *Églises romanes,* p. 178, and on that between San Michele of Clusa and Le Puy, id., *ibid.*, pp. 176, 177, and the study by E. de Dienne, Congrès archéologique de Puy, 1904. °The most recent editions of the Guide for the Pilgrims of St. James are by J. Vieillard (Mâcon, 1938), and by W. M. Whitehill (Santiago, 1944). See also P. David, *Études sur le livre de Saint-Jacques*, Bulletin des Études Portugaises, Vols. 10–12, 1946–1948.

¹⁰ It is well known that the *chansons de geste*, according to Gaston Paris, are the ultimate fruit of centuries of composition whereas for J. Bédier, *Les légendes épiques*, 2nd ed. (Paris, 1914–21), they arose from the pilgrimages themselves. Note also the observations of G. Cohen, *La civilisation occidentale au moyen âge*, p. 211, where he indicates on the one hand the part played in the poems by geography and the northern abbeys, and on the other the continuity of poetic

tradition attested by a ninth-century text such as the *Chanson de Saint-Faron de Meaux.*

[°11] H. Focillon has expressed the same views in *Vie des formes* (Paris, 1934), translated as *The Life of Forms in Art* (New Haven, 1942, and New York, 1948).

[12] *L'art religieux du XIIe siècle en France* (Paris, 1924), chaps. I, IV.

[°13] On the iconographic meaning of the Vézelay tympanum, see A. Katzenellenbogen, *The Central Tympanum at Vézelay,* Art Bulletin, 1944, pp. 141–151.

[°14] A. J. Evans, *The Earlier Religion of Greece in the Light of Cretan Discoveries* (London, 1931).

[15] See V. Cottas, *Le théâtre à Byzance* (Paris, 1931), and *Le drame Christos Paskon* (Paris, 1931).

[°16] See J. Baltrusaitis, *Art sumérien, art roman* (Paris, 1934).

[17] Bibliothèque Nationale, ms. fr. 19, 093. First published by Lassus and Darcel (1858), then by H. Omont in the series of phototype albums issued by the department of manuscripts, and most recently by Hans R. Hahnloser (Vienna, 1935).

[18] J. Baltrusaitis, *La stylistique ornementale dans la sculpture romane* (Paris, 1931), chap. 5, VII, p. 273, L'animal (genèse des monstres); VIII, p. 301, Le personnage. The method followed in this remarkable book has revolutionized the subject.

13. THE ORIGINS OF THE BAY SYSTEM

Walter Horn

INTRODUCTION

This selection is based on a paper presented by Walter Horn at the 1958 meeting of the Society of Architectural Historians in Washington. Here Professor Horn picks up Strzygowski's intuition that the origins of the bay system in medieval architecture lay in the example of wood construction and supports his thesis with convincing evidence reaching as far back as the Iron Age. This article is a fine example of the disciplined weaving together of documentary and archaeological data in support of a reexamined idea. Yet, as the reader will note in the last two paragraphs, the writer is careful to point out some alternate possibilities, however strongly he may reason against their validity.

For further reading consult Raymond Richards, *Old Cheshire Churches* (1947); Fred H. Crossley, *Timber Building in England* (1953); J. T. Smith, "Medieval Aisled Halls and Their Derivations," *Archaeological Journal*, CXII (1956); Walter Horn, "Two Timbered Mediaeval Churches of Cheshire: St. James and St. Paul at Marton and St. Oswald at Lower Peover," *The Art Bulletin*, XLIV (1962); Walter Horn, "Great Tithe Barn of Chosley, Berkshire," *Journal of the Society of Architectural Historians*, XXII (1963); Walter Horn and F. W. B. Charles, "Cruck-built Barn of Middle Littleton in Worcestershire, England," *Journal of the Society of Architectural Historians*, XXV (1966).

The selection that follows is reprinted from Walter Horn, "On the Origins of the Mediaeval Bay System," *Journal of the Society of Architectural Historians,* XVII (1958), by permission of the author.

Joseph Strzygowski advanced the theory in 1924 that the medieval bay system had its origins in northern wood construction.[1] This idea was neither accepted nor rejected by architectural historians; it simply failed to be acknowledged, as were so many of the ideas promiscuously conceived and propagated by this ingenious but undisciplined mind. Strzygowski's theory was based upon the assumption that a tradition of bay-divided wooden houses existed in the formative phases of the Romanesque, but at that date he could not point his finger to any bay-divided house that antedated the emergence of the principle of bay division in monumental medieval masonry architecture, because the first such house on the Continent had yet to be excavated. Doubtless there are striking similarities between the intensely skeletal churches of the Norman and Frankish Romanesque and certain Scandinavian stave churches, but none of the churches which Strzygowski cited in support of his theory were of a date sufficiently early to support the hypothesis that they might have been a contributing force in the formation of the Romanesque style, nor could Strzygowski demonstrate that any such churches existed in the Continental cradle areas of the Romanesque—not to speak of the fact that the stave churches to which he referred were centralized structures, and therefore not truly analogous in type to the basilican bay-divided churches of the Continent.[2]

There is no doubt, however, that timber churches were a common phenomenon even on the medieval Continent. Not only is there an abundance of documentary references to such structures,[3] but an appreciable number of them survive. Most of these churches have not been properly recorded, however, as nobody has ever gathered this material together. Thus, after some hundred years of intensive architectural research in the course of which we have measured the dimensions of even the smallest stone incorporated into the masonry of every fourth-rate medieval country church, the question of the design and constructional layout of a typical Continental medieval timber church has been almost entirely neglected.

29. Honfleur, Normandy, France. St. Catherine's Original Site, 15th Century
(Author's reconstruction based on drawings by M. Jullien)

Of the extant medieval timber churches of Continental Europe,
probably the most revealing, historically, is the church of St.
Catherine at Honfleur, in Normandy, France.[4] In its present state
this church consists of two parallel naves of equal height and two
smaller aisles. But in 1946, Monsieur Jullien, an architect of the
Monuments Historiques, made the interesting discovery that in its
original form the church was a three-aisled structure.[5] M. Jullien
observed that the octagonal wooden posts which separate the two
naves in the center still today show on their southern faces the
complete original set of the mortise holes which formed the spring-
ing of the crossbeams and bracing struts of the original aisle. I had
occasion in the summer of 1957 to check these observations and
found them to be correct in all detail. On the basis of M. Jullien's
carefully measured sections and elevations I have prepared the
perspective which is shown in Fig. 29. In this, its original form,
St. Catherine's stems most likely from the time of the general
economic resurgence which followed the eviction of the English
from this city in 1450. Some time after completion but still within
the course of the fifteenth century, as can be gathered from the
profiles of the moldings of the new work (the new work being more
complex than the original work but still late Gothic in style), the

southern aisle was taken down and replaced by a second nave, an alteration to which the church owes its present shape.

In France, St. Catherine of Honfleur is the oldest surviving building of its kind, but in England the type can be traced back to the fourteenth century, in Germany and Holland to the ninth, in Belgium to the sixth or fifth.

A late medieval church from the hamlet of Paasloo, Province Overyssel, Holland, was brought to my attention by Messrs. Jan Jans and E. Jans in Almelo.[6] The walls of the church are built in brick and date from the beginning of the sixteenth century. But the roof-supporting inner trusses of timber appear to be of an earlier date. The original timbers survived until 1954, when, suffering from a heavy infestation of death-watch beetles, they were completely replaced by modern timbers. The new work, however, is a true copy of the original work. A fifteenth-century church of practically identical construction, again unpublished, stands in the village of Nyeven, Province Drente, Holland. The record, however, becomes truly rich as we move across the Channel into England. In the county of Cheshire alone there are five aisled and bay-divided timber churches, and two of those reach back to the fourteenth century: the church of St. James and St. Paul in Marton and the church of St. Werburgh at Warburton. Two further churches of the same design, but dating from the fifteenth century, are to be seen in Lower Peover and in Holmes Chapel, Cheshire; to these can be added a fifteenth-century church in Mattingly, Hampshire, and a fifteenth-century church in Ribbesford, Worcestershire. The Cheshire churches are reproduced and discussed in Raymond Richards comprehensive volume on *Old Cheshire Churches*.[7] Numerous other churches of a similar construction type outside of Cheshire may have escaped my attention or may only be brought to light in the future, as the two great archaeological surveys of the *Victoria History of the Counties of England* and the *Royal Commission on Historical Monuments* draw toward their completion.

As in the Continental timber churches previously discussed, so in the above-named English churches the space is subdivided into a nave and two aisles by two rows of free-standing, inner uprights, which are framed together crosswise by means of tie beams and lengthwise by means of plates and purlins.

What vast distribution this construction type must have had in the Middle Ages may be gathered from a medieval timber church from Stóry-Nupur in Arnessysla, Iceland, torn down in 1875, but accurately recorded in the form of a scale model now on display in the National Museum at Copenhagen.[8] The exact date of this church unfortunately is not known, but a Norwegian Book of Homilies from the beginning of the twelfth century contains a complete description of a church which suggests that the Stóry-Nupur type of church was a common concern in the north Germanic territories of Scandinavia and the Atlantic islands.[9]

Until very recently no evidence existed that bay-divided timber churches of this type existed on the Continent during the formative phases of the Romanesque, but in 1947 P. Glazema unearthed in the villages of Buggenum and Grubbenvorst, Holland,[10] two Carolingian churches of this type. In 1948–50 their number was increased to four when the Landesmuseum in Bonn excavated in the villages of Breberen and Doveren, not far from the Dutch border, two more Carolingian churches of the same construction type on sites which had been bombed in World War II.[11] In Fig. 30 I am reproducing one of these as reconstructed by P. J. Tholen.[12] The discovery of these structures, which could be attributed to the eighth and ninth centuries by pottery shards and other accessories, brought added credence to the results of an excavation which had been made in the 'twenties in connection with the old episcopal church of Maastricht, Belgium (5th–6th centuries). In the interior of this church the excavators had discovered the remains of two ranges of flat stones, which could only have served as base blocks for two rows of wooden uprights, dividing the church lengthwise into three aisles of equal width. Albert Verbeek, who discussed this church at the Sixth Congress of German Art Historians, held at Essen in 1956,[13] pointed at the similarity of the general layout of Maastricht Cathedral to that of the pre-Carolingian churches of Worms and of St. Albans in Mainz, the roofs of which he also presumes to have been supported by two rows of wooden posts.

Taken by themselves these Carolingian and early medieval timber churches are inconsequential. Their significance lies in the fact that they tell us that the constructional layout of a Carolingian timber church was substantially that of the surviving medieval timber churches just discussed, and—if it is the constructional system of a church like St. Catherine's at Honfleur (Fig. 29) or St. James' and St. Paul's in Marton that we have to think of when we read in Thietmar's chronicle (to name just one of countless references to

30. Breberen (Near Aachen), Germany; Carolingian Timber Church (Reconstruction P. J. Tholen)

medieval timber churches that could be cited in this connection) that Bishop Unro of Verden erected in the town of Verden toward the middle of the tenth century a church in timber, and made this church "superior in scale and quality to all other churches" (*et magnitudine et qualitate caeteras precellentem*)[14]—then Strzygowski's theory of the origin of the medieval bay system in northern wood construction would indeed require reexamination.

True enough, the evidence so far available is meager, and I would hesitate to base my views about the validity of Strzygowski's theory of the origin of the medieval bay system upon the fragile pedigree of medieval timber churches above discussed. The inquiry, fortunately, is greatly simplified by the fact that the construction type with which we are here concerned—and here Strzygowski's guess, it has to be admitted, turned out to be correct—was by no means confined to the building of churches. Church construction was only one phase, and centuries before anybody had thought of applying these construction principles to churches they had been a standard procedure in house and barn construction. In Fig. 31 I show the plan and reconstruction of a prehistoric cattle barn which the Dutch anthropologist Albert Egges van Giffen excavated in 1934–36 in a hamlet called Ezinge, Province Groningen, Holland.[15] It dates from the third century B.C. The details of the roof are not assured but the roof-supporting posts and the braided wattle walls which en-

223

31. Ezinge (Prov. Groningen), Holland;
Cattle Barn, 3rd Century (Author's reconstruction, drawn by Walter Schwarz)

closed the house and subdivided the aisles into stalls for cattle were
preserved to hip and even to shoulder height, and the braided fodder
mats in front of the posts were found in such good condition that
they could be stepped upon without sustaining damage. The damp-
ness of the ground in conjunction with the acidity of the wood
retained the timbers in an unusually fine state of preservation.

This same site revealed on a lower level an entire settlement of
houses of the same design, the varying furnishings of which suggest
that we are here confronted with an all-purpose house. Depending
on the respective presence or absence of fireplaces or fodder mats,
or their combined appearance in one and the same structure, this
construction type—without undergoing even the slightest structural
alteration—could be used as shelter for humans alone, as shelter
for humans and animals combined, as shelter for animals alone, or
as shelter for the storage of produce and harvest. The arrangement
of the posts leaves no doubt, in my opinion, that these were bay-
divided structures, for although none of the actual timbers of the
upper parts of these houses are preserved, the posts could not have
successfully braced the roof against the lateral thrust of wind and
storm had they not been framed together at the top by means of
crossbeams and long-beams. Bay division lay in the nature of the
materials employed. The reconstruction reproduced in Fig. 31 [is]

my own. They do not pretend to be trustworthy in all details and, in fact, having been made some six or seven years ago do not altogether correspond to my present views. Nor do I wish to advance the claim through them that each and every three-aisled Iron Age house that has been excavated so far was bay-divided. But I feel certain that in the Iron Age, bay division was a going concern. In some of the smaller houses, if the uprights were anchored deep enough in the ground the roof might well have been capable of taking the normal thrust of the prevailing winds without having the posts connected crosswise by means of tie beams; but in the larger houses, and especially in such cases where the posts rested on base blocks rather than being sunk into the ground, the uprights must have been connected crosswise as well as lengthwise if the house were to stay up at all.[16]

The Ezinge houses [not reproduced here, but as Figs. 12 and 13 in original article] date from the fourth century B.C. When they were discovered in 1934 they were a relatively rare phenomenon. But between 1934 and 1958 over 200 houses of this construction type have been excavated in Holland, in northern Germany, in Scandinavia, and in England, and today we are able to trace their development, century by century, into the Middle Ages and through the Middle Ages to their modern survival forms.[17] The structural layout of this house-type is well exemplified in a model of a house which Werner Haarnagel excavated in 1949–50 in Wilhelmshaven-Hessens where it could be identified in settlement-horizons of the seventh, eighth, ninth, and tenth centuries;[18] and in excavations conducted in 1951–53 in Emden, the same type was discovered in settlement-horizons of the eleventh, twelfth, and thirteenth centuries.[19] For Holland a closely related house-type had been ascertained as early as 1939 for the period of 700–1000 through an excavation undertaken by van Giffen in the vicinity of the parish of Leens, Province Groningen (Fig. 32).[20]

Medieval architectural history has responded to these discoveries with a peculiar apathy, and our failure to evaluate this material in its proper context has prevented us from tackling one of the major unsolved problems of medieval architectural history—which is, in turn, of greatest importance to the excavators—that of the reconstruction of the guest and service buildings of the Plan of St. Gall.

Apart from the monastic buildings proper, i.e., the church, the claustrum, the noviciate and the infirmary, this plan[21] comprises

32. Leens (Prov. Groningen), Holland; Medieval Timber House, c. 700–1000 (Author's reconstruction, drawn by Walter Schwarz)

a host of subsidiary structures, which are as common to secular life as they are indispensable to the economy of a monastic settlement. Under this category come such installations as the granaries, the house of the gardener and his crew, the house of the duck and fowl keeper, the house of the workmen, some six or seven structures which serve as shelter for the livestock and its keepers, the so-called

"Outer School," and the two monastic guest houses: the House for Visitors of Rank and the Hospice of the Paupers. A typological analysis of the guest and service structures of the Plan of St. Gall shows that they are variants of the house type above discussed. As the Iron Age houses of Ezinge and their early medieval descendants of Wilhelmshaven-Hessens and Leens (Fig. 32), so in the guest and service structures of the Plan of St. Gall the principal portion of the house consists of a large rectangular center room which contains the hearth and serves as common living room, while the more private and more specialized functions, such as sleeping and the stabling for the livestock, are relegated to the peripheral aisles and lean-tos.

Thus in the Guest House for Visitors of Rank the center space is used as the common "dining hall" (*domus ad prandendum*), the chambers under the lean-tos as the "bedrooms for the distinguished guests" (*caminatae cum lectis*), the aisles as "servants' quarters" (*cubilia servitorum*) and as "stables for the horses" (*stabula caballorum*). By the same token, in the Hospice of the Paupers the center space serves as "living room for the pilgrims and paupers" (*domus peregrinorum et pauperum*), while the outer rooms are used as dormitories (*dormitorium*), as "quarters for the servants" (*servitorum mansiones*), as "storage room" (*camera*), and as "cellar" (*cellerarium*). Likewise in the House for the Country Servants, as well as in all of the buildings which accommodate the livestock and its keepers, viz., the sheepfold, the goat-shed and the pigsty, the large rectangular center space is designated as the "common living room" (*domus familiae, ipsa domus*, etc.), while the outer rooms serve as "sleeping quarters for the attendant servants" and as "stables" (*cubilia custodientium, cubilia opilionum, cubilia pastorum* and *cavil* or *stabula*). In order to be taken to their stalls the animals had to be led through the common center room. This held true not only for the structures specifically devised for the purpose of housing livestock, but also for buildings of such a highly residential nature as the Guest House for Visitors of Rank, where the horses, likewise, in order to reach their stables had to be guided through the common living room.

In the majority of the guest and service structures of the Plan of St. Gall the center room is surrounded by wings on all four sides, but on some of the smaller houses the aisles are confined to two or three sides only. Two typical examples of this latter kind are the House of the Duck and Fowl Keeper and the House of the Physician, while the Guest House for Visitors of Rank is, of course, a typical example of the more common type. Yet in whatever combination this house-type may appear, it is obvious that we are confronted with an all-purpose structure that served a great variety of functions, separate and combined, without entailing even the slightest changes in its basic structural dispositions: it was used in one case as shelter for humans alone, in another as shelter for humans and animals combined, and in still another as storage space for the harvest.

The only medieval house-type known to have comparable versatility of functions (while at the same time retaining unaltered all of its basic structural dispositions) is the house-type of Ezinge, Leens, and Wilhelmshaven-Hessens. The Plan of St. Gall gives us an idea of the immense distribution which this house-type must have had in Carolingian Europe—in fact, it holds the key to the entire unsolved problem of Carolingian residential and rural architecture, for granaries, cow sheds, pigsties, sheepfolds, houses for workmen, guests, and country servants belonged to a category of buildings which in the Middle Ages were even more common to secular life than they were to a monastic settlement.

If we have been negligent in keeping abreast with the discoveries made during the last two decades by our colleagues in the field of prehistory, we have been even more remiss with our own material. France and England are replete with the remains of the most extraordinary aisled and bay-divided medieval timber structures *which we have not even taken the trouble to record properly.* The oldest surviving aisled and bay-divided timber hall of Europe is the castle hall of Leicester. It dates from around 1150. The historical aspects of this structure have been competently dealt with in a study of Levi Fox,[22] but archaeologically this building is as good as uninvestigated. Reliable plans and sections have never been published and are not even locally available. While of the excavated prehistoric and early medieval houses which I discussed above only the ground or bottom timbers survive, in Leicester Castle the situation is exactly reversed. Most of the supporting frame has disappeared, but the roof is preserved. And here we have the earliest residential timber roof of Europe that is still in a perfect state of preservation—a fact which should be of primary concern to the prehistorians who have not had the good fortune as yet of finding among their excavated house remains sufficient evidence to be certain about the details of reconstruction of the roof system. I am stressing "in a perfect state of preservation" since British archaeologists have recently displayed a tendency to assume that the original twelfth-century roof of the hall of Leicester Castle might have been replaced by a new one sometime in the course of the fourteenth century. This view has been expressed by Mr. C. A. R. Radford,[23] who observed that the tie beam which lies contiguous to the southern gable wall cuts across the cornice of the arches of the Norman windows, and hence could not have been part of the original work. Mr. Radford's observation is correct, but I cannot follow his conclusion. The timber frame of the hall of Leicester Castle, while originally keyed firmly into the gable walls by means of half-beams which rested on masonry brackets, had simply sunk away from its original level early in the nineteenth century, when the wooden Norman pillars were cropped three feet below the meeting point of tie beams and plates, and then shored by modern timbers resting on modern piers of brick. In the summer of 1957 I had an opportunity to study this roof timber by timber. To my own surprise I found it to be original and homogeneous throughout. The frame is out of plumb and has buckled severely, and in places has sunk away from its original position for a distance of almost two feet, but the timbers *are Norman!* And this holds true not only for the tie beams and the rafters and all of their connecting bracing struts, but also for the heavy plates as well as for the headpieces of the supporting piers and their entire complement of bracing struts. The profiles, moldings, and scantling of these timbers are Norman and show none of the refinements and mannerisms of fourteenth-century carpentry work.

On one of the walls of the stairwell which leads to the private court rooms installed on the modern second floor of the hall there is on display a woodcut of a perspective reconstruction of the hall, which was made in 1917 by T. H. Fosbrooke of Leicester (Fig. 33).[24] Save for a few minor details which can be corrected only after the building has been systematically measured (a task which I hope to be able to undertake next summer), this reconstruction is, in my opinion, basically correct. Fosbrooke's woodcut takes us into the interior of a typical medieval castle or manor hall such as must have dotted the European countryside in the twelfth and thirteenth centuries in thousands, if not in hundreds of thousands,

33. Leicester Castle (Leicestershire), England; Interior of Great Hall (Reconstruction by T. H. Fosbrooke)

of specimens. In the homes of those of the highest social and economic level the traditional timber walls were often replaced by masonry, as is the case in Leicester, but in general they were built in timber.[25] As in the guest and service structures of St. Gall and the prehistoric and early medieval houses of Ezinge and Wilhelmshaven-Hessens, so here the hall received its warmth from an open fireplace that burned in the middle of the center aisle. The lord sat at the table on the elevated dais at one of the two narrow ends of the hall, while his retainers took their meals on benches and tables set up along the walls in the aisles of the building. The benches and tables were cleared away after the meal to make room for the bolsters and pillows on which the retainers slept. This is the architectural system of the standard hall not only of the great and powerful lords of the secular order, but also that of the hall of the overlords of the church.

One of the most beautiful feudal halls of England—entirely built in timber—is the palace hall of the Bishop of Hereford. It dates from the same general period as Leicester Hall,[26] is equally well preserved, but has received even less attention from medieval architectural historians than the hall of Leicester Castle.[27] The hall appears to have survived in its original form up to the time of Bishop Bisse (1713–1721), when it was robbed of its spatial unity by the insertion of a number of inner-wall partitions. It was subjected to further disfiguration under Bishop Atley (1868–1896), who subdivided what remaining open space there was into a jumble of separate rooms by the insertion of further cross partitions and the construction of a second story. It is in the masonry of these eighteenth- and nineteenth-century wall partitions and in the space above the plaster ceilings of the rooms installed by Bishops Bisse and Atley that three of the original wooden piers and a substantial portion of the original wooden arcades can still be seen. While only three of the original bays can now be traced, it is possible that the original structure was comprised of five bays. This at least was the view of John Clayton, to whom we owe the first description of the hall.[28]

34. Hereford (Herefordshire), England; Interior of Great Hall (Reconstruction by John Clayton)

John Clayton is the author also of the superb reconstruction reproduced in Fig. 34, which I am publishing here with the kind permission of the Lord Bishop of Hereford and the City Library and Old House Committee of this city.[29] While unreliable in many of its details—especially in the rendering of the roof and the doubtful large transverse arches—this picture nevertheless recreates in an arresting manner the sweeping spatial grandeur of a typical timbered medieval palace hall. The large and remarkable arcades of this structure, however, though entirely hewn in timber, are a design feature that is not natural to wood and which already comes, of course, under the influence of stone construction. The standard type of feudal English hall had the traditional timber system of straight long- and crossbeams, framed together with the aid of diagonal bracing struts, and in this form the three-aisled timbered hall served in the Middle Ages not only as a domestic feudal residence, but also as a barn, as a hospital, and as a market hall —even as a church.

Westminster Palace, the largest feudal hall in Europe, and the hall of the kings of England, is unfortunately not preserved in its original form. Today this hall is covered by a single span, a master-piece of hammer beam construction, which King Richard II raised at the end of the fourteenth century.[30] But prior to the invention of the arch-braced hammer beam a hall of this enormous width could not have been spanned in single trusses; for that reason there is general agreement among British archaeologists that when this hall was built by William Rufus between 1097 and 1099 its roof must have been supported, like the roofs of the halls of Leicester and Hereford, by two rows of free-standing inner timbers which divided the structure lengthwise into a nave and aisles and crosswise into a sequence of bays.[31] We can make ourselves a convincing picture of what that system must have looked like in its original form by stepping into one of the monumental tithe barns of the great monastic orders, such as the fourteenth-century tithe barn of Great Coxwell in Berkshire.[32] This is, in its essential lines, what the royal hall in the Palace of Westminster must have looked like from the time of William Rufus to that of Richard II when it was the administrative center at which a major portion of the political history of England was forged.

In medieval England hall and barn were structurally interchange-able, and if there were any difference between the two it consisted in the fact that the barns, in general, were considerably larger and infinitely more numerous than the halls. No medieval manor was in need of more than one hall, but every medieval manor needed three to five barns. We are in an excellent position to evaluate the density of distribution of medieval barns, not only because of the help provided by the Plan of St. Gall—which gives us the layout of not less than eight such structures—but also because of the survival of a number of written documents of a related nature. One of the most enlightening documents of this type is a dossier of lease agreements of the twelfth century which records the manorial holdings of the dean and chapter of St. Paul's in London.[33] From this inventory we learn that the chapter of St. Paul's derived its sustenance from a total of thirteen manors which were scattered throughout the counties of Hertfordshire, Essex, and Surrey. The number of barns on each of these manors varied from three to five. Thirteen of these barns are so well described that they can be reconstructed on a drawing board. The canon who took the inventory gives us not only the length and width of each barn but, in many cases, even such details as the height and width of the aisles, the height and width of the nave, the depth of the bays and lean-tos, the height from the floor to the crossbeam, and the distance from the crossbeam to the ridge.

In view of the crucial position which this document occupies in the history of the aisled and bay-divided medieval timber barn, I shall translate from the Latin, as a typical example, the description of one of three barns which the chapter of St. Paul's owned on its manor at Wicham, Essex.

> The third barn, which lies further east, is 49½ feet long, not counting its lean-tos, which have a depth of 22 feet. The height of this barn below the tie beam is 15 feet, and above, between the tie beam and the ridge, it is 9½ feet. The nave is 22½ feet wide, and each of its two aisles is 6½ feet wide and 8 feet high. This barn Ailwinus must render full of summer wheat from the entrance toward the east, and from the entrance toward the west it must be full of oats. The center [bay] opposite the entrance must remain empty. It is 11½ feet wide.

The largest of the barns described in the leases of St. Paul's is a barn in a place called Walton on the manor of Adulvesnasa, Essex. It measured 168 feet in length, 53 feet in width, and 33½ feet in

height. Its nave was filled to the ridge with huge stacks of oats
and summer wheat, and scattered here and there in the aisles were
heaps of barley, the dimensions of which are accurately recorded.
This description is a striking tribute to the economic acumen of
the landowning corporation which, with these details, made sure
that all such goods as a new tenant received on entering the manor
were dutifully returned at the termination of the lease.

The lease agreements of St. Paul's range in date from 1114 to
1155.[34] Obviously they establish only a *terminus ante;* they say
nothing about the age of the barns. Some of them may have been
of relatively recent date. Others may have been centuries old; in
fact, may date from any time between the date of inspection and
the original land grants in the seventh and eighth centuries.

That barns of this layout and design were as common in the
Middle Ages on the Continent as they were in England, we may
gather from a glance at Dom Milley's superb engravings of the
Abbey of Clairvaux.[35] Published in 1708, these engravings show the
settlement substantially in the form it had attained by the close
of the twelfth century. In the foreground of the bird's-eye view
which shows the monastery from the west, one recognizes two large
barns, one lying at right angles, the other parallel to the monastery
walls immediately to the right of the entrance. Dom Milley's plan
reveals that these were five-and six-aisled structures, and the scale
with which the plan is furnished permits us to establish their
dimensions as amounting to 90 by 120 feet and to 72 by 168 feet,
respectively. Inserted into the edge of Dom Milley's great perspective is a view of one of the outlying granges of Clairvaux, the grange
of Ultra Albam. It also contains two barns, one subdivided into
five, the other into seven, aisles. The larger of these two barns was
210 feet long and 108 feet wide.

The barns of Clairvaux perished when the monastery was de-
molished in the wake of the French Revolution. Their loss as
historical monuments, however deplorable it may be, is not irrepara-
ble, as a considerable number of like-type barns survive, both in
France and in England. The earliest of these appears to be the
abbey grange of Parçay-Meslay, near Tours in France (Fig. 35), a
dependency of the monastery of Marmoutier. Dom Edmond
Martène, a learned French Benedictine of the Congregation of
St. Maur (1654–1739), who was thoroughly acquainted with the
history and the archives of this monastery, lists the abbey grange

35. Parçay-Meslay (Indre-et-Loire), France; Abbey Grange, 1211–1227, Interior (Photo: Philip Spencer)

of Parçay-Meslay as belonging to a group of buildings which were erected by Abbé Hugue de Rochecorbon (1211–1227).[36] The general character of the masonry work of the barn, its profiles and its moldings, is in full accord with this date. This impressive structure has a clear inner length of 170 feet, 6 inches, a clear width of 80 feet, 2 inches, and a height to the bottom of the ridgepiece of 44 feet, 4 inches. Reliable plans and sections have never been published, but are available at the Centre de Recherches of the Monuments Historiques in Paris. Even expert photography does not render justice to this building; it is only by drawing it up that one can capture the cathedral-like appearance of this magnificent frame of timbers which penetrates the space in all directions, dividing it into parts, and at the same time braiding the parts together into an all-embracing coherent whole.

There is some question as to whether the present timbers of the barn of Parçay-Meslay are the original ones. Aymar Verdier, who discussed this building in his *Architecture Civile et Domestique*,[37] reports that Mr. Drouet, who acquired the barn after the French Revolution and saved it from demolition, was of the opinion that the original frame of timber had caught fire during the invasion of the Touraine by the English in 1437. I have no means of judging whether this view was based on any valid historical evidence. But even if the present timbers were proved to date from the fifteenth century, this would have little bearing on the basic argument of this study since we are not concerned here with the changing details of carpentry work, but with the constructional system as a whole —and a sufficient number of other thirteenth-century barns survive to indicate that no noteworthy changes took place between the thirteenth and the fifteenth centuries as far as the principle of bay-division is concerned.

A thirteenth-century barn of considerable size and beauty, the property of the Abbey of Longchamp, stood within the very boundaries of the city of Paris until the middle of the nineteenth century, when it was taken down to make room for the fashionable race tracks in the Bois de Boulogne. The timbers of the barn are gone, but they were carefully recorded before being dismantled.[38] And further north, in the abbey grange of Canteloup (Eure), in Normandy,[39] and in the abbey grange of Ter Doest in Belgium[40] there are two thirteenth-century barns of even larger dimensions, the timbers of which are still standing in an excellent state of preservation.

Vast and impressive as they are, there is nothing about these barns that is unique. Good documentary evidence suggests that by the close of the twelfth century the Abbey of Clairvaux alone possessed, on its respective granges, not less than twenty-six such structures, and the Abbey of Foigny probably as many as twenty-eight.[41] If we assume that the agricultural economy of the average Cistercian monastery required in each case a minimum of between ten and twenty barns—and the latter figure may come closer to the truth than the former—we would have to infer that by the end of the twelfth century, when the total of Cistercian foundations had risen to about 500, there were not less than 5,000 to 10,000 Cistercian barns alone.

Of the hundreds of thousands of such barns that once undoubtedly were scattered over the medieval countryside, some thirty or forty survive, and of them the most beautiful, in my opinion, is the great tithe barn of Harmondsworth in Middlesex, whose timbers are still as fresh today as they were in the thirteenth century when they

36. St. Pierre-sur-Dives (Calvados), France; Market Hall, 13th(?) Century, Exterior from SW (Photo: Philip Spencer)

were hewn and framed together. Harmondsworth barn is mentioned in a list of alien properties seized by the Crown of England from 1288–1386, in an entry which refers to the year 1293–94 (22 Edward I).[42] This barn has the distinction of having been competently described and recorded as early as 1875 by Albert Hartshorne.[43] It is also succinctly dealt with in the volume on Middlesex of the Royal Commission for Historical Monuments in England,[44] where, however, without any substantiating evidence the barn is ascribed (and wrongly, in my opinion) to the fourteenth century. Harmondsworth barn is 191 feet, 10 inches long, 37 feet, 6 inches wide, and 37 feet, 6 inches high. The feeling of grandeur which this structure evokes as one steps over its threshold into its massive forest of rising timbers, can only be compared to that experienced in entering a medieval cathedral. If I speak of this barn as the finest and most beautiful of all surviving medieval barns of England, I am referring not only to its general proportions—the full nobility of which can only be perceived on the spot—but also to a specific muscular and skeletal type of beauty that occurs only on the highest level of barn construction and finds its expression in an unusually sensitive and convincing down and upward scaling of the timbers, as the eye moves from primary to secondary to tertiary member and back again.

By the time the barns of Parçay-Meslay and of Harmondsworth were built a new variety of the type had sprung into existence, the market hall. The most impressive medieval market hall I know of is the hall of the sleepy little country town of St. Pierre-sur-Dives (Calvados), in Normandy, which is here published for the first time (Fig. 36). It is astonishing that this extraordinary structure should never have found its way into any authoritative treatise on medieval architecture. The hall is 225 feet, 6 inches long, 64 feet, 6 inches wide, and 42 feet, 6 inches high, and may go back to the thirteenth century. Unfortunately the hall was shelled in 1944, and its original frame of timber was at that time almost completely destroyed by fire. Under the competent direction of Mr. Jean Merlet, Architect-in-Chief of the Monuments Historiques, the hall was subsequently restored, and this restoration, carried out by a team of carpenters who reproduced the ancient system to its smallest detail, is one of the masterpieces of French conservationism.

Last summer, Philip Spencer and I studied and photographed altogether seven such halls, all of them unpublished. St. Pierre-sur-Dives was the largest, but its timbers are new, and as far as the scantling, the patina, and the texture of the wood are concerned, it is surpassed by a considerably smaller hall in the city of Arpajon (Seine et Oise), some thirty kilometers south of Paris,[45] which dates from the fifteenth century, and is used—even today—for the same purpose for which it was constructed five centuries ago. A hall of approximately the same dimensions, and so identical in the details of its carpentry work that it must be ascribed to the same master, stands in the nearby city of Milly-la-Forêt. It was erected by Admiral de Graville in 1479, and the patent letter of Louis XI, in which the construction of the hall is authorized, is still preserved in the city archives of Milly.[46] In the same general region of the department of Seine-et-Oise there are three more market halls of similar description—one of outstanding beauty in the city of Méréville. While they too will probably have to be dated into the fifteenth century, we have good reason to assume that the thirteenth-century halls of Paris cannot have looked much different.

I should now like to summarize what I have tried to demonstrate so far in the analytical part of this study before turning to my conclusions.

Discoveries made during the last two decades by German, English, Dutch, and Scandinavian excavators, and a roundup of a pitifully neglected—in parts even uncharted—area of medieval research, suggest that there existed in the Middle Ages an aisled and bay-

Rome: St. Paul's

Harmondsworth: Tithe Barn

Speyer: Cathedral

Amiens: Cathedral

37. Space Division in Early Christian and Medieval Architecture (Redrawn by Ernest Born after Construction of William Hill)

divided, all-purpose structure in timber, about the imposing density of distribution of which we have been deplorably misinformed in the past. The existence and general prevalence of this type of structure during the formative phases of Romanesque and Gothic architecture casts new light upon Strzygowski's abortive theory of the origin of the medieval bay-system in wood construction.

The bay system is one of the principal distinguishing features of medieval architecture and is perhaps its most distinguishing single feature. It developed on an architectural organism which by origin was not possessed of this feature, namely, that of the West Roman type of the Early Christian basilica, which, in the wake of a general process of political and cultural Romanization that seized the kingdom of Charlemagne toward the end of the eighth century—as

Richard Krautheimer has so convincingly demonstrated[47]—became a leading Frankish building type and the point of departure for the entire development which followed. This West Roman version of the Early Christian basilica was an aggregate of three or more monolithic spaces, internally undivided and of varying dimensions, which shouldered each other axially and transversely, but never intersected one another (cf. Fig. 37, diagram of St. Paul's). The relative measurements of these spaces were not regulated by any set canon of proportions and thus varied greatly. The Romanesque and the Gothic churches, which developed from this prototype form, on the other hand, are bay-divided churches, i.e., churches in which the total space is subdivided into a multitude of equal or homologous parts by means of an all-pervasive skeleton of shafts and arches which act both as divisive and as connective members (cf. Fig. 37, diagrams of Speyer and Amiens Cathedrals).

These concepts are diametrically opposed to one another, and the development which leads from the former to the latter passed through a series of clearly observable steps which have been described frequently and which I shall now recapitulate very briefly.

The first of these consisted of a general rearrangement of the primary geometrical space relationships of the church. The width of the nave and the transept were made equal, their area of intersection, the crossing unit, thus was fixed into a square, and all of the remaining parts of the church were calculated as a multiple of the crossing square. In Carolingian and Ottonian architecture we witness the gradual crystallization of this principle which reaches its apex in the so-called "square schematism" of the Romanesque—but the essential features of this system were already anticipated in the church of the famous Plan of St. Gall of around the year 820. For seven decades the emergence of this peculiar system of unit relationships has been discussed by leading architectural historians, and yet no one has ever been able to explain it. I suggest that the geometricity of the floor plan of Carolingian and Ottonian churches and the modular lay-out of their volume sequence owe their origin to the fact that these churches were constructed by men, to whom—as long as their collective memory could recall—"to build" had been synonymous with building in multiples of a basic spatial unit value.[48] Geometricity and unit sequence had been for them intrinsic elements of timbered frame construction—a feature that becomes strikingly apparent if one glances at the intensely geometrical layout of the large Iron Age cattle barn of Ezinge, Holland (Fig. 31), or the early medieval houses of the type of Wilhelmshaven-Hessens (Fig. 32).

In Ottonian architecture this steadily increasing trend of calculating the general dimensions of the principal spaces of the church as multiples of a basic unit value gathered added momentum with the introduction of the "alternating support system" which carried into the elevation of the church a rhythm of alternating vertical accents that mirrored in the columnar structure of the wall modular prime relationships which heretofore had been a property of the dimensional organization of the space alone. This was a preliminary to a second decisive step in the development of the medieval bay system which was reached when the geometrical layout of the floor plan found muscular embodiment in a system of rising shafts which were engaged into the masonry walls, and when these shafts were interconnected crosswise and lengthwise by means of arches. As soon as this point was reached the churches could be vaulted, the walls between the rising shafts and arches could be perforated and were progressively transformed into curtain walls—and thus the Early Christian basilica with its aggregate of neighboring monolithic spaces separated by rigid walls had been transformed into that intensely skeletal and bay-divided system of the Romanesque. In church construction as well as in domestic building the totality of the space was now conceived of as a multiple of equal or homologous parts, created by an all-pervasive system of structural members, in function both divisive and connective.

It is very hard for me to believe that the appearance of this concept in stone should not have been connected, developmentally, with the fact that in the territories in which this change took place these principles had been for over a millenium a traditional feature of timbered house construction. In timber this concept is old; in stone it is new. In timber it flows as a logical construction method from the natural properties of the material, and for that reason could be invented on a relatively primitive cultural level. In masonry it ushered in a conflict between style and matter such as could be handled only on a very sophisticated level of civilization, to the extent of leading in its terminal phase—the Gothic—to a complete denial of the natural properties of the stone.

The great architects of the Renaissance, to whom the Gothic was a "monstrous and barbarous" way of building, were fully aware of this dichotomy between material and style in Gothic architecture, as is expressed in no uncertain terms by Giorgio Vasari, who complained that Gothic buildings "have more the appearance of being made in paper than of stone or marble,"[49] as well as by the author of the famous "Report on the Remains of Ancient Rome" (once believed to be Raphael, but now more commonly ascribed to Bramante or Baldassare Peruzzi), who compared the soaring flight of the Gothic piers and arches with the tensile action of the trunks of living trees, and based upon this simile his puzzling theory of the origins of Gothic architecture in the wooden huts of the primitive forebearers of civilized man.[50] In order to obviate any misconceptions as to my own views in this matter, let me point out that I am not subscribing to Raphael's, Bramante's, or Peruzzi's views. The study with which I am here concerned is devoted to an analysis not of the complex phenomenon of the origins of the Gothic, but to the specific problem of the origins of the medieval bay system, a feature which is an integral part of both the Romanesque and the Gothic, without being identical with either.

If, with these qualifications in mind, then, I readvance Strzygowski's ill-conceived idea of the origins of the medieval bay system in northern wood construction, I wish to make it clear that I do not mean to imply that the architectural system of the Romanesque and Gothic emerged mechanically like a chemical formula from the simple historical superimposition or interpenetration of two formerly separate building traditions: that of the Early Christian stone basilica and that of the medieval timber house. Primarily and above all, of course, the architectural systems of the Romanesque and Gothic are the expression of a spiritual experience, and in the Middle Ages, bay division was as much of a cultural phenomenon as it was a principle of architectural composition.

Sometime between the year 1230 and 1236 a leading French .scholastic, William from Auvergne, gave the finishing touches to a book which dealt with the structure of the universe (*Liber de Universo*) and aimed at a total integration of the metaphysical concepts prevailing in his time into a rounded metaphysical vision. The universe here is envisaged as a triad of structurally related hierarchies, each a mirror reflection of the other as well as of the system as a whole with its identical subdivisions into triads of triads of ranks, and in each of these triads each subordinate rank corresponds in substance to its equivalent part in every other triad. The architectural plan that underlies this metaphysical scheme displays the most astounding analogies with that of the Gothic bay system. As in the latter, so here the whole "is arranged according to a system of homologous parts, and parts of parts"—if I may be permitted to apply to the *substance* of a metaphysical concept a definition which Panofsky in his brilliant essay on Gothic architecture and scholasticism has coined with regard to the *formal layout* of the scholastic treatise.[51]

In its ultimate analysis, then, I would say the problem of the medieval bay system cannot be separated from the rank division of the feudal order, the ecclesiastical order, and the celestial order, and it is in these areas, of course, that we must search for the primary spiritual forces that brought about the transformation of that sluggish organism of the Early Christian basilica into that highly flexible, highly complex, incredibly sophisticated, but equally emotive, organism of the Gothic cathedral. In order to be expressive of the thinking of that period, architecture required a style in which the whole could be conceived as a multiple of homologous parts, and in order to create such a style the rigid Early Christian basilica had to be converted from a monolithic into a cellular and from a crustacian into a skeletal structure. In facing this task, medieval architects had the signal advantage of being able to draw on a tradition in which bay division and skeletal construction had been for over a millenium a guiding principle of construction for the houses in which they dwelled, the halls from which they ruled and governed their land, the barns in which they sheltered their livestock and harvest, the markets in which they traded their produce and even, to some extent, the churches in which they worshiped.

In submitting this theory I should like to end on a precautionary note. I have stressed the native northern aspect of the medieval bay system because this aspect has been generally neglected. But in strongly underscoring what I feel to be in need of primary emphasis I do not mean to diminish the importance of other factors which also may have had a bearing on this matter. While the bay system in the form in which it is here defined is, in my opinion, a typical medieval feature, its primary constituent part—the bay—was known to the Romans, and the morphology of the vaulted canopies of stone which frame the bays of Speyer Cathedral is, of course, a direct derivative of the Roman groin vault, of which the medieval masons had learned to make use, first in the crypts, then in the aisles, and finally in the naves of their churches. It is an incontrovertible historical fact, however, that the vaulted Roman canopy had not found a place of survival in any of the principal spaces of the large Early Christian basilicas of the western type from which the medieval development took its point of departure. Nevertheless there existed, in the sixth century, two churches in northern Syria which had their nave divided into large bays by means of large transverse arches: the basilica of St. Sergios at Rusafa and the Bissos church at Ruweha.[52] I consider it unlikely that either of these two churches exercised appreciable influence upon the development of the medieval bay system. They lie in territory which early in the seventh century had fallen into the hands of the Arabs and which remained outside the sphere of western accessibility even during the time of the Crusades, not to mention the fact that by the time the earliest Crusade took place, in 1096, the medieval bay system had already found its full embodiment in the Cathedral of Speyer.

Yet even if I should be wrong in this assumption—or if it could be demonstrated that similar or related types were known to medieval masons and architects—it must still be pointed out that in Rusafa and in Ruweha bay division remained confined to the nave of the church and was not extended to the church as a whole. The Rusafa-Ruweha bays actually are large compartments rather than bays, and were created by the simple insertion into the nave of the church of two monumental transverse arches carried by elongated piers, but the masonry of the nave walls—diminished as it may be by arcades of extraordinary width—is not reduced to an analogous system of structural members. It is in the full absorption of mass in structure on the one hand, and in the development of an all-pervasive armature of space-dividing and space-connecting shafts and arches on the other hand, that I see the common denominator of the bay division of the Romanesque and Gothic and the bay division of the timbered halls and houses of transalpine Europe.

The Origins of the Bay System

NOTES

[1] Josef Strzygowski, "Die Europäische Kunst," *Belvedere*, 26 (1924), pp. 35–55; cf. in particular p. 43. The idea is voiced again in Strzygowski's *Nordischer Heilbringer und Bildende Kunst* (Vienna and Leipzig, 1939), p. 233.

[2] On the derivation of the Scandinavian stave churches from central prototypes see Gerda Boëthius, "Stavkyrkans Ursprung och Utveckling," *Festskrift Johnny Roosval* (Stockholm, 1929), pp. 18–33.

[3] For rapid, if only partial, orientation see the references listed under the terms *ligneus* or *bois* in the indices of the following works: Otto Lehmann-Brockhaus, *Schriftquellen zur Kunstgeschichte des 11. und 12. Jahrhunderts für Deutschland, Lothringen und Italien* (Berlin, 1938); Victor Mortet, *Recueil de textes relatifs à l'histoire de l'architecture en France au Moyen Age, XIe-XIIe siècles* (Paris 1911); Victor Mortet and Paul Deschamps, *Recueil de textes relatifs à l'histore de l'architecture en France au Moyen Age, XIIe-XIIIe siècles* (Paris, 1929).

[4] St. Catherine's is briefly dealt with by M. de Caumont in *Statistique Monumentale du Calvados* (Paris-Caen, 1862), IV, pp. 323–338, but has never become the subject of a special monograph, which is badly needed.

[5] Monsieur Jullien's observations have not been published but are incorporated into a set of carefully measured drawings which are on file in the Centre de Recherches of the Monument Historiques in Paris. Prints of these I owe to the kindness of Mlles. Bertholier and Bloch of the Monuments Historiques.

[6] . . . [To] Messrs. Jan and E. Jans of Almelo . . . I am indebted for the following historical information conveyed to me by Pastor H. L. Lieve of Paasloo: Permission to build a church at Paasloo was granted in 1336 by the chapter of St. Clement's in Steenwyk, according to a document in the archives of St. Clement's. Judging from foundations which were discovered some three feet inward of the walls of the present church, this building must have been a little smaller than the present church. Until 1486 the church of Paasloo was the principal church of the district. Thereafter it sank into the status of a chapel, and Oldemarkt became the seat of the principal church.

[7] Raymond Richards, *Old Cheshire Churches* (London, 1947). For Marton, cf. pp. 229–231; for Warburton, pp. 339–341; for Lower Peover, pp. 200–204; for Holmes Chapel, pp. 186–190. Most of the churches listed above are also dealt with in Fred H. Crossley, *Timber Building in England* (London-New York, 1951), pp. 32 ff., where one will also find a reproduction of the handsome late medieval timber church of Coppenhall, Cheshire, which was torn down in 1821. For a description and photographic reproductions of the church of Mattingly, cf. *Victoria History of the Counties of England, Hampshire* (London, 1911), IV, pp. 50 ff.; for Ribbesford, *ibid., Worcestershire*, (London, 1924), IV, pp. 312–314.

[8] The church is mentioned in Daniel Brunn, *Fortidsminder og Nutidshjem paa Island* (Copenhagen, 1898), p. 212.

[9] Gamal Norsk Homiliebok, Cod. AM 619, ed. Gustav Ludvig Indrebø, *Norske historiske kjeldeskriftfond, Skifter*, Vol. 54 (Oslo, 1931).

[10] Dr. P. Glazema, "Outheidkundige opgravingen in door de oorlog verwoeste Limburgse Kerken," *Publications de la Société Historique et Archéologique dans le Limbourg*, 84 (1948), pp. 226–232, 252–258.

[11] Kurt Böhner, Peter Joseph Tholen, and Rafael von Uslar, "Ausgrabungen in den Kirchen von Breberen und Doveren," *Bonner Jahrbücher*, Heft 150 (1950), pp. 192–228.

[12] Reproduced after *Werdendes Abendland an Rhein und Ruhr* (Ausstellung in Villa Hügel, Essen, 18 May–15 September, 1956), p. 95, Fig. 9.

[13] Albert Verbeek, "Eine merovingische Kathedrale?", *Kunstchronik*, 9 (1956), 280–281, with plan on p. 280.

[14] Cf. Otto Lehmann-Brockhaus, *Die Kunst des 10. Jahrhunderts im Lichte der Schriftquellen* (Akademische Abhandlungen zur Kulturgeschichte, 3rd series [Strassburg, 1935]), VI, pp. 13 ff. To the incident mentioned above I add here at random two further typical examples. After the destruction of the Cathedral of Hamburg by the Slavs, Bishop Unwanus (who acceded to the episcopal see in 1013) rebuilt the episcopal "church and all of its appendices in timber" (*ecclesiam et diversoria . . . omnia lignea*). (Cf. Otto Lehmann-Brockhaus, *Schriftquellen zur Kunstgeschichte des 11. und 12. Jahrhunderts für Deutschland, Lothringen und Italien* [Berlin, 1938], pp. 108–109.) Even as late as 1184 the Emperor Frederic Barbarossa erected in the triangular plain formed by the confluence of the rivers Rhine and Main "a church of considerable size and a stately palace in timber" (*ecclesiam maximum et palatium de lignis honestissime fieri iusserat*), "together with numerous other structures of varying description for the purpose of celebrating in the most magnificent manner the great feast of Joy" (i.e., the coronation of his son Henry as King of Germany). And the reason for this was "the narrowness of the streets in the city of Mainz and the bad air prevailing there." Cf. *Arnoldi Chronica Slavorum*, ed. Heinrich Pertz (Hannover, 1868), p. 88.

[15] Albert Egges van Giffen, "Der Warf in Ezinge, Prov. Groningen, Holland und seine Westgermanischen Häuser," *Germania*, 20 (1936), pp. 40–47.

[16] This holds true for a three-aisled Iron Age house which was excavated in 1940 on the Aalburg, near Belfort, Luxembourg, and which even antedates the earliest Ezinge houses (cf. Gustav Riek, "Ein Fletthaus aus der Wende ältere-jüngere Hunsrück-Eiffelkultur bei Belfort, Luxemburg," *Germania*, 26 [1942], pp. 26–34). The reconstruction problems of this, as well as many other Iron Age houses are discussed authoritatively by Adelhart Zippelius, in "Das vormittelalterliche dreischiffige Hallenhaus in Mitteleuropa," *Bonner Jahrbücher*, 153 (1953), pp. 13–45.

[17] I am confining myself here to the most summary bibliography. The material excavated in Holland and in Germany is not summarized at any place, so far as I know, and is scattered through a vast array of prehistoric and regional periodicals, many of which are not easily available in this country. Good surveys of the Swedish material are to be found in such works as: John .Nihlen and Gerda Boëthius, *Gotländska gårder och byar undre äldre järnaldern.* (Stockholm, 1933); Mårten Stenberger, *Öland under aldre järnaldern* (Stockholm, 1933), and Mårten Stenberger, *Vallhagar, A Migration Period Settlement on Gotland, Sweden* (2 vols.; Copenhagen, 1955). The Norwegian material excavated prior to 1942 is summarized in Sigurd Grieg, "The House in Norwegian Archaeology," *Acta Archaeologica*, 13 (1942), pp. 169–178; for the Danish material excavated prior to 1937 see

Gudmund Hatt, "Dwelling Houses in Jutland in the Iron Age," *Antiquity,* 2 (1937), pp. 162–173. For later material cf. Paul Nørlund, *Trelleborg* (Copenhagen, 1948). For Iceland, cf. Mårten Stenberger, *Forntida Gårdar I Island* (Copenhagen, 1943). A royal Anglo-Saxon palace of the seventh century, comprising a total of twenty-five houses, was excavated in the summer of 1956 in Northumbria, England, by Mr. Brian Hope-Taylor. The results of this excavation are in process of being published by the Ministry of Works. The earliest bay-divided timber house known so far was unearthed in the summer of 1954 in a place called Jemgum, near Emden, Germany. It dates from the period of transition from the Bronze Age to the Iron Age (seventh-sixth centuries, B.C.) and is dealt with in Werner Haarnagel, "Die spätbronze-, früheisenzeitliche Gehöftsiedlung Jemgum bei Leer auf dem linken Ufer der Ems," *Die Kunde,* Neue Folge, 8 (1957), pp. 1–43.

[18] Cf. Werner Haarnagel, "Das nordwesteuropäische dreischiffige Hallenhaus und seine Entwicklung im Küstengebiet der Nordsee," *Neues Archiv für Niedersachsen,* 4 (1950), pp. 88–89, and, same author, "Die Flachabdeckung der Wurt Hessens am Jadebusen bei Wilhelmshaven und ihr vorläufiges Ergebnis," *Germania,* 29 (1951), pp. 223–225.

[19] Cf. Werner Haarnagel, "Die frühgeschichtliche Handelssiedlung Emden und ihre Entwicklung bis ins Mittelalter," *Friesisches Jahrbuch* (1955), pp. 9–78.

[20] Albert Egges van Giffen, "Een Systematic Onderzoek In Em Der Tuinster Wierden Te Leens," *Jaarsverslag Van Den Vereeniging Voor Terpenonderzoek,* 20–24 (1935–1940), pp. 26–117.

[21] A full-scale, eight-color, offset facsimile reproduction of the Plan of St. Gall was published in 1952 under the auspices of the Historische Verein des Kantons St. Gallen, and can be obtained through the Fehr'sche Buchhandlung in St. Gall, Switzerland. The facsimile was accompanied by a study of Hans Reinhardt, *Der St. Galler Klosterplan* (92. Neujahrsblatt herausgegeben vom Historischen Verein des Kantons St. Gallen [St. Gall, 1952]).

[22] Levi Fox, "Leicester Castle," *Leicester Archaeological Society Transactions,* 21, part 2 (1942–1943), pp. 127–170.

[23] In a footnote of C. A. R. Radford's report on "Oakham Castle," published in *Archaeological Journal,* 112 (1956), pp. 181–184; cf. note 1, p. 183.

[24] Fosbrooke's reconstruction is mentioned by Margaret Wood, "Norman Domestic Architecture," *Archaeological Journal,* 92 (1935), 191. For a copy of this woodcut, which is here published for the first time as far as I know, I am greatly indebted to Mr. Albert Herbert in Leicester.

[25] New light has recently been thrown upon the problem of the aisled medieval timber hall by J. T. Smith in an article entitled "Medieval Aisled Halls and Their Derivatives," *Archaeological Journal,* 112 (1956), 76–93. Mr. Smith has also recently made the interesting discovery that the hall of Stokesay Castle was in its original form a three-aisled structure (cf. J. T. Smith, "Stokesay Castle," *Archaeological Journal,* 113 [1957], pp. 211–214).

[26] The editors of the Royal Commission on Historical Monuments, *Herefordshire* (London, 1931), Vol. 1, where the hall is dealt with on pp. 116–117, date it into "the late 12th century." Margaret Wood in her "Norman Domestic Architecture," *op. cit.,* p. 188, dates the hall "*c.* 1160." The Rev. Francis T. Havergal in *Fasti Herefordenses and other Antiquarian Memorials of Hereford* (Edinburgh, 1869),

p. 136, attributes the hall to Bishop William de Vere (between 1174 and 1199). No record as to the name of the builder of the hall or its date of construction exists, but the Norman character of the work is beyond question.

[27] The hall has never been the subject of a special monograph, which is badly needed.

[28] John Clayton discussed the hall in 1847 in a paper read before the Royal Institute of British Architects. Extracts of this discussion are to be found in *Fasti Herefordenses, op. cit.,* pp. 136–138.

[29] Clayton's reconstruction is mentioned in Wood, "Norman Domestic Architecture," *op. cit.,* p. 188. It was not included in John Clayton's work, *Ancient Timber Edifices of England* (London, 1948). A copy of a woodcut fashioned after Clayton's original drawing is in the Refectory Hall of the Bishop's Palace at Hereford, and the City Library of Hereford has a second one. To the Lord Bishop of Hereford as well as to Miss Penelope Morgan and Mr. F. C. Morgan of the Cathedral Library I wish to express my deepest appreciation for their gracious assistance in my studies at Hereford Palace.

[30] Westminster Hall is dealt with in W. R. Lethaby, "The Palace of Westminster in the Eleventh and Twelfth Centuries," *Archaeologia,* 60 (1906), pp. 131–141, and by the Royal Commission on Historical Monuments, *London (West)* (London, 1925), pp. 121–123. For the roof specifically cf. Herbert Cescinski and Ernest R. Gribble, "Westminster Hall and Its Roof," *Burlington Magazine,* 40 (1922), pp. 76–84.

[31] The belief that Westminster Hall in its original state must have been divided into a nave and aisles by two rows of intermediary supports was first expressed by Sidney Smirke in 1836 ("Remarks on the Architectural History of Westminster Hall," *Archaeologia,* 26 [1836], p. 416). Smirke's opinion is shared by every authoritative student of the subject, including the late Director of Works, Sir Frank Baines, Cf. Lethaby, *op. cit.,* p. 136; Cescinski and Gribble, *op. cit.,* p. 76; Royal Commission on Historical Monuments, *op. cit.,* p. 121, and Geoffrey Webb, *Architecture in Britain, The Middle Ages* (Baltimore and Harmondsworth, 1956), pp. 66 and 67, Fig. 38.

[32] Some good photographs and a cross section of this extraordinary structure have been published by Ralph Tubbs, *The Englishman Builds* (Harmondsworth, 1945), pp. 20–21, but otherwise this barn has not been studied.

[33] Published by William Hale, *The Domesday of St. Paul's of the Year MCCXII . . . and other Original Documents Relating to the Manors and Churches Belonging to the Dean and Chapter of St. Paul's in London, in the Twelfth and Thirteenth Centuries,* printed for the Camden Society (London, 1858). The first to draw attention to this precious document was Sidney Oldall Addy, *The Evolution of the English House* (London, 1898), pp. 67, 129 ff.

[34] For the dates see Hale's introductory notes, *op. cit.,* pp. xc-c.

[35] One complete set of these engravings is now in the Cabinet des Estampes of the Bibliothèque Nationale at Paris (Topographie de la France, Aube, Arondissement Bar-sur-Aube, fol. 27, 28, and 29); a second one is available in the Archives de l'Aube at the city of Troyes (Bibliothèque de Troyes, Carteron 1, Planches 2, 3, and 4). The best reproductions are to be found in Alphonse Roserot, *Dictionnaire*

Historique de la Champagne Méridionale (Aube) des Origines à 1790 (Langres, 1942), I, pp. 392 ff.

[36] Dom Edmond Martène, "Histoire de l'Abbaye de Marmoutier" (publié et annoté par M. l'abbé C. Chevalier), *Mémoires de la Société Archéologique de Touraine*, 25 (1875), p. 200.

[37] Aymar Verdier and F. Cattois, *Architecture Civile et Domestique au Moyen Age et à la Renaissance* (Paris, 1864), pp. 27–35.

[38] Cf. Viollet-le-Duc, *Dictionnaire Raisonné de l'Architecture Française du XIe au XVIe siècle* (Paris, 1863), VI, 43, with plan, section, and elevation.

[39] The barn of the abbey grange of Canteloup is summarily described by Phillippe Lemaitre, "Notes sur Quelques Granges Dimiéres du Departement de L'Eure," *Bulletin Monumental*, 15 (1849), pp. 196–197, but plans and sections are not available.

[40] For plan, section, and elevation of this structure (not altogether reliable, however), see Thomas H. King, *The Study-Book of Mediaeval Architecture and Art* (Edinburgh, 1893), II, Fig. 137; there listed under "Lissewegh."

[41] These figures are based on the rough assumption that every grange dependent on the mother settlement required for its agricultural economy a minimum of two barns, like the abbey grange of Clairvaux, and the outlying grange of Ultra Albam. Clairvaux had a total of 12 granges, and six of those had already been established during the lifetime of St. Bernard (d. 1153); Foigny had a total of 14 (cf. Marcel Aubert, *L'Architecture Cistercienne en France* (Paris, 1947), II, pp. 60–161.

[42] This document is to be found on Exchequer, Queen's Remembrancer, *Extents, etc., of Alien Priories*, Bundle 2, No. 1, mem. 1 (Reference E. 106/2/1: date 22 Edw. I) and was quoted, but not without errors, in Hartshorne's article mentioned in note 43.

[43] Albert Hartshorne, "The Great Barn at Harmondsworth," *London and Middlesex Archaeological Society, Transactions*, 4 (1875), pp. 417 ff.

[44] Royal Commission on Historical Monuments in England, *Middlesex*, (London, 1937), pp. 61–62. To Miss Vera Dallas, Secretary of the Royal Commission on Historical Monuments, I should like to express on this occasion my deepest appreciation for the generous assistance and support which she has extended to me over a period of many years in my research on aisled medieval barns and halls in England.

[45] Photographs, plans, and sections of the market hall of Arpajon have never been published, to my knowledge, but are on file in the Centre de Recherches of the Monuments Historiques in Paris.

[46] The hall of Milly is briefly dealt with in a booklet by Georges Lasserre entitled *Les Rues de Milly* (Etampes, 1925), pp. 6 ff. For access to this booklet, a copy of which I could not otherwise have obtained, I am greatly obliged to the Comte de St. Périer of Morignon. The patent letter of Louis XI which authorizes the establishment of the market and the construction of the hall of Milly has also never been published, but an exact transcript of this important document has been transmitted to me by Mr. Raymond Geber, member of the Commission des Antiquités et des Arts de Seine-et-Oise, to whom I am deeply indebted for his

kindness. I should also like to express my gratitude at this point to my friend Peter Harnden of Orgival, who was the first to draw my attention to this extraordinary group of medieval market halls.

[47] Richard Krautheimer, "The Carolingian Revival of Early Christian Architecture," *Art Bulletin*, 24 (1942), pp. 1–38.

[48] I do not contend that this explains the entire problem of geometricity in medieval architecture, since intensely geometrical concepts appear in many other areas of medieval art, especially in the field of book illumination where they cannot be explained as an offspring of an architectural way of thinking. The problem of medieval geometricity hence has still another dimension and can only be solved in its full complexity when it is possible to define the general mental (or metaphysical?) concepts which underlie these other forms of geometricity. But it cannot be denied that in timbered frame construction geometricity and unit sequence have an immediate constructional rationale which will have to be taken into consideration in any future discussion of this problem.

[49] "Et hanno più il modo da parer fatte di carta che di marmi." See Erwin Panofsky, "Das erste Blatt aus dem 'Libro' Giorgio Vasaris; eine Studie über die Beurteilung der Gotik in der italienischen Renaissance, etc.," *Städel-Jahrbuch*, VI (1930), pp. 25–72 . . . (cf. p. 43), translated into English in Panofsky's *Meaning in the Visual Arts* (New York, 1955), pp. 169–235 (cf. p. 189).

[50] Cf. Panofsky, *op. cit.*, *Städel-Jahrbuch*, pp. 39–40. *Meaning in the Visual Arts*, p. 182.

[51] Erwin Panofsky, *Gothic Architecture and Scholasticism* (Latrobe, 1951), p. 45.

[52] For Rusafa and Ruweha see Howard Crosby Butler, *Early Churches in Syria* (Princeton, 1929), pp. 145 ff., 161 ff. [A] reconstruction of St. Sergios basilica at Rusafa [is] reproduced in Friedrich Sarre and Ernst Herzfeld, *Archäologische Reise im Euphrat—und Tigris—Gebiet* (Berlin, 1920), II, 4, Fig. 133.

14. THE ICONOGRAPHY OF A ROMANESQUE TYMPANUM AT VÉZELAY

Adolf Katzenellenbogen

INTRODUCTION

This selection examines the arrangement and subject matter of the central tympanum in the narthex of Sainte-Madeleine at Vézelay, and proposes a web of meanings in which the prophecies of Isaiah, the old mission of the Apostles, and the new mission of the crusaders have been harmonically interwoven. A fine example of iconographical analysis, this selection has the added interest of linking the complex program of this tympanum to the historical events of the era and to the guiding genius of the theologian, Peter the Venerable.

Among other works by the late Adolf Katzenellenbogen are *Allegories of the Virtues and Vices in Mediaeval Art* (1939); "The Prophets on the West Facade of the Cathedral of Amiens," *Gazette des Beaux-Arts,* S.6, XL (1952); and *The Sculptural Programs of Chartres Cathedral* (1959), which was awarded the Charles Rufus Morey Prize by the College Art Association as the best book in the history of art to be published in 1959.

T he central tympanum in the narthex of the Abbey Church of Sainte-Madeleine at Vézelay, which was created between about 1120 and 1132, has proved to be one of the most tempting and brittle iconographical enigmas of medieval art (Fig. 38). Its explanation has been attempted time and again with a wide variety of results.[1] In more recent years the conflicting opinions have been narrowed down to two different interpretations, established by Émile Mâle and Abel Fabre.[2]

Émile Mâle has related the program of the tympanum to the events on the day of Pentecost. He has explained the central scene as the *Descent of the Holy Spirit* with Christ Himself bestowing the rays of heavenly grace on His apostles. The numerous groups of figures surrounding the central scene in the eight compartments of the archivolt and on the lintel represent those nations to whom the apostles will preach the gospel, now that they are endowed with the power to speak in all languages. Monstrous races are among these nations. According to medieval belief, they live at the ends of the earth. In the archivolt some people are characterized as being sick. They are already experiencing the miracle-working of the apostles. On the left side of the lintel, however, the groups who offer their gifts and bring a sacrificial bull still remain faithful to their old erroneous belief, but the word of the Lord will reach them too.

According to Abel Fabre the central scene represents the Mission which Christ gave to His apostles immediately before His Ascension.

The apparent discrepancy between the two interpretations which relate the central scene either to the Pentecost or to the day of Ascension may find a solution if one considers briefly the meaning of the tympanum decorating the western portal of the church at Anzy-le-Duc (*c.* 1125).[3] Here the problem is similar, although less complex. The tympanum represents the *Ascension of Christ,* a favorite theme of Burgundian Romanesque sculpture. The enthroned Christ, whose mandorla is held by two angels, occupies the center of the tympanum, while Mary and the twelve apostles, who are

38. Tympanum: The Mission of the Apostles, Center Portal of Narthex, Ste-Madeleine, Vézelay, 1120–1132 (Marburg-Art Reference Bureau)

the witnesses of the Ascension, are rendered on the lintel. Yet the program of the tympanum is not restricted to this event. It also gives visible form to the prediction of the second coming of Christ which the two Men in White made to the apostles: "This same Jesus, which is taken up from you into heaven, shall so come in like manner as ye have seen Him go into heaven."[4] The second coming of Christ, an event still remote at the time of His Ascension, does not remain just a prediction, but is actually represented. In the archivolt the twenty-four Elders are shown as the witnesses of His coming at the end of time. Thus the tympanum gains a twofold meaning. If Christ is considered in context with the figures on the lintel, He is the Christ of the Ascension, if in context with the Elders of the archivolt, the apocalyptic Christ. Two events are clearly telescoped to make the meaning of the tympanum more comprehensive. The triumphant return of Christ to heaven is merged with His triumphant reappearance to judge mankind.

The fact that different events are telescoped here may justify an analogous interpretation of the more complicated aspects of the Vézelay tympanum. Its main literary source may be found in Acts 1:4-9. Just before He was taken up and received by a cloud, Christ prophesied to His apostles that they would receive the power of the Holy Spirit and be His witnesses unto the uttermost part of the earth. In my opinion, just as at Anzy-le-Duc the theme of the *Ascension of Christ* is expanded by giving visible form to the prediction of His second coming, so at Vézelay the *Ascension of Christ* is supplemented by the sculptural rendering of His predictions. The promise of the giving of the Holy Spirit is represented by the rays emanating from His hands. The reference to the future missionary work of the apostles is illustrated on lintel and archivolt by the representatives of the various nations, some of whom were supposed to live at the edge of the world. Thus the representation of the ascending Christ who leaves His apostles and is received into a cloud is merged with the *Mission of the Apostles* and with the giving of complete and final power through the Holy Spirit in what may be called an encyclopedic representation of the Mission. Such a telescoping might have been suggested by the summarizing sentence (Acts 1:2): "Until the day in which He was taken up, after that He through the Holy Ghost had given commandments unto the apostles whom He had chosen."

This interpretation may also be corroborated by the fact that until the fourth century A.D. the Ascension of Christ was celebrated on the afternoon of the day of Pentecost and that a continuous pictorial tradition represents the two events on the same page of manuscripts or even fuses them in a compositional unity.[5]

It seems to me that a more precise analysis, which is based not only on the text of the New Testament, but considers also certain passages of the Old Testament and the historical situation in the epoch of the crusades, can further clarify the meaning of the tympanum. Not merely a general idea is represented here; a program of an astonishing preciseness, of an encyclopedic complexity and of a crystalline clarity seems to have been translated into visible terms. It must have been conceived by an outstanding theologian.

I shall first try to analyze this program, then to relate it to the historical events at the time of its creation. Finally I shall venture to identify the author of the program.

I

The encyclopedic *Mission* on the Vézelay tympanum seems to be strongly influenced by Old Testament prophecies referring to the coming salvation of mankind. It also indicates in a definite manner three specific tasks and the power to perform them, which Christ had given to His apostles:

He had given them the power to save or to condemn (Matt. 18:18; Mark 16:16; John 20:23).

He had sent them out into the world to preach the gospel to all the nations (Matt. 28:19), or, as St. Mark says, to every creature (16:15), so that they would be His witnesses unto the uttermost part of the earth (Acts 1:8).

He had given them the command and the power to heal the sick and to drive out devils (Matt. 10:1, 8; Mark 16:17, 18; Luke 9:1).

The task of saving or condemning is indicated in the central scene and in the four lower compartments of the archivolt. The task of preaching the gospel to all the nations is represented on the lintel. The task of healing the sick and of driving out devils is indicated in the four upper compartments of the archivolt. First I shall analyze the central scene, then the lintel and the archivolt.

In the central scene the apostles at Christ's right, the side where, in the Last Judgment, the blessed appear, are shown in the process of saving mankind. The apostle at the extreme left takes the lock away from his book. The next one holds his open book on his lap. His neighbor, probably St. John, shows the open book even more emphatically before his chest, before his heart. St. Peter, next to Christ, holds the key which will open paradise to the blessed. There is an increase in the size of the apostles toward the mighty, towering central figure of Christ. And to this increase in size corresponds a gradual increase in the intensity of the gestures and attributes of salvation. On the left side of Christ, however, the apostles have their books closed, thus indicating that they can condemn. St. Jerome expressed the same idea when he wrote that the apostles reveal the Savior to those who believe, but hide Him from those who do not believe.[6] This conception is also reflected in the clouds which flank the upper side of Christ's mandorla. On His right they are calm. On His left they look like thunderclouds.

The central scene, the final empowering of the apostles by Christ Himself, radiates into the subordinated scenes of the lintel and archivolt, where many of the small figures point with ecstatic gestures toward the center.

The apostles must preach the gospel to every creature. They must convert mankind. This task is represented on the lintel. From both sides approach groups of people engaged in vehement discussions. The procession coming from the right is received by St. Peter, the dispensator, with the keys of the heavenly kingdom, and St. Paul, the teacher of the gentiles. They are the princes of the apostles, also the traditional patrons of the abbey.[7]

At the extreme left the procession begins with a group of barefoot men mostly clad in short tunics and armed with bows and arrows. The next group brings offerings, a bowl full of fruit, a special cake, a fish, an object which is now partially destroyed, probably a box with incense, and a pail with wine or milk in it. Near the center of sacrificial scene is represented, obviously influenced by some classical prototype.[8] A sacrificial bull stands there among priests and helpers of the sacrifice.

At the right side, a soldier clad in mail and armed with a shield hands his sword with its point down to the apostles. He leads a group of other soldiers and men, who have not taken sufficient time to arm themselves, so eager are they to rush toward salvation. There is a pygmy, an inhabitant of Africa, who mounts a horse from a ladder.[9] Close to him at the left stands another pygmy, now partly destroyed, to whom a man of normal size talks in an emphatic manner. The procession is still extremely dramatic at the end, where two family groups gesticulate violently. The group at the very right has a monstrous appearance. It belongs to the fabulous race of the Panotii, the people with large ears. Classical and medieval writers report that they live in India or on some island far in the north.[10]

How are we to explain these two processions? Immediately before His Ascension Christ tells His apostles that they shall be His witnesses unto the uttermost part of the earth (Acts 1:8). The gospel according to St. Mark (16:15) relates that Christ gives His apostles the command to preach the gospel to every creature. These passages suggest in a general manner the idea of representing various and even monstrous peoples as the object of the missionary work of the apostles. Yet they say nothing about a frantic procession, where people admonish and push each other. It is rather the prophecies of the Old Testament which foretell, and in an emphatic manner, the effect of the coming salvation on mankind. Isaiah has described this in great detail. We know that these prophecies were quoted again and again early in the twelfth century.

Isaiah predicts that nations from afar will come that they may be saved: "Behold, these shall come from far, and, lo, these from the north and from the sea, and these from the land in the east" (49:12).[11] He speaks not only of the known peoples, but of the unknown peoples, too: "Behold, thou shalt call a nation that thou knowest not, and nations that knew not thee shall run unto thee" (55:5). Among these unknown peoples the Middle Ages include the pygmies and the Panotii. Even those of unusual appearance, like the man, the woman, and the child with large ears, would be saved. . . .

On the right side of the lintel the people are clearly more bewildered than on the left. Some, as we have seen, are talking vehemently. No better description of their attitudes and gestures could be given than that one provided by another prophecy of Isaiah: "The ends of the earth were afraid, drew near and came. They will help everyone his neighbor, and everyone will say to his brother: 'Be of good courage'" (41:5, 6).

Thus Isaiah's prophecies seem to be translated on the lintel out of dramatic pictorial language into dramatic relief sculpture. And another passage seems to have exerted an even more direct influence. This is the famous crowning prophecy in the last chapter, where the Lord says: "And I will set a sign among them, and I will send those of them that are saved to the nations in the sea, to Africa and Lydia that draw the bow, to Italy and Greece, to the isles afar off, to those that have not heard of me, neither have seen my glory; and they shall declare my glory among the gentiles" (66:19). This passage was interpreted by medieval theologians as the sending out of the apostles to all these nations[12] which, it seems, are represented on the lintel. . . .

The meaning of the lintel is even more complex. Not only do the peoples mentioned by Isaiah seem to be represented here, but they stand at the same time for different classes of humanity. We see the hunters with bow and arrow, the peasants and the fishermen, who bring the fruits of the soil, of the trees, and of the water. We see the priests, the soldiers, and the savage races. These different classes of humanity are arranged in a hierarchical order. The lowest classes form the ends of the two processions, at the extreme left the hunters, at the extreme right the savages. The highest classes, the priests and the soldiers, are accorded the favored places at the heads of the processions.

The other tasks of the apostles are represented in the eight compartments of the archivolt. Here groups of people, who by their appearance and costumes represent different races, discuss in a passionate manner the mission of the apostles and the power which Christ bestowed upon them. Some of them have again a monstrous appearance. There are the sick who will be healed by the apostles, and those whose souls will be saved by them. Specific examples illustrate the tasks of the apostles. The four upper compartments, which show different examples of physically and mentally defective people, are a kind of an encyclopedia of these defects which the sculptor renders in extremely dramatic terms. With feverish gestures some of these sick people express their hopes of being healed. They point toward the central scene, as if the realization of these hopes were now at hand. . . .

The program of the archivolt stresses the idea that the grace about to be accorded to the gentiles descends upon them by degrees. The two compartments at the top show people laboring under the severest permanent physical defects. In the next two transient or minor ailments are shown. These defects and ailments can only be cured by the working of miracles. The following pair of compartments refers to those who can be saved by conversion, while in the lowest pair the effects of grace are already apparent. In a similar manner the groups on the lintel are arranged in graduated symmetry from the ends toward the center. What is true of iconography also applies to form: the idea of gradation is expressed in the very scale of all the sculptured figures. Largest of all is Christ in the center. His size stresses His all-pervading power. By their smaller size the apostles are characterized as His helpers. Still smaller, and therefore least important, are the peoples at the periphery. They are only the objects of the work of salvation which Christ performs through His apostles.

The violent gestures of the little figures show how the grace of the Holy Spirit radiates immediately throughout the world. The *Mission of the Apostles* has a world shaking, cosmic aspect. This cosmic aspect is further enlarged by the outer archivolt, which comprises the twelve signs of the zodiac and little scenes portraying the occupations of the twelve months.[13] Christ is not only the ruler over space, over all the races of the world, but also over time, over the cycle of the year and its activities. . . .

II

The central tympanum at Vézelay was created between the first and the second crusades, in an epoch which gave a new impulse to religious feeling and broadened the outlook of medieval thinkers. It was created in Burgundy, in the center of France, at a place which played a prominent role in the history of the crusades.

In 1095, on the eve of the first crusade, Urban II, the Cluniac Pope of French descent, had planned, according to William of Tyre,[14] to hold a council either in Vézelay or in Le Puy, but decided in favor of Clermont. There he called upon clerics and laymen to rescue the Christians of the East, to liberate by a pilgrimage in arms Jerusalem and the Oriental churches which had been overrun by the Moslems and were suffering so miserably. That was about thirty years before the tympanum was created. About fifteen years after its completion it was in Vézelay that St. Bernard preached the second crusade in 1146 and Louis VII, the king of France, took up the cross. Again it was from Vézelay that, in 1190, Richard Coeur de Lion and Philip Augustus, the French king, started for the third crusade. . . .

The canonical Acts of the Apostles and apocryphal acts report how the twelve apostles had, each in his allotted region, conquered the world for the Christian faith. They had established the Church unto the ends of the world. But later, with the coming of the Arabs, infidels had gradually overrun many parts of the world: all of Asia and Africa, and even parts of Europe.

In 1095, at the end of the Council of Clermont, Pope Urban II addressed the assembly. His speech, as different writers relate it in different versions, sounds like the proclaiming of a new mission which set a twofold task to the clerics and one to the laymen. The clerics alone were urged to persuade men of all ranks to take up the fight against the Moslems. According to Fulcher of Chartres, the Pope said: "Qua de re supplici prece hortor, non ego, sed Dominus, ut cunctis cuiuslibet ordinis tam equitibus quam peditibus, tam divitibus quam pauperibus, edicto frequenti vos, Christi praecones, suadeatis, ut ad id genus nequam de regionibus nostrorum exterminandum tempestive Christicolis opitulari satagant."[15] But both clerics and laymen were called upon to reconquer the lost parts of the world for the Christian faith and to liberate Jerusalem, the navel of the earth, and the Lord's Sepulcher. . . . What had been achieved by the apostles had to be achieved again, at the end of the eleventh century. The clerics were urged to preach the crusade in their districts, and they were sent out, together with the laymen, to reconquer the lost parts of the world which once had been conquered by the apostles. Thus the choice of the subject to be represented in the tympanum just at this time seems to bear a deeper meaning. The encyclopedic *Mission of the Apostles* prefigures the new mission of the crusaders. . . .

We have seen that the prophecy in the last chapter of Isaiah was very likely the main literary source of the lintel. Medieval writers believed that it had been fulfilled by the apostles, but it seemed to be fulfilled again in the first crusade. This is the opinion of Peter the Venerable. Once the prior of Vézelay, he had become abbot of Cluny in 1122. In his sermon *In laudem sepulcri Domini* he quotes this very prophecy which, he believes, came true again, when the crusaders liberated the Holy Sepulcher from the rule of the infidels and "purified with their holy swords the place and habitation of heavenly purity."[16] This idea has its counterpart on the lintel where the foremost soldier on the right, who may be considered as a prototype of the crusading knights, presents his sword to the apostles that it may be made holy.

Some other very characteristic elements in the program of the tympanum seem to reflect quite closely ideas which the abbot of Cluny has expressed in his writings. We have seen that the prophecies of Isaiah may have played a paramount part in the conception of the program. It is this same prophet whom Peter the Venerable likes to quote as his primary witness. He invokes him as "eximie prophetarum" or "maxime prophetarum."[17] "Audite divinum prophetam," he says in his sermon on the Holy Sepulcher, "immo praecipuum in prophetis ad vos ante multa saecula propheticum oculum convertentem."[18]

Shortly after quoting the prophecy of the last chapter of Isaiah, Peter the Venerable gives a list of miracles. He mentions first the giving of sight to the blind, then the restoring of hearing to the deaf and of speech to the dumb.[19] These are the three organic defects, which are represented in the same sequence in the topmost compartment at the left. . . .

Since so many ideas which are expressed in the tympanum can be found in the writings of Peter the Venerable, may we not draw the conclusion that he may have worked out the program to be sculptured in the narthex at Vézelay? Peter the Venerable was a great theologian who took a keen interest in the liberation of the Holy Land. The Abbey of Vézelay was closely affiliated with Cluny and Peter had once been its prior. All this may speak in favor of his authorship. He might even have conceived the program while he was still there, although the actual sculpturing of the tympana was done during his abbotship at Cluny. In any case, the deep and complex meaning of the central tympanum betrays ideas of a great theologian. According to his program, prophecies of the Old Testament, their fulfillment by the *Mission of the Apostles* and their refulfillment by the new mission of the crusaders are interwoven here into a grandiose, cosmic, encyclopedic and at the same time beautifully dramatic unity.

NOTES

NOTE: This article grew out of a lecture given in April, 1943, at The Pierpont Morgan Library, New York.

[1] See, for instance, G. Sanoner, "Portail de l'abbaye de Vézelay," *Revue de l'art chrétien*, LIV (1904), pp. 448 ff.; L. Eugene Lefevre, "Le symbolisme du tympan de Vézelay," *ibid.*, LVI (1906), pp. 253 ff.; Paul Mayeur, "Le tympan de l'église abbatiale de Vézelay," *ibid.*, LVIII (1908), pp. 103 ff.; Paul Mayeur, "Les scènes secondaires du tympan de Vézelay," *ibid.*, LIX (1909), pp. 326 ff.

[2] Émile Mâle, *L'art religieux du XII siècle en France* (Paris, 1922), pp. 326 ff.; Abel Fabre, "L'iconographie de la Pentecôte," *Gazette des Beaux-Arts*, 65° année (1923), II, pp. 33 ff. See also A. Kingsley Porter, "Spain or Toulouse? and Other Questions," ART BULLETIN, VII (1924–25), p. 20.

[3] A. Kingsley Porter, *Romanesque Sculpture of the Pilgrimage Roads* (Boston, 1923), Figs. 96, 97. Conant has recently reinterpreted in a similar manner the tympanum which once decorated the great portal at Cluny. See Kenneth John Conant, "The Third Church at Cluny," *Medieval Studies in Memory of A. Kingsley Porter*, II (Cambridge, 1939), pp. 335, 336.

[4] Acts I:II.

[5] The two events are represented on the same page, for instance, in the Carolingian Bible of S. Paolo fuori le mura, fol. 292v (Amédée Boinet, *La miniature carolingienne* [Paris, 1913], pl. CXXVIII). See also the Golden Gospel Book from

Echternach, late tenth century (Gotha, Landesbibliothek, Ms. 1.19, fol. 112v; Albert Boeckler, *Das goldene Evangelienbuch Heinrichs III* [Berlin, 1933], Fig. 173). Both events are merged in a miniature of a Gospel Book from Seitenstetten of the early thirteenth century (Pierpont Morgan Library, Ms. 808, fol. 24; *Catalogue of the Renowned Collection of Western Manuscripts the Property of A. Chester Beatty*, II [London, 1933], pl. 18). In some eleventh-century illustrations of the *Ascension of Christ* rays emanate from the clouds on which Christ stands. See Ernest T. Dewald, "The Iconography of the Ascension," *American Journal of Archaeology*, XIX (1915), pp. 277 ff.; Figs. 19, 20.

[6] *Commentaria in Isaiam*, lib. III, cap. 6 (*Patrologia Latina*, 24, col. 96).

[7] See Hugo of Poitiers, *Historia Vizeliacensis Monasterii*, lib. III (*Patrologia Latina*, 194, col. 1605): "Ecclesia Vizeliacensis ab inclito Gerardo comite nobiliter fundata, nobilius ab eodem attitulata beatorum Petri et Pauli apostolorum nomini ascripta, juri assignata, regimini credita, protectioni commissa." Cf. also the beginning of a privilege granted by Pope Leo IX in 1050: "Leo episcopus, servus servorum Dei, Gaufrido abbati Vizeliacensis coenobii, quod est in honore Domini nostri Jesu Christi et veneratione ejusdem genitricis et beatorum apostolorum Petri et Pauli et beatae Mariae Magdalenae, ejusque successoribus in perpetuum" (*Patrologia Latina*, 143, col. 642).

[8] See Jean Adhémar, *Influences antiques dans l'art du moyen âge français*, Studies of the Warburg Institute, no. 7 (London, 1939), pp. 177 ff.

[9] Pliny, *Natural History*, VI. 35. 188, ed. H. Rackham, II (London and Cambridge, 1942), p. 478. They are also mentioned as inhabitants of India.

[10] Pliny, *op. cit.*, IV. 13, 95; VII. 2. 30, ed. Rackham, II, pp. 192, 526; C. Julius Solinus, *Collectanea Rerum Memorabilium*, XIX. 8, ed. Th. Mommsen (Berlin, 1895), pp. 93, 94; Isidore of Seville, *Etymologiae*, XI. 3. 19, ed. W. M. Lindsay, Oxford.

[11] Cf. also Isaiah 2:2–4; Jeremiah 16:19; Zechariah 8:20–23.

[12] St. Jerome, *Commentaria in Isaiam*, lib. XVIII, cap. 66 (*Patrologia Latina*, 24, cols. 692 ff.); Isidore of Seville, *De Fide Catholica*, lib. I, cap. 55 (*ibid.*, 83, cols. 493, 494); Haymo of Halberstadt, *Commentaria in Isaiam*, lib. III, cap. 66 (*ibid.*, 116, col. 1082); Hugo of St. Victor, *Sermo de quibuslibet Apostolis* (*ibid.*, 177, cols. 1039 ff.).

[13] The chronological cycle consists of twenty-six medallions, comprising the twelve signs of the zodiac, the twelve labors of the months, and two extra medallions, i.e., the third from below on either side. Four additional medallions, which do not refer to the cycle of the year, form the topmost arc of the semicircle.

The two extra medallions which are inserted in the cycle of the year represent at the left, a man warming himself at a fire and another taking off his garment, at the right, a bearded man carrying a wrapped woman on his shoulders. These four figures may personify the four seasons. The four medallions at the top show an eagle, a dog (?), a man and a siren. One might think that three elements are symbolized by them, air by the eagle, earth by dog and man, and water by the siren. May one even go a step farther and see fire symbolized by the adjoining sign of the lion? Such groups of cosmological significance already frame late antique Mithraic reliefs, thereby stressing the power of the pagan god. On the relief of the *Birth of Mithras* from Trier, for instance, the zodiac and the four winds are grouped around the new-born god, while symbols of the four elements are represented in the crowning gable. See Fritz Saxl, *Mithras* (Berlin, 1931), Fig. 199.

[14] *Historia Rerum in Partibus Transmarinis Gestarum*, lib. i, cap. 14 (*Patrologia Latina*, 201, col. 231).

[15] "Wherefore, I exhort with earnest prayer—not I, but God—that, as heralds of Christ, you urge men by frequent exhortation, men of all ranks, knights as well as foot-soldiers, rich as well as poor, to hasten to exterminate this vile race from the lands of your brethren, and to aid the Christians in time" (August C. Krey, *The First Crusade* [Princeton and London, 1921], p. 29). I am greatly indebted to the Princeton University Press for the kind permission to quote this and other translations from Krey's book. For the original text, see *Fulcheri Carnotensis Historia Hierosolymitana*, lib. i, cap. 3, ed. Heinrich Hagenmeyer (Heidelberg, 1913), pp. 134, 135.

Cf. also the command, as reported by Balderic, Archbishop of Dol, in his *Historia Hierosolymitana*, lib. i, cap. 4: "Et conversus ad episcopos: 'Vos,' inquit, 'fratres et coepiscopi, vos consacerdotes et cohaeredes Christi, per ecclesias vobis commissas id ipsum annuntiate, et viam in Jerusalem toto ore viriliter praedicate. Confessis peccatorum suorum ignominiam, securi de Christo celerem paciscimini veniam'" (*Recueil des historiens des croisades, Historiens occidentaux*, iv, [Paris, 1879], p. 15).

[16] *Patrologia Latina*, 189, col. 985.

[17] *Tractatus adversus Judaeorum inveteratam duritiem*, cap. 1 (*ibid.*, col. 509); cap. 5 (*ibid.*, col. 608).

[18] "Listen to the divine prophet, yes indeed to the foremost among the prophets, who has turned his prophetical eye towards you many ages ago." For the original text, *see ibid.*, col. 982.

[19] *Ibid.*, col. 986.

15. MEDIEVAL

ICONOGRAPHY

Emile Mâle

INTRODUCTION

Since its publication in 1898, Emile Mâle's *L'Art Religieux du XIIIe Siècle en France* has enjoyed an important place in the literature dealing with the iconography of medieval art. The English translation of 1913 (available in paperback as *The Gothic Image*) is the source for the selection in this anthology. In this work the imagery of Gothic cathedral decoration is related to the theological literature of the Middle Ages, particularly to the *Speculum* of Vincent of Beauvais, which supplies the framework for Mâle's study. Since Mâle is primarily concerned with the meaning of the images in Gothic decoration, one should read in conjunction with it Erwin Panofsky's *Gothic Architecture and Scholasticism* (1951), which emphasizes the role played by the diffusion of a scholastic "mental habit" in establishing relationships between scholastic thought and Gothic architecture.

For the iconography of Christian art there are a number of works in English. The numerous volumes by Anna B. Jameson are still valuable references: *The History of Our Lord,* 4th ed., 2 Vols. (1881); *Sacred and Legendary Art*, 2 Vols. (1911); *Legends of the Monastic Orders* (1911); *Legends of the Madonna* (1911). Other studies are Adolphe Didron, *Christian Iconography*, trans. by E. G. Millington, 2 Vols. (1896), and Maurice Drake, *Saints and Their Emblems* (1916). For the iconography of the Renaissance there is Erwin Panofsky's brilliant *Studies in Iconology* (1939), of which the introductory chapter is an excellent orientation to the whole subject of meaning in a work of art. It is also available in a paperbound edition. For mythological themes in art, there are such works as E. Panofsky and F. Saxl, "Classical Mythology in Medieval Art," *Metropolitan Museum Studies*, IV, 2 (1933); Kurt Weitzmann, *Greek Mythology in Byzantine Art* (1951); and Jean Seznec, *The Survival of the Pagan Gods* (1953).

The selection that follows is from the book *The Gothic Image: Religious Art in the Thirteenth Century* by Emile Mâle. Translated by Dora Nussey. Reprinted by permission of E. P. Dutton & Co., Inc.

GENERAL CHARACTERISTICS OF
MEDIEVAL ICONOGRAPHY

The Middle Ages had a passion for order. They organized art as they had organized dogma, secular learning and society. The artistic representation of sacred subjects was a science governed by fixed laws which could not be broken at the dictates of individual imagination. It cannot be questioned that this theology of art, if one may so put it, was soon reduced to a body of doctrine, for from very early times the craftsmen are seen submitting to it from one end of Europe to the other. This science was transmitted by the Church to the lay sculptors and painters of the thirteenth century who religiously guarded the sacred traditions, so that, even in the centuries in which it was most vigorous, medieval art retained the hieratic grandeur of primitive art.

These are the general principles which it concerns us to state at the outset as briefly as possible.

I

The art of the Middle Ages is first and foremost a sacred writing of which every artist must learn the characters. He must know that the circular nimbus placed vertically behind the head serves to express sanctity, while the nimbus impressed with a cross is the sign of divinity which he will always use in portraying any of the three Persons of the Trinity.[1] He will learn that the aureole (*i.e.* light which emanates from the whole figure and surrounds the body as a nimbus) expresses eternal bliss, and belongs to the three Persons of the Trinity, to the Virgin, and to the souls of the Blessed. He must know that representations of God the Father, God the Son, the angels and the apostles should have the feet bare, while there would be real impropriety in representing the Virgin and the saints with bare feet. In such matters a mistake would have ranked almost as heresy. Other accepted symbols enabled the medieval artist to express the invisible, to represent that which would otherwise be beyond the domain of art. A hand emerging from the clouds, making the gesture of benediction with thumb and two fingers raised, and surrounded by a cruciform nimbus, was recognized as the sign of divine intervention, the emblem of providence. Little figures of nude and sexless children, ranged side by side in the folds of Abraham's mantle, signified the eternal rest of the life to come.

There are also accepted signs for objects of the visible world which the artist must learn. Lines which are concentric and sinuous represent the sky, those which are horizontal and undulating represent water. A tree, that is to say a stalk surmounted with two or three leaves, indicates that the scene takes place on the earth; a tower pierced by a doorway is a town, while if an angel watch on the battlements it is the heavenly Jerusalem.[2] Thus we have a veritable hieroglyphic[3] in which art and writing blend, showing the same spirit of order and abstraction that there is in heraldic art with its alphabet, rules and symbolism. . . .

II

The second characteristic of medieval iconography is obedience to the rules of a kind of sacred mathematics. Position, grouping, symmetry and number are of extraordinary importance.

To begin with, the whole church is oriented from the rising to the setting sun, a custom dating back to primitive Christian days for it is found even in the *Apostolical Constitutions*. In the thirteenth century Gulielmus Durandus cites this as a rule without exception:—"The foundations must be disposed in such a manner that the head of the church lies exactly to the east, that is to the part of the sky in which the sun rises at the equinox." And, as a matter of fact, from the eleventh to the sixteenth century it is difficult to find a badly oriented church. Like other traditions of medieval art the rule fell into neglect toward the time of the Council of Trent, the Jesuits being the first to violate it.

Each cardinal point has its significance in churches oriented in this way. The north, region of cold and darkness, is usually consecrated to the Old Testament, and the south, bathed in warm sunlight is devoted to the New, though there are many exceptions to the rule.[4] The western façade—where the setting sun lights up the great scene of the evening of the world's history—is almost invariably reserved for a representation of the Last Judgment. The medieval doctors, with their curiously bad etymology, connected *occidens* with the verb *occidere,* and the west became for them the region of death.

After orientation it was relative position which most engrossed the artist, here again at one with the theologian. In early times certain passages in the Bible led to the belief that the right hand was the place of honor. Is it not written, for example, in the Psalms: "Adstitit regina a dextris tuis in vestitu deaurato?" In the *Shepherd* of Hermas which belongs to primitive Christian literature, the right is the place given to those who are marked out for honor. In the account of the third vision it is said that the Church caused Hermas to be seated on a bench at her side. When he would have seated himself to her right she signed to him to pass to the left, because the right is reserved for those who have suffered in the name of God. The medieval theologians in their turn laid great stress on the dignity of the right hand place, and the artists did not fail to conform to so well-established a doctrine. When, for example, the Savior is represented in the midst of His apostles, St. Peter—first in dignity—occupies a place to the right of the Master.[5] In the same way in the scene of the Crucifixion or in that of the Last Judgment, the Virgin is to the right, St. John to the left.

Again, the higher place was considered more honorable than the lower, and from this some curious compositions resulted. Of these the most striking is that of the figure of Christ in Majesty supported by the four beasts of the Apocalypse. The four beasts, symbols of the evangelists as we shall show later, were placed according to the excellence of their natures—man, eagle, lion and ox. When it was a question of disposing them in a tympanum, the dignity conferred by the higher and that conferred by the right hand place had to be taken into consideration. The following arrangement was the one generally adopted. The winged man was placed at the top of the composition and to the right of Christ, the eagle at the top to the left, the lion at the bottom to the right, the ox at the bottom to the left[6] (Fig. 39). . . .

But no disposition met with more favor than that controlled by symmetry. Symmetry was regarded as the expression of a mysterious inner harmony. Craftsmen opposed the twelve patriarchs and twelve prophets of the Ancient Law to the twelve apostles of the New,

39. Tympanum: Christ as Judge and Ruler of the Universe with Symbols of Evangelists, Central Portal, West Façade, Chartres Cathedral, *c.* 1150 (Marburg-Art Reference Bureau)

and the four major prophets to the four evangelists. A window in the south transept at Chartres shows—with audacious symbolism—the four prophets Isaiah, Ezekiel, Daniel and Jeremiah bearing on their shoulders the four evangelists, St. Matthew, St. John, St. Mark, St. Luke. In this way the artists would tell us that although the evangelists rest upon the prophets, yet from their spiritual vantage-ground they have a wider outlook. The four and twenty elders of the Apocalypse frequently correspond to the twelve prophets and the twelve apostles. . . .

Schemes of this kind presuppose a reasoned belief in the virtue of numbers, and in fact the Middle Ages never doubted that numbers were endowed with some occult power. This doctrine came from the Fathers of the Church, who inherited it from those Neoplatonic schools in which the genius of Pythagoras had lived again. It is evident that St. Augustine considered numbers as thoughts of God. In many passages he lays it down that each number has its divine significance. "The Divine Wisdom is reflected in the numbers

270

impressed on all things."[7] The construction of the physical and moral worlds alike is based on eternal numbers. We feel that the charm of the dance lies in rhythm, that is in number; but we must go further, beauty is itself a cadence, harmonious number.[8] The science of numbers, then, is the science of the universe, and from numbers we learn its secret. Therefore the numbers met with in the Bible should be considered with reverent attention, for they are sacred and full of mystery.[9] He who can read them enters into the divine plan. . . .

A few examples will give some idea of the method. From St. Augustine onward all theologians interpreted the meaning of the number twelve after the same fashion. Twelve is the number of the universal Church, and it was for profound reasons that Jesus willed the number of His apostles should be twelve. Now twelve is the product of three by four. Three, which is the number of the Trinity and by consequence of the soul made in the image of the Trinity, connotes all spiritual things. Four, the number of the elements, is the symbol of material things—the body and the world—which result from combinations of the four elements.[10] To multiply three by four is in the mystic sense to infuse matter with spirit, to proclaim the truths of the faith to the world, to establish the universal Church of which the apostles are the symbol.[11]

Computations of this kind were often more than ingenious, and at times reached real grandeur. The number seven, regarded by the Fathers as mysterious above all others, intoxicated the medieval mystic. It was observed first of all that seven—composed of four, the number of the body, and of three, the number of the soul—is preeminently the number of humanity, and expresses the union of man's double nature. All that relates to him is ordered in series of sevens. Human life is divided into seven ages with each of which is associated the practice of one of the seven virtues. The grace necessary for the practice of these seven virtues is gained by addressing to God the seven petitions of the Paternoster. The seven sacraments sustain man in the exercise of the seven virtues, and guard him from falling into the seven deadly sins.[12] The number seven thus expresses the harmony of man's nature, but it also expresses the harmonious relation of man to the universe. The seven planets govern human destiny, for each of the seven ages is under the influence of one of them. Thus seven invisible threads connect man with the scheme of the universe.[13] . . .

271

III

The third characteristic of medieval art lies in this, that it is a symbolic code. From the days of the catacombs Christian art has spoken in figures, showing men one thing and inviting them to see in it the figure of another. The artist, as the doctors might have put it, must imitate God who under the letter of Scripture hid profound meaning, and who willed that nature too should hold lessons for man.

In medieval art there are then intentions a knowledge of which is necessary to any real understanding of the subject. When for example in scenes of the Last Judgment we see the Wise and Foolish Virgins to the right and left hand of Christ, we should thereby understand that they symbolize the elect and the lost. Upon this all the commentators on the New Testament are agreed, and they explain it by stating that the five Foolish Virgins typify the desires of the five senses, and the five Wise Virgins the five forms of the contemplative life. To take another example, it is not as rivers that the four rivers of Paradise—the Gihon, Phison, Tigris, and Euphrates—are represented pouring water from their urns towards the four points of the compass, but as symbols of the evangelists who flooded the world with their teaching like four beneficent streams.

An Old Testament personage in the porch of a cathedral is but a type, an adumbration of Christ, the Virgin, or the future Church. At Chartres the form of Melchizedek, priest and king, bearing the bread and wine to Abraham, should remind men of another priest and king who offered bread and wine to His disciples. At Laon Gideon calling down rain from heaven on to the fleece he had laid on the earth, reminds men that the Virgin Mother was this symbolic fleece on whom fell the dew from on high.

A detail of apparent insignificance may hide symbolic meaning. In a window at Bourges the lion near to the tomb from which the risen Christ comes forth is a type of the Resurrection. It was generally believed in the Middle Ages that for three days after birth the cubs of the lioness gave no sign of life, but that on the third day the lion came and with his breath restored them to life. And so the apparent death of the lion represents the sojourn of Jesus in the tomb, and its birth was an image of the Resurrection.

In the art of the Middle Ages, as we see, everything depicted is informed by a quickening spirit.

Such a conception of art implies a profoundly idealistic view of the scheme of the universe, and the conviction that both history and nature must be regarded as vast symbols. We shall see later that this undoubtedly was the view of the medieval mind. Further, it should be remembered that such ideas were not the property of the great thirteenth century doctors alone, but were shared by the mass of the people to whom they had permeated through the teaching of the Church. The symbolism of the church services familiarized the faithful with the symbolism of art. Christian liturgy like Christian art is endless symbolism, both are manifestations of the same genius. . . .

From what has been said it is evident that medieval art was before all things a symbolic art, in which form is used merely as the vehicle of spiritual meaning.[14]

Such are the general characteristics of the iconography of the Middle Ages. Art was at once a script, a calculus and a symbolic code. The result was a deep and perfect harmony. There is something musical in the grouping of the statues in the cathedral porches, and in truth all the elements of music are present. Are there not here conventional signs grouped according to the law of numbers, and is there not something of the indefinite quality of music in the infinite symbolism dimly discerned behind the outward forms? The genius of the Middle Ages, so long misunderstood, was a harmonious genius. Dante's Paradiso and the porches at Chartres are symphonies. To thirteenth century art more truly perhaps than to any other might be given the title of "frozen music."

METHOD USED IN THE STUDY OF
MEDIEVAL ICONOGRAPHY

THE MIRRORS OF VINCENT OF BEAUVAIS

The thirteenth century was the century of encyclopedias. At no other period have so many works appeared bearing the titles of *Summa*, *Speculum* or *Imago Mundi*. It was in this century that Thomas Aquinas coordinated the whole body of Christian doctrine, Jacobus de Voragine collected the most famous legends of the saints,

Gulielmus Durandus epitomized all previous writers on the liturgy, and Vincent of Beauvais attempted to embrace universal knowledge. Christianity came to full consciousness of its own genius, and the conception of the universe which had been elaborated by previous centuries received complete expression. It was believed to be possible to raise the final edifice of human knowledge, and in the universities which had recently been founded throughout Europe—above all the young university of Paris—the work was carried on with enthusiasm.

While the doctors were constructing the intellectual edifice which was to shelter the whole of Christendom, the cathedral of stone was rising as its visible counterpart. It too in its fashion was a *Speculum*, a *Summa*, an *Imago Mundi* into which the Middle Age put all its most cherished convictions. These great churches are the most perfect known expression in art of the mind of an epoch. We shall attempt to show that in them a whole dogmatic scheme found expression in concrete form.

The difficulty lies in grouping in logical sequence the innumerable works of art which the churches offer for our study. Surely we have hardly the right to dispose of the matter according to some arbitrary scheme which appears to us harmonious. It is necessary to discard modern habits of mind. If we impose our categories on medieval thought we run every risk of error, and for that reason we borrow our method of exposition from the Middle Age itself. The four books of Vincent of Beauvais's *Mirror* furnish us with the framework for the four divisions of our study of thirteenth century art.

If Aquinas was the most powerful thinker of the Middle Ages, Vincent of Beauvais was certainly the most comprehensive. He might well be called an epitome of the knowledge of his day. A prodigious worker, he passed his life like the elder Pliny in reading and making extracts. He was called "librorum helluo," the devourer of books. St. Louis threw open to him the fine library containing virtually all the books procurable in the thirteenth century, and at times came to visit him at the abbey of Royaumont, where he loved to hear him talk of the wonders of the universe.

It was probably toward the middle of the century that Vincent of Beauvais published the great *Mirror*, the *Speculum majus*, which to his contemporaries seemed the supreme effort of human learning. Even today one cannot but admire so stupendous a work.[15]

His learning was immense, yet it did not overwhelm him. The order which he adopted was the most imposing which the Middle Age could conceive—the very plan of God as it appears in the Scriptures. Vincent of Beauvais's work is divided into four parts—the Mirror of Nature, the Mirror of Instruction, the Mirror of Morals[16] and the Mirror of History.

In the Mirror of Nature are reflected all natural phenomena in the order in which they were created by God. The Days of Creation mark the different chapters of this great encyclopedia of nature. The four elements, the minerals, vegetables and animals are successively enumerated and described. All the truth and the error which had been transmitted by antiquity to the Middle Ages are found there. But it is naturally on the work of the sixth day—the creation of man—that Vincent of Beauvais dwells at greatest length, for man is the center of the universe and for him all things were made.

The Mirror of Instruction opens with the story of the Fall, the recital of the drama which explains the riddle of the universe. Man has fallen, and only through a Redeemer can he hope for salvation. Yet in his own strength he can begin to raise himself, and through knowledge to prepare for grace. There is in knowledge a quickening power, and to each of the seven Arts corresponds one of the seven Gifts of the Spirit. After expounding this large and humane doctrine Vincent of Beauvais passes in review all the different branches of knowledge; even the mechanical arts are included, for by the labor of his hands man begins the work of his redemption.

The Mirror of Morals is closely connected with the Mirror of Instruction, for the end of life is not to know but to act, and knowledge is but a means to virtue. Out of this springs a learned classification of the virtues and vices, in which the method, divisions and often the very expressions of Aquinas are found—for the *Speculum morale* is the *Summa* in abridged form.

The last division is the Mirror of History. We have studied human nature in the abstract, and we now turn to man himself, watching his progress under the eye of God. He invents arts and sciences, he struggles and suffers, choosing sometimes vice, sometimes virtue in the great battle of the soul which is the sum of the world's history. It is hardly necessary to observe that for Vincent of Beauvais, as for Augustine, Orosius, Gregory of Tours and all the historians of the Middle Ages, true history is the history of the Church, the City of God, which begins with Abel the first just man. There is a chosen people and their history is the pillar of fire which lightens the darkness. The history of the pagan world is deserving of study only with reference to the other; it has merely value as a synchronism. It is true that Vincent of Beauvais did not scorn to tell of the revolution of empires, and even delighted in speaking of pagan philosophers, scholars and poets, but such subjects are really incidental. The dominant thought of his book—the idea which gives it unity—is the unbroken line of saints of the Old and New Testaments. Through them and them alone the history of the world becomes coherent.

Thus was conceived this Encyclopedia of the thirteenth century. In it the riddle of the universe finds solution. The plan is so comprehensive that the Middle Ages could conceive of nothing which it did not include, and until the Renaissance the following centuries found nothing to add to it.

Such a book is the surest guide that we can choose for our study of the great leading ideas which lay behind the art of the thirteenth century. Striking analogies are noticeable, for example, between the general economy of the *Speculum Majus* and the plan followed in the porches of the cathedral of Chartres. As was first pointed out by Didron in the authoritative introduction to his *Histoire de Dieu*, the innumerable figures which decorate the porches may well be grouped under the four heads of nature, instruction, morals, and history. We do not know whether that great decorative scheme was directly inspired by Vincent of Beauvais's book with which it was almost contemporaneous, but it is obvious that the arrangement of the *Speculum Majus* belonged not to him but to the Middle Ages as a whole. It was the form which the thirteenth century imposed on all ordered thought. The same genius disposed the chapters of the *Mirror* and the sculpture of the cathedral. It is then legitimate to seek in the one the meaning of the other.

We shall therefore adopt the four great divisions of Vincent of Beauvais's work, and shall try to read the four books of the *Mirror* in the façades of the cathedrals. We shall find them all four represented, and shall decipher them in the order in which the encyclopedist presents them. Each detail will in this way find its place, and the harmony of the whole will appear.

THE MIRROR OF NATURE

. . . The Mirror of Nature is carved in brief on the façades of most of the French cathedrals. We find it at Chartres, at Laon, at Auxerre, Bourges and Lyons, treated in a restrained and conventional way. At Chartres a lion, a sheep, a goat and a heifer stand for the animal world, a fig tree and three plants of indeterminate character represent the vegetable kingdom; there is an element of greatness in this summing up of the universe in some five or six bas-reliefs. Some naïve details are full of charm. In the representation at Laon the Creator sits in deep reflection before dividing the darkness from the light, and counts on His fingers the number of days needed to finish His work. Later in the series, when His task is accomplished, He sits down to rest like a good workman at the end of a well-spent day, and leaning on His staff He falls asleep.

One might well feel that these few typical forms were inadequate representations of the wealth of the universe, and might accuse the thirteenth-century craftsmen of timidity and want of power, did the animal and vegetable worlds really occupy no further place in the cathedral scheme. But a glance upward shows us vines, raspberries heavy with fruit and long trails of the wild rose clinging to the archivolts, birds singing among the oak leaves or perching on the pillars. Beasts from far-off lands side by side with homely creatures of the countryside—lions, elephants and camels, squirrels, hens and rabbits—enliven the basement of the porch, while monsters securely fastened by their heavy stone wings bark fiercely at us from above. How little do these old masters with their unequalled, if naïve love of nature deserve the reproach of lack of power or invention. Their cathedrals are all life and movement. The Church to them was the ark to which every creature was made welcome, and then—as if the works of God were not sufficient for them—they invented a whole world more of terrible beings, creatures so real that they surely must have lived in the childhood of the world. . . .

There are few cases in which it is permissible to assign symbolic meaning to animal forms, but they are of such a kind that through literary references one may reach sure conclusions.

The four beasts surrounding the figure of Christ in Glory, found in the porch of so many churches, form the first class of representations in which the symbolic meaning cannot be mistaken. The motif of the four creatures—the man,[17] the eagle, the lion and the ox—so frequent in the Romanesque period, became more rare in the thirteenth century though not entirely discarded. The four creatures are seen, for example, on the Porte du Jugement of Notre Dame at Paris. It is true they no longer have the breadth, the heraldic boldness which is so striking at Moissac, and they no longer fill the tympanum but hide humbly in the lower portion of the doorway.

From earliest Christian times the man, the eagle, the lion and the ox, first seen in Ezekiel's vision by the river Chebar and later by St. John round the throne of God, were accepted symbols of the four evangelists.

. . . The emblem of St. Matthew is the man, because his gospel begins with the genealogical table of the ancestors of Jesus according to the flesh. The lion designates St. Mark, for in the opening verses of his gospel he speaks of the voice crying in the wilderness. The ox—the sacrificial animal—symbolizes St. Luke, whose gospel opens with the sacrifice offered by Zacharias. The eagle—an echo of the natural history of the Bestiaries—who alone of created things was reputed to gaze straight into the light of the sun, is the emblem of St. John, who from the first transports men to the very heart of divinity. Again, these same creatures are symbols of Christ, for in them may be seen four great mysteries in the life of the Savior. The man recalls the Incarnation, and reminds men that the Son of God became man. The ox, victim of the Old Law, calls to remembrance the Passion—the Redeemer's sacrifice of His life for mankind. The lion, which in the fabled science of the Bestiaries sleeps with open eyes, is the symbol of the Resurrection, for therein, says the lectionary, is a figure of Jesus in the tomb. "For the Redeemer in virtue of His humanity appeared to sink into the sleep of death, but in virtue of His divinity He was living and watching." Lastly, the eagle is a figure of the Ascension. Christ rose to Heaven as the eagle rises to the clouds. Summing up its teaching in a precise formula, the lectionary lays it down that Christ was man in His birth, ox in His death, lion in His Resurrection, eagle in His Ascension.[18]

But the four creatures have yet a third meaning, and express the virtues necessary for salvation. Each Christian on his way to divine perfection must be at once man, ox, lion and eagle. He must be man because man is a reasonable animal, and he who treads the path of reason alone deserves that name. He must be ox because the ox is the sacrificial victim, and the true Christian by renouncing worldly pleasures sacrifices himself. He must be lion because the lion is the most courageous of beasts, and the good man having renounced all worldly things fears nothing, for of him it is written, "The righteous are bold as a lion." And he must be eagle because the eagle flies in the heights looking straight into the sun, type of the Christian who with direct gaze contemplates the things of eternity.

This is the Church's teaching on the four creatures, but only one of these interpretations, that likening the apocalyptic beasts to the evangelists, survived medieval times. The others shared the fate of all the old mystical theology, and at the Reformation fell into oblivion. But Protestants themselves remained faithful to tradition on the first point, and in the seventeenth century Rembrandt painted his sublime St. Matthew of the Louvre listening with all his soul to the words of an angel who, deep in shadow, whispers to him of eternal things. . . .

THE MIRROR OF INSTRUCTION

The world has come into being. The work of God is finished and perfect, but the harmony is destroyed for man has misused his liberty. Sin has brought misery into the world, and henceforth mankind is like the wretched Adam and Eve who at the top of Notre Dame at Paris seem to shiver in the mist and the rain.[19]

The Church proclaims through her art that fallen humanity can only be restored through the grace of God and the sacrifice of Christ, but that man must merit grace and must take his part in the work of redemption. In the preface to his *Speculum doctrinale* Vincent of Beauvais expresses the conviction—"Ipsa restitutio sive restauratio per doctrinam efficitur" and, as the sequel shows, by "doctrina," he understands work of every kind, even the humblest. The Middle Age was not only the age of contemplation, it was also the age of work accepted and conceived not as servitude but as enfranchisement. Manual labor—in substance we quote Vincent of Beauvais—delivers man from the necessities to which since the Fall his body is subject, while instruction delivers him from the ignorance which has weighed down his soul.[20] And so in the cathedrals, where all medieval thought took visible shape, knowledge and manual

279

labor are given a place of equal honor. In the church where kings, barons and bishops fill so modest a place we find representations of almost every craft. At Chartres and Bourges, for example, in the windows given by the guilds, the lower part shows the donors with the badges of their trade—trowel, hammer, wool-carding comb, baker's shovel and butcher's knife.[21] In those days no incongruity was felt in placing these pictures of daily life side by side with scenes from the legends of the saints. The dignity and sanctity of labor were expressed in this way. . . .

But it was to the primeval work of tilling the soil, the task which God Himself imposed on Adam, that the Church seems to have given the foremost place. In several French cathedrals the cycle of the year's work is carved round the orders of the arch or on the basement of the porch.[22] A sign of the zodiac accompanies each scene of harvest, tillage or vintage. Here are really "The Works and Days."

The custom of decorating the churches with calendars in stone was well-established in primitive Christian times, for we know that the pavements of early basilicas were sometimes engraved with symbolic figures of the seasons. The mosaic from a church at Tyre given to the Louvre by the Renan mission represents scenes of the hunt and vintage accompanied by figures of the months.[23] This work is classical in character, and probably came from some thermæ or villa. The Church did not scruple to borrow pagan forms, and to hallow them by reading into them a Christian meaning. The sequence of the months became a reminder not only of the cycle of labor, but also of the cycle of the Christian year—the round of prayers and festivals.

The Romanesque churches, whose pavements were so often decorated with the signs of the zodiac, show how faithfully the traditions of earlier centuries were preserved. . . .

At Chartres[25] and Paris[26] the signs of the zodiac and the rural scenes which accompany them were disposed so as to follow the course of the sun. The signs of the months mount like the sun from January to June and descend from June to December. . . .

From manual labor man rises to instruction which by dissipating error enables him in some measure to raise himself after the Fall. The Seven Arts (the Trivium and the Quadrivium) open out seven paths of human activity. On the one side are grammar, rhetoric, dialectic, on the other arithmetic, geometry, astronomy and music.

Above the Liberal Arts stands Philosophy, the mother of them all.
Philosophy and the Arts contain all the knowledge possible for man
to acquire apart from revelation.[27]

The artists of the thirteenth century, intent upon embracing the
whole domain of human activity, did not fail to include on the
façades of their cathedrals the eight Muses of the Middle Ages.
These queenly figures—youthful and serious—were never denizens
of this world; they live enthroned above it like the Ideas of which
Goethe speaks. . . .

The cathedral teaches that work of any kind demands respect.
Another lesson she would teach men is to expect neither riches from
manual labor nor fame from learning. Work and knowledge are the
instruments of man's inner perfection, and the things which his
activities gain for him are of a material and fleeting nature.

In the cathedral at Amiens a curious figure embodies this moral
truth. There is in the upper part of the south porch a kind of
half-wheel round which seventeen small figures are arranged. Eight
of them seem to be carried up with the wheel, and eight others
descend with it. At the top a man is seated, his head crowned and
a scepter in his hand, motionless while all around him moves. Is
this, as Didron tried to prove, an allegory of the different ages of
man?[28] We do not think so. The figures descending so abruptly with
the wheel are dressed in rags, and have bare feet or shoes through
which their toes appear. This surely must convince one with Jourdain
and Duval that this symbolic half-circle is not the wheel of Life, but
the wheel of Fortune.[29] A miniature in an Italian manuscript of the
fourteenth century supports this interpretation.[30] Near to the figure
which seems to mount the wheel is written "regnabo," near to that
enthroned at the summit "regno," near to those descending on the
other side "regnavi" and "sum sine regno." The subject is certainly
power, riches, glory, pomps and vanities of the world, and the wheel
expresses the instability of these things. . . .

THE MIRROR OF MORALS

Nature, knowledge, virtue—that is the order in the *Speculum
majus*. It will be remembered that these are the three worlds of
Pascal, the world of material things, the world of mind and the
world of love. The unity of Christian thought is so marked that
one finds it unchanged through the centuries. Virtue is higher than

knowledge or art, said the Middle Ages, it is man's goal. But curiously enough the artists have sometimes placed the highest in the lowliest position. At Paris and Amiens the twelve pensive maidens who symbolize the virtues are not enthroned above the doorway with the angels and the blessed, but are placed at the level of men's eyes so that in passing to and fro they may learn to know them well. Age after age, worn by the rubbing of countless hands, covered with the dust from countless feet, they stand indeed one with the life around them. . . .

Apparently it was Tertullian who first represented the Virtues as warrior-maidens struggling with the Vices in the arena. "See," says he, "wantonness overthrown by chastity, perfidy killed by honesty, cruelty thrown down by pity, pride conquered by humility; these are the games in which we Christians receive our crowns." [31] . . . He was the first to give naïve expression to the profound teaching that Christianity had not brought peace to the world but a sword, and that the soul had become a battlefield. In its ignorance of the true nature of man the ancient world tried to establish a harmony which is not of this world, for so long as man lives will the conflict between his two natures exist. The drama which to the ancients was the struggle of man with Fate is in reality a conflict raging within the soul.

The idea of an inner battle, or Psychomachia, does not indeed belong to Tertullian since it is one of the fundamental ideas of Christianity, but to his imagination is due its concrete embodiment. . . .

From the twelfth century onward the theologians, and after them the artists, began to see the opposition of the virtues and the vices under new aspects. Honorius of Autun, one of the perennial sources of inspiration for medieval art, conceives virtue as a ladder which links earth to heaven.[32] He interprets the vision of Jacob in a moral sense. Each of the fifteen rungs of the ladder is a virtue, and he gives their names—patientia, benignitas, pietas, simplicitas, humilitas, contemptus mundi, paupertas voluntaria, pax, bonitas, spirituale gaudium, sufferentia, fides, spes, longanimitas and perseverantia. . . .

About the same time another metaphor appeared. The theologians of the twelfth and thirteenth centuries who studied the connection between virtues and vices with such diligence, frequently compared them to two vigorous trees. Hugh of St. Victor, one of the first to present this new idea in fully developed form, gives a name to each branch of the two trees.[33] One is the tree of the old Adam and has pride as its root and main stem. From the trunk spring seven great boughs, envy, vainglory, anger, sadness, avarice, intemperance, luxury. In its turn each bough divides into secondary branches. For example, from sadness grow fear and despair. The second tree is the tree of the new Adam with humility for its trunk, and the three theological and the four cardinal virtues as its seven main branches. Each virtue is subdivided in its turn. From faith grow the shoots of chastity and obedience, from hope come patience and joy, from charity concord, liberality, peace and mercy. The first of these trees was planted by Adam and the second by Christ, it is for man to choose between them. One of the most famous of thirteenth-century books, the *Somme le Roi* written in French for Philip the Bold by Brother Laurent, his Dominican confessor, presents Hugh of St. Victor's idea under new forms. The author begins by showing the two trees of good and of evil, but with a deeper knowledge of human nature he gives love, that is charity, as the root of the first tree, and desire, that is egoism, as the root of the second. Thus all the vices spring from love of self, as all the virtues from forgetfulness of self.

THE MIRROR OF HISTORY

So far the subject of our study has been man in the abstract—man with his virtues and his vices, with the arts and sciences invented by his genius. We now turn to the study of humanity living and acting. We have reached history.

The cathedral recounts the history of the world after a plan which is in entire agreement with the scheme developed by Vincent of Beauvais. At Chartres, as in the *Speculum historiale,* the story of humanity is virtually reduced to the history of the elect people of God. The Old and the New Testament and the Acts of the Saints furnish the subject matter, for they contain all that it is necessary for man to know of those who lived before him. They are the three acts in the story of the world, and there can be but three. The course of the drama was ordained by God Himself. The Old Testament shows humanity awaiting the Law, the New Testament shows the Law incarnate, and the Acts of the Saints shows man's endeavor to conform to the Law. . . .

But since the Council of Trent the Church has chosen to attach herself to the literal meaning of the Old Testament, leaving the symbolic method in the background. And so it has come about that the exegesis based on symbolism of which the Fathers made constant if not exclusive use, is today generally ignored. For this reason it seems useful briefly to set forth a body of doctrine which so often found expression in art.

God who sees all things under the aspect of eternity willed that the Old and New Testaments should form a complete and harmonious whole; the Old is but an adumbration of the New. To use medieval language, that which the Gospel shows men in the light of the sun, the Old Testament showed them in the uncertain light of the moon and stars. In the Old Testament truth is veiled, but the death of Christ rent that mystic veil and that is why we are told in the Gospel that the veil of the Temple was rent in twain at the time of the Crucifixion. Thus it is only in relation to the New Testament that the Old Testament has significance, and the Synagogue who persists in expounding it for its own merits is blindfold.

This doctrine, always held by the Church, is taught in the Gospels by the Savior Himself, "As Moses lifted up the serpent in the wilderness, even so must the son of man be lifted up," [34] and again, "Even as Jonah was three days and three nights in the belly of the whale, so shall the Son of man be three days and three nights in the depths of the earth." [35] . . .

An immense popular literature relating to the Bible arose in the East. These legends have a very different character according as they refer to the Old or the New Testament. The traditions relating to the Old Testament, which first claim our attention, are full of marvels, and introduce us to a fairy world as strange as that of the *Thousand and one Nights*. The rabbis with their commentaries and the Arabs with their stories created a new Bible, all dream and phantasy;[36] amendment and expansion of the sacred text occur in every line. . . .

Such stories bear the mark of their origin. In the burning deserts of the East the imagination seems to have something of the nature of that light which creates the unreal world of mirage.

All of these marvellous stories were not known to the Middle Ages, though some travelled as far as the West and were accepted by the commentators. Some of them were inserted by Peter

Comestor in the *Historia Scolastica* and by Vincent of Beauvais in the *Speculum historiale.*

At times the artists drew inspiration from them. . . .

No figure in the New Testament owes more to legend than that of the Virgin. The Gospel account in which she rarely appears, and still more rarely speaks, soon seemed inadequate to men who would know of her family, her childhood, the circumstances of her marriage, her latter years and her death. And so there arose in primitive times the apocryphal stories which charmed the Middle Ages. The figure of the Virgin is seen against a background of legend, as in the pictures of the old German masters she is seen against a hedge of roses. . . .

The cult of the Virgin which grew up in the twelfth century developed in the thirteenth. The bells of Christendom began to ring the Angelus, the Office of the Virgin was recited daily, and the finest cathedrals arose under her patronage. Christian thought, meditating through the centuries on the mystery of a virgin chosen of God, anticipated the dogma of the Immaculate Conception, and as early as the twelfth century the mystical church of Lyons celebrated that festival. The monks ever thinking of the Virgin in their solitude extolled her perfections, and more than one of them deserved the title of Doctor Marianus, which was given to Duns Scotus. The new orders, Franciscans and Dominicans, true knights of the Virgin, spread her cult among the people. . . .

The history of the Christian world is presented in the cathedrals as it is in Vincent of Beauvais's *Speculum historiale,* where periods are reckoned not by the deeds of emperors and kings but by the lives of saints. The windows and statuary of the churches proclaim that since the coming of Christ the really great men are the doctors, confessors and martyrs. Conquerors who filled the world with their fame appear in the humblest of attitudes; tiny figures smaller than children, they kneel at the feet of the saints.

We know from the *Speculum historiale* that such was the medieval conception of history. Nothing could be more surprising than the scheme of the great work from which so many generations of men—and the kings themselves—learned history. At the beginning of each chapter Vincent of Beauvais mentions the emperors of the East and of Germany and the kings of France, and devotes a few lines to their battles and their treaties. He then reaches his subject, the story of the saints who were contemporaries of these kings and emperors. His heroes are abbots, anchorites, young shepherdesses, beggars. The translation of relics, the founding of some monastery, the healing of a demoniac, the retreat of a hermit to the desert, are to him the most important facts in the history of the world. . . .

In the eyes of the thirteenth century the real history of the world was the story of the city of God. It is necessary to bear in mind such a conception of history in order to understand the innumerable legends of saints which are painted or carved in the cathedral of Chartres, where each window or bas-relief is like a chapter from the *Speculum majus*. In this reading of history the enormous number of images of saints which decorate the churches find at least partial explanation. . . .

The cathedral is as we have seen the city of God. In it the righteous, and all who from the beginning of the world have worked at the building of the holy city have their place. But those who are descended, as St. Augustine has it, not from Abel but from Cain, are not found there whatever the part they may have played in life. There is no place for Alexander or for Caesar.

The Christian kings themselves are rarely seen there. The honor was not given to all, but was reserved for those who were pre-eminent as workers for the kingdom of God—for Clovis, Charlemagne and St. Louis. And so profane history when it does appear in thirteenth-century glass may in a sense also bear the name of sacred history. . . .

CONCLUSION

In one of the chapters of *Notre Dame de Paris,* that book in which rare rays of light break through the darkness, Victor Hugo says: "In the Middle Ages men had no great thought that they did not write down in stone." What the poet grasped with the intuition of genius we have labored to demonstrate.

Victor Hugo was right. The cathedral is a book. It is at Chartres, where each Mirror finds its place, that this encyclopedic character of medieval art is most evident. The cathedral of Chartres is medieval thought in visible form, with no essential element lacking. Its ten thousand figures in glass or in stonework form a whole unequalled in Europe.

It may be that other great French cathedrals were originally as complete as Chartres still is, but time has dealt more harshly with them. Yet nowhere else appears so coherent an effort to embrace the whole of the universe. Either intentionally or because the loss of neighboring work has destroyed the balance, each of the other great cathedrals seems designed to place in relief some one truth or doctrine; a diversity which is not without its charm. One chapter for instance is developed at Amiens, another at Bourges.

Amiens is the messianic, prophetic cathedral. The prophets of the façade stand like sentinels before the buttresses and brood over the future. All in this solemn work speaks of the near advent of a savior.

Notre Dame at Paris is the church of the Virgin, and four out of six portals are dedicated to her. She occupies the center of two of the great rose-windows, and round her are grouped the saints of the Old Testament or the rhythmical sequence of the works of the months and the figures of the virtues. She is the center of all things. Never weary, the centuries sang her praises turn by turn, the twelfth century in the Porte Sainte-Anne, the thirteenth in the Porte de la Vierge, and the fourteenth in the bas-reliefs on the north side. Nowhere was she more beloved.

Laon is the cathedral of learning. Knowledge is there placed in the forefront, and the Liberal Arts accompanied by Philosophy are sculptured on the façade and painted in one of the rose-windows. The Scriptures are presented in their most mystical form, and the truths of the New Testament are veiled under the symbolism of the Old. Famous doctors, one feels, must have lived beneath her shadow. She has indeed something of their austerity of aspect.

Reims is the national cathedral. Others are catholic, she alone is French. The baptism of Clovis fills the angle of the gable, and the kings of France occupy the windows of the nave. The façade is so rich that on a coronation day it needs no further decoration, for tapestries of stone hang in the porches. She is ever ready to receive kings.

Bourges celebrates the virtues of the saints. The windows illustrate the *Golden Legend*. Round the altar the life and death of apostles, confessors and martyrs form a radiant crown.

The doorway at Lyons recounts the wonders of creation. Sens unfolds the immensity of the world and the diversity of the works of God. Rouen is like a rich book of Hours in which the center of the page is filled with figures of God, the Virgin and the saints, while fancy runs riot in the margin.

Though in each cathedral one chapter of the Mirror is, as we see, developed by preference, it is seldom that the others are not at least indicated, thus suggesting the desire to give encyclopedic teaching. Aware of the power of art over childlike and humble souls, the medieval Church tried through sculpture and stained glass to instill into the faithful the full range of her teaching. For the immense crowd of the unlettered, the multitude which had neither psalter nor missal and whose only book was the church, it was necessary to give concrete form to abstract thought. In the twelfth and thirteenth centuries, doctrine was embodied both in the drama of the liturgy and in the statues in the porch. By its marvelous inner force Christian thought created its own medium. Here again Victor Hugo saw clearly. The cathedral was the people's book of stone rendered gradually valueless by the coming of the printed book. "The Gothic sun," he says, "set behind the colossal press at Maintz."

At the end of the sixteenth century Christianity had lost its plastic power, and had become solely an inward force.

NOTES

[1] It is not our object, as we have said, to write the history of the nimbus nor of the other attributes passed in review in this chapter. The greater number date back to remote antiquity, and some (like the nimbus) to pagan times. The question has been fully treated by Didron, *Hist. de Dieu*, pp. 25–170.

[2] All these symbols are constantly used in glasspainting.

[3] The word hieroglyphic does not seem too strong if one remembers that the evangelists were sometimes represented in the form of men with the head of the ox, the eagle and the lion (see capital in the cloister at Moissac). Here medieval art joins that of ancient Egypt, and is perhaps even derived from it through the Christian art of Alexandria.

[4] It was scrupulously observed at Chartres. The heroes of the Old Covenant are sculptured in the north porch, those of the New in the south porch. In Notre Dame at Paris the great rose-window to the north is devoted to the Old Testament, that to the south to the New. At Reims the rose-window to the north (mutilated) again shows scenes from the Old Testament (the Creation, Adam, Cain, Abel, &c.), that to the south (restored in the sixteenth century, but doubtless on the old model) is filled with figures of Christ and the apostles. It is curious that the rule is still observed in the fifteenth century. At St. Ouen at Rouen and at St. Serge at Angers

the windows to the north portray the prophets, those to the south the apostles. The practice was also known to the East. In the monastery of Salamis the Old Testament is to the left, that is to the north, and the New to the right, the south. See Didron and Durand, *Iconographie chrétienne. Traduction du manuscrit byzantin du Mont Athos* (Paris, 1845), 8vo, p. xi. On the symbolism of the north and south see especially G. Durand, *Ration.*, lib. IV., cap. xxiii., xxiv.; and Rabanus Maurus, *De Universo,* ix., *Prol.* "auster sancta Ecclesia est fidei calore accensa."

[5] There are a few exceptions to prove the rule. In the great porch at Amiens, for example, St. Paul is to the right of Christ and St. Peter to the left. This arrangement takes us back to primitive Christian art. In early times St. Paul was placed to the right and St. Peter to the left of Christ to mark the substitution of the Gentile for the Jew. This is the reason given even in the twelfth century by Peter Damian in a treatise he wrote on representations of the two chief apostles (*Patrol.*, cxlv.). St. Paul, he said, placed the hosts of the Gentiles on the right hand of God. And he adds, St. Paul was of the tribe of Benjamin, and Benjamin means "son of the right hand." The old doctrine is perpetuated in the papal bull, where St. Paul is seen to the right and St. Peter to the left of the Cross.

[6] Old porch at Chartres.

[7] St. Augustine, *De libero arbitrio,* lib. II., cap. xvi. *Patrol.*, Vol. xxxii, col. 1263.

[8] *Id., ibid.*

[9] St. Augustine, *Quaest. in Heptateuch.; Patrol.*, Vol. xxxvi.–xxxvii., col. 589; see also St. Augustine's treatise *De Musica,* chapter "De numeris spiritualibus et æternis," vi. xii., *Patrol.*, Vol. xxxii., col. 1181.

[10] St. Augustine, *In Psalm.*, vi.; *Patrol.*, Vol. xxxvi.–xxxvii., col. 91. "Numerus ternarius ad animum pertinent, quaternarius ad corpus," and Hugh of St. Victor, *Patrol.*, Vol. clxxv., col. 22.

[11] On the number twelve see Rabanus Maurus, *De Universo,* xviii. 3; *Patrol.*, Vol. cxi., "Item duodecim ad omnium sanctorum pertinent sacramentum, qui, ex quatuor mundi partibus per fidem Trinitatis electi, unam ex se faciunt ecclesiam"; and Hugh of St. Victor, *De scripturis et script. sacris, Patrol.*, Vol. clxxv., col. 22.

[12] On the number seven see Hugh of St. Victor, *Exposit. in Abdiam, Patrol.*, Vol. clxxv., col. 400 *sq.*

[13] Subtle and learned Italy connected the planets with the seven ages of man on the capitals of the Ducal Palace at Venice, and in the frescoes in the Eremitani at Padua. *Annales archéol.*, t. xvi. pp. 66, 197, 297.

[14] A question which has given rise to lengthy controversy in medieval archaeology is that of the deviation of the axis of churches, so frequently noticed in the choir. Is such an irregularity due to chance, to necessities of a material order, or has it a symbolic intention? Was it not done in remembrance that Christ, of whom the church is an image, inclined His head when He died on the Cross? Viollet-le-Duc does not commit himself, though recognizing that such an idea would be in harmony with all that we know of the genius of the Middle Ages (*Dictionn. raisonné de l'architect.*, article *Axe*). For my part I was long disposed to interpret the deviation of the axis in a mystical sense. The notable memoir that M. de Lasteyrie devoted to this question, (*Mém. de l'Acad. des Inscript. et Belles-Lettres*, Vol. xxxvii. (1905), has convinced me that this deviation could have no symbolic meaning. When not due to the necessities of the site, it resulted from

an error in measurement, and always corresponds to a break in the work of building. The precise examples given by M. de Lasteyrie must surely remove all doubt. M. Anthyme Saint-Paul, so long one of the champions of symbolic interpretation, almost immediately on the publication of the *Mémoire* signified his adhesion to M. Lasteyrie's theory *Bullet. monum.* (1906). This symbolism discarded, what remains of the ingenious deductions of Mme. Félicie d'Ayzac who had tried to show that the small door in the side of Notre Dame at Paris, the *porte rouge*, was the figure of the wound made by the lance in the right side of Jesus, *Revue de l'art chrétien* (1860 and 1861)? Symbolism has too large a place in medieval art to leave room for the fancies of modern interpreters.

[15] *Speculum majus*, Douai (1624), 4 Vols., folio. This is the reprint made by the Jesuits. We shall constantly refer to this edition.

[16] Vincent of Beauvais had not time to write the *Mirror of Morals*, and the work that bears that title dates from the beginning of the fourteenth century. (See *Histoire littér. de la France*, Vol. xviii. p. 449.) But it is evident that the *Speculum morale* was part of his original plan, and that is all that concerns us here.

[17] The first is not an angel, as is often stated, but a man. It will be seen that he expressly symbolizes human nature.

[18] The miniaturists gave artistic form to this symbolism. Near to the man (St. Matthew) they sometimes represented the Nativity, near to the ox the Crucifixion, near to the lion the Resurrection, and near to the eagle the Ascension. Examples of this practice are known from the tenth century (*Evangeliarium* of the Emperor Otto *Bull. Monum.* [1877], p. 220), down to the fourteenth (Bibl. Mazarine, MSS. 167, f. 1, *Postilla* of Nicolas de Lyra).

[19] The statues of Adam and Eve are modern, but are reproductions of the originals.

[20] *Speculum doctrinale*, I. ix. The same idea is developed by Honorius of Autun in his *De animae exsilio et patria, Patrol.*, clxxii., col. 1241. The idea is this: the soul's exile is ignorance, the native land is wisdom, the Liberal Arts are so many cities on the road which leads there.

[21] At Chartres there are as many as nineteen craft guilds. See Bulteau, *Monogr. de la cath. de Chartres*, i. p. 127.

[22] E.g. Senlis (west porch); Semur (north porch); Chartres (old porch, north porch, window in choir); Reims (west porch, mutilated series); Amiens (west porch); Notre Dame at Paris (west porch and rose-window to the west); Rampillon (Seine-et-Marne) (west porch). The rose-window in Notre Dame at Paris as reproduced in Lenoir's *Statistique monumentale de Paris*, Vol. ii., Pl. XIX., is the outcome of several restorations, but the original state is given by Lasteyrie, *Hist. de la peint. sur verre*, p. 141. Didron thought to recognize a third Zodiac at Notre Dame at Paris—west façade, left doorway, trumeau. I do not share his view. The artist did not set out to represent the labors of the months, but to make a sort of thermometer. At the bottom there is a man warming himself before a good fire, higher up a man looking for wood, then a man taking a walk but still wearing a cloak, then a curious figure with two heads and two bodies, one body clothed, the other nude, evidently an expression of the sudden variations of temperature in spring. Then one sees a figure clothed only in breeches, and lastly an entirely nude figure. On the other side of the trumeau there is a ladder of the ages of man.

[23] Reproduced in the *Ann. arch.*, Vol. xxiv.

[24] See the pavements in the church at Tournus, in Saint Rémi at Reims (now removed), in Saint-Bertin at Saint-Omer, and in the church at Aosta. Suger, faithful to tradition, had the works of the twelve months executed in mosaic on the façade of St. Denis (see fragment in the Musée de Cluny).

[25] The archivolts of the north porch.

[26] West façade, Portail de la Vierge; pillars.

[27] Augustine, treatise, *De ordine*, ii. 12. *Patrol.*, xxxii., col. 1011.

[28] Didron, *Iconographie chrétienne. Guide de la peinture du Mont-Athos*, p. 408, note. This theme of the ages of man is not unknown in French medieval iconography. I believe they are to be seen at Notre Dame at Paris (west front, left porch, to the right on the trumeau). There are six ages beginning with adolescence ("infantia" is missing).

[29] Jourdain and Duval, *Le Portail Saint-Honoré ou de la Vierge dorée à la cathédrale d'Amiens* (Amiens, 1844), 8vo.

[30] The miniature was published by G. de Saint-Laurent, *Guide de l'art chrétien*, iii. p. 346.

[31] Tertullian, *De Spectaculis*, xxix. On this subject see Puech, *Prudence* (Paris, 1888), 8 vo, p. 246.

[32] Honorius of Autun, *Scala coeli minor*, col. 869; *Spec. Eccles.*, col. 869; *Patrol.*, clxxii. He did not invent the metaphor, but took it from St. Joannes Climacus.

[33] Hugh of St. Victor, *De fructibus carnis et spiritus. Patrol.*, clxxvi., col. 997.

[34] St. John 3:14.

[35] St. Matthew 12:40.

[36] The Jewish and Arabic traditions relating to the chief persons of the Old Testament are collected in Migne's *Dictionnaire des apocryphes*, 2 Vols., 4to (1858).

16. THE GOTHIC

Paul Frankl

INTRODUCTION

Paul Frankl's *The Gothic: Literary Sources and Interpretations Through Eight Centuries* is not only a thorough review of the literature on the Gothic, but it examines as well a number of special problems, of which the sections on the rib and the cross-ribbed vaults are of particular interest. The selections on vaulting chosen for this anthology, taken together with Walter Horn's article on the origins of the bay system (pp. 217) should provide a good basis for understanding the structural principles of medieval architecture. The selection on mysticism treats an aspect of the Gothic that is difficult for the modern observer to comprehend. Mystical experience has not been characteristic of our age, but some notion of what it involved is essential to an adequate understanding of Gothic art and architecture. Frankl's remarks on mysticism, however difficult, are therefore rewarding passages.

A fine summary of the general problems of the Gothic style can be found in Part Two of Frankl's *Gothic Architecture* (1962). Erwin Panofsky's *Gothic Architecture and Scholasticism* (1951) is especially valuable in drawing attention to correspondences between the form of medieval scholastic writings and the form of Gothic architecture, based on a pattern of thought common to both. Clarence Ward's *Medieval Church Vaulting* (1915) is still most useful and Joan Evans, *Art in Medieval France* (1948) is a fine survey. Works dealing with specific aspects of the Gothic are Otto von Simson, *The Gothic Cathedral* (1956); Adolf Katzenellenbogen, *The Sculptural Programs of Chartres Cathedral* (1959); and James S. Ackerman, " 'Ars sine scientia nihil est.' Gothic Theory of Architecture at the Cathedral of Milan," *The Art Bulletin*, XXXI (1949), in conjunction with which one should read Paul Frankl, *The Gothic*, pp. 57–86.

GOTHIC MYSTICISM

To speak of mysticism to people who have themselves never had any mystical experience is as difficult as to talk of color to the blind. In the age of Gothic men were predisposed to mysticism by tradition, and prepared for it by example and precept. It is, therefore, hardly possible to separate the scholars of the time into scholastics and mystics. They were always both at once, some inclined more strongly toward scholasticism, others toward mysticism.

As we have seen, mysticism does not take things as symbols. But art, thus also architecture, since it is itself a form symbol, can by its form symbolize the mystic. Therefore it is correct to say that Gothic symbolizes mysticism, but Gothic itself is not identical with mysticism; it *is* not a personal state of mind, though it *symbolizes* one and can induce one. It arouses a definite conception of a particular kind of other world, just as a sculptured *crucifixus* symbolizes a particular conception of Christ, one specific one by means of Romanesque form, another by means of Gothic. The Romanesque *crucifixus* can be broadly characterized as the expression of the words: "Thy will be done," the Gothic, correspondingly, as: "My God, why hast Thou forsaken me," as the expression of suffering and immediate longing for God. Both states can also be expressed by architectural forms. Neither, however, is mysticism or symbol of mysticism. What Albrecht intended in his temple of the Grail, on the other hand, *is* mysticism.

Here we enter for the first time a field that is immediately connected with Gothic. But one should not succumb to the temptation of characterizing mysticism at the time of Gothic as likewise Gothic. Mysticism is fundamentally a very simple, indeed the simplest and most immediate, if also the strangest experience and in all ages and in all cultures the same, even though individual peoples and schools of mysticism have different methods of contemplation and attain, or differentiate, different stages.[1] It is true that there is an Indian, Oriental, and a European mysticism, but when any one refers to each individual type, he means the outer coloring, the trappings, not the inner essence. So one can also speak of Gothic mysticism, if one means the Gothic coloring: for example, the veneration of Mary for men, of Christ for women (*Gottesminne*). Actually, however, the expression "Gothic mysticism" ought to refer to something Gothic in mysticism itself, not merely to a connection with religious ideas typical of the time.

"Gothic mysticism" found the Gothic light of stained glass one of the most convincing form symbols. Stained glass existed before Gothic but the new style reveals a reciprocal effect: the more people became aware of the effect of the light, which "falls dimly through painted panes," the larger they made the windows, and the larger the window surfaces became, the more possibilities they were for the glass painters to carry out their experiments in color and to revel in the effects. Gothic stained glass belonged to Gothic as an integrating, mystical building material, so to speak, just as much as stone or brick.

The history of stained glass shows that the degree of brightness, or of dimness, was not the same in all generations, but rather that a lightening of its scale was already begun in the fourteenth century and that at times toward the end of Late Gothic a brightness was reached that displeased conservative souls. For this there is a curious piece of evidence in a chronicle of Chemnitz, printed in 1716,[2] in which the author quotes the Humanist and monk Niavis (Schneevogel), who had still seen the old church of Annaberg and who wrote of it as follows: "that it was a strongly built but old-fashioned building and not light, because people formerly thought that it encouraged religious fervor when a church was not too light" (fit enim saepe in saeculo, ubi ecclesias habent prorsus lucidas, ut dediti homines libidini, quum inspiciunt amantes, plus cupidini operam dant quam orationibus).[3] In any case, his chief aim seemed to be to recommend the mystic light of ancient tradition. As soon as one becomes acquainted with the entire context of this passage, which describes "the old mountain monastery and present castle," one is inclined to question the advisability of mentioning it at all when mysticism is being discussed. For Niavis begins with a description of the monastery beer and with the admission that it tastes better to him than that of Kempten; then we hear of the pleasure garden with sweet smelling and medicinal herbs; further, of a crucifix with a crooked or distorted mouth ("Maul" in the German);

then comes the sentence about light, after which the description turns to the fishpond, the forests in which the abbot goes hunting, the bathroom where the monks bathe every fortnight, the stables and their animals, the plants that are grown for their efficacy against vermin, the many hens, because the monks ate chiefly eggs, and so on. Niavis' "mystical" note is thus embedded in an account of cheerful, everyday affairs and the enjoyment of life; perhaps it is well to remind modern scholars who are hunting for analogies to Gothic that even the monks who knew how to appreciate Gothic light did not live by it alone, and that the task of proving a parallelism to Gothic in the styles of agriculture might be difficult.

The situation with respect to the favorite comparison of Gothic with scholasticism is similar to that regarding mysticism. Dehio summed up the usual points of comparison well: in both there was a high intellectual accomplishment and an artistic composition, "common to both is the enthusiasm in the work, common also the method of thought; both have the same combination of boldness and sobriety, the same strictly rational development of arbitrary premises, the same heady enjoyment of logical formalism. . . . As scholasticism begins its doctrinal structure at the top, as it were, from whence it derives everything else deductively, so in Gothic everything is the result of a particular system of vaulting. As scholasticism proves the unprovable with the help of the authority of revelation lying outside thought, so Gothic produces the miracle of its vaulted halls resting on incredibly weak supports with the help of the system of buttresses lying outside the building itself." [4] Though such comparisons are beguiling on a first reading they do not stand the test of more serious consideration. The Doric temples were also built with enthusiasm for the work, intelligence, artistic composition. The Eiffel Tower is also bold and sober; every vaulted structure, even the un-Gothic Pantheon in Rome, is begun with the consideration of the top, that is, with the vault. The comparison of the buttresses with revelation we would read with friendly sympathy in Durandus, but not in a modern historian of architecture. Dehio says in conclusion: "When scholasticism tries to solve the riddle of existence by such means it does not convince us; the symbolical solution by Gothic still has power over our spirits." [5] If Gothic convinces us and at the same time is supposed to be the expression of scholasticism, why then does not scholasticism convince us? It is because Gothic architecture is not the expression of scholasticism at all. Both are contemporaneous states of two different spheres of activity and intellect.

Insofar as scholasticism is natural science, dependent on or independent of Aristotle and the Arabs, it is just as rational in its tendency as it is irrational in its metaphysical quality, but not more so. It did not gain complete freedom to trust to native reason and to question nature methodically by experiment in order to arrive at general principles. But there was a preliminary stage of modern natural science in the Middle Ages that reveals a greater variety within the limits defined by the Church than the popular conception of the "dark Middle Ages" would lead one to suspect.[6] Geometry and natural science, with mechanics at their head, resulted from practical work. Both, geometry and mechanics, we have met— geometry on the building site and mechanics in the Lodge Book of Villard de Honnecourt, in the Milanese records, and so on. One can perhaps clarify the general question as to Gothic culture most easily if one turns it into the specific question as to whether there is a Gothic geometry. There was, of course, a "Gothic" structural geometry if one means by that a method of building measurement practiced at the time of Gothic, such as we learned especially from the Milanese expertises. But no one can call the half diagonal of the square as such Gothic. The method served indeed to measure the Gothic churches but the mensuration itself is not Gothic.

Even in the case of the automata the description "Gothic automata" is questionable. When Villard caused the figure of an angel to turn in such a way that it always points toward the sun, the idea was presumably connected with the metaphysics of light, but this, as we have seen, is not Gothic, any more than the wheel-work itself that was described by Villard. The angel, which he did not draw, would doubtless have been just as Gothic a sculpture as the angels of Reims Cathedral, but that is again form symbolism, in other words, art, and the works within the automaton, the wheels that were never intended to be seen, had no sort of form symbolism. If one were to argue that the automata really represented wonders, that is, miracles, then the answer would be that miracles are not per se Gothic.

As long as one asks whether the individual cultural spheres have a direct effect on one another, the answers received are always in the negative. Architecture has no effect on scholasticism, and vice versa. The corresponding is true of the other spheres. On the other hand, sculpture and painting influence each other, which, however, cannot surprise us since they are both fundamentally the same, that is, are representation, be it of an idea or of a real model, and differ only in the number of dimensions. In the Middle Ages they are also dependent on architecture, from which result again direct and even reciprocal influences. Moreover, sculpture, painting, and architecture are *arts*, they all speak the same language of form symbolism. If now the other spheres as well—theology, metaphysics in all its variations, and so on—are connected with art, the explanation lies in the fact that they are all held together by a common center. One can distribute the various subjects, such as economics, technology, politics, science, philosophy, art, as individual points on a circle and then observe that the periphery connects them only slightly or superficially. On the other hand, all these points are firmly united with each other across the center. In this case one can, for example, say that architecture in Point A is connected across the Center M with the other Points B, C, D, and so on. This Center M is man. In him is united everything that we have touched upon and that could still be added in a long series. In him everything finds its unity, because every individual has a tendency toward harmony or at least toward the assimilation of his experiences. Man has an astounding ability to unite in himself disparate elements as well, but then he often feels inwardly torn. He seeks the harmony of all spheres of life and constantly destroys it himself by forwarding the continual evolution of each sphere individually, a contradiction that reveals itself to be almost the root of all historical happenings.[7]

The statement that man forms the center of all the areas of culture is, of course, a generalization, inasmuch as it is entirely a matter of utterly different individuals, an intellectual stratum within a broad, anonymous, and relatively unintellectual mass. In this culture-bearing stratum each is influenced by each. All are united by a common tradition of education, the coworkers in each individual field of activity being especially close to each other. It is the "subject" that has its own inner logic and of itself urges the specialists on to a common goal. Architecture, once having entered upon a particular tendency, for example, Gothic, demands of the architects a continued development in liturgical, technical, aesthetic, and specifically stylistic fields; theology, once having taken the direction of so-called scholasticism, demands of its scholars likewise that the way adopted be continued as a result of the "subject"—that

is, of its specific subject matter. In every intellectual field of endeavor there is a similar *immanent* logic of evolution, which is in
turn always *extramanent* for all the other fields. From this it would
seem to follow that all fields will develop with no reference to
each other and under certain circumstances will even develop
divergently. But these fields do not hover isolated in the air but
are all united in Man. When specialized fields diverge, it is man,
or rather society, that forces them to converge again. One can
visualize this process by returning to the figure used above and
imagining man in his intellectual development not as the center
M of a circle but as an ascending line, that is, as the axis of a
cylinder. In man and his desire to form a unity, harmonious in itself,
would reside the power of attraction by means of which the diverging evolutionary lines of the specialized fields, ascending on the
periphery and standing, as it were, on the peak of a cone, would
be forced together, so that they do not separate toward the outside
but remain parallel as on the surface of a cylinder. Object and
person are mutually affected. The "person" is inclined to believe
that he has full mastery over the "object," and often does not notice
how much he is dominated by the latter. One can see this in its
crassest form in our present situation where the development of
physics with its immanent logic has arrived at results that threaten
the existence of all the other fields, which were thought to be able
to progress independently in their own way and are now forced
to a revision and assimilation; so that all these diverging lines of
economics, politics, military science, and the like, are compelled
to adopt a parallel course in order to allow "the" human being
his harmony. Such has been the case, however, to a greater or lesser
degree, in all ages, and very often there has occurred, as today,
a radical change in the fundamental attitude of an entire culture.
One should, however, not take this geometrical figure of the evolution of culture in the sense of dead mechanics but substitute, for
"the" human being universal spirits like Albertus and Thomas.

To the all pervading basic ideas of the Middle Ages belong those
of Christianity, in the stage which it reached in the course of the
development of the twelfth century. The inclination to carry out
in real life the doctrines of the New Testament was inhibited by
definite inclinations of society in a secular direction. The papacy,
the church, monasticism, and the knights of the militant orders were
opposed by the secular empire and feudalism, in the later Middle

Ages by the citizen class as well. In the early part of the period the church Christianized the laity; in the latter half of the Middle Ages the ideas of the laity secularized the church. In the former case the solution of all problems was sought in the so-called other world, that is, in our own spirituality, in a redemption from sinfulness and worldliness. As long as this ideal dominated, natural science was not permitted to develop freely, but the authority of the Bible and the tradition of recognized authors was in the ascendancy. Through the influence of Petrarch, classical philology and, even more important, the Humanistic idea were strengthened in the fourteenth century. With the resurgence of the classical spirit men slowly became free to investigate the world and prepare the way for modern natural science. In all this the spirit of Christianity itself was not lost; it merely slowly changed its relationship to the "world." Thus it was classical philology as a particular, limited, specialized field that offered to comprehensive minds the means of changing gradually the predominantly Christian basic idea of culture, and that, therefore, as a transformed "object" transformed the "person."

The picture of culture and its development that has been sketched here really becomes alive only when one studies the great personalities of the Middle Ages. In the case of Suger it is extraordinary how much of what filled the minds of the men of his age is apparent in his writings. He is both particular and universal. The more universal men are the more they are representatives of their time and even include in themselves all the fields about which they are silent. It is their universality that also connects them with Gothic, although they may have written nothing about it, as in the case of Albertus Magnus and Thomas Aquinas.

This becomes clear by pointing to Dante Alighieri (1265–1321). Nowhere in his work do we find anything said about Gothic, yet it would be leaving an unpardonable gap to discuss Gothic and not think of Dante. It would be false to try to consider his *Divine Comedy* as architecture; it has no place in a chapter on architectural fantasies. His hell, with its funnel shape, is to be compared to a classical arena or the Colosseum rather than to a Gothic cathedral. But the *Divine Comedy* is Gothic in the sense we mean when we talk of Gothic culture.

Understanding of Dante is a touchstone for the understanding of Gothic. Anyone who despises Dante and who nevertheless main-

tains that he loves the Gothic cathedrals probably has not understood the cathedrals—at least not in the way that they were
intended in their time. Of course, much of Dante is strange to us,
but this is equally true of the cathedrals. They are just as fearful,
just as purifying, just as paradisiacal as the three parts of the *Divine
Comedy*. They are just as unbourgeois, extravagant, magnificent,
adventurous, fantastic, ambiguous, obscure, and at the same time
irradiated and suffused with unaccustomed light. Dante was the
universal spirit of his time, very much of his earthbound world with
all his hatred, bitterness, defiance, ambition as a Florentine nobleman, delivered into the power of fellow citizens who shared his
vices without having his greatness, his inexhaustible force and
freedom of imagination, or his stringency of form. But these country-
men did share with Dante scholastic education, mysticism of the
Franciscan provenience, knowledge of classical literature, and the
Christian metaphysics of the age; there were specialists in all these
fields, but Dante comprised them all, because he was, we may say,
a "specialist for poetry." Dante is hard to understand; one must
work at him if one does not merely wish to be carried away by
the melody of his speech; and likewise one must first seek the way
to the cathedrals. One of these ways is through Dante's poem.

In his many-sidedness Dante also wrote theoretical treatises on
politics, poetics, and so on, but these prose works are today read
by only a small group of specialists. The poem, in spite of its
difficulties, with or without commentaries, is open to everyone—as
the cathedrals are. Here we do not stand before two disparate
intellectual fields. Both are works of *art*. Even though medieval
aesthetic theory had not yet recognized the fact, architecture and
poetry were analogously constructed: art or *form symbols* expressed
in different media. We have traced the medieval epics from the
Grail to Chaucer and Lydgate on the basis of points of external
resemblance between the temple of the Grail and the temple of
glass. Chronologically the description of the temple of the Grail
of about 1270 is followed by the *Divine Comedy* around 1300.[8] It is
the next religious epic, thoroughly imbued with the spirit of the age,
with the Christian doctrine of salvation and Christian ethics, with
Christian belief in the spirit and the other world, with classical
mythology, with astrology and astronomy, with metaphysics of light,
scholastic and mystic, with politics, physics and magic of stones, with
history, contemporary reporting, and autobiography. An incalculable

mass of persons appears on this infinite stage of the world. Dante's journey through Hell, his ascent of the mountain of Purgatory to the spheres of the planets and up to the highest heaven is a spiritual and, on the whole, mystical progress, attributed indeed to one individual and inwardly experienced by that individual but representative, nevertheless, of humanity's purification and redemption through mystical experience. At first Dante submits himself to the guidance of his friend Vergil, then to that of Beatrice, the perfect beloved, in whom Dante's Christian love is merged with the personal. Only through her does he attain the highest level and the ultimate vision.

In the *Divine Comedy* Dante mentioned Giotto. The latter was also active in architecture and built the Gothic campanile of the Cathedral of Florence, but Dante speaks of him only as a painter (Purg. xi, 95). He was in Padua in 1306 when Giotto was painting in the chapel of the Arena. There he immortalized Dante in a portrait in the *Last Judgment.* Those are direct links between Dante and the painting of High Gothic, and this illustrates what was said above about the connection of all fields of culture.

If one were to compare the *Divine Comedy* with the cathedral of Florence one would find the task insoluble, and in connection with this unreasonable demand one would be somewhat taken aback that an Italian poet should be recognized as the representative of Gothic when, after all, Italian Gothic is not taken quite seriously by admirers of French Gothic. And yet that is justified. Dante is a "European," his horizon embraces the whole Catholic world of his day, including France and the domains of the Roman emperors of the German nation.

These remarks ought to have made it clear that all poetic and scientific literature of that time can be considered a source of Gothic, the important thing being, of course, to interpret it correctly. On no account should one deprive historical reality of its richness, its irrationality, its incalculable and unpredictable freedom, because of a preconceived idea that all contemporaneous intellectual movements must also automatically tend in the same direction. Its preestablished harmony and, as it were, preestablished disharmony have their origin in the profound mystery of the life process, itself rooted in the mystery of the spiritual.

What has been discussed here must be understood in relation to what was said in the chapter on the architectural fantasies. We comprehend the spiritual entity of Gothic itself all the more deeply the more we are acquainted with the entire literature of the time, but the form of Gothic must be grasped as an architectural problem. If we succeed in the latter effort, something essential is then reflected from this knowledge back to the understanding of the literature and "culture" of the age of Gothic.

Dante has been taken here as *one* example. Many others can be mentioned; and the more of them one learns to know, the more vivid does the outline sketched above become. Master Eckhart (1260?–1327) is, because of his linguistic power, as great in the German field as Dante, his contemporary, in the Italian. He is a preacher, not a poet, and as a mystic he is more profound than Dante. His best interpreter, Rudolf Otto, called him a "Gothic man par excellence" and immediately thereafter referred to Worringer.[9] But, when we spoke above of "the" human being, it was not done in order to support the generalization of the "Gothic man." We may well speak, however, of Gothic society, or of the Gothic stratum which created and fostered the culture that is called Gothic.

Because the word Gothic, originally introduced only for architecture,[10] was extended not only to sculpture and painting but also to all spheres of culture developing simultaneously with Gothic architecture, the problem arose as to how far these had something in common, that is, something Gothic. As is well-known, Gothic architecture developed step by step and so also did, for example, medieval metaphysics. Even as early as the lifetime of Dante and Eckhart, the dispute between *realism* and *nominalism* came to a head. It seems as though even today it has not been completely laid to rest. By realism was meant the thesis that reality should be ascribed to general concepts; from the universal ideas individuals were supposed to be derived, and the problem was to explain the *principium individuationis* by which from the idea "horse" the individual horses eventuated. The theory of nominalism declared, on the contrary, that the general concepts were only *nomina*, empty sound; only the individuals were real. To speak, however, of the "Gothic man" is realism (in the sense of the scholastic use of the term). If, however, we speak of Giotto, Dante, Eckhart, Occam, we mean, in the sense of nominalism, the real and living individuals, to whom we apply the adjective "Gothic" after we have created a general concept that is intended to include the most diverse phenomena, for example, even two such different theses as those

304

of scholastic realism and scholastic nominalism; both are for us "Gothic."

Gothic society consisted of innumerable individuals living in their cultural atmosphere that was common to all of them; they themselves created the continuously changing web. In modern terms culture is a "configuration," "Gestalt," but a dynamic, labile, fluid configuration. It has been very convincingly proven that just that fundamental contrast between realism and nominalism can be demonstrated in sculpture, painting and in the poetry of the Middle Ages as well and the conversion to subjectivism discovered everywhere.[11] Recently the rise of perspective, or of its forerunner, the oblique parallel projection, in Duccio and Giotto has also been brought under the general heading of subjectivism, and the same thing has been claimed for the interior aspect of Late Gothic churches.[12] It is here, however, more a question of the method of the cultural historians and their enlargement of the concept of Gothic, than of the details.

The web of intellectual connections among contemporaries, their exposure to the patterns of thought of the particular past and present, can be spun out three-dimensionally and the comprehensive minds seen as large, thick knots in the web, their function being to receive the threads in tangled form and spin them out in their own spirit as a particular clue. The more they comprehend of the fields of contemporary life and gather productively into a personally colored unity, the more they appear to us as representatives of their age.

Yet despite all this, it remains astonishing that the word Gothic, which has prevailed for architecture only since the seventeenth century, was chosen to designate the "common denominator." We should be content that such a term has become adopted and as Neo-nominalists not demand more of it than it has to give. Above all, one should cease to exaggerate analogies or indeed to insist on them where they are not present. Our task is rather to define precisely the extended concept Gothic, and for that, as will be seen, we do not need at all this hunt for analogies.

The field that lies closest to church architecture is that of the liturgy. The architectural program is conditioned by the purposes and needs of the liturgy; and when the latter changes, the architect must adapt himself to the innovations. The best general account of this subject is still the chapter that Dehio wrote on the architectural program in Gothic.[13] He describes in detail seven components of the church building: the enlargement of the choirs; the transference of the relics to the upper church and in connection with that the abandonment of crypts; the introduction of the rood loft and choir screens in order to protect the clergy from disturbances during their seven daily canonical offices; the increase in the number of masses and therefore in both altars and chapels; the increase in the number of towers, or their abolition among the puritanical Cistercians and the mendicant orders; the increasing significance of the sermon, especially in the parish churches, combined with the latter's ambition to vie in externals with the cathedrals; and, finally, the relationship of the church proper to its adjuncts, the chapter houses and cloisters. Much has been written about the influence of the architectural program in the case of the Cistercians and the mendicant orders. To Dehio's list might be appended the question what was the liturgical significance of the transept, which was sometimes left out and sometimes, on the other hand, doubled (in Cluny and England), if it had any liturgical significance at all.[14]

Since Dehio only Mayer has, as far as I know, treated this subject of the liturgy.[15] Although he is influenced by Dehio, he tries to penetrate to a deeper level, that of history of ideas. From the great mass of relevant literature he took the suggestion of the subjectivity of the emotional life that also extended to the piety of the time. He finds in representational art and poetry, the tendency toward multiplication of forms, intensification of means of expression, the realistic urge to grasp concrete details (realism here in the sense of modern usage), particularization, and he discerns analogies in the cumulation of masses and prayers, sees a multiplication in the rosary, also in the increase in the number of the saints, and finally, he stresses the humanization of Joseph, the foster father, St. Anne, and even Jesus. In this category belongs also the rise of the worship of the heart of Jesus. Of interest is what he says about the elevation of the host: it was to be seen by all.

Presumably much more can still be explored from this point of view; we feel, however, that the question of style cannot be exhausted in such digging for intellectual roots. Dehio's concrete observations are in themselves correct, but it suffices to reflect in the case of the first of his seven programmatic points, the arithmetically calculable enlargement of the choirs (he gives ratios of the choirs to transept and nave), that Strasbourg Cathedral is Gothic in spite of its apse preserved from Romanesque time. To be sure, this is an exception that does not essentially change anything in Dehio's thesis, especially since Strasbourg had a rood loft, acquired two chapels—and yet, more important than the size of the choir, for example, that of Cologne Cathedral, are its specifically Gothic structural forms. The forms of the piers, arches, and so on, are the real problem, whether the choir be large or small.

Perhaps from here we can find the key to this whole problem that troubles us so much today. In Gothic architecture the spatial form, looked at *roughly,* is often explained by the architectural program, and if this is derived from a changed conception of the liturgy, there is here revealed *one* thread leading directly to *one* of the many spheres of life. This analysis—one might almost say anatomy of the intellectual system—is indicative of the method to be followed for all similar inquiries. But what one means by "Gothic" in the history of culture as well as art is something deeper; it is the common root from which spring the changes in the liturgy and those in the architectural forms, even if these are not themselves simply determined by the liturgy.

We know that there are today adherents of the materialistic conception of history, which seeks to derive and explain all intellectual processes by way of economic requirements. Literature on economics during the period of Gothic is sparse. Dehio said very little on the subject; above all, he stresses the fact that in the first period of the Middle Ages an agrarian economy prevailed, while in the second the system of money economy began in the second half of the twelfth century, that is, contemporaneously with Gothic.[16] It would be interesting to read the paradoxical proof of how Gothic poetry, and so on, can be derived from the system of money economy in strictly materialistic fashion. But anyone who does not believe this theory dogmatically knows that economics are always a factor, but never explain everything. Thus it would be hopeless to try to explain Gothic from *this* root alone, and we may add that the root we seek is itself complicated and branching. Following this casual remark on money economy, Dehio said that economy of materials and therefore of cost of transportation was to many a patron "more interesting than any questions of style." What was saved on materials and transportation, however, was expended on more elaborate stone masons' work, high towers, and so on. Thus Dehio's statement has no real basis. Moreover, we should not forget that, not only for Suger, relics and later indulgences also represented a most important source of income. Money flowed in rivers—sometimes, only drop by drop—as soon as the spiritual attraction was there. Economics always is based on "spirit." In this case the spirit was "Gothic." But this by no means implies that money economy is simply and always Gothic.

To approach a real insight even more closely, a last example may be adduced: that of the Crusades.[17] They originated as armed pilgrimages and were then idealized as "holy wars," for pacifistic ears a contradiction in terms. What they actually were is well-known: the interplay of political forces from about 1096 to 1291. The chief protagonists were the popes with their religiously colored rallying-cries—war on the "infidels," more properly, those of other faiths, the freeing of the Holy Sepulcher—and with the princes of Europe, as military leaders, each with his own personal claim to power, the emperors of Byzantium, the many Mohammedan potentates in Asia Minor, Syria, Egypt, the commercial city-states of Genoa, Pisa, Venice, that possessed the indispensable fleets but put them at the disposal of the Crusades only when the undertaking spelled profits. This drama of two hundred years in length is, from the psychological point of view, a paradigm of all human frailty and inner contradictions. On the whole it was a failure, at least with respect to the original goal, but in widening geographical horizons, fostering an upsurge of commerce and the prosperity of cities, and making European Christianity receptive to new ideas it was enormously successful. The Crusades are politically the most important factor in the first two centuries of Gothic. They gave birth to the militant orders that accomplished the miracle of fusing the ideals of monasticism with the chivalric values of heroism, forcefulness, and soldierly honor. These orders functioned as patrons, and the Teutonic Order, like the Cistercians and the mendicant orders, evolved its own architectural characters within the later stages of Gothic. For the early period of Gothic, however, it has been assumed that there was direct influence from local specimens of architecture in the East, and the spread of the pointed arch in France has been attributed to the Dome of the Rock in Jerusalem. The First Crusade ended on July 15, 1099, with the storming of Jerusalem, and after a senseless and brutal massacre in the streets, the blood-spattered noble lords met in the church of the Holy

Sepulcher for a service of thanksgiving and a few days later in the Dome of the Rock for a council. It is a very romantic idea to mingle the fundamental idea of the Crusades, namely, mass murder in the name of Christ, with the pointed arches of the Dome of the Rock, and in this way to see the birth of Gothic as a divine reward. Of course, this has never been so explicitly expressed, but it can be read between the lines in Wren's theory of the derivation of Gothic from the Saracens. Today we are of the opinion that the quadripartite ribbed vaults were more important for the initial development of Gothic than the pointed arches, and we know that the former were already introduced some years before the First Crusade. Gothic and the Crusades run on parallel courses, they are connected by some threads, and in that fact, if anywhere, must be sought their common root.

It was natural that the Franks who founded kingdoms in the Levant and in Cyprus should transplant their Gothic architecture to the Orient and that, conversely, borrowings and reminiscences of the Orient should be demonstrable in the West. Before the knights and their vassals left the homeland, they dedicated themselves to their holy mission in *Gothic* churches, at least from the Second Crusade on (Suger's period). Many never reached the Holy Land; many remained there and died in exile; many returned home, most of them disillusioned and skeptical. A whole literature arose seeking to explain the failures. Gothic, on the other hand, had no failures. It built at home places of divine worship for the same God who let the Crusades be wrecked, who allowed even the initial successes to be lost in personal jealousies. The Crusades are the real world, real humanity, real history; Gothic is also absolute reality, but it is the realization of that ideal or, more properly ideated, intended, dreamed of world, humanity, and history. Albrecht's temple of the Grail is as poetry, in addition to all else, liberated from any cares of practice, procurement of materials, costs, statics; it is Gothic, if we call that *dream* which impelled the knights and the armed pilgrims to take the cross Gothic. This dream is the root for which we are seeking.

But is this not true of every epoch of cultural history? Certainly. What we mean from the point of view of history of ideas, the dream, the imaginative conception, which society in its generations creates by common intellectual effort, is always a wish image that occupies the mind as much as wishing and desiring. It is now clear that the root of culture is not *one* of its threads but always and from the very beginning a many-colored, loose tissue composed of all. In this colorfulness there is a dominant shade. We have met it over and over again in the case of the culture of the Gothic age. Spirituality, the idea of the other world, the concern for the forgiveness of sins, all accompany the cult of the carts and the Crusades. Crimes and violations of the laws promulgated by the state, sins and transgressions against divine commandments: redemption from sin is the religious as well as ethical basic conception, and within its confines the change to nominalism, to subjectivism, to this-worldliness could and did occur, without loss of the spiritual, mystic fundamental attitude.

The architecture of Gothic symbolized through its forms that which was the great theme in all the individual areas of contemporary culture. This may perhaps only be expressed with complete clarity at the end of this book, but it can already be seen at this point that the literary sources for Gothic go far beyond the texts quoted and that the answer to the question of how the contemporaries of Gothic felt about this style will only then be full and resonant when we include the scholasticism and mysticism of the period, the fantastic Crusades, the poetry of Albrecht and Dante, not as a beautiful background but as the Fata Morgana that hovered before men's minds and gave direction to their lives, their deeds, their writings, their sculpture and paintings, and thus also to their buildings, secular as well as sacral. If we want to express it in the style of that age we may say that the idea of Gothic was the pillar of fire, showing the way to the pious amid the wilderness of the reality of human passions.

The cult of relics was in itself not Gothic, the same is true of the belief in miracles, of the magic of precious stones, of symbolism, of the metaphysics of light, or of the entertaining automata, but they all, as parts of the total culture, as a new "configuration," acquired a common hue: everything is miracle, even the automata share in it, everything is Grace, for man alone is frail. We have seen how many names of architects have come down to us from the age of Gothic, but the men behind these names are for us almost without exception pale shades. Even today the great cathedrals seem to us like miracles. He who sees them as such, despite all his knowledge of their statics and rationality, sees Gothic architecture with the eyes of the Gothic.

Yet, if scholars insist on getting at the root of Gothic culture, comprising scholasticism, mysticism, liturgy, crusades, cult of relics, asceticism, poetry, and all the other components, then the answer has to be that the root of all roots is Jesus from Nazareth. In the language of symbolism he could be identified with the pillar of fire in the desert of life, himself not "Gothic." The ideal of following his teaching generated different styles before Gothic and afterwards. The common root feeds different blossoms; they are alike Christian, only in different degrees and according to other interpretation. Gothic culture seems to be the purest and most intensive realization of the spirit contained in the New Testament.

PROBLEMS CONNECTED WITH THE RIB

. . . By far the most complete survey of medieval vaulting systems was given by Clarence Ward (b. 1884);[18] this applies both to his information about vault types in their relation to the various parts of the church interior—nave, aisles, ambulatories, chapels, and so on—and to his data about the structures themselves in France and England as well as other countries.

But our knowledge of the geometry of vaults is not definitive. Future investigations will have to continue the trend represented excellently by John Bilson and Charles Herbert Moore (1840–1930), the endeavor to make exact measurements of all the extant Romanesque and Gothic cross vaults and thus transform our hitherto relative conception of chronology into an absolute one—as far as this is attainable.

Modern scholarship has been more interested in the statics of ribbed vaults than in their geometry, especially with regard to the question of whether the rib carries.

. . . In 1906 Bond observed that the flying buttresses remained standing even when the vaults had collapsed. Porter's objections of 1911 followed.[19] He was of the opinion that the value of the rib as a carrying member had been "grossly exaggerated" for there were ruins where the ribs had broken off and yet the vaults held. In 1915 Gall wrote that the early ribs were curved in the form of a segmental arch and thus had scarcely any statical value but that later the secret of their usefulness was discovered and the ribs consequently became *also* statically useful; he really saw in them, however, more the "decorative" factor.

Alfred Hamlin (1855–1926), whose uncommonly lucid arguments have been rather overlooked, had doubts of a much more general nature.[20] He criticizes Viollet-le-Duc: "The leitmotif of Viollet-le-Duc's discussions on French Gothic is the word and idea of *logique.*"[21] He finds it incredible that such great works of art should be supposed to have been inspired by cold logic. The structural lines, he says, may indicate the logic of the construction, but the details encompassed by these structural lines cannot be explained by logic. He admires the *Dictionnaire raisonné*—like everyone else—but "it takes the French cathedrals to pieces."

His chief criticism is directed against the statical interpretation of the flying buttresses and pinnacles. The former merely transmit the load, they do not oppose the counterload (Hamlin, page 109). The latter, the pinnacles, are much too light to be really able to paralyze the thrust of the flying buttresses and the vaults, they have an "imaginary value." The thrust of the flying buttresses against the clerestory wall is indeed minimal—especially when they are supported at this point by a pier or a column. Really statically effective is the external buttress (rising along the aisles). The situation in the ruin of Melrose can be explained in that way. Some people committed the error of assuming that the flying buttress pushed against the vault, whereas it pushes only against the outer buttress. If, therefore, the vault should collapse, there is no reason for the flying buttress to overthrow the wall. The vertical buttress simply remains standing, together with the arch, which now presses on the piers with its own weight only, no longer with that of the vault.

But Hamlin continues inexorably. The engaged shafts are unnecessary; they only *appear* to carry (page 110); consoles would suffice and have often done so. They are "aesthetic logic" in contrast to structural logic and also to scientific logic. Aesthetic logic is, to be sure, a *contradictio in adjecto* but an uncommonly happy paradox. Everyone understands immediately what is meant. Hamlin lists under the heading of this "logic" "the gables, lofty spires, openwork gables, wall traceries, niches, and tabernacles having no function in the structural framework." One ought not first to derive Gothic from structure and then try to eliminate from it everything that is not structure.

Hamlin therefore approves of Late Gothic buildings unreservedly. He quotes Ralph Adams Cram (1863–1942) to the effect that whatever they may lack of the shining and divine serenity of the thirteenth century, they nevertheless belong among the loveliest works of human hands, and discusses the point in some detail. His conclusion is: "Architecture is, after all, not all science; it is preeminently an art in which imagination and the love of pure beauty of form have their place." [22] This is directed against Viollet-le-Duc, and at a later date Marcel Aubert (b. 1884) said something similar. What seems so much a matter of course became clearer and clearer, namely that architecture is made up of construction *and* imagination and does not consist merely of one of them. It was, however, easier to acknowledge this fact than to determine conceptually the relationship of the two factors.

The fresh ruins of the First World War afforded a sad opportunity of examining the actual statical conditions. Roger Gilman (b. 1874) studied principally Reims and Soissons. [23] The result of his unprejudiced and very conscientious investigation was surprising, for the ruins showed that the ribs were in some cases noncarrying and, on the other hand, in many other cases carrying. Consequently Viollet-le-Duc's theory seems to be neither refuted nor proved. Gilman, too, does not regard the flying buttresses as having the function of exercising a thrust against the vault: transmission of the load rather than equilibrium, he says, is what we recognize as the truth of this matter (page 65). This approximates Hamlin's opinion that the statically important structural member is the outer pier buttress (rising outside of the aisle). It must be so stable that it will not collapse outward when the thrust of the vault is transmitted to it. Gilman reflected in general on just what is "logical" in Gothic and concluded that neither the enormous height of the French cathedrals nor the dissolution of the wall and stained glass can be called logical. To erect a solid wall of cut stone would have cost far less in France because building material could be had abundantly and cheaply. Dehio had already written on occasion that the treatment of the stone in Gothic cathedrals cost far more time and consequently money than simple masonry (as in Romanesque buildings). After considering many aspects of the subject Gilman, too, came to the conclusion that Gothic is indeed strikingly logical in its construction but not *merely* logical, and he remarked that it sometimes happens that such a principle (of logic) is transformed in spirit from a means to an end in itself. . . .

Henri Focillon (1881–1943) continued the fight on Viollet-le-Duc's side but without calling the opposing party entirely wrong. He asks: "What is the true function of the rib? Does it carry? Does it support, does it relieve the vault? . . ."[24] . . . Focillon thinks the rib is found at the point of greatest pressure; its spur has a contributory effect since it is of better, harder material and can be constructed in a pure line before the cells are filled in with masonry. He differentiates the various stages of construction. The medieval architect thought much as Viollet-le-Duc did. But—and now comes the chief point—he did not merely *think*. Architecture is visible, it has light and shade. "To fail to appreciate the plastic elements—and even the effects of the illusion—would be to commit as grave an error as to describe an edifice according to its plan alone. The rib is of a *constructive, structural,* and *optical* value."[25] Focillon remarks here rather casually that a *purer line* could be constructed by means of the rib. It is convincing that this desire for the pure line as opposed to the imprecise one of the groins was the real reason for the introduction of the rib.

Focillon did not enter into a discussion of the details of this debate. And, for that matter, how could historians of art be expected to reveal the mysteries of statics and technics? We can get a clearer picture of the present state of the problem by formulating a few groups of questions after we have come to the realization that the ribs and, like them, the other structural members of Gothic, have both a purely practical (nonartistic) and an aesthetic (or even artistic) aspect. The former is called abbreviatedly and inexactly the constructive, the latter, also inexactly, the decorative. Let us turn to the former.

1. What did the architects of Gothic think about the "constructive" aspect of the ribbed vaults? We have only one single piece of evidence for that, the expertise of Chartres from the year 1316, where it is said that the four transverse arches that help to *carry the vault* are good and strong and that the four ribs that *carry* the keystone are good and strong. This proves that the masters of 1316, who knew something about the matter if anyone did, believed that the *transverse arches carried;* one *can* interpret the passage to mean that they also believed that the *ribs* carried. The latter point is not so absolutely certain.

314

2. What actually takes place in the vaults? The Gothic masters built on the basis of their progressing experiments. Their knowledge of mechanics and mathematics was not sufficient to explain what actually happens in the vaults and their supports. Can we do that today? The differences of opinion among the various writers on the subject can only make us very skeptical. Today we know more than Viollet-le-Duc knew but we have lost all certainty of judgment. The historian of art who has learned enough mechanics and mathematics to be able to read this branch of the literature intelligently is nevertheless not qualified to decide whether the rib carries, or sometimes carries, and when. He can, however, collect the material and pass it on to the physicist. The student who hears for the first time what a cross vault is rejoices when he has happily comprehended that it is a penetration of two half cylinders. Anyone who then continues to concern himself with cross vaults for the next fifty years discovers that there are very different cross vaults even among the groined vaults and certainly among the ribbed vaults. He finds, furthermore, that things become more and more complicated the more he goes into them. A ribbed vault is constructed in two stages. First the ribs are erected and, when they have set, the cells. But in the case of the latter one can proceed in different ways. Assuming that the movable arch form (cerce) is used, the builder is still free to lay the stones parallel to the line of the crown or diagonally. And the statics always differs according to this position of the stones, the material of the rib, of the cells, and the mortar. For the mortar one even needs a chemist as well! But what concern is all this of ours? Certainly it is interesting, but we should do better to wait until the physicists have agreed among themselves.

3. In the meantime we can turn our attention to the second aspect of the ribbed vault, that called "decorative." And therewith we come back to Abraham. If the whole complicated apparatus is unnecessary from a rational point of view, what is its significance *aesthetically?* Abraham answers that all those structural members —ribs, transverse arches, engaged shafts—have the function "of creating a plastic illusion." And how is the rib to be explained? "There is obviously a discord, there is a rupture in the edifice between the vertical parts and the vaults. The transverse arch will be a first means of continuing in the vaults the stability of the pier, of having good and precise work, rich stonework from the ground level to the top of the building. But if the transverse arch suffices

to regularize the barrel vault, it is insufficient for the groined vault and much more so for the dome. The diagonal arches will therefore satisfy one or the other of these two cases. With their help not only the groined vaults and the domes but also the intermediate vaults between these types . . . can become as stable in aspect as the piers themselves: the stonework of the whole building will have become homogeneous in appearance." [26]

THE AESTHETIC AND STYLISTIC FUNCTION OF
THE CROSS-RIBBED VAULT

. . . It should be added here that the rib presumably originated because of the unprecise groin curves that were obtained as a result of the intersection of the wooden planking, for the intersection produced curves of double flexure and the weight of the stones embedded in mortar pressed the wooden sheathing out of shape. If the builders began instead with *centerings for the groins themselves,* there was a better prospect of obtaining *precise lines.* The radical solution was the *stone rib,* that is to say, the *transference* of the transverse arch to the place of the groin. Inasmuch as the transverse arches were a preliminary to this process it is a legitimate task to be on the lookout for transverse arches in barrel vaults (Bayeux, etc.) and domes and half domes in apses. But whereas these never produced a Gothic, the ribbed cross vaults were the beginning of Gothic—even in their initial stage when the ribs were segmental arches (because the builders wanted to approach the form of the ellipse).

The ribbed quadripartite vault destroyed the unity of the Romanesque style, which was based (among other things) on frontality and addition. Faced with the question of whether the cross rib should therefore be abandoned, the generation of around 1090 in Durham and Normandy decided in the negative because the aesthetic advantage of clean lines could be achieved in no other way. The retention of the rib meant that everything else had to be *adapted* to it, and just that process is the history of Gothic as an architectural style.

But despite its aesthetic advantage of replacing the ugly, depressed lines of the groins by means of regular curves, the rib would not have been retained had it not been in complete harmony with the spirit of the age. Diagonality and spatial subdivision were welcome because they were symbols of the union of fragmentary parts and men were themselves tending to adopt this attitude toward life. The rib is an "architectonic" structural member—only later did it become "decorative," in the reticular, star, and fan vaults; it is spatial, optical, and an expression of a force. It is all of these things at one and the same time, and immediately or soon after its introduction proved itself to be useful for and during the process of building. Insofar as it also corresponded to the spirit of the age it was still more: it was the symbol of that new spirit.

NOTES

[1] Rudolf Otto, *West-Östliche Mystik* (Gotha, 1926).

[2] Cornelius Gurlitt, in *Kunst und Künstler* . . . (cited above, p. 124n [in Frankl], called attention to this source; it comes from A. D. Richter, *Chronik der Stadt Chemnitz* (Annaberg, 1753 or 1767); it is reprinted *in extenso* in Appendix II.

[3] ". . . for it often happens in the secular world where there are utterly well-lighted churches that people given to libidinousness, when looking at lovers, pay more attention to lewdness than to the sermons."

[4] Georg Dehio, *Die kirchliche Baukunst* . . . , II, p. 15.

[5] *Ibid.*, p. 15.

[6] Charles Homer Haskins, *Studies in the History of Mediaeval Science* (Cambridge, Mass.: *Harvard University Historical Studies*, xxvii, 1924).

[7] Wilhelm Weber commented on this passage: "In the case of such universal minds as Albertus Magnus and Thomas Aquinas the effect of the center M is obviously much stronger than the theory indicates. Should we not imagine that the architects of the same age, who invented and executed such daring structures, felt, thought, planned, and acted just as universally?" Weber's question is justified, but we know too little about the great architects of Gothic to be able to attribute to them the same universality as to an Albertus Magnus or a Thomas. In the case of philosophers of such powers, we may say, using that geometrical figure, that the whole circle, i.e. its periphery, is included in the personalities themselves, but that in the case of the architects the majority of the periphery lies outside them. However, this objection of mine cannot be proved; even with regard to Villard de Honnecourt it is not known how extensive his knowledge was of all areas of life lying outside his art. That is a subject for a longer investigation.

[8] There is no evidence as to when Dante began the *Divine Comedy;* the various views are brought together by Friedrich Schneider-Jena, *Dante,* 4th ed. (Weimar, 1947), pp. 124 ff. Dante had already begun the *Inferno* before his banishment in the year 1302. The work was perhaps completed by 1317. The best introduction to the study of Dante is Karl Vossler's, *Die göttliche Komödie, Entwicklungsgeschichte und Erklärung,* 2nd ed. (Heidelberg, 1925).

[9] Rudolf Otto, *op. cit.* Cf. also Georg Weise, "Das Schlagwort vom gotischen

Menschen," *Neue Jahrbücher für Wissenschaft und Jugendbildung,* VII (Leipzig and Berlin, 1931), p. 404.

[10] The history of the word Gothic will be discussed later.

[11] Georg Weise, *Die geistige Welt der Gotik und ihre Bedeutung für Italien* (Halle a.S., 1939).

[12] Erwin Panofsky, *Gothic Architecture and Scholasticism* (Latrobe, 1951).

[13] Georg Dehio, *Die Kirchliche Baukunst des Abendlandes,* II (Stuttgart, 1901), p. 24.

[14] Since this was written the article of George H. Forsyth, Jr., has been published: "The Transept of Old St. Peter's at Rome" (in *Late Classical and Mediaeval Studies in Honor of Albert Mathias Friend* [Princeton, 1955], p. 56) showing convincingly that the transept was first created in St. Peter's in Rome about 340 to permit pilgrims as part of the liturgy to pass around the tomb of the Apostle. In later churches the copy of the transept was independent of pilgrimage, keeping only the aesthetic function that it already had in its first appearance.

[15] Anton L. Mayer, "Die Liturgie und der Geist der Gotik," *Jahrbuch der Liturgiewissenschaft,* VI (Münster i.W., 1926), p. 68.

[16] Dehio, *op. cit.,* II, p. 19; cf. more recently Heinrich Bechtel, *Wirtschaftsstil des deutschen Spätmittelalters* (Munich and Leipzig, 1930); to the older investigations belong those of Stephan Beissel, S.J., *Die Bauführung des Mittelalters, Studie über die Kirche des hl. Victor in Xanten* (Freiburg i.b., 1889), and Josef Neuwirth, *Die Wochenrechnungen und der Betrieb des Prager Dombaus in den Jahren 1372–1378* (Prague, 1890).

[17] Eduard Heyck, *Die Kreuzzüge und das heilige Land* (Monographien zur Weltgeschichte, XII) (Bielefeld and Leipzig, 1900). Further, Ernest Barker's article in the *Encyclopaedia Britannica,* s.v. Crusades, where further literature is given.

[18] Clarence Ward, *Mediaeval Church Vaulting* (Princeton, 1915).

[19] Porter also talks of "logic," but this is meant with regard to economy of centering. [See A. K. Porter, *The Construction of Lombard and Gothic Vaults* (1911).]

[20] A. D. F. Hamlin, "Gothic Architecture and its Critics," *Architectural Record,* XXXIX, 1916, pp. 338 ff., 419 ff.; XL, 97; XLI, p. 3.

[21] Hamlin, *op. cit.,* XL, p. 101.

[22] *Ibid.,* XL, p. 113.

[23] Roger Gilman "The Theory of Gothic Architecture and the Effect of Shell-fire at Rheims and Soissons," *American Journal of Archaeology,* XXIV, 1920, p. 37.

[24] Henri Focillon, *Art d'occident, Le Moyen-âge roman et gothique* (Paris, 1938), p. 143. . . .

[25] *Op. cit.,* p. 147: "Méconnaítre la part des données plastiques—et même des effets d'illusion—serait commettre une erreur aussi grave que de définir un édifice d'après son seul plan. L'ogive est valeur *constructive, structural* et *optique.*"

[26] . . . Pol Abraham, *Viollet-le-Duc et le rationalisme médiéval* (1934), p. 110.

17. PAINTING IN FLORENCE AND SIENA AFTER THE BLACK DEATH

Millard Meiss

INTRODUCTION

Painting in Florence and Siena After the Black Death examines the emphatic shift of style and mood in Tuscan painting around the middle of the fourteenth century in the context of a series of social and economic setbacks climaxed by the dreadful circumstances of the Black Death. Meiss contends that these disastrous events influenced the character of the art, turning it away from the gentle Franciscan-inspired painting of the earlier decades of the century, exemplified by Giotto and his followers. The new art, pessimistic and guilt-ridden, became more Dominican in tone and appealed to the conservative taste of a new population drawn largely from provincial backgrounds. In linking together the experiences of a society and the temper of its art, Meiss has developed a fascinating—and penetrating—study of some of the determinants involved in changes of style. The range of this work is such that it must be considered essential not only to students of the history of art, but to students of cultural history generally.

Other works that examine art in its social context—from a Marxist point of view—are George Plekhanov, *Art and Society* (1937) and Frederick Antal, *Florentine Painting and Its Social Background* (1948). Francis Klingender, *Art and the Industrial Revolution* (1947) deals with questions regarding the relationship between developments in British art and the impact of industrialization. A general history of this type is Arnold Hauser's

Social History of Art (1951). In conjunction with the selection that follows, one might read the reviews in *The Journal of Aesthetics and Art Criticism,* XI, 4 (1953) and *The Art Bulletin,* XXXIV, 4 (1952).

INTRODUCTION

In one of his *Trecento novelle*, written around 1390 toward the end of his life, Franco Sacchetti relates the following incident: "In the city of Florence, which has always been rich in talented men, there were once certain painters and other masters who were at a place outside the city called San Miniato al Monte for some painting and other work that had to be done in the church; after they had had a meal with the abbot and were well wined and dined, they began to converse; and among other questions, this was posed by one of them called Orcagna, who was head master of the noble oratory of Our Lady of Orto San Michele: 'Who was the greatest master of painting that we have had, who other than Giotto?' Some replied Cimabue, some Stefano, some Bernardo [Daddi], others Buffalmacco, and some named one master, and others another. Taddeo Gaddi, who was one of the company, said: 'Certainly there have been plenty of skillful painters, and they have painted in a manner that is impossible for human hand to equal; but this art has grown and continues to grow worse day by day.'"[1]

The story, which has come down to us incomplete, then takes a jocular turn in the remarks of the sculptor Alberto di Arnaldo. He belittles the opinions of the others, saying that excellent painters, the equals of Giotto, were working at that very moment—the Florentine women, whose skill in cosmetics corrects the defects of the greatest painter of them all, God.

The proposals for Giotto's nearest rival have an authentic ring, and it is generally agreed, though we cannot be certain, that the story reflects a conversation at a gathering at S. Miniato in the late 'fifties.[2] We know all the artists present and those mentioned in the discussion—one group, Taddeo Gaddi, Orcagna, Bernardo Daddi, Cimabue, Alberto di Arnaldo by their works, another, Stefano and Buffalmacco (the St. Cecilia Master?), by reputation. We should expect the assembled masters to accept the preeminence of Giotto without question. And as for the choices expressed by the group, they are remarkable, so far as we can judge, only for the omission of Maso, surely Giotto's greatest follower, and perhaps Nardo. Taddeo Gaddi himself was not proposed, possibly because he was present; nor Orcagna, who was both present and the proponent of the question. Quite surprising, however, at least on first consideration, is the statement of Taddeo Gaddi. For it goes beyond an acceptance of the superiority of Giotto, already dead some twenty-three years, to assert a continuous decline of the art into the present moment.[3]

Though laments about the state of contemporary art are common enough in history, precisely in the fourteenth and fifteenth centuries they were exceedingly rare. Taddeo's pessimistic opinion is thus exceptional in its time, and it is all the more remarkable because of the occasion on which it was expressed. For it was spoken in the very presence of Orcagna, certainly the greatest Florentine Trecento painter after Giotto, excepting only Maso di Banco. And it ignores the stature not only of Orcagna but of his brother Nardo and of Andrea Bonaiuti, who were inferior to Maso but no less gifted than any of the other masters of the earlier part of the century, Bernardo Daddi and Taddeo Gaddi himself included.

The significance of this extraordinary judgment may be grasped, I believe, if we consider the historical position and the taste of its author. Taddeo Gaddi was the most devoted pupil of Giotto. He had worked with him, according to Cennino Cennini, for twenty-four years, and in the later 'fifties he was the only veteran of Giotto's circle still alive. His insights and his taste were those of an earlier time, and the utter failure to recognize the greatness of Orcagna, if we may trust Sacchetti, suggests an important truth—the profound difference of the art of this painter and his contemporaries from that of Giotto and his successors in the earlier part of the century.

This difference implies not only that people with a taste formed in the earlier Trecento might fail to understand Orcagna, but also that some members of Orcagna's generation might feel less enthusiastic than their elders about Giotto. Possibly we may find an intimation of this in a rather cryptic comment of a writer of the time. In the great chorus of approval of the painting of Giotto that begins with Dante and Riccobaldo and extends into the fifteenth century there was only one discordant note. It was introduced by a writer just a few years younger than Orcagna, Benvenuto da Imola. Though

Benvenuto was not Florentine, he lived for a time in Florence[4] and he was quite familiar with Florentine critical and historical thought. In his commentary on the *Divine Comedy*, which he wrote *c.* 1376, he upheld the reputation and the superiority of Giotto, but qualified it with what, in the light of earlier and later opinion, amounts to heresy. "Giotto," he said, "still holds the field because no one subtler than he has yet appeared, even though at times he made great errors in his paintings, as I have heard from men of outstanding talent in such matters."[5]

These are serious charges against the man who had been widely hailed as the founder of modern painting and the greatest master since the Greeks. They have been ignored by almost all later historians, and recently one scholar has attempted to dispel them by attributing their meaning exclusively to their context. Benvenuto's statement occurs in the course of his discussion of Dante's famous passage on the transitory nature of fame. The poet says that the renown of Oderisio the miniaturist was short-lived because he was immediately succeeded by Franco, just as Cimabue was eclipsed by Giotto.

> O vana gloria dell'umane posse,
> Com' poco verde in su la cima dura,
> Se non è giunta dall'etadi grosse!
> Credette Cimabue nella pittura
> Tener lo campo, ed ora ha Giotto il grido,
> Sì che la fama di colui è oscura.[6]

It has been suggested that Benvenuto's reference to the great errors of Giotto was simply contrived *ad hoc*, to extend to this painter also Dante's thought about the brevity of fame.[7] But neither the verses themselves nor Benvenuto's comments permit this interpretation. Dante was concerned first of all with reputation and renown, not with problems of criticism and value. Benvenuto himself understood this, devoting most of his commentary on the passage to a discussion of Dante's condition for the loss of fame. The glory of Plato, he says, was dimmed by Aristotle. But since Aristotle was not followed by a philosopher equally as subtle, his reputation survived to the present day.[8] Virgil enjoyed a similar good fortune, for similar reasons, while Cimabue was unlucky enough to find himself not "in aetatibus grossis" but "subtilioribus." Giotto on the other hand, Benvenuto says, *had* no equally subtle successor. Benvenuto would have been inconsistent then if he had supposed a necessary decline in Giotto's reputation; and if he himself had for some personal reason felt called upon to detract from it, would he not have written simply and vaguely that nowadays "some people are no longer unqualified in their praise" rather than the careful statement "he made great errors, as I have heard from outstanding critics"? It seems indeed quite probable that Benvenuto's comment was not provoked by Dante's text alone, but reflected current criticism of Giotto's pictorial style.[9]

Whatever the real meaning of Benvenuto's remarks, a certain kind of adverse criticism of the work of Giotto and his followers was certainly common at this time in the paintings themselves. Every one of the younger masters after 1345–1350 rejected, at least in part, Giotto's most easily imitable accomplishment, linear perspective. None attempted to rival the equilibrium in his art between form and space, or his supple figures moving freely in a measured, easily traversible, receptive world. And which of these masters subscribed without equivocation to his conception of the divine immanent in an exalted and profoundly moral humanity? In all these respects Maso di Banco, of whose activity we do not hear after the early 'forties, was Giotto's last follower. It is striking that the influence of this major master was not dominant in the late 'forties and 'fifties. He had no real succession among the younger painters, who turned unanimously to Orcagna and Nardo.[10]

All of this is indicative of an important change in style and in taste around the middle of the fourteenth century. Variety and change there was of course in the preceding years, too, however dominant the figure of Giotto. The space with which he had surrounded his figures was extended and deepened, the environment made more specific and more familiar. In the hands of Taddeo Gaddi his massive forms became ponderous and rather assertive, in Bernardo Daddi refined and lyric. Maso introduced a marvelous subtlety of color, and gave to the ambience of the figures a wholly new intensity of form and meaning. Other painters, the S. Cecilia Master, Pacino, Jacopo del Casentino, the Biadaiolo Master, whose work has been defined in recent years chiefly by Richard Offner,[11] heeded Giotto's example relatively little, seeking an effect of greater animation and spontaneity, and a more fluid mode of expression. They avoided the grave and the monumental. Unlike Giotto and

Taddeo and Maso they were more effective in smaller works —tabernacles, miniatures, little histories in altarpieces—than in fresco. The departures of the mid-century from Giottesque style, however, are not connected with differences of scale or technique or the conditions of exhibition: they appear in large murals as well as in retables, tabernacles, and miniatures. And whereas some of the masters of the earlier part of the century are un-Giottesque, most of the later ones are, in a sense, anti-Giottesque.

There were similar changes in Siena, too, around the middle of the century. The great styles that succeeded one another during the preceding fifty years—those of Duccio, Simone Martini, Pietro and Ambrogio Lorenzetti—show despite their diversity many related qualities and a certain community of purpose. They constitute a rather orderly development, the younger painter in each instance developing one or another aspect of the older master's style. Around 1350 this continuity seems interrupted. Though the influence of the earlier tradition persists, many of its fundamental elements were rejected, and others were combined in a new and wholly different way. These transformations occurred despite the fact that only one of the painters active at this time, Barna, approximated in stature the great masters of the preceding years. He belonged to an earlier generation, however, and with all his originality he remained in many ways more fully within the tradition of the first half of the century. The younger painters, Bartolo di Fredi, Luca di Tommè, Andrea Vanni, were all less gifted, but they created distinctive forms nevertheless, very similar to one another and related to those of contemporary Florence without being dependent upon them.

Previous accounts of Sienese painting of this period have been devoted less to the analysis of its distinctive character than to its dependence upon the art of the earlier part of the century.[12] It has always, furthermore, been studied separately from Florentine. And when these studies have been part of a comprehensive account of Italian painting, they have emphasized the differences between the two schools rather than the similarities, although they have pointed to the influence upon the Florentines of the earlier art of Simone Martini and the Lorenzetti.[13] Without minimizing these differences, our present purpose is to consider those aspects of the form and content of the two schools that are related.

These similarities between the painting of the two towns are interesting in the light of the remarkably similar circumstances surrounding their appearance. Though the history of the two city-states had corresponded in many ways from the late twelfth century onward, the resemblances between them were especially numerous just before and after the middle of the fourteenth century. During this brief period, both the Sienese and Florentines lived through a series of deeply disturbing events, which provoked in each a social, moral, and cultural crisis. For what light it may throw on the similarities of their painting, therefore, we shall consider the history of the two people together—their common experience of economic failure, pestilence and social conflict, their fear, their sense of guilt, and the varieties of their religious response.

THE TWO CITIES AT MID-CENTURY

For both Florence and Siena the first forty years of the fourteenth century had been generally years of great prosperity and of political stability. Already at the beginning of this period the two cities had risen to European prominence as centers of finance and manufacture. Just before 1300 the contest between the rising middle class and the long-established noble landholders had ended in a victory for the former. The middle class acquired complete control of the state. Though many noble families, particularly in Florence, had entered trade or banking and had merged to a great extent with the business groups, they were, like all the members of their class, excluded from communal offices.

As in other late medieval towns, Florentine and Sienese society was organized for political and economic purposes in a series of guilds. Citizenship depended upon membership in one of them. The thousands of workers in the chief industry, the manufacture or refinement of woolen cloth, were forbidden to form or to join guilds, and they thus had no political rights whatever. The guilds of the great merchants, bankers, industrialists, and professional men (jurists and physicians) formed the Greater Guilds, or *Arti Maggiori*. The shopkeepers and artisans were members of the more numerous *Arti Minori*. The state, which shortly before 1300 had assumed the form of a bourgeois republic, was actually administered by a wealthy oligarchy centered within the *Maggiori*. Their rule, as well as the guild structure which supported it, lasted in both cities for about half a century.

Painting in Florence and Siena after the Black Death

The great entrepreneurs were engaged in production for foreign more than for local consumption, and with their large accumulation of capital they financed the Papacy as well as many princes throughout Europe. Seeking wider markets in their own regions, they pursued a policy of local "imperialism." During their rule almost all of Tuscany was brought under the domination of one or another of the two cities. As long as the oligarchy succeeded in maintaining a high level of prosperity, it was not seriously challenged in either Florence or Siena.

Though political power was thus highly concentrated, the form of the state reflected a libertarian ideal. The oligarchy sought to maintain the approval of the entire middle class, which believed it had the right to determine the policy of the government, and at times of crisis, as in Florence in 1343, exercised it. The republican principle, which implied the evolution of a nonhierarchical, more horizontal social order, was apparent also in other forms of association—in the guilds, for instance, with their elected captains. It was apparent also, within the sphere of religion, in the confraternities. These societies, formed by laymen for purposes of worship and mutual aid, grew rapidly from the late thirteenth century on. Their members, though subject to canon law, lived in the world without taking vows or adhering to a fixed rule. They were drawn from all classes; priests and friars were admitted too, but they had no special rights or privileges. The fraternities were governed, and their religious services conducted, by lay rectors elected for short periods of time. On the altar of the chapel that each of these societies possessed there stood almost invariably a retable that was the visible center of the cult. There the members assembled periodically, singing hymns to the Virgin before her painted image. No phenomenon of town life was more expressive of its democratic and lay tendencies, and none impinged more directly upon the art of painting.

As in other advanced European centers, but nowhere more than in Florence and Siena, the new competitive economy fostered (as well as it implied) independent individual inquiry and action in all fields of endeavor, and it stimulated a greater measure of individual self-consciousness. The middle class, concerned with the techniques of manufacture and the kinds of calculation required by production and banking on an unprecedented scale, developed increasingly empirical, inductive, and quantitative modes of thought. The burghers emphasized family and civic responsibilities and they val-

40. Giotto, Meeting of Joachim and Anna, Fresco, 1305–06 (Scrovegni [Arena] Chapel, Padua)

ued circumspection, moderation, and, above all, industriousness.[14] Though they remained deeply pious, they believed with increasing assurance that they could enjoy themselves in this world without jeopardizing their chances in the next. Their optimism seemed to be confirmed by the prosperity and the comparative peace of the first forty years of the century.

The arts flowered as at few other moments in history. The painters and sculptors, developing a more naturalistic style, created an image of an orderly world, substantial, extended, traversable. They endowed the people in it with a new range of intellectual and emotional awareness, and great moral strength. The realm of human values was immeasurably enlarged, the relation of man to man becoming as important as the relation of man to God. It is no accident that the most memorable episodes in the Arena Chapel include the return of Joachim to his sheep, his meeting with Anna at the Golden Gate (Fig. 40), and the lament over the dead body of Christ. These are scenes that had held only a subordinate meaning in earlier Christian art or had only recently been represented at all. In the early Trecento cycle they seem more congenial to the painter and more deeply felt than the episodes involving the prophetic and the symbolical (Last Supper), or the supernatural (Wedding at Cana, Ascension, Pentecost—the last executed by an assistant). Giotto's human sympathy and insight reach an astonishing profundity in the wonderful soldier standing at the left in the Massacre of the Innocents, a wholly unprecedented figure who, though traditionally on the side of brutality and evil, now withdraws in anguish from the bloody work of his men.

THE ECONOMIC CRISIS

From about 1340 on, the whole of Florentine and Sienese society was shaken by a series of increasingly disastrous events. The persistent and costly attempt of Florence to add Lucca to its domain was frustrated in 1341 by the capture of that city by the Pisans. The expansion of Milan under the Visconti began to present a serious threat,[15] and the burden of meeting this, together with the failure of the English branches of two of the largest Florentine banks, provoked an economic and then a political crisis. In 1343 the great house of the Peruzzi declared bankruptcy, and it was followed by the Accaiuoli, the Bardi (1345) and almost every other bank and mercantile company in Florence.[16] Many of the Sienese houses were brought down also. Throughout the cities workshops and stores closed because commissions were lacking and funds were not available for the purchase of materials or the payment of wages.[17] The crash plunged the towns into an unprecedented depression. Long after it had passed it continued to weigh upon the spirit of enterprise, engendering a more cautious and conservative attitude. For many years, fear of comparable loss tended to divert investment from trade and manufacture to farms and land. The merchant and chronicler Giovanni Villani, who himself suffered severe reverses and who was even thrown into the Stinche for inability to pay his debts, reported that by 1346 the Florentine companies had lost around 1,700,000 florins. No such calamity, he said, had ever overtaken the commune.[18] He wrote this judgment on the eve of a far greater one, in which he lost not his fortune but his life.

POLITICAL AND SOCIAL CHANGE

The ruling merchants and bankers in Florence tried to meet the mounting crisis by the usual method of the Italian communes in time of distress—transference of municipal authority to a dictator. In 1342 the Duke of Athens was called to Florence and given supreme power in the state. But this expedient, which in many other cities had resulted in the permanent loss of republican government, proved unsatisfactory to all sections of the Florentine middle class. Rallying to the cry of liberty, they united to expel the Duke in 1343. The republic was restored, but with new provisions that curtailed the power of the great merchants, industrialists, and bankers who had controlled the state almost uninterruptedly since the end of the thirteenth century. Weakened by the failure in the Lucchese war, the financial collapse, and the necessity of relying upon other groups to expel the *signore* whom they had installed, they were obliged to admit to the priorate representatives of sections of the middle class that had not previously had a voice in its councils. . . .

If the smaller entrepreneurs and the professional men, the *mezzani* of the Greater Guilds, were actually dominant in the government of Florence from 1343 to 1378, this era was not quite so "democratic" as many historians have maintained.[19] But in any event the oligarchy was overthrown, the new priorate was more widely representative, and the lower middle class did acquire a share in the regime. There were, moreover, corresponding readjustments of power within the guilds themselves, so that the consequences of the revolution were felt through Florentine society.[20] The rise to power of the *mezzani* and the necessity for the political recognition of the lower middle class shattered the confidence of the very wealthy, which had already been shaken by the crash. They and all those in the city who depended upon, or sympathized with, the old oligarchy bitterly opposed the new government. In 1345 Giovanni Villani ridiculed the rulers of Florence as "artisans and manual workers and simpletons."[21]

In Siena during these years there was a corresponding series of revolutions, though they occurred at different intervals of time and on the whole the swing to the left extended farther than in Florence.[22] . . .

During the years of lower middle class participation and ascendancy, several Sienese painters—Andrea Vanni, Bartolo di Fredi, Luca di Tommè, Giacomo di Mino—were active in the political parties and in the government, occupying a variety of offices and serving as municipal envoys.

THE BLACK DEATH

During the 'forties, just after the fall of the oligarchy in Florence and several years before it was overthrown in Siena, both cities suffered seriously from lack of grain.[23] The bankruptcies reduced the financial resources of the cities and weakened the influence of the great Florentine houses of the Accaiuoli and the Bardi in Naples, so that normal imports from that region were not forthcoming.[24] On top of this, crops failed throughout Tuscany in 1346, and they were badly damaged in 1347 by exceptionally heavy hailstorms. Weakened and terrified by these deprivations, which they attributed to divine displeasure, the Florentines and Sienese attempted to appease God. They engaged in collective prayer and public displays of repentance. Giovanni Villani tells of great processions, in one of which, continuing for three days, he marched himself.[25] These had scarcely disbanded when an unimaginable catastrophe struck both towns.

Suddenly during the summer months of 1348 more than half the inhabitants of Florence and Siena died of the bubonic plague.[26] By September only some 45,000 of the 90,000 people within the walls of Florence were still living; Siena was reduced from around 42,000 to 15,000.[27] Never before or since has any calamity taken so great a proportion of human life. The plague struck again in 1363 and once more in 1374, though it carried off far fewer people than in the terrible months of 1348.[28]

The survivors were stunned. The Sienese chronicler Agnolo di Tura tells of burying his five children with his own hands. "No one wept for the dead," he says, "because every one expected death himself."[29] All of Florence, according to Boccaccio, was a sepulcher. At the beginning of the Decameron he wrote: ". . . they dug for each graveyard a huge trench, in which they laid the corpses as they arrived by hundreds at a time, piling them up tier upon tier as merchandise is stowed in a ship . . ."—sights not unfamiliar to modern eyes. For years the witnesses were haunted by memories of bodies stacked high in the streets and the unforgettable stench of flesh putrefying in the hot summer sun. Those fortunate few who were able to escape these horrible scenes by fleeing to isolated places were, like Petrarch, overwhelmed by the loss of family and friends.

The momentous nature of the experience is suggested by the words of Matteo Villani as he undertook after a few years to continue the chronicle of his dead brother:

> The author of the chronicle called the Chronicle of Giovanni Villani, citizen of Florence and a man to whom I was closely tied by blood and by affection, having rendered his soul to God in the plague, I decided, after many grave misfortunes and with a greater awareness of the dire state of mankind than the period of its prosperity had revealed to me, to make a beginning with our varied and calamitous material at this juncture, as at a time of renewal of the world. . . . Having to commence our treatise by recounting the extermination of mankind . . . my mind is stupefied as it approaches the task of recording the sentence that divine justice mercifully delivered upon men, who deserve, because they have been corrupted by sin, a last judgment.[30]

Though the rate of mortality was doubtless somewhat greater among the poor, about half of the upper classes succumbed. Agnolo di Tura's comments about Siena are significant: four of the nine members of the oligarchic priorate died, together with two of the four officers of the *Biccherna,* the *podestà,* and the *capitano di guerra.*[31] The painters were not spared. The plague carried off Bernardo Daddi, the most active and influential master in Florence, and perhaps also his associate whom Offner has called the "Assistant of Daddi,"[32] It is generally assumed that the disappearance of all references around this time to Ambrogio and Pietro Lorenzetti signifies their death in the epidemic.[33] Undoubtedly a great many minor painters suffered a similar fate. This sudden removal at one stroke of the two great Sienese masters and of Daddi along with numerous lesser painters produced a more than ordinary interruption in pictorial tradition. It gave to the surviving masters, especially the younger ones, a sudden, exceptional independence and a special freedom for the development of new styles.

ECONOMIC AND SOCIAL
CONSEQUENCES OF THE PLAGUE

In the immediate wake of the Black Death we hear of an unparalleled abundance of food and goods, and of a wild, irresponsible life of pleasure. Agnolo di Tura writes that in Siena "everyone tended to enjoy eating and drinking, hunting, hawking, and gaming,"[34] and Matteo Villani laments similar behavior in Florence:

"Those few sensible people who remained alive expected many things, all of which, by reason of the corruption of sin, failed to occur among mankind and actually followed marvelously in the contrary direction. They believed that those whom God's grace had reserved for life, having beheld the extermination of their neighbors, and having heard the same tidings from all the nations of the world, would become better men, humble, virtuous, and Catholic; that they would guard themselves from iniquity and sins; and would be full of love and charity for one another. But no sooner had the plague ceased than we saw the contrary; for since men were few, and since by hereditary sucession they abounded in earthly goods, they forgot the past as though it had never been and gave themselves up to a more shameful and disordered life than they had led before. . . . And the common people (*popolo minuto*), both men and women, by reason of the abundance and superfluity that they found, would no longer work at their accustomed trades; they wanted the dearest and most delicate foods for their sustenance; and they married at their will, while children and common women clad themselves in all the fair and costly garments of the illustrious ladies who had died."[35]

This extraordinary condition of plenty did not, of course, last very long. For most people the frenzied search for immediate gratification, characteristic of the survivors of calamities, was likewise short-lived. Throughout the subsequent decades, however, we continue to hear of an exceptional indifference to accepted patterns of behavior and to institutional regulations, especially among the mendicant friars. It seems, as we shall see, that the plague tended to promote an unconventional, irresponsible, or self-indulgent life, on the one hand, and a more intense piety or religious excitement, on the other. Villani tells us, in his very next sentences, of the more lasting consequences of the epidemic:

"Men thought that, through the death of so many people, there would be abundance of all produce of the land; yet, on the contrary, by reason of men's ingratitude, everything came to unwonted scarcity and remained long thus; . . . most commodities were more costly, by twice or more, than before the plague. And the price of labor, and the products of every trade and craft, rose in disorderly fashion beyond the double. Lawsuits and disputes and quarrels and riots arose everywhere among citizens in every land, by reason of legacies and successions; . . . Wars and divers scandals arose throughout the world, contrary to men's expectation." [36]

Conditions were similar in Siena. Prices rose to unprecedented levels.[37] The economy of both Florence and Siena was further disrupted during these years by the defection of almost all the dependent towns within the little empire of each city. These towns seized as an opportunity for revolt the fall of the powerful Florentine oligarchy in 1343, and the Sienese in 1355. The two cities, greatly weakened, and governed by groups that pursued a less aggressive foreign policy, made little attempt to win them back.

The small towns and the countryside around the two cities were not decimated so severely by the epidemic, but the people in these regions felt the consequences of it in another way. Several armies of mercenaries of the sort that all the large states had come to employ in the fourteenth century took advantage of the weakness of the cities. Sometimes in connivance with the great enemy of the north, the Duke of Milan, they invaded, or threatened to invade, the territory of Florence and Siena. These large marauding bands— the companies of the Conte Lando, of John Hawkwood, and of Fra Moriale, the Company of the Hat and the Company of St. George— hovered in the neighborhood throughout the 'fifties and 'sixties, a continual threat to the peace of the *contado* and a serious drain on the already shrunken communal treasuries. Florence, the stronger of the two cities, was less troubled by them. Siena paid out huge ransoms,[38] in twenty years some 275,000 florins, but even then its lands were pillaged and the people on the farms and in the villages lived in constant terror. For them the story of Job, an old paradigm of trial and affliction, acquired a specially poignant meaning. Not only did Job suffer from a disease whose outward symptoms were like those of the plague; his cattle were driven off and his children

334

killed. It is not surprising that his history, rarely if ever represented in earlier Tuscan panels and frescoes, should now have been portrayed several times. . . .

The ravages of the merchant companies accelerated a great wave of immigration from the smaller towns and farms into the cities that had been initiated by the Black Death. Most of the newcomers were recruits for the woolen industry, who were attracted by relatively high wages. But the mortality offered exceptional opportunities also for notaries, jurists, physicians, and craftsmen. In both Florence and Siena the laws controlling immigration were relaxed, and special privileges, a rapid grant of citizenship, or exemption from taxes were offered to badly needed artisans or professional men, such as physicians.[39] . . .

In addition to bringing into the city great numbers of people from the surrounding towns and country, the Black Death affected the character of Florentine society in still another way. Through irregular inheritance and other exceptional circumstances, a class of *nouveaux riches* arose in the town and also in decimated Siena.[40] Their wealth was accentuated by the impoverishment of many of the older families, such as the Bardi and the Peruzzi, who had lost their fortunes in the financial collapse. In both cities, too, many tradesmen and artisans were enriched to a degree unusual for the *popolo minuto*. Scaramella sees as one of the major conflicts of the time the struggle between the old families and this *gente nuova*.[41] Outcries against both foreigners and the newly rich, never lacking in the two cities, increased in volume and violence. Antagonism to "the aliens and the ignorant" coalesced with antagonism to the new municipal regime; the government, it was said, had been captured by them. . . .

THE EFFECT UPON CULTURE AND ART

The painting of the third quarter of the century, more religious in a traditional sense, more ecclesiastical, and more akin to the art of an earlier time, may reflect these profound social changes in Florence and Siena, or rather the taste and the quality of piety that they brought into prominence. For these *homines novi*, the immigrants, the newly rich and the newly powerful, had not on the whole been closely identified with the growth of the new culture in the first half of the fourteenth century. They adhered to more traditional

335

patterns of thought and feeling, and it may well be that their ideal of a religious art was still the art of the later thirteenth century—an art that was still visible almost everywhere in the cities, and even more in the churches of the *contado*. At other times, less educated, provincial people have clung to an art that had been supplanted for as long as fifty years, and we are given hints that this was so around the middle of the fourteenth century. Writing in 1361 in his will about a Madonna by the "outstanding" painter Giotto, Petrarch says that though its beauty is a source of wonder to the masters of the art, the ignorant do not understand it.[42] Boccaccio wrote that, as a poet and a student of classical antiquity, he was regarded as a sorcerer in the town of Certaldo.[43] Elsewhere he attacked the noisy adversaries of poetry (primarily ancient poetry) who, ignorant of its character and its true meaning, constantly opposed religion to it.[44] There is no reason to suppose that these ready "theologians" or the friars and other groups whom he ex-coriates for similar reasons were any less antagonistic to certain aspects of the more advanced style of the Trecento in the figure arts. We cannot expect them to have proved anything but hostile to Ambrogio Lorenzetti's fascination with ancient sculpture. One of the known objects of his fascination, a newly discovered statue by Lysippus, was broken into bits by frightened members of the Sienese public. It may be that these same groups were unsym-pathetic also to the assimilation of ancient forms in the work of Ambrogio or Cavallini or Nicola Pisano. We cannot then suppose them to have been much more friendly to all those dispositions and qualities of the new style that lie behind such assimilations—in other words, to the essence of the new style itself. Because known com-ments on painting and sculpture in the fourteenth century are few, and limited mostly to scholars, writers, and the artists themselves, such attitudes are difficult to ascertain. It is notable, however, that Fra Simone Fidati seems to disapprove, by implication at least, the warm relationship between man and wife in paintings such as Giotto's. And in the *Meditations on the Life of Christ*, oddly enough in the very treatise that exercised so great an influence on painting, we find the old antagonism to the arts themselves reasserted. Except for their employment in the cult, they are, the Franciscan writer says, stimulants of a "concupiscenza degli occhi."[45]

Whether or not conservative tastes of this sort were felt by the painters at the moment of decisive change and innovation around the middle of the century, their wider diffusion and their prevalence among people who had acquired wealth and influence as patrons at least broadened the acceptance of the new styles and helped to maintain them. A painting such as Giovanni del Biondo's St. John the Evangelist trampling on Avarice, Pride, and Vainglory (Figs. 41, 42)[46] may thus have struck an immediate response because of its older symbolic pattern and the austere frontality of its chief figure. The panel was doubtless widely approved for its subject, too, particularly the representation of the conquest of avarice. At this time avarice was, as we have mentioned, associated especially with the unlimited desire for profit and accumulation that had already

41. Giovanni del Biondo, *St. John the Evangelist*, c. 1370 (Uffizi, Florence)

42. Detail Fig. 40

become characteristic of early capitalism. Neither this motive nor the new economic system had been accepted by a considerable part of society. They were often opposed, it seems safe to assume, by the same people who were conservative in other spheres also, particularly religion and the arts. These people clung to the medieval belief in a just price and the limitation of wealth to the amounts needed for a livelihood by persons in the several stations of life.[47] Their antagonism to the new system and its values was certainly more assured after the bankruptcies and other events of the 'forties. Segre states that in 1354 twenty-one Florentine bankers were fined for usury, and in tracing the fluctuating policy of Florence on the lending of money at interest, he implies a greater opposition to loans in the second half of the fourteenth century.[48] At this time many people undoubtedly took a special pleasure in the sight of a defeated Avarice sprawled on the ground and ignominiously trodden underfoot.

Though the *gente nuova* was doubtless pleased by this portrayal of the triumph of St. John, it is questionable whether any of them played a leading part in the selection of the painter or the determination of the subject. The work was actually commissioned, as we have seen, by the *Arte della Seta*, one of the seven greater Florentine guilds. Though within it, as in all the other guilds, there were during this period certain shifts of responsibility and power, it was still dominated by established merchants and industrial entrepreneurs.[49] These were, in fact, the chief patrons of painting at the time, just as they had been earlier in the century. It was the Tornaquinci who commissioned the frescoes by Orcagna in the choir of S. M. Novella, the Strozzi who employed Orcagna and Nardo for the altarpiece and murals of their chapel, one of the Guidalotti who provided the funds for the frescoes in the Spanish Chapel, though they were executed after his death. But, these wealthy patricians were deeply affected, too, by the events of the 'forties and 'fifties. They had never freed themselves of doubt as to the legitimacy of their occupation. The Church had not explicitly sanctioned either their activities or their profits, and "manifest" usury it strongly condemned. The distinctions between usury of this kind and permissible interest, while precise, were very fine, and in advanced age merchants and bankers quite commonly sought to quiet their conscience and assure their salvation by making regular provision for corporate charity and by a voluntary restitution of wealth that they judged was improperly acquired. As the most eminent living student of Floretine economic history has written: "Reading the last wills of the members of the Company of the Bardi . . . there becomes evident and dramatic the contrast between the practical life of these bold and tenacious men, the builders of immense fortunes, and their terror of eternal punishment for having accumulated wealth by rather unscrupulous methods."[50]

The guilt of the entrepreneurs and bankers was greatly quickened around the middle of the century. The bankruptcies and the depression struck just as hard at their conscience as at their purse. The loss of exclusive control of the state and the terror of the Black Death seemed further punishments for dubious practices. Giovanni Villani attributed the failure of the companies of the Bardi and the Peruzzi, in the second of which he himself had invested money before he joined the Buonaccorsi, to the "avarizia di guadagnare," and his strictures imply a condemnation not so much of poor judgment in this single instance as of all financial practices that involve great risks. Since few large ventures of the time could be undertaken without such risks, Villani comes close to turning his back on capitalism itself, and he had earlier signified that moneylending was a disreputable occupation.[51]

In the wake of the disasters of the 'forties and 'fifties, then, the established wealthy families of Florence very probably welcomed a less worldly and less humanistic art than that of the earlier years of the century. Their own position seriously threatened, they felt sustained by the assertion in art of the authority of the Church and the representation of a stable, enduring hierarchy. Their taste would have tended to converge, then, with that of the *gente nuova,* who emerged from circles that still clung to a pre-Giottesque art in which very similar qualities inhered.

All sections of the middle class were, in any event, clearly united in their desire for a more intensely religious art. It was not only great merchants such as Giovanni Colombini, with their own special reasons for remorse, who vilified and abandoned their former mode of life. Masses of people, interpreting the calamities as punishments of their worldliness and their sin, were stirred by repentance and religious yearning. Some of them joined groups that cultivated mystical experiences or an extreme asceticism; many more sought salvation through the traditional methods offered by the Church. Several painters—Orcagna, Luca di Tommè, Andrea da Firenze—

339

were, as we have seen, moved to a greater piety or a mystical rapture. Others who were less deeply stirred saw fit nevertheless, as the craftsmen of images for the cult, to adopt many of the new values and the new artistic forms, though in a more conventional way. For the painting of the time this religious excitement, and the conflict of values which it entailed, was a crucial cultural event. . . .

GUILT, PENANCE, AND RELIGIOUS
RAPTURE

The years following the Black Death were the most gloomy in the history of Florence and Siena, and perhaps of all Europe. The writing of the period, like the painting, was pervaded by a profound pessimism and sometimes a renunciation of life.[52] "Seldom in the course of the Middle Ages has so much been written," Hans Baron has said recently, "concerning the 'miseria' of human beings and human life."[53] Though religious thought throughout the Middle Ages had dwelt on the brevity of life and the certainty of death, no age was more acutely aware of it than this. It was preached from the pulpits, most vividly by Jacopo Passavanti, and set forth in paintings, both altarpieces and murals. . . .

The majority of the people expressed their devotion within the traditional patterns established by the Church. In Florence they were inspired chiefly by the great Dominican preacher, Jacopo Passavanti. Passavanti, who was born in Florence at the beginning of the century, became a preacher at S. M. Novella in 1340 after a period of study and teaching in Paris and Rome. From the late 'forties on he was in charge of maintenance and construction, and from 1354 to his death in 1357 he served as prior.[54] During this period the new church was completed, the Spanish Chapel was built, and funds were received for its frescoes. Orcagna, furthermore, painted the altarpiece of the Strozzi Chapel and Nardo its walls, and the former may also have undertaken the mural cycle in the choir. Much of this activity was due to Passavanti's influence, and all of it was under his supervision. The existence of iconographic similarities between the paintings in the Strozzi and Spanish Chapels is therefore not surprising, even though the latter were not executed until some years after his death.

Passavanti's thought has been preserved in a treatise called "Lo Specchio di Vera Penitenza."[55] In it he brought together in a systematic way ideas expressed in his sermons, especially those delivered in 1354. They center on the necessity, or rather the urgency, of penitence, for which he accumulates evidence among the writers of the past, and which he makes vivid for his contemporaries by numerous "esempi," brief but highly colored images or stories interspersed through his more formal discourse. His thought and his mood are closely related to contemporary painting. Man appears a perpetual sinner, hovering in the shadow of death and judgment. His only hope lies in penitence, a mordant contrition that continually torments the spirit. Recalling the common experiences of 1348, Passavanti describes for his audience the frightful decay of human flesh, more odorous, he insists, than that of putrefying dogs or asses.[56] He tells of skeptics who, uttering words of doubt, were struck by lightning and immediately reduced to ashes.[57] He follows them to hell, lingering with their tortures and listening for their anguished shrieks, as though he were under the spell of Orcagna's fresco in S. Croce, where the faces of the damned are torn by the claws and teeth of wildly sadistic devils. Passavanti tries to convey by calculation the incalculable endlessness of their doom. "One day," he says "a French nobleman wondered if the damned in hell would be freed after a thousand years, and his reason told him no; he wondered again if after a hundred thousand years, if after a million years, if after as many thousands of years as there are drops of water in the sea, and once again his reason told him no."[58]

To Passavanti sin is a demonic power and life a relentless struggle against it, grimly maintained because of fear of something worse. And in many paintings of the time, devils, the embodiments of guilt, become more prominent, more aggressive and more vengeful, attacking the lost souls in Orcagna's Hell, menacing the patriarchs in Andrea's Limbo[59] [Andrea da Firenze, in Spanish Chapel, S.M. Novella, Florence], and the unrepentant thief in Barna's Crucifixion, the most intense image of guilt and fear in the art of the fourteenth century [Collegiata, S. Gimignano]. In the fresco of Limbo one devil munches ecstatically on a human head, and in Orcagna's Hell a group of them lacerate the faces and bodies of their victims. For Giotto, on the other hand, hell is a place more of disorder than of excruciating pain [in *Last Judgment*, Arena Chapel, Padua]. The damned and all the devils except Satan are reduced in scale. Hell is more remote and less substantial than heaven. Indeed Giotto's outlook, serene and assured, differs from that of these later masters in much the same way as Giotto's Dominican contemporary Domenico Cavalca (c. 1270–1342) differs from Jacopo Passavanti. Of these two preachers De Sanctis wrote: "Cavalca's muse is love, and his material is Paradise, of which we get a foretaste in that spirit of charity and gentleness which gives his prose so much softness and color. But Passavanti's muse is terror, and his material is vice and hell, pictured less from their grotesque and mythological sides than in their human aspects, as in remorse and the cry of conscience. . . ."[60] Can we avoid thinking of Giotto and Orcagna?

NOTES

[1] Sachetti, *Novella* 136.

[2] Orcagna was capomaestro of Or S. Michele from 1355 to 1359, and both Taddeo Gaddi and Alberto di Arnaldo were in Florence at that time (see J. von Schlosser, *Quellenbuch für Kunstgeschichte*, XLVIII [Vienna, 1896], p. 349).

[3] The story has been mentioned by previous writers simply as evidence of the pessimism, the "Epigonengefühl," of all the artists present. See J. V. Schlosser, in *Kunstgeschichtliches Jahrbuch der K. K. Zentralkommission*, IV, 1910, p. 126; P. Toesca, *Florentine Painting of the Trecento* (New York, n.d.), p. 50 (the translation in part incorrect); W. R. Valentiner, in the *Art Quarterly*, XII, 1949, p. 48 (Taddeo's reply incorrectly read).

[4] From 1357 to 1360 and in 1373–1374 (see P. Toynbee, *Dante Studies* [London, 1902], pp. 218–222).

[5] *Comentum super Dantis Aldigherii Comoediam*, ed. (Florence, 1887), III, p. 313.

[6] "O empty glory of human powers! How short the time its green endures at its peak, if it be not overtaken by crude ages! Cimabue thought to hold the field in painting, and now has Giotto the cry, so that the fame of the former is obscured." (*Purgatorio*, XI, 91–95.)

[7] R. Salvini, *Giotto* (Rome, 1938), p. iii.
A later Dante commentator, perhaps under the influence of Benvenuto, also imputed errors to Giotto, but in architecture, where they are far less significant. The Anonimo, writing about 1395, says that he made two errors in the Campanile, of which he was aware and which led him to die of a broken heart. . . . (see Milanesi in Vasari, I, p. 371). Schlosser, *op. cit.*, p. 124, refers to changes in the design made by Giotto's successors as a possible source of the Anonimo's fable.

[8] *Commentum cit.*, p. 311.

[9] It is true that eulogies of Giotto were not lacking around this time. Petrarch spoke admiringly of him in a letter, and in his will of 1361 he referred to the praise of the "magistri artis" as Benvenuto had of the "ingenii." But Petrarch,

living far from Florence, may not have been in close touch with the growth of Florentine opinion on the arts. Boccaccio's famous statement in the Decameron was written in 1350–1352, thus at the very beginning of a profound change of taste in Florence. (For the passages in Petrarch and Boccaccio, see Salvini, *op. cit.*, pp. 4–5.)

[10] This statement seems to me essentially correct even though some elements of Maso's style were assimilated by two or three younger masters, among them the author of the frescoes of the Nativity and Crucifixion in the Chiostrino of S. M. Novella (Van Marle, *The Development of the Italian Schools of Painting* [The Hague, 1924], III, Fig. 241), and Orcagna himself.

[11] *Studies in Florentine Painting* (New York, 1927), pp. 3–42, and *Corpus of Florentine Painting* (New York, Sec. III, Vols. I, 1931, and II, 1930).

[12] See for instance C. Weigelt, *Sienese Painting of the Trecento* (New York, 1930), pp. 56–57.

[13] Resemblances between Florentine painting of the period and Bartolo di Fredi have already been observed, however, by G. Gombosi (*Spinello Aretino* [Budapest, 1926], p. 14) and F. Antal (*Florentine Painting and its Social Background* [London, 1947], p. 205). But I cannot agree with Antal's belief that Giovanni del Biondo and several contemporary Florentine painters were influenced by Fredi.

[14] See, for instance, a collection of middle class precepts such as that of Paolo di Messer Pace, *Il libro di buoni costumi*, ed. by S. Morpurgo (Florence, 1921). For burgher modes of thought, see also the comments below on the Villani chronicles (note 17 . . .).

[15] The growth of the power of Milan weighed so heavily upon the minds of the Florentines that a large part of Matteo Villani's chronicle from 1351 on (book II) is devoted to it. For the consequences of the Milanese threat see H. Baron, in *Annual Report of the American Historical Association for 1942* (Washington, 1944), pp. 123–138.

[16] See A. Sapori, *La crisi delle compagnie mercantili dei Bardi e dei Peruzzi* (Florence, 1926); also A. Doren, *Italienische Wirtschaftsgeschichte* (Jena, 1934), pp. 464 ff.

[17] Sapori, *op. cit.*, p. 140.

[18] "Maggiore ruina e sconfitta che nulla che mai avesse il nostro comune" (book XII, chap. 55). Villani was a *socius* of the Buonaccorsi Company.

[19] This government, furthermore, suppressed as firmly as the oligarchic one preceding it the *sottoposti* of the woolen guilds, who comprised the great majority of the working population of Florence (see G. Capponi, *Storia della Repubblica di Firenze* [Florence, I, 1875], p. 245).

[20] See, for instance, the changes within the guild of the physicians and apothecaries to which the painters belonged, described by R. Ciasca, *L'arte dei medici e speziali* (Florence, 1927), pp. 86 ff., and A. Doren, *Entwicklung und Organization der florentiner Zünfte* (Leipzig, 1897), pp. 51–59.

During these years the painters acquired greater independence and influence within the guild, but this was in part the consequence of special factors, chiefly the greater public esteem won by this craft during the course of the fourteenth century. The painters entered the guild in 1314 as dependents of the *membrum* of the apothecaries, classified simply as men who buy, sell, and work colors. In the guild lists of the 'forties or 'fifties painters of panels and frescoes are called *dipintori,* and differentiated from painters of chests and furniture. Not long afterward the *dipintori* became dependents of the physicians, the only professional group in the guild. Finally, in 1378 the group of painters was authorized to form an independent *membrum* because, as the record states, "aveva conseguito una grande importanza nella vita dello stato, ed appariva già maturo per la vita dello stato" (Ciasca, *op. cit.,* p. 131).

[21] "Signori artefici e gente manovali e idioti" (book XII, chap. 43). In 1340, before the revolution, Villani had advocated a government representative of all classes (book XI, chap. 118).

[22] See G. Luchaire, *Documenti per la storia dei rivolgimenti politici del comune di Siena dal 1354 al 1369* (Lyons, 1906); P. L. Sbaragli, "I mercanti di mezzana gente al potere in Siena," in *Bullettino senese di storia patria,* VIII, 1947, pp. 35 ff.; F. Schevill, *Siena* (London, 1909), pp. 213–228; L. Douglas, *A History of Siena* (New York, 1902), pp. 149 ff.

[23] See N. Rodolico, *Il popolo minuto* (Bologna, 1899), p. 51.

[24] See Doren, *Italienische Wirtschaftsgeschichte,* p. 391.

[25] Book XI, chap. 21.

[26] In a previous epidemic, during the spring of 1340, 15,000 Florentines died, according to Giovanni Villani (book XI, chap. 114).

[27] These estimates of Doren (*op. cit.,* pp. 634–635) are conservative. Others suppose a higher rate of mortality. N. Rodolico, *La democrazia fiorentina nel suo tramonto* (Bologna, 1905), pp. 7, 32, 35, gives an overall figure for Florence in 1347 of 120,000; after the plague 25,000 to 30,000, a death rate of four-fifths. Boccaccio in the Decameron said that 100,000 Florentines died, and the Chronicle of Stefani puts the figure at 96,000. Matteo Villani gives a general death rate of three-fifths (see note 30).

Agnolo di Tura seems to say that 80,000 Sienese died, leaving only 10,000 alive (*Rerum Italicarum scriptores,* xv, part VI, ed. by A. Lisini and F. Iacometti, Bologna, 1932, p. 555) and an anonymous chronicler (*ibid.,* p. 148) asserts that the "grande morìa" carried off three-fourths of the people. A. Lisini, commenting on this statement (*ibid.,* p. 148 note 2), says that if three-fourths did not die, at least a half did. Lisini estimates as many as 70,000 people in Siena before the plague. Commenting on Siena, Matteo Villani (book I, chap. 4) says "non pareva che fusse persona."

[28] See for Siena, W. Heywood, *"Ensamples" of Fra Filippo* (Siena, 1901), pp. 80 ff., and for Florence, F. T. Perrens, *Histoire de Florence* (Paris, 1888–90), IV, pp. 379 ff. The plague of course became endemic, reappearing in 1400, 1411, 1424, and thereafter, but with a greatly diminished rate of mortality.

[29] *Rerum Italicarum scriptores,* xv, part 6, pp. 555–556.

[30] Book I, end of chap. 1 and beginning of chap. 2.

The entire passage is interesting for its careful, precise account of the spread of the plague through Italy and Europe. Villani is assiduous in the collection of facts and opinions but cautious in accepting them, and he frequently records them with skepticism or with contrary argument. Thus he tells about the reports of a great fire in Asia, and the belief that the plague originated in areas ravaged by it, but adds, "ma questo non possiamo accertare." To the assertion of the astrologers that the plague resulted from the conjunction of three superior planets in the sign of Aquarius, he replies that a similar conjunction had occurred in the past without producing such dire results. He is quick to calculate, and to propose laws and principles: on the basis of reports from many countries, he says that the pestilence may be said usually to last five months in a given region. It normally carried away three out of every five persons.

[31] Agnolo di Tura, *op. cit.*, p. 555–556. One hundred and thirteen of the friars in S. M. Novella in Florence died (C. di Pierro, in *Giornale storico della letteratura italiana*, xlvii, 1906, p. 14), and in Avignon nine cardinals and seventy prelates, despite the great fires which were maintained in the papal palace to purify the air (P. Schaff, *History of the Christian Church*, (New York, 1910), v, part 2, p. 100).

[32] *Corpus*, sec. iii, vol. v, p. 119.

[33] Their names are lacking not only in all documents, but in the list of the best Sienese painters compiled around 1349 for the *operaii* of S. Giovanni, Pistoia (C. von Fabriczy, *Repertorium für Kunstwissenschaft*, xxiii, 1900, pp. 496–497).

[34] Agnolo di Tura, *op. cit.*, p. 560.

[35] Book i, chap. 4. A translation of the entire chapter—upon which the above is based—may be found in G. C. Coulton, *The Black Death* (London, 1929), pp. 66–67.

[36] Book i, chap. 5.

[37] Chronicle of Neri di Donato, *Rerum Italicarum scriptores*, xv, pp. 633–636. On the inflation throughout Europe after the Black Death see J. W. Thompson, in *American Journal of Sociology*, xxvi, 1920–21, p. 565, and Kovalevsky in *Zeitschrift für Sozial- und Wirtschaftsgeschichte*, iii, 1895, pp. 406–423.

[38] Twenty thousand florins, for instance, to Lando in 1356 (see Neri di Donato, *op. cit.*, p. 585). On the merchant companies and Florence, see especially Perrens, *op. cit.*, iv, pp. 424, 457–470.

[39] See R. Ciasca, *op. cit.*, p. 291. Despite these inducements the number of physicians did not increase as rapidly as the shopkeepers and tradesmen in the same guild (*ibid.*, p. 117). For immigration into Florence see also N. Rodolico, *I ciompi*, pp. 40–42, and *idem, Democrazia fiorentina*, pp. 36 ff. For Siena, see Kovalevsky, *op. cit.*, p. 421 and L. Douglas, *op. cit.*, pp. 155–156. All these writers comment only very briefly on the immigration. The entire phenomenon, and its consequences for contemporary society and culture, has not hitherto been given adequate attention.

[40] Agnolo di Tura (*op. cit.*, p. 560) wrote that "tutti li denari erano venuti a le mani di gente nuova." See also Matteo Villani (book iii, chap. 56); Perrens, *op. cit.*, iv, p. 391.

[41] *Op. cit.*, p. 34. Through Scaramella does not observe it, all references that he cites to the *homines novi* are from the period after the plague (Matteo and Filippo Villani, Giovanni di Paolo Morelli, etc.).

[42] ". . . tabulam meam sive iconam beatae Virginis Mariae . . . cuius pulchritudinem ignorantes non intelligunt, magistri autem artis stupent." See R. Salvini, *Giotto* (*Bibliografia*) (Rome, 1938), p. 5.

[43] H. Hauvette, *Boccace* (Paris, 1914), p. 464.

[44] See books xiv and xv of the *Genealogia degli dei*, trans. by C. G. Osgood, *Boccaccio on Poetry* (Princeton, 1930).

[45] *Meditations*, chap. xii (see the edition of the Italian text by A. Levasti,

Florence, 1931, pp. 46–47): "Cotali cose [i.e. lavorìo curioso, bello, . . . delicato] sono concupiscenza degli occhi, lo quale vizio è uno de' tre peccati, ai quali tutti gli altri si riducono." The author condemns works of craft and of art also because they waste time, promote vanity, and are contrary to poverty.

The passage in the *Meditations* is based on ideas about the *concupiscentia oculorum* expressed by St. John (First Epistle, 2:16) and developed by St. Augustine (*Confessions*, book x, esp. chap. 34), after whom they became part of the medieval tradition. The latter speaks of the "attractions" that men, with the aid of the arts, have added to paintings and other things.

[46] The association of these vices with St. John is probably connected with the passage from this saint cited in the previous note and later interpretations of it.

[47] See Paolo di Messer Pace da Certaldo, *Il libro di buoni costumi*, ed. by S. Morpurgo (Florence, 1921), p. CL (Paolo is mentioned in documents from 1347 to 1370). The writer, son of a jurist, recounts the perils of avarice, and then concludes: "Sia temperato in se, e non disiderare più che'l tuo stato richegha."

[48] A. Segre, *Storia del commercio* (Turin, 1923), p. 223.

[49] A. Doren, *Entwicklung und Organization der florentiner Zünfte* (Leipzig, 1897), p. 71, pointed to the greater recognition given at this time to silk weavers and dyers in a guild that continued to be dominated by silk merchants. See also *idem, Florentiner Zunftwesen* (Stuttgart and Berlin, 1908), p. 199.

[50] A. Sapori, in *Archivio storico italiano*, III, 1925, p. 250. On the subject of voluntary restitution, see B. N. Nelson, in *Tasks of Economic History*, supplement VII, 1947, to the *Journal of Economic History*. Even in the fifteenth century, Cosimo dei Medici sought the advice of Pope Eugene IV on the restitution of money that he confessed had been illegitimately gotten.

[51] Book VII, chap. 147.

[52] See, for instance, the beginning of Sacchetti's *Trecento novelle:* "Considerando al presente tempo, ed alla condizione dell' umana vita, la quale con pestilenziose infirmità, e con oscure morti, è spesso vicitata; e veggendo quante rovine, con quante guerre civili e campestre in esse dimorano; e pensando quante populi e famiglie per questo son venute in povero ed infelice stato, e con quanto amaro sudore conviene che comportino la miseria, là dove sentono la lor vita esser trascorsa; e ancora immaginando, come la gente è vaga d'udire cose nuove, e spezialmente di quelle letture che sono agevoli a intendere, e massimamente quando danno conforto, per lo quale tra molti dolori si mescolini alcune risa; . . ." (Franco Sacchetti, *Proemio del Trecento novelle*).

[53] *Speculum*, XIII, 1938, p. 12. Baron discusses the diffusion of stoicism and the ideal of poverty in the period following the epidemic.

For the preoccupation with death, see A. M. Campbell, *The Black Death and Men of Learning* (New York, 1931), pp. 172 ff.

[54] C. di Pierro, "Contributo alla biografia di Fra Jacopo Passavanti," *Giornale storico della letteratura italiana*, XLVII, 1906, pp. 1–24.

[55] Ed. by M. Lenardon (Florence, 1925). See also N. Sapegno, *Storia letteraria d'Italia, Il trecento* (Milan, 1942), pp. 505–510; A Levasti, *I mistici del duecento e del trecento* (Rome, 1935), pp. 64 ff.; A. Monteverdi, "Gli esempi di Jacopo Passavanti," *Giornale storico della letteratura italiana*, LXI, 1913, pp. 266 ff., and LXIII, 1914, pp. 240 ff.

[56] *Specchio, cit.,* pp. 307–308.

[57] See A. Monteverdi, *op. cit.,* 1914, pp. 249, 287. The monastery of S. M. Novella itself was struck by lightning several times during the priorate of Passavanti. In 1358 the choir was hit and the frescoes of Orcagna damaged (see Matteo Villani, book VIII, chap. 46).

[58] Monteverdi, *op. cit.,* 1913, p. 305.

[59] Antal, *op. cit.,* p. 202, has pointed to the prominence of the devils in this scene, connecting them with "popular taste."

[60] F. De Sanctis, *History of Italian Literature,* trans. by J. Redfern (New York, 1931), I, p. 123.

18. JAN VAN EYCK AND
ROGER VAN DER WEYDEN

Erwin Panofsky

INTRODUCTION

It is fitting that the final selection in this volume should concentrate on Jan van Eyck and Roger van der Weyden. The art and lives of these two painters from the Lowlands are particularly resonant in communicating both the continuity of northern Gothic traditions and the accelerated conquest of pictorial means that characterized the art of the early fifteenth century in the north as it had in Italy. Granting that it smacks of mere academic exercise—however entertaining it may be—to debate the question of whether Jan van Eyck and Roger van der Weyden are "Late Gothic" or "Renaissance" artists, the very existence of the question implies a degree of ambivalence regarding the extension of the idea of a Renaissance to the Lowlands in the early fifteenth century. It is appropriate, therefore, to conclude this volume with the late Erwin Panofsky's discerning remarks on both the social status and the painting style of each of these artists, for, whatever the classificatory preferences of the reader, Panofsky provides in the passages that follow numerous indications of the productive interlace of tradition with innovation in early Netherlandish art.

The new English translation of Max J. Friedlaender's essential fourteen-volume work, *Die altniederlandische Malerei* (1924–37), will join the same author's *Early Netherlandish Painting from Van Eyck to Bruegel*, 2nd ed. (1965), and Erwin Panofsky's *Early Netherlandish Painting*, 2 Vols. (1953) as the best sources for further information on the early artists of the Lowlands. Other studies of special interest are Erwin Panofsky, "Jan van Eyck's Arnolfini Portrait," *Burlington Magazine*, LXIV (1934); Millard

Meiss, "Light as Form and Symbol in Some Fifteenth-Century Painting," *The Art Bulletin,* XXVII (1945); by the same author, "Highlands in the Lowlands: Jan van Eyck, the Master of Flemalle and the Franco-Italian Tradition," *Gazette des Beaux-Arts,* s. 6, LVII (1961); Jules Desneux, "Underdrawings and *Pentimenti* in the Pictures of Jan van Eyck," *The Art Bulletin,* XL (1958); and Karl M. Birkmeyer "The Arch Motif in Netherlandish Painting of the Fifteenth Century," *The Art Bulletin,* XLIII, 1–2 (1961).

JAN VAN EYCK

Jan van Eyck is first heard of as painter and *varlet de chambre* to John of Bavaria, the unconsecrated Bishop of Liége who, after the death of his brother, William VI of Holland, had usurped the territory of his niece, Jacqueline, and established residence in the Hague. He employed Jan for the decoration of his castle from October 24, 1422 (at the latest) until at least September 11th, 1424. And since Jan is already referred to as "master" at the time of his appointment we may assume that he was born not later than *c.* 1390. There is also some doubt as to his birthplace. For many centuries it has been taken for granted that both brothers were born at "Eyck," viz., Maaseyck, some eighteen miles north of Maastricht. Recently it has been proposed that they were natives of Maastricht itself where the name "van Eyck" is not uncommon as a family name. But since the evidence for this hypothesis is as yet inconclusive, I am inclined to accept, for the present, the traditional view.

At the end of his employment in Holland, Jan van Eyck repaired to Bruges, but stayed there for only a short time. On May 19, 1425, he was appointed as painter and *varlet de chambre* to Philip the Good of Burgundy and moved to Lille prior to August 2 of this year. Here he resided, with major and minor interruptions, until the end of 1429, having married, at an undetermined date, a lady of whom nothing is known except that her Christian name was Margaret, that she was born in 1406, and that she presented him with no less than ten children. Soon after, presumably in 1430, he established himself at Bruges for good and spent the rest of his life in a stately house "with a stone front" (acquired in 1431 or 1432), combining the office of a court artist with the normal activities of a bourgeois master painter who would not consider it beneath his dignity to accept such commissions as the coloring and gilding of the statues on the façade of the Town Hall. He died on July 9, 1441.

Throughout the sixteen years of their association the Duke and his painter—the first Early Flemish master to sign his works and, so far as we know, the only one to imitate the nobles in adopting a personal motto, the famous *Als ich chan*, "As best I can," in which becoming pride is so inimitably blended with becoming humility— lived on terms of mutual esteem and confidence. Philip the Good not only admired Jan van Eyck as a great artist but also trusted him as a familiar and a gentleman. As early as 1426 the painter undertook, in the name of his master, certain confidential pilgrimages and "secret voyages," and during the following years he was a member of two embassies to the Iberian peninsula. After two previous marriages, both terminated by death, Philip the Good was still without an heir, and the first of the voyages overseas, lasting from early summer to October, 1427 (when Jan van Eyck received his *vin d'honneur* at Tournai on the eighteenth), was undertaken, it seems, in order to negotiate a marriage with Isabella of Spain, daughter of James II, Count of Urgel. This having failed for reasons unknown, another mission was dispatched to Portugal in order to obtain the hand of the eldest daughter of King John I, also named Isabella. This time the envoys succeeded, though only at the price of two exceedingly rough and dangerous crossings—entailing lengthy stopovers in England on both trips. They started on October 19, 1428, and returned—with the Infanta—as late as December, 1429; the marriage took place on January 10, 1430.

Apart from another "secret mission" in 1436, the Duke of Burgundy honored his painter by at least one personal visit to his workshop, showed him his favor by all kinds of extra payments and an occasional gift of silver cups, exempted him from a general cutback in jobs and salaries decreed in 1426, and acted as godfather by proxy (at the sacrifice of another half dozen silver cups) when a child of Jan's was baptized sometime before June 30, 1434. He even extended his affection beyond the grave. After Jan van Eyck's death his widow received a substantial gratuity "in consideration of her husband's services and in commiseration with her and her children's loss"; and nine years later, in 1450, his daughter Livina (Lyevine) was enabled to enter the Convent of St. Agnes at Maasseyck by a special grant from Philip the Good.

On one occasion, when the bureaucrats in Lille had made some difficulties about Jan's salary, the Duke came down upon them with an order that has the ring of the Italian High Renaissance rather than of the Northern Middle Ages. He enjoined them, under threats of gravest displeasure, to honor the claims of Jan van Eyck without delay or argument; for he, the Duke, "would never find a man equally to his liking nor so outstanding in his art and science": "nous trouverions point le pareil a nostre gré ne si excellent en son art et science."

What may be dismissed as humanistic hyperbole in Bartolommeo Fazio, who praises Jan van Eyck as a man of literary culture (*litterarum nonnihil doctus*), proficient in geometry, and a master of "all arts that may be added to the distinction of painting," is thus borne out by the testimony of Philip the Good. By the very wording of his reprimand (*art et science,* a phrase not uncommon in the early fifteenth century) he implies that the achievement of an artist, and particularly those of his favorite painter, had to be considered not only as a matter of superior skill but also of superior knowledge and intelligence.

This judgment is confirmed by Jan van Eyck's pictures. Only a keen intellectual curiosity could have devoted so much interest to theological texts, chronograms, astronomical details, cabilistic invocations and even paleography. Only a logical mind could have so thoroughly refined and systematized the principle of "disguised symbolism" that in his world, as I expressed it, "no residue remained of either objectivity without significance or significance without disguise." Only the instinct of a historian could have rediscovered the indigenous Romanesque and recaptured its spirit in all its phases and manifestations. And only an imagination controlled and disciplined by geometry, the "art of measurement," could have determined the impeccable proportions of Eyckian architecture.

That Jan was also an expert in alchemy, as Vasari would have it, is of course an assumption derived from the belief that he was the inventor of oil painting. This belief, we know, can no longer be maintained. Yet the fact remains that he must have devised certain improvements unknown before—improvements which enabled him to surpass both in minuteness and in luminosity whatever was achieved by his predecessors, contemporaries and followers. Whether he distilled new varnishes, driers and diluents—and in this case Vasari's reference to alchemy and his amusing tale of Jan's innovations having started with the development of a quick-drying varnish might, after all, contain a grain of truth—or merely applied the processes of the *nouvelle pratique* with greater sophistication, it is difficult to say. Certain it is, however, that in his pictures the oil technique, though not invented by him, first revealed itself in its full glory, the translucency of the colors—"radiant by themselves without any varnish"—enhanced by an increasingly economical use of lead white which he employed (apart, of course, from the rendering of linen, etc.) for luminary surface accents rather than the construction of plastic form.

From the sheer sensuous beauty of a genuine Jan van Eyck there emanates a strange fascination not unlike that which we experience when permitting ourselves to be hypnotized by precious stones or when looking into deep water. We find it hard to tear ourselves away from it and feel drawn back by what Magister Gregorius, compelled to revisit a statue of Venus again and again although it meant a walk of more than two miles, described as "some kind of magical persuasion." Whoever has tried to give a fair amount of conscientious attention to other paintings hung in the same room will remember that even a Rubens may strike him as "just a painting," a mere semblance as opposed to a reality, when looked at with an eye still carrying the imprint of a Jan van Eyck. In fact, a picture by Jan van Eyck claims to be more than "just a painting." It claims to be both a real object—and a precious object at that— and a reconstruction rather than a mere representation of the visible world.

The first of these claims is stressed by the very treatment of the frames which he invariably provided himself and which have come down to us in at least eight instances. Setting aside the exceptional case of the Ghent altarpiece, these frames are elaborated into complex moldings and painted so as to simulate marble or porphyry. Moreover, this marbleization is carried over to the back of the panel, and carefully lettered inscriptions are seemingly incised into the artificial stone. By this legerdemain, which may seem reprehensible to the purist, Jan van Eyck not only showed off his virtuosity (as did the Limbourg brothers when they fooled the Duc de Berry with the wooden dummy of a gorgeous Book of Hours) but also emphasized and glorified the materiality of the picture. The modern frame is nothing but a device for isolating the picture space from the space of nature. The Late Medieval frame, exemplified by the van Beuningen altarpiece with its carved rosettes, or, more extravagantly, by the "Carrand diptych" with its elaborate gilt tracery, is an ornamental setting which compasses the picture as chased metal does a precious stone. Jan van Eyck's frames are, in a sense,

354

both. In subduing them coloristically, he stressed the modern idea of the panel as a "picture," that is, as the projection plane of an imaginary space. But in transfiguring them into what looks like marble, he retained the idea of the panel as a tangible piece of luminous matter, united with its frame into a complex *objet d'art* composed of many precious materials.

The impression that paintings by Jan van Eyck confront us with a reconstruction rather than a mere representation of the visible world is more difficult to rationalize. Very tentatively, we may say this: the naturalists of the fifteenth century, avid for observation yet in many ways committed to convention, were plagued by the problem of striking a balance between the general and the particular—between the total aspect of a face or hand and the wrinkles of the skin, between the total aspect of a piece of fur or fabric and its individual hairs or fibers, between the total aspect of a tree and its individual leaves. Before Jan van Eyck, these details, if not entirely suppressed, tended to remain distinct from each other as well as from the whole and give the impression either of a whole incompletely differentiated or of a mass of details incompletely unified. The hand of the St. George in the "Madonna van der Paele," however much detailed, remains a totality so that no contradiction is felt between its complexity and the simplicity of the polished armlet from which it emerges (Fig. 43). The face of the Giovanni Arnolfini in the London double portrait, smooth though it is, seems sufficiently rich in detail to harmonize with the intricacies of the plaited Italian straw hat and fur collar.

This Eyckian miracle was brought about by what may be likened to infinitesimal calculus. The High Renaissance and the Baroque were to develop a technique so broad that the details appeared to be submerged, first in wide areas of light and shade and later in the texture of impasto brushwork. Jan van Eyck evolved a technique so ineffably minute that the number of details comprised by the total form approaches infinity. This technique achieves homogeneity in all visible forms as calculus achieves continuity in all numerical quantities. That which is tiny in terms of measurable magnitude yet is large as a product of the infinitesimally small; that which is sizable in terms of measurable magnitude yet is small as a fraction of the infinitely large.

Thus Jan van Eyck's style may be said to symbolize that structure of the universe which had emerged, at his time, from the prolonged

43. Jan van Eyck, Madonna of Canon van der Paele (Musée Communal, Bruges)

discussion of the "two infinites"; he builds his world out of his pigments as nature builds hers out of primary matter. The paint that renders skin, or fur, or even the stubble on an imperfectly shaved face seems to assume the very character of what it depicts; and when he paints those landscapes which, to quote Fazio once more, "seem to extend over fifty miles," even the most distant objects, however much diminished in size and subdued in color, retain the same degree of solidity and the same fullness of articulation as do the very nearest. Jan van Eyck's eye operates as a microscope and as a telescope at the same time—and it is amusing to think that both these instruments were to be invented, some 175 years later, in the Netherlands—so that the beholder is compelled to oscillate between a position reasonably far from the picture and many positions very close to it. And while thus being reminded of the limitations of nature, we share some of the experience of Him

Who looks down from heaven but can number the hairs of our head.

However, such perfection had to be bought at a price. Neither a microscope nor a telescope is a good instrument with which to observe human emotions. The telescopic view tends to reduce human beings to those "figures of diminutive size" which people distant landscapes; the microscopic view tends to magnify their very hands and faces into panoramas. In either case the individual is apt to be de-emotionalized, whether he be reduced to the status of a mere part of the natural scenery or expanded into a small universe.

By nature, Jan van Eyck was by no means an impassive artist, and where occasion demanded it—as in the animated Genesis scenes on one of the capitals in the "Rolin Madonna" or in the truly terrifying "Slaying of Abel" in the Ghent altarpiece—he could be as dramatic as any other artist of his time. But in the "classic," unanimously accepted works of his maturity these dynamic elements are relegated to the background. The emphasis is on quiet existence rather than action, and with the significant exception of the Annunciate in the comparatively early picture at Washington, who retains, in much attenuated form, the emotional *contrapposto* attitude of her Italianate predecessors, the principal characters are nearly motionless, communicating with each other only by virtue of spiritual consubstantiality. Measured by ordinary standards, the world of the mature Jan van Eyck is static. . . .

ROGER VAN DER WEYDEN

Roger van der Weyden was born, we recall, at Tournai in 1399 or 1400, the son of a master cutler named Henry. Nothing is known of his boyhood and early youth except that he was not at Tournai on March 18, 1426, when the house of his father, recently deceased, was sold without his participation. In the same year he married (as can be concluded from the fact that his first child, a son named Corneille, was eight years old in 1435), and this marriage, too, would seem to have taken place outside Tournai: his bride, Elizabeth Goffaerts, hailed from Brussels. Her mother, Cathelyne, however, bore the same family name, van Stockem, as did the long-suffering wife of Robert Campin, and this very fact lends further support to the assumption that it was the latter, alias the Master of Flémalle, whose workshop Roger entered on March 5, 1427, and left as "Maistre Rogier" on August 1, 1432.

Where the young master turned immediately upon his "graduation" is unknown. Certain it is, however, that he was most successful from the outset and ultimately settled in the native city of his wife. As early as October 20, 1435, he was able to invest a considerable sum of money in Tournai securities, and on May 20, 1436, the city fathers of Brussels resolved not to fill the position of City Painter ("Portrater der stad van Brussel" or "der stad scildere") after Roger's death—a resolution from which we learn that this position was his at the time and may infer that it had been especially created for him not long before. Whether he was appointed for the express purpose of supplying the courtroom of the Town Hall with the "Examples of Justice" that were to delight eight generations of travelers is not known. Certain it is, however, that these four celebrated panels are not mentioned until 1441, and that the first pair of them was not completed until 1439. It was about this time that he was granted the privilege of wearing the same particolored cloak (*derdendeel*) as did the "geswoerene knapen" of the city of Brussels.

Internationally famed and financially prosperous (further purchases of Tournai securities are recorded for 1436–1437, 1442 and 1445, and in 1449 he gave 400 crowns to Corneille who wished to enter the Charterhouse of Hérinnes), Roger van der Weyden represents, perhaps even more paradigmatically than Jan van Eyck, the novel type of bourgeois genius. Though honored by princes and dignitaries at home and abroad, he lived the dignified and uneventful life of a good citizen charitable to the poor, generous to religious institutions, intent upon the welfare of his community, and solicitously providing for his wife and children. He received splendid commissions from Spain and Italy, yet did not disdain to polychrome and emblazon a stone relief in the Minorites' Church or to attend to the coloring of twenty-four brass statuettes. And except for occasional business trips and a pilgrimage to Italy in the Holy Year of 1450, nothing seems to have interrupted his quiet, laborious life until it ended on June 18, 1464.

Of Roger's personality we know little more than that he was a man of integrity and rare unselfishness. It was to him that people turned as an arbitrator when a dispute arose between a fellow painter and his clients. On May 7, 1463, the Duchess of Milan,

Bianca Visconti, effusively thanked her "noble and beloved master Roger of Tournai, painter in Brussels" for the courtesy and kindness which he had shown to her young protégé, Zanetto Bugatto, and the unstinting generosity with which he had instructed him "in everything he knew about his art." And in 1459 the Abbot of St. Aubert at Cambrai noted with gratification that Roger had improved and considerably enlarged the stipulated dimensions of an altarpiece commissioned in 1455 "pour le bien de l'oeure." These are small things, perhaps, in themselves, but not quite usual at a time when painters were secretive about their methods and even the greatest were paid according to working hours and the cost of materials used.

Happily such scanty records are supplemented, and corroborated, by two portraits which, however inadequately, inform us of Roger's physical appearance. His features are known, first, from an inscribed drawing in the "Recueil d'Arras"; and, second, from his self-portrait in one of the "Examples of Justice" which is transmitted to us through the Berne tapestry. In spite of the indifferent quality of the Arras drawing and the inevitable distortion of the woven copy, we feel at once that we are in the presence of greatness, and this impression is borne out by no less illustrious a witness than Nicolaus Cusanus. In an attempt to describe the way in which God looks at the world, the Cardinal refers to "that face of the outstanding painter Roger in the most precious picture preserved in the Town Hall at Brussels" (*facies illa . . . Bruxellis rogeri maximi pictoris in preciosissima tabula quae in praetorio habetur*). Though a motionless image, he says, this face seems to pursue the beholder with its glance wherever he goes as does the eye of God which observes the human being "wherever he may be" and is fixed on him "as though on him alone." After an established custom of medieval scholasticism, Cusanus endeavored to carry the mind of his readers to that which is divine by means of a *similitudo* taken from human activity. But he might not have chosen this particular simile had his imagination not been stirred by this thoughtful, deadly-serious face and deep, bitter folds around a wide, generous mouth and enormous, visionary, indeed inescapable eyes.

"Jan van Eyck," Max J. Friedlaender once aptly remarked, "was an explorer; Roger van der Weyden was an inventor." Not that Roger was unable to do justice to what may be called the surface blandishments of the visible world. There are enchanting details in many of his pictures, and in sensibility to color he was second to none. No visitor to Beaune or Philadelphia will ever forget the modulations of blue in Roger's "Last Judgment" or the polyphony of warm, lilac-rose, pale gray-blue, flaming vermilion, drab gray, and gold in his "Calvary." But it is true that Roger substituted for Jan van Eyck's pantheistic acceptance of the universe in its entirety a principle of selection according to which inanimate nature and man-made objects are less important than animals, animals less than man, and the outward appearance of man less than his inner life. One of his contemporaries admired his paintings for *sensuum atque animorum varietas,* and Carel van Mander praised him for having improved the art of the Lowlands by an increase in movement and, most particularly, by the "characterization of emotions such as sorrow, anger or joy as was required by the subject."

Thus Roger's world is at once physically barer and spiritually richer than Jan van Eyck's. Where Jan observed things that no painter had ever observed, Roger felt and expressed emotions and sensations—mostly of a bitter or bittersweet nature—that no painter had ever recaptured. The smile of his Madonnas is at once evocative or motherly affection and full of sad foreboding. The expression of his donors is not merely collected but deeply pious. Even his design is expressive rather than descriptive; it was he, for instance, who discovered how much the pathos of a Crucifixion might be intensified by contrasting the rigidity of the Body with the undulating movement of a billowing loincloth. His iconographic innovations, too, were often designed to create new emotional situations. He permitted donors directly to participate in sacred events and, conversely, introduced contemporary personages into Biblical narratives as *dramatis personae* who, as Leone Battista Alberti would say, "attract the eyes of the beholder even though the picture may contain other figures more perfect and pleasing from an artistic point of view." He combined half-length portraits with half-length Madonnas into diptychs in which the sitter is represented in prayer. And it seems to be he who if not invented, at least reformulated and popularized the subject of St. Jerome compassionately extracting the thorn from the foot of his faithful lion.

When we compare, for example, Jan van Eyck's "Madonna van der Paele" [Fig. 43] with the central panel of Roger van der Weyden's "Columba altarpiece" (so called after the Church of St.

44. Roger van der Weyden, Columba Altarpiece, *c.* 1460; Center Panel, 54⁵⁄₁₆″ by 60¼″; Each Wing 54⁵⁄₁₆″ by 27⁹⁄₁₆″ (Alte Pinakothek, Munich)

Columba in Cologne which was its home from 1493) we perceive what seems to be an irreconcilable contrast. The "Madonna van der Paele" is strictly symmetrical, and its weighty, immobilized figures, receding from the central plane as well as from each other, are painted as though they were crystallizations of light itself. Its style is static, spatial and pictorial. In the Columba altarpiece (Fig. 44) the central group is shifted to the left and the slender, supple figures of St. Joseph and the Magi, all in action, are pressed against the picture plane so as to form a sharply delineated pattern; its style is dynamic, planer and linear. Roger's composition looks almost like a throwback to the fourteenth, if not the thirteenth century, and he has often been said to represent a kind of Gothic counterrevolution against Jan van Eyck. However, while it is true that Roger's style has fundamental characteristics in common with what we call High Gothic and that he revived a number of motifs and devices nearly forgotten for half a century or more, he was not, as has occasionally been said, a "reactionary." He arrived at his apparently archaic solutions not only from an entirely "modern" starting point but also for a very "modern" purpose: far from simply opposing to the ideals of Jan van Eyck and the Master of Flémalle those of an earlier period, he attempted to break new ground by the old device of *reculer pour mieux sauter.*

Jan van Eyck had not so much resolved as negated the problems posed by the great painter of Tournai; he had eliminated the tensions and contradictions characteristic of the latter's manner by abolishing their very *raison d'être*. Where, as in Jan's mature style, all physical and emotional action was absorbed into pure existence there could be no conflict between movement and rest. Where all surface relations were transposed into space relations there could be no conflict between two-dimensional design and composition in depth. Where all details were perfectly integrated with total form there could be no conflict between a pictorial and a linear mode of presentation. Roger van der Weyden, however, set out to develop the expressive and calligraphical possibilities inherent in the style of the Master of Flémalle without forfeiting the consistency and purity attained by Jan van Eyck.

While Roger's figures are more dynamic than Jan's their movements are both more fluent and more controlled than the Master of Flémalle's. And while their grouping is denser and more diversified than in an Eyckian composition it is less crowded and more coordinated than in a Flémallesque one. It is as though a living chain of figures were thrown across the picture plane—a chain whose links remain distinct though conjoined by artful repetition and variation. And the component parts of every figure, body and garments alike, are both articulated in form and function and unified by an uninterrupted flow of energy. In short, Roger van der Weyden may be said to have introduced into Flemish fifteenth-century art the principle of *rhythm* in contradistinction to meter—definable as that by which movement is articulated without a loss of continuity.

This rhythm unfolds within a kind of foreground relief neatly divorced from the space behind it. But both foreground relief and background space are what I should like to call "stratified" into a series of planes deliberately frontalized yet interconnected in depth. The entire picture space is thus made to obey a common principle analogous to the "rhythmical" organization of figure movement: articulation is accomplished without destroying continuity. In the central panel of the Columba altarpiece this system of interlocking frontal planes is particularly evident, not only in the general disposition of the figures, the succession of piers, arches and posts in the building, and the stratification of the landscape but even in inconspicuous details. The donor on the extreme left looks on from a plane located between that of the St. Joseph and the pillar behind him. The little greyhound on the extreme right attaches the figure of his master to the very front plane (the hat in front of the oldest king, incidentally, fulfills a similar function) and the rigidly frontalized animals behind the Virgin Mary obligingly bend their heads into the planes in front of them.

As the principle of rhythm overcomes the tension between movement and rest in the behavior of the figures, and between surface and depth in the organization of space, so does it overcome the tension between the pictorial and the graphic in the presentation of plastic form as such; and this, I believe, is the very essence of Roger van der Weyden's "linearism." As in all Early Flemish painting, his lines are not abstract contours separating two areas of flat color, but represent a condensation or concentration of light or shade caused by the shape and texture of the objects. However, in Roger's paintings these forms assume a linear quality without relinquishing their luminary significance. Eyebrows or eyelids, the bridge of a nose, the edge of the lips, strands of hair, or, for that matter, the borders and folds of a garment are indicated by lines designed with the precision of an engineering drawing yet innervated by a vital force that sharpens their angles and intensifies their curvature. While never disrupting the unity of plastic shapes and color areas, they achieve a purely graphic beauty and expressiveness.

Index

Index

Bricks (Roman), 135
  brick-facings, 140, 141
  "flexible" use of, 138
  kiln-fired, 136
  structural need for, 143
Bruges, Belgium, 351
Brussels, Belgium, 357, 358, 359
Bubonic plague, *see* Black Death
Buffalmacco, 321
Bugatto, Zanetto, 359
Buggenum, Holland, 222
Bull
  Assyrian, 11
  Cretan, 13
Buonaccorsi, 339
Burckhardt, J., 98
Byzantine art, 164
  "bath of Child Christ" motif, 171–175
  Christ in, 170–175
  Descent from the Cross theme, 102
  emotion in, 101, 178–185
  eroticism and, 170
  gold in, 178
  Hellenistic influences on, 167–186
  illusionism in, 176–178
  landscape painting, 175–176
  Octateuchs, 179
  pastoral idyls in, 170
  Roman art and, 185
  themes of, 91

Cairo, Egypt, 7
"Calvary" (van der Weyden), 360
Cambrai, 359
Campania, Italy, 136
Campin, Robert (Master of Flémalle), 357, 361, 362
Canteloup abbey grange (Normandy), 236
Capua, 125
Carolingian art, 194–196
  architecture, 240
  bay-divided timber churches, 222–223
Carrand Diptych (Florence), 170, 354
Casa del Menandro, 173
Casentino, Jacopo del, 324
Castelseprio, 169
  frescoes, 177
  mosaics, 176
Catacomb art, 155–156
Cathedral, Gothic, 164
  as "city of God," 286
  see also names of cathedrals
Cavalca, Domenico, 342

Cavallini, 336
Cennini, Cennino, 322
Certaldo, Italy, 336
Chalcis, 84
"Chancellor Rolin Madonna" (van Eyck), 357
Charlemagne, 239, 286
Chartres Cathedral, 26, 272, 273, 286–287
  guild windows, 280
  Mirror of Nature, 277
  portrayal of story of humanity, 283
  ribbed vaulting, 314
  zodiac signs, 280
Châteaumeillant, 204
Chaucer, Geoffrey, 302
Chemnitz, 296
Cheshire County, Eng., medieval timber churches in, 221
Chiusi, Etruria, 68
Christian art, 101
  Byzantine influence, 163–164, 165–166
  catacomb frescoes, 155–156
  Christ in, 158–160
    medieval iconography, 269, 278
    miracles of Christ, 156
    Vézelay tympanum, 253–260
  Egyptian, 158–159
  Hellenistic influence on, 155
  New Testament subjects in early Church art, 158–161
  Old Testament influence on, 155–158, 284
    Vézelay tympanum, 256–258, 261, 262
  origins of, 153–166
  Russian ikons, 158
  tombs, 155–156
Church of the Holy Apostles, 174
Churches
  medieval timber church construction, 220–223
  Romanesque, 197–215
  stave churches, 219
  see also Basilicas; Cathedral; Temples
Cimabue, 321, 323
Cistercian order, 306, 308
  monastery barns, 236
Clairvaux Abbey, barns of, 234, 236
Claudianus (poet), 172
Clayton, John, 231, 232
Clermont, Council of, 260
Clermont, France, 260
Clovis, 286, 287
Cluny, 199, 261, 262, 306

Index

Index

Index

Index

Index